DATE DUE

Demco, Inc. 38-293

OWEN JONES

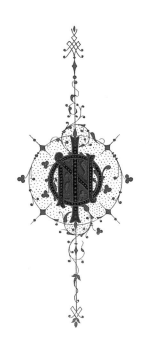

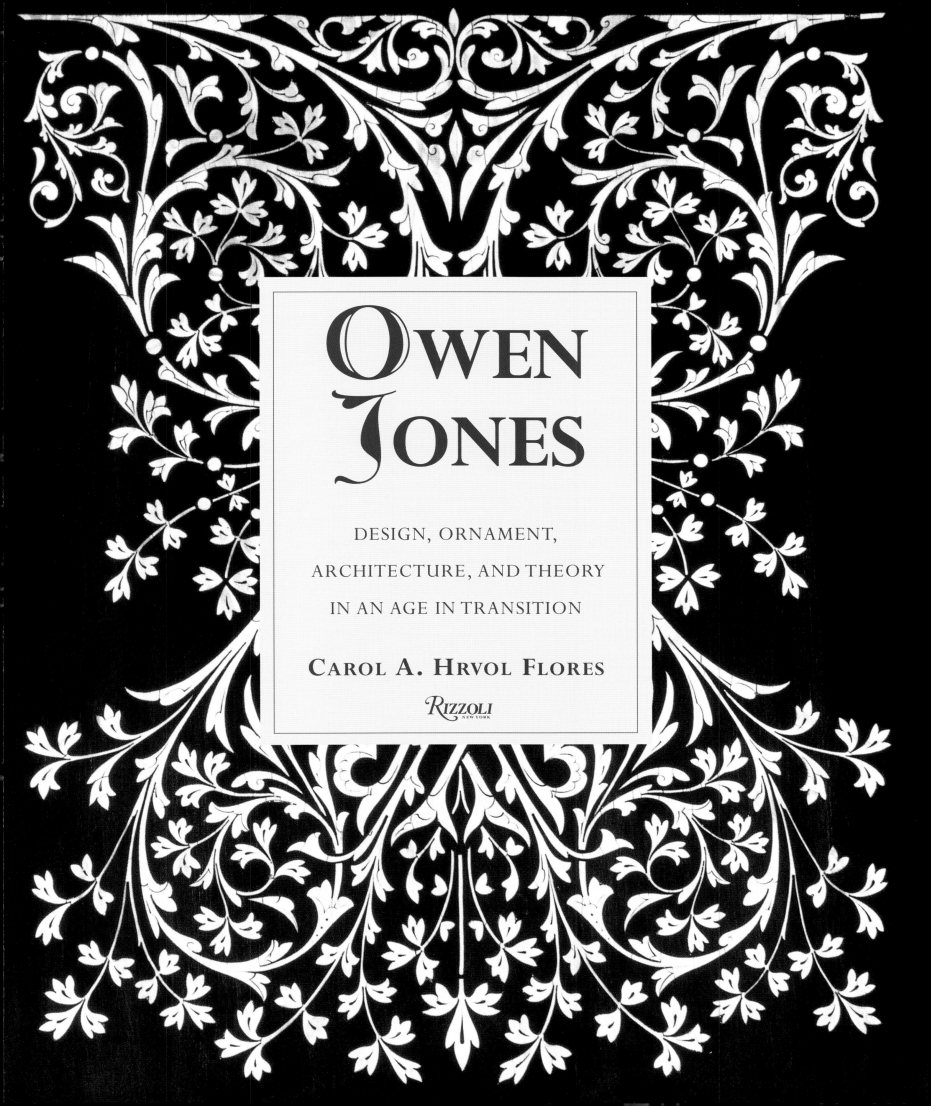

Owen Jones

DESIGN, ORNAMENT,
ARCHITECTURE, AND THEORY
IN AN AGE IN TRANSITION

Carol A. Hrvol Flores

RIZZOLI
NEW YORK

PAGE 1 *Owen Jones's monogram for* The Prism of Imagination, *1844*

PRECEDING PAGES *Detail of Alfred Morrison monogram inlaid in ivory in ebony upright case, 1863 (See Figs. 4.17 and 4.18.)*

First published in the United States in 2006 by
Rizzoli International Publications, Inc.
300 Park Avenue South
New York, NY 10010

Copyright © 2006 Carol A. Hrvol Flores

ISBN-10: 0-8478-2804-2
ISBN-13: 978-0-8478-2804-3

Library of Congress Control Number: 2005936755

2006 2007 2008 / 10 9 8 7 6 5 4 3 2 1

Designed by Abigail Sturges

Printed in China

CONTENTS

ACKNOWLEDGMENTS

Like thousands of others, I was introduced to Owen Jones through *The Grammar of Ornament,* I found the book on a sale table in a college bookstore and was fascinated with the illustrations. After reading Jones's principles, I wanted to know more about him and his designs. The search for this information has been a great adventure, made special by the people I have met, the archives and places I have visited, and the materials I have studied. I am deeply grateful to all those who have shared their knowledge or facilitated my research in some way.

I am particularly indebted to the wisdom of Ronald Lewcock, the mentoring of Betty Dowling, the camaraderie of Annibel Jenkins, and the patience of Fran Flores.

Special thanks are also extended to Michael Darby, Martin Levy, Robert Thorne, Jan Piggott, G. Michael Bott, Valerie Phillips, and Reverend Christopher Ivory.

Many individuals have been generous with their time and expertise and have my admiration and appreciation. These individuals include: Verity Andrews, Megan Aldrich, Stephen Astley, Michael Barker, Karen Beauchamp, Robin de Beaumont, Roger Bowdler, Kathy Brackney, Lady Brassey, the late George Chadwick, Michael Chrimes, Peter Cormack, Elizabeth Darby, Andrew De la Rue, John and Barbara De la Rue, Max Donnelly, Katherine Ferry, Vanessa Fleet, Marie Frank, Michael Goodall, Rosemary Hill, Hermione Hobhouse, Simon Jervis, John Kresten Jespersen, Paul Johnson, Sue Kerry, Tim Knox, Frederick R. Koch, Julie Anne Lambert, Julian Litten, Harry Lyons, David Mason, Frederica McRae, Peter Meadows, Wayne Meyer, Nicholas Olsberg, Paul Ojennus, Linda Parry, Andrew Peppitt, Geraint Phillips, Jessie Poesch, John Powell, Andrew Saunders, Larry Schaaf, John Scott, Barry Shifman, John P. Smith, Gavin Stamp, Annamarie Stapleton, Roger Taylor, David Temperley, Michael Twyman, Sellayah Viji, the late Clive Wainwright, Robert Welsh, Michael Whiteway, Glennys Wild, Stephen Wildman, Richard Guy Wilson, and Christine Woods.

Images are critical to an appreciation of the designs and publications of Owen Jones. I am deeply grateful for the expert photography of John Huffer in preparing the new images for this text. Several other individuals have been key in procuring photography or permissions; these include: Mike Bott, Peter Cormack, Martin Durrant, Giles French, Eliana Glicklich, Penny Haworth, Paul Johnson, Martin Levy, Jonathan Makepeace, Janet Parks, Roxanne Peters, Jan Piggott, Vivienne Rudd, Florian Schweizer, Annamarie Stapleton, Colleen Thorne, and Ann Wise.

I am also grateful to several individuals and institutions for providing funding, accommodations, photography, or permissions. In the United States, these include Winterthur Museum, the Victorian Society, and Ball State University. At Ball State, I wish to thank Jon Coddington, Warren Vander Hill, Joe Bilello, Beverly Pitts, Brian Sinclair, and John Straw. In the United Kingdom, I wish to thank Ralph Waller and Judith Nesbit at Harris Manchester College, Oxford University, Michael Bott at Reading University, H. Blairman & Son, the Fine Arts Society, The Crown Estate, and the Whitworth Art Gallery.

Finally, my thanks to the staffs of the following: Art Resource, Artists Rights Society, Avery Architectural and Fine Arts Library, Bodleian Library, Braintree District Museum (Ann Wise), British Library, British Museum, Cambridge University, Carnegie Museum of Art, Cecil Higgins Musuem, The Charles Dickens Museum, Christie's, Cole & Sons, The Crown Estate, Derby City Museum and Art Gallery, Elvehjem Museum of Art, Emory University (Archives & Special Collections), Fondation Le Corbusier, Georgia Institute of Technology (Architecture Library), Guildhall Library, the *Illustrated London News,* Kensington Central Library, Library Company of Philadelphia, Library of Congress, London Metropolitan Archives, the Metropolitan Museum of Art (New York), The National Archives (UK), The National Library of Wales, National Monument Records, the National Museum of Wales, Reading University (Archives & Special Collections), The Royal Academy, The Royal College of Art, The Royal Commissioners of 1851 Exhibition, The Royal Institute of British Architects, The Royal Society of Art, Arthur Sanderson and Sons, Ltd., Soane Museum, Steedman Library, Victoria and Albert Museum (Martin Durrant, Roxanne Peters, Charles Newton), and William Morris Gallery.

Finally, the preparation of this book has been achieved through the efforts of a dedicated team of professionals assembled by Rizzoli, and I am profoundly grateful for their contributions. In this regard, I wish to recognize the vision of David Morton and Charles Miers, the management of Douglas Curran, the artistry of Abigail Sturges, and most especially, the editorial expertise of Isabel Venero.

FACING PAGE
Textile design in chintz for 84 Westbourne Terrace, London, 1850

7

INTRODUCTION

FACING PAGE
Wallpaper design, c. 1860

Within two weeks of Owen Jones's death on April 19, 1874, a committee was formed to organize an unprecedented event: a memorial exhibition of the works of an architect held immediately after his death.[1] The tribute was planned to honor the man many considered most responsible for improving British design. Jones's international stature prompted the committee to include the display as part of the 1874 London Exhibition. Several hundred items were assembled, including textiles, furniture, and drawings from over eighty completed architecture commissions.

Unfortunately, the records and most of these works have disappeared. The scarcity of surviving buildings and documents explains why one of the most important theorists and designers of the nineteenth century has never had a book dedicated to his work, even though Nikolaus Pevsner warned about this "serious gap in the historiography of Victorian design" over three decades ago and Pevsner and Henry-Russell Hitchcock referred to Jones's significant contributions in their nineteenth-century studies.[2] Instead, this void has been filled by texts on other architects, with the result that Jones's contributions have been overlooked, while architects of lesser stature are celebrated and studied.

Fortunately, scholars have addressed aspects of Jones's work. The broadest investigations include two unpublished dissertations: Michael Darby's "Owen Jones and the Eastern Ideal" (1972), my "Owen Jones, Architect" (1996), and Simon Jervis's biographical essay in the *Dictionary of Design and Designers*. Most studies have focused on particular areas of Jones's work, including Michael Darby and David Van Zanten's article "Owen Jones's Iron Buildings of the 1850s," John Kresten Jespersen's dissertation "Owen Jones's *The Grammar of Ornament* of 1856: Field Theory in Victorian Design at the Mid-Century," and my article "A Colorful Context: Owen Jones's Designs for the Manchester Art Treasures Exhibition Building." Van Zanten established Jones's significance with regard to architectural polychromy, and other noted scholars, including E. H. Gombrich, Oleg Grabar, Stuart Durant, and Thomas Beeby have discussed Jones's theories, ornamental patterns, and designs. Jones's decorative arts have been considered in Mary Schoeser's *Disentangling Textiles*, Marilyn Oliver Hapgood's *Wallpaper and the Artist*, and Charlotte Gere and Michael Whiteway's *Nineteenth-Century Design from Pugin to Mackintosh*.

These studies contribute to our knowledge of Jones, but as the work of various experts, they are divided among architecture, theory, and several areas of specialization; consequently, we are left with a fractionalized understanding, since one writer presents Jones as a theorist, another celebrates him as a colorist, and yet another defines his work within the context of Orientalism. Jones is greater than the sum of these parts, however, and my goal for this book is to present his theory and accomplishments within the context of nineteenth-century British architecture and culture. In this format, Jones's standing and prominence are restored and his unusual ability to translate theory into practice is revealed. This format also facilitates comparisons of Jones's theory with the ideas of his contemporaries and indicates the influence of his ideas on later generations.

Studies of nineteenth-century architecture have relevance today, since the questions debated by the Victorians remain critical to good design. We are still responsible for the condition of our environment, for the aesthetics with which we choose to live, and for the legacy we will leave. Whether we choose to develop a better understanding of the impact of design and its potential for contributing positively to improved health and harmony, or negatively by assisting in agitation and dysfunction, is our choice, but we should not act in ignorance.

The designs and theory of Owen Jones have particular significance, since we live in a period when the importance of art to society is devalued and efforts to reintroduce color and ornament in architecture seem empty and superficial. Jones has much to tell us in this regard and his design philosophy and achievements in establishing a new style of architecture are shared in this book.

CHAPTER ONE

A NEW
UNDERSTANDING
OF
ARCHITECTURE

By the mid-nineteenth century, a sense of crisis and anxiety pervaded Britain, prompted by decades of extraordinary growth and accelerated change. Contemporaries saw themselves as living in a transitional age and tried to mitigate the uncertainty of the mutable present and to prepare for a radically different future by identifying the basic principles governing all areas of knowledge. In architecture, this new spirit of inquiry encouraged serious study, expanded publication, and intensified debates.

Key theorists emerged in England, France, and Germany. This book focuses on the theory and designs of one of them, the British architect Owen Jones (1809–1874; Fig. 1.3). Throughout a career spanning four decades, Jones proved to be a talented designer, perceptive theorist, and insightful critic, introducing ideas and concerns that became central to architectural understanding and debate for the remainder of the century.

The profession of architecture was still in a state of infancy in England during the first decades of the nineteenth century. The eighteenth-century gentleman-architect, serving an enlightened aristocratic patron, was disappearing, replaced by the businessman-designer. Such a man supervised a large office of draftsmen and clerks and produced designs to accommodate unprecedented public and private demand. The expansion of industry and trade, and dramatic changes in social conditions, required new types of buildings at a larger scale; the selection of architects and the designs for these new public and commercial buildings was often determined by committees through open or invitational competitions. The unscrupulous administration of the competitions, the lack of design education on the part of committee members, and, most of all, the introduction of new technologies and materials, challenged both the role of the designer and the practice of architecture. Other prob-

lems involved the decline of craftsmanship, an uneven and unsatisfactory system of training, and divisions between architects and other practitioners, including engineers, building contractors, and surveyors. To respond to these conditions architects formed two groups: the Architectural Association (1831) and the Royal Institute of British Architects (1834). The former was intended to improve training in design and practice, and the latter to raise the practice of architecture to professional status.

Publishing and debates about architecture intensified during the same period. Debates were largely focused on one theme: the origin and nomenclature of Gothic architecture, the popular style of the period.[1] Although publications proliferated, scholarship was perfunctory. The majority of books contained picturesque cottage and villa designs and lacked perceptive stylistic analysis or profound insight into the theory of architecture.[2] The practice-oriented training of British architects may have contributed to this problem.

The preparation for practice involved a three-to-five-year apprenticeship in an architect's office. Although some practitioners were seriously committed to training students, many apprentices were employed for menial tasks and were given limited design experience. Some students enhanced their education with drawing classes and European travel. Students financed their apprenticeships, their instruments and supplies, as well as the optional classes and travel; as a result, the profession continued to be populated by gentlemen who could afford the average seven years spent in apprenticeship and touring.

In Owen Jones's case, the provision for training came through inheritance. He was the son and namesake of a prosperous London furrier, antiquarian, and philanthropist. His father, also known as "Owain Myfyr" (1741–1815), founded the Gwyneddigian Society for the encouragement and study of oral and written Welsh. He collected over one

FACING PAGE
AND LEFT
*Figs. 1.1 and 1.2.
Designs for De la Rue,
1867*

hundred volumes of poetry and prose to preserve Welsh literature at a time when England was trying to suppress the language, and published some of this material, at a cost of over 1000 pounds, as *The Myvyrian Archaiology of Wales*. Upon his death, his literary collection was sold and subsequently became the foundation of the British Library's Welsh archive.[3] He left his birthplace, Llanvihangel, an eight-hundred-acre estate in North Wales, to his son. At the time, an estate of this size ranked in the top 2 percent of landholdings in Britain and the rents from this property provided income for the boy's education.[4]

At the age of fifteen, Jones began his apprenticeship with Lewis Vuillamy (1791–1871), a leading London practitioner.[5] Vuillamy had been articled to Sir Robert Smirke (1780–1867) and had attended the Royal Academy. The academy was the official institution for all of the arts in England, but paid relatively little attention to architecture. Six lectures a year and a limited collection of books in the library were devoted to the subject. The few students who gained admission, after submitting a drawing portfolio for review, were exposed to the work of contemporary British architects and were permitted to join them in competing in academy-sponsored exhibitions and contests. As a student, Vuillamy won a silver and gold medal, and a four-year travel scholarship (1818). He published the drawings from his study tour in *The Bridge of Sta. Trinità at Florence* (1822) and *Examples of Ornamental Sculpture in Architecture from Greece, Asia Minor, and Italy* (1823).[6]

An apprenticeship with Vuillamy was desirable, since his pupils worked to high standards and had the opportunity to develop proficiency in a wide range of styles. During the five years Jones worked in the office, classical schemes included the Corn Exchange, Bishop's Stortford, Hertfordshire (1828); an addition to the Assembly Rooms, Queen's Street, Wolverhampton, Staffordshire (1829); and

early Greek Revival designs for the Law Society's Hall, Chancery Lane (1828–32). Gothic ecclesiastical commissions included St. Bartholomew's Church, West Hill, Sydenham (1826–31); St. Barnabas, Addison Road, Kensington, (1828–9); St. James's Church, Park Hill, Clapham Common (1828–9); St. Paul's Church, Burslem, Staffordshire (1828–30); and St. John the Divine, Richmond-upon-Thames, Surrey (1829–31). Vuillamy used Tudor Revival and a variety of other styles in his residential schemes.[7]

Jones followed Vuillamy, applying to the Royal Academy and gaining acceptance on June 25, 1830.[8] The exhibition in progress displayed works by John Soane, Charles Barry, and C. R. Cockerell. Soane's entry used a new type of bird's-eye perspective for the Bank of England; Barry illustrated two schemes for an addition to the Pitt Press at Cambridge, and Cockerell submitted *The Western Pediment of the Temple of Minerva Parthenon, at Athens*.[9]

Jones also traveled that year (1830), visiting Paris, Milan, Venice, and Rome. When he returned, he entered the office of the surveyor William Wallen. While "surveyor" was the term used by many practical architects, surveyors' offices were also places of employment for aspiring architects interested in obtaining the measuring skills required for serious studies of ancient architecture. This is most likely the motivation for Jones, who left Wallen after a few months to begin an extended tour of Europe and the Middle East, including Italy, Sicily, and Greece (1831), Egypt and Constantinople (1832–3), and Spain and France (1834).[10] Vuillamy may have inspired Jones's itinerary, since Vuillamy was one of the first British architects to visit the Middle East. Surviving drawings of the Yeni Valide Camii and the Sehzade Camii in Istanbul by Vuillamy and Jones support this idea (Pl. 1.1). These drawings also demonstrate Jones's proficiency in preparing the on-site studies important in the architectural education of the period. Students measured, rendered, and sometimes produced reconstruction drawings of the monuments and ruins they observed. These representations filled portfolios and books intended to impress prospective clients and to establish a reputation in the profession. Like Vuillamy, Jones produced two books based on his travels: *Views on the Nile from Cairo to the Second Cataract* (1843; Figs. 1.4 and 1.5) and *Plans, Elevations, Sections, and Details of the Alhambra* (1842–5). (Sections of his book on the Alhambra were sold beginning in 1836, prior to the first bound edition in 1842.) These books were not, however, the young architect's first significant contributions to British architecture. That event occurred on the evening of December 1, 1835, when the twenty-six-year-old architect delivered a talk entitled "On the Influence of Religion upon Art" to the members of the Architectural Association. Jones began by saying that he intended to review several styles of architecture to show the close connection between them and the religious institutions of the country where they originated, and finally to deduce from this review some of the causes contributing to the current state of the practice of architecture. Although the connection between architecture and society seems both obvious and fundamental today, this concept was revolutionary when Jones introduced it. Particularly, the beliefs and practices of a society often based, as they were, on religion. To prove his hypotheses, Jones summarized the convictions and motivations of the Egyptians, Greeks, Romans, and the followers of Christ and Mohammed, demonstrating the relationship between the art and architecture produced by each of these groups and the depth of their religious commitment. He developed his case chronologically, pointing to the direct correlation between changes in style and the way the religion was inspired by, or rejected, previous dogma. He also argued that changes within styles corresponded to the rise, progress, and decline of a society and its religious institutions.

Jones found that the monuments constructed by the ancient Egyptians formed a comprehensive chronicle of the history and religious beliefs of the people. He cited the richly colored bas-reliefs on both the interior and exterior walls of Egyptian temples as examples, observing that the innermost walls reported the genealogy, attributes, and appropriate religious ceremonies associated with each deity. In contrast, the hieroglyphs on the public portions of the temples told the story of kings and political events, while private tombs recorded daily life through depictions of the arts and commerce. Jones interpreted the absence of remains of private dwellings as evidence that the wealth and art of the community had been concentrated in erecting temples for the gods, palaces for the kings, and tombs for the dead.

If Jones had concluded his remarks at this point, the lecture would have considerably advanced British theory by establishing the link between the "world-views" of societies and their architecture. Jones continued, however, and took another bold step, criticizing British architecture as inappropriate and expressionless. He delivered his attack through a series of contrasts, comparing the positive attributes of earlier buildings with the negative qualities of contemporary designs, a technique soon to be adopted by the architect A.W.N. Pugin in his book *Contrasts*.

Jones blamed the Reformation for severing the connection between religion and art, since the Reformation had destroyed the unity of Christian belief and produced numerous sects with divergent dogma. Jones concluded that this fragmentation prevented a cohesive society and a unified religious architecture that would be legible to future generations. Later, Pugin, John Ruskin, and others also condemned the Reformation for destroying the unity of the Christian religion.

Jones argued that, unlike earlier societies whose architecture reflected religious belief, the fracture and decline of faith in the nineteenth century could only produce buildings representing the new forces of Science, Commerce, and Industry; consequently, the best works being produced were the result of building science, or engineering—not art. The engineers were erecting the new types of structures required, such as bridges, train sheds, and industrial buildings, while the architects continued designing conventional structures in historicist styles. Jones understood the changes taking place in design and construction. While the eighteenth-century amateur architect could give a sketch or plan with approximate measurements to a builder who determined the best way to execute the design, nineteenth-century building conditions were more complex. The architect had to communicate his designs to untrained competition committees and to building contractors, many of whom were more adept at negotiating business transactions than carrying out construction. Jones realized that architects, in order to be effective, needed a greater understanding of advances in materials and construction. To make his point, he used the treatment of cast iron, criticizing his peers for ignoring the

Fig. 1.3.
Charles Baugniet,
Owen Jones, *1843.*
Lithograph,
13½ x 10½ in.

14 *Chapter One*

benefits of the material and the opportunity for new design. Instead of accepting the fact that a six-inch iron column was as strong as a twenty-inch stone pillar, architects encased the cast-iron column to imitate the stone column. Jones maintained that all previous periods of architecture were true to the materials available and that local materials, climate, and religion, were the factors responsible for the style of architecture a country produced. In a radical departure from prevailing theory, he challenged his audience to abandon the imitation of former styles and create original designs using new materials and construction techniques. He explained that invention would result from fashioning connecting and terminating pieces for the undisguised cast-iron column and other materials. He recognized these experiments as the natural process of creating architecture and argued that the ancients had used the knowledge and materials at their command and would have produced a far different architecture if cast iron had been at their disposal. He condemned contemporary historicism as meaningless and dishonest, criticizing shops suggestive of princely palaces as imitation, not architecture, and called for buildings true to the times, as new and progressive as technological advances permitted. He also wanted architects to study the needs and occupations of society to produce structures capable of contributing to the facility and civility of life.

"On the Influence of Religion upon Art" established Jones's position as a scholar, critic, and major figure in the debates on the practice and theory of architecture. In differentiating the characteristics of early nineteenth-century Britain from preceding periods and defining the "spirit of the age" in terms of contemporary industrialization and the inadequacy of organized religion to provide a unifying spirituality, Jones shared the concerns and thinking of Fichte, Hazlitt, Carlyle, and Mill.[11] His original contributions involve the identification of key concepts that profoundly influenced the understanding and approach to architecture of his contemporaries and later generations. These concepts include the connection between a society's culture and its architecture; the importance of the principle that architecture should be true to the materials of its construction; and the need for a new style reflective of the capabilities, lifestyle, and needs of the age. These insights, communicated powerfully and simply, predate the treatises of Pugin, Ruskin, and E. E. Viollet-le-Duc, and constitute an important step in the development of architecture theory.

The year 1835 marks two other important initiatives for Jones. First, two of his watercolors were displayed in the Architectural Drawings Section of the Royal Academy exhibition at Somerset House. These depicted the ruins of the Great Temple at Karnak and a restoration of an interior in the Alhambra looking toward the Court of the Lions. Reviews elevated Jones's use of color and the quality of the renderings over the entries of Soane and Vuillamy.[12] Second,

Jones began preparing his book on the Alhambra, one that substantially advanced the state of architecture publishing in England.

The Alhambra was a popular destination and subject for study in the 1830s and 1840s. The noted Islamic scholar Oleg Grabar identified two types of studies undertaken of the Spanish palace. The first type involved a search for the picturesque by members of the French literati and the English aristocracy emphasizing the exoticism and sensuousness of the medieval palace. Théophile Gautier's description of the Alhambra as an "earthly paradise" and Washington Irving's characterization of its "barbaric magnificence" are typical of this viewpoint. The second type of inquiry entailed deeper research for "new doctrines and new ideas about the arts and especially about ornament." Grabar identified Jones and the French architects Jules Goury and Girault de Prangey as exemplars of the second group. Grabar notes that the extensive copying of the designs of Jones, Goury, and de Prangey resulted in their association with the romantic images presented by Washington Irving, Chateaubriand, and others, and with the places of sensuous leisure (hotels, bars, and movie theaters) called "Granada" or "Alhambra."

Fig. 1.4. Page from Views on the Nile from Cairo to the Second Cataract, 1843

The Alhambra presented an opportunity for Jones and Goury to become authorities in an undeveloped area of architecture research, since most architects who visited the Middle East had dismissed the architecture as insignificant, seeing originality only in secondary structures such as kiosks, fountains, and *caravanserai*.[13] The Alhambra also offered the opportunity to investigate the colors used by the Moors, since the study of polychromy (color in ancient architecture) was a subject of increasing interest and scholarship. Attention to the topic started in the eighteenth century when archaeologists and architects, including Stuart and Revett, reported pigment on Greek and Roman buildings. In 1806, Antoine-Chrysostome Quatrèmere de Quincey (1755–1843) invented the term *polychromie* to dis-

Fig. 1.5. Page from Views on the Nile from Cairo to the Second Cataract, 1843. British Library, BL135826

cuss the Greeks' use of semiprecious stones, gold, and paint in the decoration of interior sculptures and presented his theory to the French Academy.[14] Other architects and theorists studied exterior polychromy. For example, Franz Christain Gau (1790–1853), an architect teaching in Paris, published *Antiquitées nubiennes* in 1822; Thomas Leverton Donaldson (1795–1855) issued the findings of English architects in 1824 and several French students prepared reconstructions and new design schemes involving polychromy as part of their studies at the Académie de France in Rome during the late 1820s; this group included Henri Labrouste (1801–1875), Félix-Louis-Jacques Duban (1797–1870), and Théodore Labrouste (1799–1885). The French architect Jacques-Ignace Hittorff (1792–1867) collaborated with Karl Ludwig von Zanth (1796–1857) and published polychrome restorations of the temples of Selinunte and Agrigento in 1827. Hittorff presented these drawings in the Paris Salon of 1831, where the intense primary colors applied to the entire facades of the temples sparked considerable criticism and controversy. Jones may not have seen these images, but would have been familiar with the debate and with the fourth volume of *Antiquities of Athens* (released between 1825 and 1830) showing Donaldson's colored reconstruction of the Temple of Apollo Epicurius at Bassae and Cockerell's Temple of Jupiter Olympius at Agrigentum. Jones's travel itinerary suggests a desire to study color in ancient architecture, since his choices of Italy, Sicily, and Greece are consistent with the areas most researched.

When Jones arrived in Athens in 1831, he met Jules Goury (1803–1834) and the German architect Gottfried Semper (1803–1879), a former pupil of Gau's, who were conducting chromatic studies of ancient monuments.

Semper described Goury as "an excellent artist, strong in mind and body, whose level of energy and activity was equal to his talent" and praised his portfolio as "the most complete and most reliable collection on Polychromy" produced. Goury left Semper in Athens and spent the next several years (1831–4) studying architecture in Turkey, Egypt, and Spain with Jones. The noted Egyptologist Joseph Bonomi described the pair working together in Thebes:

. . . the two architects set to work with an extraordinary enthusiasm, and cleared out one of those crude brick arches which surround the Memnonium, and converted it into a comfortable residence, employing the fellaheen, and some of their boats even, to build a wall across the arch separating the kitchen from the studio, which was lighted by a large hole in the roof. I was struck by the facility with which the Arabs seemed to understand them with the smallest amount of words of a polyglot dialect, chiefly composed of French, and the discipline and order they had obtained in the arrangement of their folios and drawing implements.

From this improvised abode the two architects used to sally forth with Arabs carrying their ladders, boards, and implements for measuring, and return in the evening with a store of architectural knowledge derived from the surrounding remains that was quite astounding for accuracy and detail, with sometimes not a few picturesque sketches in water-colour of the ruins and their present occupants. Never has it seemed to me did two men work together in better harmony and success.[15]

Jones and Goury demonstrated this same intensity in their study of the Alhambra, and within six months produced hundreds of measured drawings, paper tracings, and plaster casts, recording in infinite detail the plans and patterns of the Moorish palace. Their study ended with Goury's death

Fig. 1.6. "General Plan of the Fortress of the Alhambra," Pl. I from Plans, Elevations, Sections, and Details of the Alhambra, *vol. I, 1842*

from cholera on August 28, 1834. Jones visited his friend's family in France and continued on to England to publish their research. The result, the *Plans, Elevations, Sections, and Details of the Alhambra*, in two volumes, revolutionized the reporting of architecture in Britain through the comprehensiveness of Jones and Goury's investigation, the originality of their findings, and the quality of their analysis.

In addition, Jones's success with color printing improved the accuracy and consistency of representation and design communication. Before *Alhambra*'s publication, almost all books and illustrations were printed with black ink on a white page. Text could be printed in colored inks but illustrations required hand coloring, a costly, labor-intensive process. Experiments with colored illustrations printed from lithographic plates had been conducted with some success in France, Germany, and England, but no London publisher was competent to render the volume and complexity of designs Jones desired.[16] When the plates he commissioned from Day and Haghe proved unsatisfactory, he began experimenting with printing from zinc plates and then moved to the new process of chromolithography, or colored printing, from stones.[17]

Chromolithography demands precision in each stage of production. First, the image to be printed is transferred to a lithographic stone. The lithographer retraces the outline on the stone in chalk or black ink, adding desired shading. The printer etches the image by applying acid to the stone. An impression on thin paper is made for each color to be used; each impression is placed on a stone and passed through a lithographic press, imprinting the outline of the first, or key stone, on the other stones. An artist indicates the amount and location of color to be used on each stone, one stone per color. Finally, the image is printed on a sheet of paper and the impressed paper is attached to each of the stones successively and aligned so the colors fall in their proper places or "register." Seven stones, prepared in this manner, were required for many of the illustrations in Jones's text.

The young architect was not dissuaded by the difficulty of the process. He established a workshop at 11 John Street, Adelphi, with a staff of ornament draftsmen and two experienced lithographic printers. Their experiments were slow, frustrating, and costly, forcing Jones to mortgage his Welsh property to finance the operation. He also sold subscriptions for *Alhambra*, issuing the two volumes in parts and selling the sections as they were produced, a popular method of receiving income during the publishing process and increasing sales, since individuals were able to purchase a book in sections, spreading the cost over an extended period rather than in one large payment. This method was particularly suited to expensive professional publications intended for students as well as practitioners.

The text was also issued in two sizes: the large folio format used for major architecture publications and a smaller, more affordable version. The first volume, with all ten parts, appeared in 1842 and cost 21 pounds in the large-paper format (*folio grand aigle*) and 12 pounds 10 shillings in the smaller format (*folio colombier*). The second volume, containing two parts, was released in 1845 at a cost of 10 pounds 10 shillings in the large format and 6 pounds 6 shillings in the smaller edition; combined editions of both volumes cost 36 pounds 10 shillings and 24 pounds, respectively.[18] Although these prices were too high for most architects, the price is modest when compared with Thomas Daniell's (1749–1840) earlier *Oriental Scenery* (1808), containing 144 aquatints at a price of 210 pounds.[19]

Fig. 1.7. "Rafters," Pl. XXXV from Plans, Elevations, Sections, and Details of the Alhambra, *vol. II, 1842*

Fig. 1.8. "Facade Court of the Mosque," Pl. XXV from Plans, Elevations, Sections, and Details of the Alhambra, *vol. I, 1842*

In addition to drastically reducing the cost of colored illustrations, chromolithography improved the speed and volume of production. J. B. Waring (1823–1875) explained the impact of chromolithography on publishing in *Masterpieces of Industrial Art and Sculpture at the International Exhibit of 1862*. Waring said that, before colored lithography, it would have taken one artist a minimum of 42 years to produce the 300 plates in his text and one printer, working ordinary hours, 104 years to print them.[20]

The plates in Waring's text and *Alhambra* remain rich and vibrant more than a century after their printing. Even more impressive, however, is the unsurpassed quality and detail of the drawings and the archaeological and architectural content of *Alhambra*. Jones's text continues to be an authoritative source for scholars and for architects engaged in restorations of the medieval palace.

Jones used a variety of graphic techniques, in addition to color, to enhance the reader's understanding of the architecture. Black-and-white images range from simple outlines and picturesque sketches to complex sections and exacting renderings. The first woodblock print shows Jones's intention to provide significant information as well as showcase his graphic talent. The print provides a distant view of the Spanish acropolis to introduce the reader to the site. The scene is not depicted from a particular vantage point but through a composite of several perspectives combined to provide a sense of the place based on accurate depictions of the buildings (Fig. 1.6).[21]

Jones often presents a wealth of information in a single plate. For example, some plates show comparative studies of particular elements, such as column capitals, spandrels, and decorative panels. These plates illustrate the stylistic characteristics and components of each piece as well as the variety possible. Other arrangements present plans, elevations, details, and profiles of elements in a particular part of the palace on the same page (Figs. 1.7, 1.8, and Pl. 1.4).

Jones preceded his text with two title pages: one calligraphic and one conventional. Both pages identify the book as the *Plans, Elevations, Sections, and Details of the Alhambra, from drawings taken on the spot in 1834 by the late M. Jules Goury and in 1834 and 1837 by Owen Jones, Archt. with a complete translation of the Arabic inscriptions, and an Historical Notice of the Kings of Granada, from the Conquest of that City by the Arabs to the Expulsion of the Moors, by Mr. Pasqual de Gayangos* (Pl. 1.2). He also added a dedication to Goury and an excerpt from Victor Hugo's *Les Orientales*, celebrating the Alhambra as the "Palace that genius / Has gilded like a dream and filled with harmony."[22]

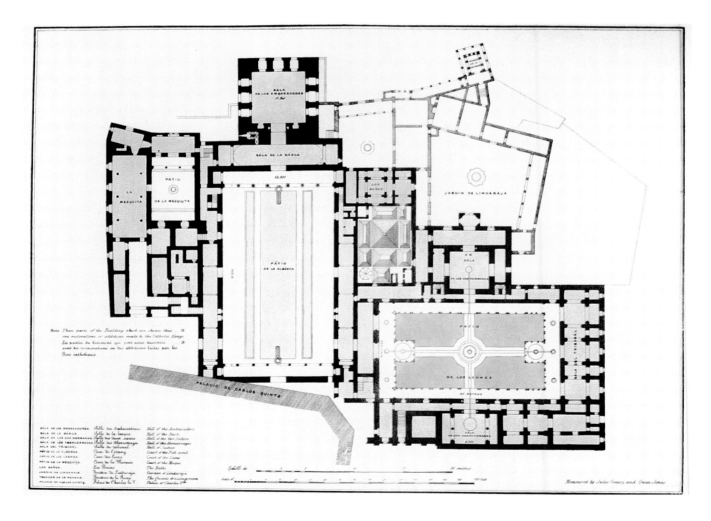

Fig. 1.9. "Plan of the Royal Arabian Palace in the Ancient Fortress of the Alhambra, measured by Jules Goury and Owen Jones," Pl. III from Plans, Elevations, Sections, and Details of the Alhambra, *vol. I, 1842*

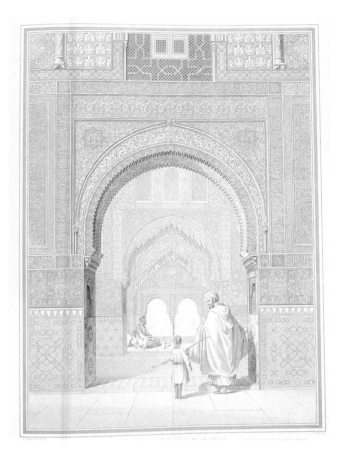

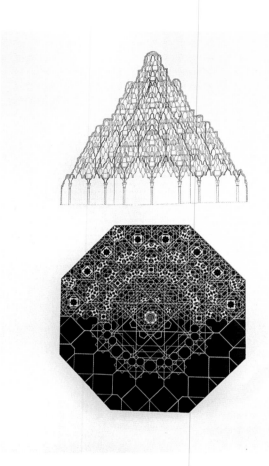

Fig. 1.10. *"View of the Hall of the Two Sisters,"* Pl. XIX *from* Plans, Elevations, Sections, and Details of the Alhambra, *vol. I, 1842*

Fig. 1.11. *"Details of the Great Arches, Hall of the Bark,"* Pl. X *from* Plans, Elevations, Sections, and Details of the Alhambra, *vol. I, 1842*

The decision to include a history of the palace accords with Jones's belief in the relationship between culture and architecture. His choice of the noted Arabic scholar, Pasqual de Gayangos (1809–1897) to prepare the history conforms to the serious pursuit of scholarship evident throughout Jones's work.[23] The focus of the book, however, is the architecture of the palace. The first volume contains plates and texts providing information on the materials, construction, and the decoration of the building. The second volume presents large-scale details of elements shown in the first volume.

Volume I begins with measured plans of the Alhambra complex by Jones and Goury and text in English and French explaining the original functions of structures and spaces as well as their contemporary state and applications. As a result, the reader learns that the ancient citadel is now used to house prisoners and that the houses, gardens, and convent situated in the areas identified as Calle San Francisco and Alhambra Alta occupy the place of the former mosque and the house of the Cadi (Fig. 1.9).

Jones explains that the Arabic architecture reflects religious belief in the same way that Gothic architecture reflected Christian values. He said the Islamic prohibition of representing animal life fostered the use of other motifs, including inscriptions containing passages from the Koran, interwoven with geometrical patterns and abstracted

flowers. He described these conventionalized designs as having been "translated through the loom" and said "The Arabs, in changing their wandering for a settled life . . . transferred the luxurious shawls and hangings of Cachmere, which had adorned their former dwellings, to their new . . . changing the tent-pole for a marble column, and the silken tissue for gilded plaster"[24] (Fig. 1.10).

Jones identifies, explains, and depicts many examples of the influence of Islam in the palace's architecture, including the construction of *mihrabs* (Pl. XXV) and the use of lattice screens to enable members of the harem to observe the feasts below undetected (Pl. XIX). The descriptions provide insights into the construction, materials, and functions of the spaces within the palace. For example, Jones discovered the mathematical basis of the *muqarnas*, or stalactite domes, that mystified Western visitors (Figs. 1.11 and 1.12). He recognized that the ceilings were made of wood and the pendentives were composed of reed and plaster. He identified the seven shapes used to form the complex stalactites and recognized these forms as derivatives of the right-angle triangle, the isoceles triangle, and the rectangle. He observed that the straight and curving surfaces of the pieces allowed them to be joined on several sides forming "combinations as various as the melodies which may be produced from the seven notes of the musical scale."[25]

Jones's investigation of the stalactite domes is a good example of his analytical technique. First, he presents factual data, such as the statistic that the dome in the Hall of the Two Sisters contained almost five thousand plaster prisms; second, he determines the mathematical and physical basis of the construction, and finally, he interprets the "wonderful power and effect obtained by the repetition of the most simple elements." He provides plans and drawings to illustrate the text. Jones describes the fabrication of other types of ceilings and architectural components, including column capitals, spandrels, cornices, arches, porticoes and pavilions, windows and doors, within the palace.[26]

Jones also identified the materials used throughout the palace and noted their condition. He recognized substitutions and suggested the original materials based on his knowledge of architecture and of other Islamic structures.[27] He concluded that most of the flooring was not original, since pavements had been raised throughout the palace, obscuring some of the mosaic patterns on the lower wall surfaces. He also observed that the existing marble-and-brick flooring was less consistent with the general decoration of the halls and courts than the colored tiles found in several places, including a section in an alcove of the Hall of Justice. He believed that the Arabs, like the Greeks, had created harmonious aesthetic arrangements where every

TOP *Fig. 1.14. "Frets from Different Halls," Pl. XXXVIII from* Plans, Elevations, Sections, and Details of the Alhambra, *vol. I, 1842*

ABOVE *Fig. 1.15. "Mosaic Dadoes on the Pillars Between the Windows in the Hall of the Ambassadors," Pl. XL from* Plans, Elevations, Sections, and Details of the Alhambra, *vol. I, 1842*

pattern and element contributed to a unified concept and that the exceptions were introduced by later Christian inhabitants and restorers unaware of the original concept. The strength of this conviction prompted Jones to look beyond what was in front of him and to reconstruct patterns and materials. An example of this practice occurs in his rendering of the Court of the Fish-Pond from the Hall of the Barck, Patio de Comares, where he replaces the existing flooring with a pattern of tiles consistent with the rest of the design (Fig. 1.13).

Jones marveled at the durability and intense colors of the mosaics and tiles used in dados and pavements and speculated on their method of manufacture (Figs. 1.14 and 1.15). He distinguished tiles and mosaics formed by different processes, such as *azulejos*, consisting of an earthenware body covered with white slip, painted and then fired, and tessellated tiles, formed by pressing wet clay into molds, impressing patterns into the clay, then filling the depressions with colored liquid and firing.[28]

Jones's interest in tile production was both archaeological and contemporary. The use of tiles in architecture had increased in France and Germany at the beginning of the nineteenth century, when architects realized the potential of replacing the fragility of painted surfaces with permanently colored materials (permanent polychromy) resistant to the dirt that blackened urban buildings.[29] Although no similar movement occurred in England, limited experiments had been conducted in tile production. Jones called attention to these experiments, citing the tile-making machinery designed by Henry Pether and improved by a Mr. Singer of Vauxhall Pottery in an endnote accompanying Plate XXXIX. Singer's machine produced a large quantity of tiles at one time by cutting clay in thin layers of biscuit (unglazed tile). The uniform pieces were glazed, fired, and then embedded in cement slate or stone slabs about 18 inches square for installation quicker than the placement of individual pieces.[30]

Jones, Pugin, and M. Digby Wyatt collaborated with manufacturers and led the promotion of England's emerging tile industry during the 1840s. Tiles were significant for Pugin in replicating the substance and aesthetic of medieval churches and, therefore, contributed to the archaeologically correct revival of Gothic architecture he sought; in contrast, Jones and Wyatt produced geometric patterns intended for contemporary schemes (Fig. 1.16). Jones produced designs for Maw and Co. and for John Marriott Blashfield, a partner in the firm of Messrs. Parker and Wyatt and a pioneer in mosaic and tessellated-tile production. Blashfield, an original subscriber to *Alhambra*, asked Jones to produce tile patterns for publication. Jones illustrated ten composite patterns in the chromolithographic plates of *Designs for Mosaic and Tessellated Pavements* published by John Weale in 1842 (Figs. 1.17–1.21). These designs demonstrated the potential for realizing new patterns by varying color and patterns. Jones also prepared plates for *Encaustic Tiles* (1843), showing ninety-six ancient schemes at half scale, plus other floor patterns.[31]

In 1844, Jones developed patterns and specified tiles and other materials for all of the floors in the Palace of Westminster (Houses of Parliament). He submitted his detailed plans in the competition held to determine the decoration of the new Palace of Westminster. He adopted a new large-scale format, creating a 25-by-12-foot entry enhanced with samples of the encaustic tiles and Staffordshire and Derbyshire marbles to be used in implementing his designs. He chose marble for the halls and galleries, encaustic tiles and porcelain mosaics for the corridors, inlaid woodwork for other rooms, and asphalt for the open courts.

In an exhibition of the entries, the *Athenaeum* praised the attractiveness and comprehensiveness of Jones's plan and recognized his submission as the only entry providing valuable assistance on what ought to be done in the building.[32] The reviewer said several of Jones's floor patterns showed

Fig. 1.16. Tile patterns, c. 1855

"great beauty and appropriateness" and noted, in particular, that the designs for the landing of the peers' private staircase and the gallery of the speaker's house (number eighty-nine) showed Jones's ability to invent new patterns without a Moorish character.[33] Ironically, the reviewer for the *Builder* had the opposite impression, criticizing the design for being in the Moresque style and admonishing Jones for being unable to abandon Moorish patterns.[34] This criticism suggests the possibility, advanced by the noted historian Henry-Russell Hitchcock, that Jones's original work was often misinterpreted and called Moorish Revival because of the geometry in the patterns and Jones's association with his book *Alhambra*.[35] It is interesting to note that the reviewer for the *Times* described design number eighty-nine as "very chaste, and remarkable for the brilliancy of the effect as well as the purity of the devices" and observed that this scheme would greatly enhance any Gothic interior and would be particularly effective in the building for Parliament.[36] The *Illustrated London News* reporter agreed,

Figs. 1.17–1.21. Pages from Designs for Mosaic and Tessellated Pavements, *1842*

finding the geometrical patterns of Jones's designs "very beautiful and the colours extremely gorgeous," but the reporter for the *Civil Engineer and Architect's Journal* thought they were most laborious and inferior to earlier designs by Jones.[37] The 1959 edition of *The Oxford History of English Art* states that some of the designs Jones submitted to the 1844 competition were used for the floors of Westminster but no evidence has been found to support this statement; however, Barry and Pugin may have accepted Jones's recommendations of the materials to be used in particular areas, since the flooring installed matches the materials specified in Jones's plan.[38]

The attention to materials and provision of pragmatic information presented marked differences between Jones's investigation of the Alhambra and previous texts. For example, James Cavanaugh Murphy's *Arabian Antiquities* (1815), considered the first important study of Islamic architecture produced in England, was superficial and full of inaccuracies. Murphy misidentified materials and committed so many errors in identifying the functions, names, and details of rooms that one writer said it was difficult to believe Murphy had ever visited the site.[39] In contrast, every description and drawing in Jones's text indicates his thorough understanding of the elements comprising the palace and his desire to educate the reader.

A particularly significant example of Jones's insight and comprehensive investigation occurs in his attention to the hundreds of epigraphs found on every surface of the palace. Jones believed the inscriptions were critical to understanding the ideas, attitudes, and feelings of the Alhambra's designers, builders, and patrons; consequently, he traced or made a plaster cast of each message and commissioned Gayangos to translate the passages. Earlier studies of ancient architecture recorded inscriptions, and sometimes reconstructed missing text, but did not provide translations. Murphy did translate a few common quotations, such as: "There is no conqueror but God" and "Praise be to God!" but Jones's comprehensive translation was unique and, as he predicted, revealed important information about the motivations and convictions of the builders and the purposes of objects and spaces in the palace.

Contemporary scholars identify the Arabic calligraphy gracing the walls of the Alhambra as Kufic and Naskhid-Thuluth scripts; Gayangos described the characters as "Arabic," "Cufic," or "African." Gayangos distinguished three types of inscriptions: *ayát*, verses from the Koran; *asja'*, pious or devout adages not from the Koran, and *ash'ar*, poems that praise the builders, occupiers, or spaces within the palace. Gayangos observed that the *ayát* and *asja* were usually composed of Kufic characters shaped so that each quotation could be read backward or forward, up or down, without altering the meaning (Fig. 1.22). He noted that other verses and long poems were composed of characters unique to the conquerors of Spain and called this script

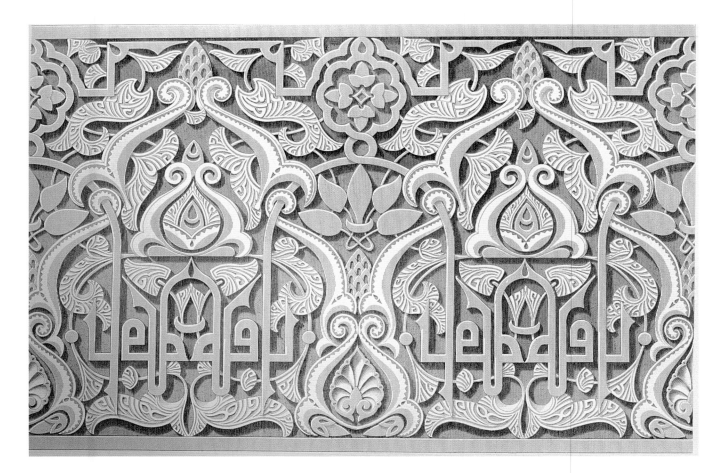

Fig. 1.22. "Frieze in the Hall of the Two Sisters," Pl. IV from Plans, Elevations, Sections, and Details of the Alhambra, *vol. I, 1842*

"African." Some of these passages divulge the purpose of a particular space or object, and Grabar notes that many of these poems are written in the first person so that the building itself seems to be speaking; for example, a text on the throne in the Hall of the Ambassadors explains: "From me thou art welcomed every morning and evening, with the tongues of blessings, prosperity, happiness, and friendship . . ." and an inscription appearing in a niche for a watercooler in the Hall of the Two Sisters reads: "The water vase within me, they say is like a devout man standing towards the *Kiblah* of the *Mihrab*, ready to begin his prayers."[40]

Jones appreciated the importance of the epigraphs on several levels. At the most basic, the passages replaced the mimetic images and symbolism of other religions and cultures and brought pleasure to the viewer (Figs. 1.22, 1.23, and Pl. 1.7). He explained this concept by saying they "address themselves to the eye of the observer by the beautiful forms of the characters; exercise his intellect by the difficulty of deciphering their curious and complex involutions; and reward his imagination, when read, by the beauty of the sentiments they express, and the music of their composition." In *The Sense of Order: A Study in the Psychology of Decorative Art*, E. H. Gombrich distinguishes the theories of Jones from Ruskin, Semper, and Pugin, observing that Jones introduced the psychology of perception into the study of nineteenth-century architecture. Well before Gestalt and information theories had been developed, Jones

realized that individuals were actively engaged in viewing their world and interpreting input according to a predilection for order. He understood that this process was made easier and more agreeable through recognition and repetition and described the secret of creating satisfying ornament as the repetition of a few simple elements to produce a broad general effect. He realized that too simple a design, endlessly repeated, produces monotony and boredom and that a sense of pleasure and beauty results from viewing patterns that require a higher mental effort. Jones believed that the eye read script and ornament in the same way and, therefore, when the eye followed the continuous curves of Arabic scripts a sense of pleasure would be derived from viewing the sensuous lines of the calligraphy and deciphering the message.[41]

Gombrich and Grabar observe that written images have universal aesthetic appeal independent from textual comprehension. They cite inscriptions composed of meaningless combinations of letters and Chinese and Islamic scripts that garner international admiration from viewers unable to read the text but who are drawn to the artistic appeal of the characters.[42] Moreover, Grabar observes that calligraphy, or writing intended to be beautiful, often confuses interpretation by manipulating the characters and adding excessive flourishes. It's interesting to note that Jones included elaborate calligraphic title pages in some of his publications (Fig. 1.35 and Pl. 2.1).

Fig. 1.23. "Small Panel in the Jamb of a Window, Hall of the Two Sisters," Pl. XXVII from Plans, Elevations, Sections, and Details of the Alhambra, *vol. II, 1845*

Fig. 1.24. *Drawing of the interior, Christ Church, Streatham, London, c. 1851*

Although Jones did not discuss redundancy, or the ability of a listener or viewer to anticipate words or sounds after seeing or hearing only the first part of the message, this principle is significant in allowing a designer to incorporate a wealth of text to enrich a visual pattern, proclaim the nature of a space, and elicit desired responses without overwhelming the viewer with too much information. The viewer recognizes the inscription by the initial elements, eliminating painstaking interpretation. Jones understood that in Islamic architecture, familiar passages from the Koran or aphorisms fulfill the dual function of stimulating piety or contemplation, while providing a rich tapestry of ornamentation. Customary examples include: "Praise [be given] to God, the only one. Thanks be likewise [returned] to God"; "There is no conqueror but God," and "Glory to God! God is eternal! God is [our] refuge in every trouble." Jones believed the familiar curving forms of these passages satisfied the eye and pleasantly engaged the intellect, creating the pleasure he described as the "repose which the mind feels when the eye, the intellect, and the affections, are satisfied by the absence of any want."[43]

By calling attention in *Alhambra* to the beauty and substance of the inscriptions, Jones demonstrated the potential of writing as a decorative device and helped revive the use

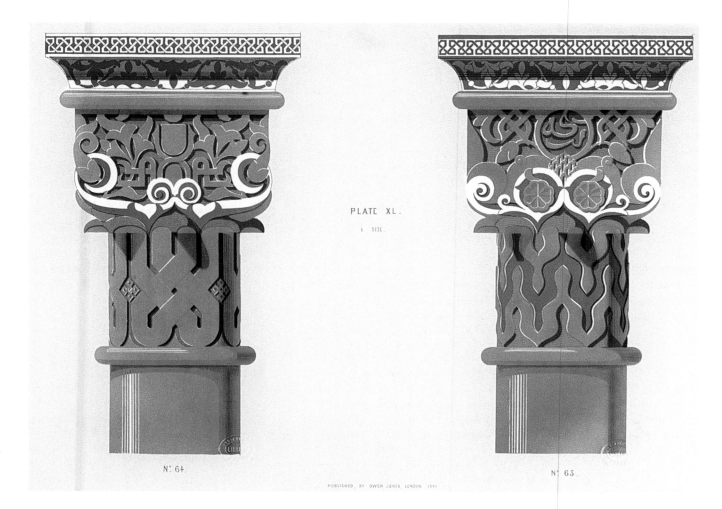

Fig. 1.25. *"Capitals of Columns, Court of the Lions," Pl. XL from* Plans, Elevations, Sections, and Details of the Alhambra, *vol. II, 1845*

of text as ornament, a technique that became important in the Gothic Revival, the Arts and Crafts Movement, and the Aesthetic Movement. Jones used inscriptions and monograms prominently in his work throughout his career. In his early schemes, he displayed an ornamental frieze on his competition submission for St. George's Hall, Liverpool (1839) and painted the customary Apostles' Creed and Ten Commandments in the sanctuaries of Christ Church, Streatham (1851; Fig. 1.24) and St. Bartholomew, Sutton Waldron (1854). He created monograms and books of initial letters for monograms (Pls. 1.9 and 1.10). In the 1850s, Jones emphasized inscriptions in the celebrated Fine Arts courts in the Crystal Palace, Sydenham (1854) and in the guidebooks that interpreted them.[44] His last commissions include monograms and mottoes for Alfred Morrison (Pages 2–3 and fig. 4.18) and James Mason.

In analyzing the Alhambra's ornamentation, Jones discovered that the Arabs' techniques for creating geometrical motifs and two-dimensional patterns were based upon grids of equidistant horizontal and perpendicular lines or diagonals (Figs. 1.26 and 1.27). He realized that the grid configurations offered an infinite variety of patterns achieved by changing the colors of the ground or the surface lines and that every change emphasized particular elements in the design, creating interlaces and other patterns.[45]

These discoveries led Jones to promote the use of geometric patterns and conventionalized forms from nature in place of the florid realism popular at the time. His arguments, combined with the ideas of Henry Cole (1808–1882), Richard Redgrave, and others, led to flat pattern being adopted as the standard in the English Reform Movement and the associated schools of design. The techniques advocated by Jones revolutionized the design of British carpets, fabrics, and wallpapers at mid-century and contributed to the later Arts and Crafts and Aesthetic movements.[46]

Jones also identified factors affecting the perception of ornament, including distance, color, and lighting. He explained that at a distance the eye discerns the outline of forms and masses and, moving nearer, discovers more information. He used the details of an arch in the Hall of Justice to make his point, saying that, at a distance, only the principal forms of ornament are visible. These elements include an inscription, a rosette, the profile of the archivolt and a gold flower on the upper surface of the spandrel. Moving nearer, details such as the blue flowers beneath the inscription and in the spandrels become apparent, and close examination reveals small flowers painted on the archivolt.[47]

Jones maintained that balanced compositions of primary colors produce a lively "bloom" at a distance, while combinations of secondary and tertiary colors dissipate into lifeless shadow; in contrast, colors viewed at close range are distinct. Jones observed that the Moors used the primary colors (blue, red, yellow or gold, and gilding) on ceilings

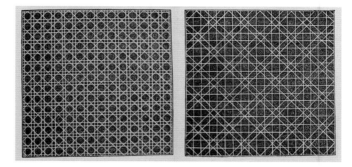

Fig. 1.26. Grids discussed with Pl. XXXVII from Plans, Elevations, Sections, and Details of the Alhambra, *vol. I, 1842*

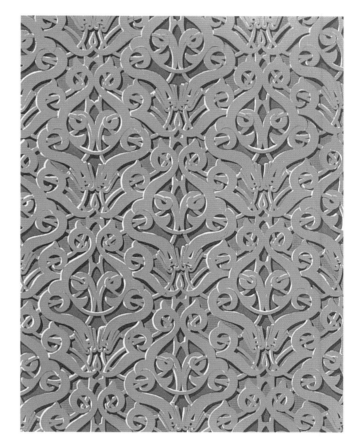

Fig. 1.27. "Ornament in Doorway at the Entrance to the Ventana, Hall of the Two Sisters," Pl. XIII from Plans, Elevations, Sections, and Details of the Alhambra, *vol. II, 1845*

and the upper surfaces of walls and placed the secondary colors (purple, green, and orange) in dados to provide visual relief from the brilliant coloring above. He explained that the green grounds in much of the Alhambra's decoration were a result of the original blue changing over time and noted that particles of blue were still visible in crevices throughout the palace. He said restorations commissioned by the Spanish kings were easy to identify by the coarseness of the execution of their green and purple grounds and the contrast they produced to the harmonious compositions of the Moors.[48]

Jones based his theory of ancient polychromy on these observations and those made during his travels. He applied Aristotle's concept of the decline of art to color saying that the Egyptians, Greeks, and Arabs used primary colors during periods of high art and that secondary colors dominated in periods of decline.[49] He noticed that the capitals of columns throughout the Alhambra revealed the remains of red and blue pigments and gilding, but the shafts showed no traces of color (Pl. 1.8). He reasoned that the shafts originally had been gilded to achieve harmony with the capitals but the gold was removed during later restorations to avoid the cost of regilding (Fig. 1.25).[50] Jones's theory paralleled Hittorff's contention that the Greeks had developed a harmonious system of polychromy comparable to their system of form and, thereby, a trained eye could assess the accuracy of a color scheme based on the degree of harmony represented.[51]

Jones's hypothesis was accepted by many of his contemporaries, a fact demonstrated in the popular writing of Washington Irving. Irving revised his 1832 edition of *The Alhambra* in 1865, adding a section entitled "Note on Morisco Architecture."[52] The new material involves a discussion of the Arabs' use of stucco and the brilliant "primitive" colors used by the Egyptians, Greeks, and Arabs in their early periods of art.[53] Irving does not credit Jones for this information but reveals his source when he describes the pillars in the Court of the Lions as "originally gilded," since Jones was alone in advancing this theory.[54]

The influence of the medieval Islamic aesthetic and the emblematic inscriptions introduced into architecture through Jones's publication is evident in the work of Pugin, an original subscriber to both volumes and the major proponent of a return to an archaeologically correct Gothic style of architecture.[55] Pugin's extensive knowledge of the Middle Ages developed under the tutelage of his father, Augustus-Charles Pugin, a French émigré to England, noted for his books of illustrations, particularly his depictions of Gothic structures and details.[56] The young Pugin assisted his father in the preparation of these texts, accompanying him on extensive travels in England and France to study, sketch, and collect artifacts. By age fifteen, the son's knowledge and skill were so advanced he was given a commission to design Gothic-style furniture for Windsor Castle.[57]

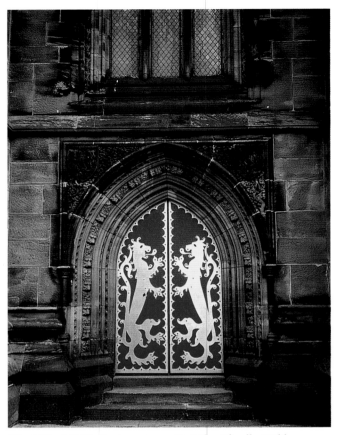

Fig. 1.29. A.W.N. Pugin, entrance, St. Giles, Cheadle, 1846

At twenty-two, he had converted to Roman Catholicism and produced a book entitled *Contrasts; or, a Parallel between the Noble Edifices of the Fourteenth and Fifteenth Centuries, and Similar Buildings of the Present Day: Showing the Present Decay of Taste* (1836). This ascerbic polemic established Pugin's influence and initiated his revival of Gothic architecture. *Contrasts*, and Pugin's other writings, condemn the ideas and practices instituted within society and the Roman Catholic church during and after the Reformation. While these texts reveal that Pugin shared Jones's belief in architecture as the embodiment of a specific culture, they also indicate Pugin's unique conviction that the only way grand and sublime architecture could be achieved again required the total reformation of society to the level of harmonious integration present during the Middle Ages.[58]

Pugin's medievalism was emotional rather than intellectual, based on the passion of his religious conviction and not on scholarship. He read very little, had minimal formal education, and his library contained "few theoretical treatises, either religious or architectural."[59] It is not surprising, then, that Pugin would have accepted Jones's study of Europe's best-preserved medieval palace as a textbook offering well-documented evidence of a style uncontaminated by the ideas of the Renaissance and the Reformation, and, like Gothic, to some extent a derivative of Byzantine architecture.[60]

Pugin would have seen texts in Gothic buildings before reading Jones's book and, in fact, his first building, a house

Fig. 1.28. A.W.N. Pugin, floor tiles in nave, St. Giles, Cheadle, 1846

for himself at St. Marie's Grange (1835–6), exhibits a religious scripture in the place normally reserved for a decorative frieze.[61] He also emphasized moral inscriptions in his first major commission, the Gothicizing of Scarisbrick Hall (1837). In *The Victorian Country House*, scholar Mark Girouard speculates that Pugin's liberal use of pious texts in the decoration of Scarisbrick is an early example of what would become an obsessive Victorian habit. Girouard cites the text embellishing the great hall, which reads "Except the Lord buildeth the house, they labour in vain that build it" as an example of a quotation that became fashionable in both English and Latin. Pugin's decorative schemes include both English and Latin versions of this quotation, producing an effect of familiar visual variety analogous to the Moors' repetition of the same verse in various Arabic scripts described in *Alhambra*.[62] What is more important, however, is the fact that the isolated moral references adopted in St. Marie's Grange and Scarisbrick Hall are replaced in the work Pugin produced after *Alhambra*'s publication by a tapestry of quotations from the Bible, excerpts from the Catholic mass, and phrases from hymns of praise covering every surface. Here, as in the Alhambra, phrases and words become a calligraphic part of the pattern and the method of design emphasizes the importance of the associations stimulated by the visual presence and appearance of the text and not the meaning of each individual line. Other significant changes observable in Pugin's work consistent with the ideas and techniques explained in Jones's text include the introduction of strong, primary colors and gilding. Pugin's work also exhibits a new preference for the abstract ornamentation, placement of decoration, and the two-dimensional designs discussed and illustrated in Jones's study. In addition, Pugin incorporates chromolithographed plates in his books, sharing Jones's desire to accurately depict the color and patterns of the designs discussed.

Medieval architecture, particularly the Decorated Style in Britain (1240–1360), was informed and transformed by the art of the book.[63] Buildings throughout Europe influenced by the Decorated, or "Illuminated," Style exhibited the same bold use of primaries, black lettering, decorative diaper patterns, and extravagant use of gilding characteristic of contemporary scholarly books, with one major distinction: the medieval manuscripts were meant to be read and were valued for their content as well as for their beauty. In contrast, the inscriptions on medieval architecture were decorative and subordinate to the figural sculpture and vast narrative mosaic schemes advocated by Gregory the Great, the ecclesiastic who promoted "sacred images as the written language of the illiterate."[64] Consequently, Gothic script appeared in captions identifying religious figures or labeling particular places and in scrolls within narrative panels on windows, walls, and sculpture, indicating spoken words and prophecies. Even the illiterate understood these phrases as the word of God, adding sanctity to a particular place. However, the high level of illiteracy, plus

the difficulty of deciphering the small, tightly packed words within the dimly lit interiors affirms the subordinate position of inscriptions within the decorative schemes of the medieval period. Scholar Armando Petrucci appropriately summarizes their role as commemorative and symbolic rather than transmissive and expressive.[65]

The best example of Pugin's intended liturgical, architectural, and iconographical reform occurs in the church of St. Giles, Cheadle, Staffordshire (1841–6), built for John, the sixteenth earl of Shrewsbury. Shrewsbury's sympathetic ideology and generous financial support gave the young architect the chance to realize his vision of "'an English parish church restored with scrupulous fidelity,' to which people might come for artistic and religious inspiration in the moment of the birth of admiration for 'Catholic antiquity.'" Consequently, investigation of this idealized "fourteenth-century" church presents the dual opportunity of studying the sources and methods Pugin used to arrive at his conception of "perfection in the whole and in every detail" and identifying the numerous changes and elements that suggest the influence of Jones.[66]

Recent scholarship reveals that Pugin drew from a wide range of German, French, Flemish, and English sources in preparing the plans and furnishings of Cheadle. He assembled casts of medieval sculpture to serve as carving models and acquired religious artifacts, such as a fifteenth-century Flemish corona to be reused in the new sanctuary. He also made an intense study of Norfolk parish churches and incor-

Fig. 1.30. A.W.N. Pugin, view toward altar, St. Giles, Cheadle, 1846

porated many of the elements he observed in the objects he designed for Cheadle; for example, the pattern of the brass embellishments on an antique hymnal owned by the cathedral at Mayence reappears in his design for a missal.

By 1840, he had completed the construction drawings for St. Giles, producing a scheme for "a plain parochial country church" with unpainted walls. This scheme is in marked contrast to the richly embellished completed work. The well-known Pugin authority Phoebe Stanton offers several explanations for the change. First, she observes that Pugin made bold experiments with scale in his later designs for Cheadle to communicate his evolving vision for the Gothic revival. For example, she cites the overscaled gilt lions, adapted from the earl's coat of arms, applied to the west doors of the church (Fig. 1.29) as Pugin's way of saying that "magnification and legible meaning would play an important part in the design of the building."[67] Moreover, her study of the correspondence between Pugin and his patron revealed that "the inspiration to decorate had come from a building or project with which the Earl and Pugin had become acquainted while the church was under construction."[68] The most obvious projects during this period include Viollet-le-Duc's restoration of Ste.-Chappelle in Paris (which he visited frequently) and Jones's publication of *Alhambra*.

A review of the completed decoration of Cheadle is essential to determine how these contemporary events may have influenced the ardent Pugin to revise his thinking and replace his simple devotional scheme with an intense program of symbolism achieved through "hundreds of painted patterns, each with its special iconographic meaning."[69] The initial powerful impact results from his adoption of strong colors. The interior blazes with brilliant red, bold blue, and bright gilding. Pugin's use of the primaries is consistent with the Decorated Style, with Viollet-le-Duc's

Fig. 1.31. A.W.N. Pugin, dining-room frieze, Ramsgate, Kent, 1843

restoration of Ste.-Chappelle, and with Jones's discussion of the use of primaries in *Alhambra*.[70] The richly painted walls, deeply stained glass, new encaustic tiled floors and risers all explode with color (Fig. 1.30). The encaustic tiles, suggestive of the mosaics and pavements used in the medieval structures of Islam and Christianity were introduced into nineteenth-century architecture by Jones and Pugin, who worked with manufacturers to produce tiles with two-dimensional patterns and inscriptions. For Cheadle, Pugin commissioned Minton to manufacture the tiles for the floors and for the Islamic-style four-foot dado on the walls of the sanctuary.

The texts appearing in the floor tiles of both porches initiate the preparation for worship, stating: "WE WILL GO INTO THE HOUSE OF THE LORD WITH GLADNESS." Immediately inside the doors, the floor tiles read: "GOOD CHRISTIAN PEOPLE PRAY FOR THE ESTATE OF JOHN XVI EARL OF SHREWSBURY OF WHOSE GOOD THIS CHURCH WAS BUILT (Fig. 1.28)." The tiles used for the floor of the nave and side aisles display excerpts from the consecration of the church, including the passage "BENE FUNDATA EST DOMUS DOMINI SUPRA FIRMAM PRETRAM" ("The Lord's house is well founded on a firm rock," adapted from Matthew vii, 25) and the floor of the Blessed Sacrament Chapel reveals the message "DOMINE NON SUM DIGNUS . . ." ("Lord I am not worthy that thou shouldst enter under my roof. Say but the word and my soul shall be healed"). Tiles also exhibit prominent scripture on the risers of the steps in the chancel and in the entrance to the Blessed Sacrament Chapel.[71]

Pugin's decorative scheme for the church he called his "perfect Cheadle" also relies upon excerpts from the liturgy and phrases from hymns of praise to adorn the walls, windows, and furnishings.[72] The architect used the texts to identify specific spaces, actions, and appropriate attitudes for worship. A typical example of his method occurs in the Blessed Sacrament Chapel where every element represents a Eucharistic text or emblem.

Although Pugin boasted of a faithful restoration of a fourteenth-century parish church, reinterpretation would be a better description, since the chapel, adjacent to the main altar, was his own creation. In the same way, the decorative scheme of the interior is Pugin's own design. The chapel's decoration begins with a quotation in Latin on the risers of the steps leading into the chapel, translated as "He gave them bread from heaven. Man ate the bread of angels" (Psalm 77: 24-5). Inside the chapel, the theme of communion continues with the words "SANCTUS, SANCTUS, SANCTUS" or "Holy, Holy, Holy" carved into the altar, gilded on the walls, and inlaid in the floor in tribute to the portion of the Mass reserved for the consecration of the bread and the wine. Above the chapel's altar, the central stained-glass window depicts an image of Christ over a quotation from the sixth chapter of St. John deciphered as "Amen, Amen. I say to you I am the living bread which came down from

32　*Chapter One*

heaven." Finally, when exiting the chapel, the worshiper is encouraged to "Let us adore for ever the most Blessed Sacrament."[73] This method of decoration, the icongraphic theme, and the redundancy of the textual messages, is consistent with the practice and creations of the Islamic architects in Granada described by Jones. For example, Jones's description of the Gate of Justice, the principal entrance to the ancient fortress, contains an inscription over the doorway reading: "This gate, called *Bab-al-shari'ah* [the Gate of Law]—May God prosper through it the law of Islam! as He made this a lasting monument of glory—May the Almighty make this [gate] a protecting bulwark, and write down [its erection] among the imperishable actions of the just!"[74] In the same way, the text accompanying Plate XXI in Volume I demonstrates the Moors' use of inscriptions to distinguish particular spaces with the quotation: "I am the garden, and every morn am I revealed in new beauty. Observe attentively how I am adorn'd, and thou wilt reap the benefit of a commentary on decoration." Moreover, Jones's text includes examples of inscriptions embellishing column capitals, architectural elements, and objects, such as vases, in the same manner as employed in Pugin's chapel. Pugin's serious commitment to a scheme displaying inscriptions on everything from candlesticks to stained glass can be determined from his decision to substitute common metals for silver in the church's vessels and to select some ready-made items in order to reserve the funds necessary for the extensive array of objects he designed with religious texts.

The profusion of text represents one of the principal differences between Pugin's "perfect Cheadle" and Viollet-le-Duc's decorative scheme for the restoration of the Ste. Chappelle. Scholars have suggested that Pugin may have been influenced by Viollet-le-Duc's contemporary work in Paris; certainly, both schemes offer dazzling interiors enriched through luminous coloration, gilding, and two-dimensional flat-surface patterns. The major difference between the two works, however, is in the methods chosen to create and embellish the sacred spaces and to communicate with the devout. Viollet-le-Duc's scheme restores the French Rayonnant Style of the chapel built by Louis IX (1241–8) to house prized fragments from the True Cross and the Crown of Thorns.[75] In the chapel's second story, the substantial masonry has been replaced by screens of stained glass, creating a transcendental, glittering boundary and infusing the space with the mystical beauty of colored light. Huge statues of the apostles were mounted on piers around the perimeter of the chapel to involve the worshiper in the beliefs of the Church. This type of direct narrative contrasts with the indirect associations established through Pugin's extensive use of text. Pugin's work differs substantially from the typical subordination of text in Christian medieval architecture.

Pugin's generous use of inscriptions is also characteristic of his elaborate scheme for the decoration of the Palace of

Fig. 1.32. A. W. N. Pugin, stained-glass window, The Grange, Ramsgate, Kent, 1843

Westminster (Houses of Parliament), where text appears on ceilings, walls, floors, and furniture in carving, gilding, stained glass, paint, tiles, and painted canvas. Pugin prepared the plans and instructions for the palace's ornamentation as Superintendent of the Works of Wood Carving under Sir Charles Barry. Although Barry, the architect of this prodigious commission, had final approval, Pugin's input to the decorative design was critical. Not surprisingly, he advocated an ecclesiastical iconography, but Barry prevailed with a program of heraldry.[76] This theme emphasized epigraphs and coats of arms symbolizing Queen Victoria and earlier monarchs. The queen is indicated throughout by the prominent display of her monogram, VR, for Victoria Regina; "*Dieu et Mon Droit*," the royal motto of England; plus Latin and English versions of "God Save the Queen" and "Long Live the Queen."

At first the effusive use of text on both the interior and exterior of the Palace of Westminster presents the impression of an encyclopedia of quotations, but repeated site visits suggest that what appears complex is, in actuality, the successful repetition of a few inscriptions offered in different languages, mediums, and composition. For example, the phrase "*Dieu et Mon Droit*," meaning "God and my right," is engraved in the brass gates and over the door at the entrance to the House of Lords. This same phrase is repeated in diagonal bands in the stained-glass windows along the corridors and imprinted in white letters on a deep blue background in the Minton floor tiles of the Peers Lobby. Inside the House of Lords, this motto is carved in a blue horizontal band on the canopy of the throne, carved and gilded on ceiling beams, and painted on armorial panels in between the ceiling beams.

As in Cheadle, the way the inscriptions are displayed suggests a link between the ornamentation of the new

A New Understanding of Architecture 33

Fig. 1.33. A.W.N. Pugin, floor tiles, St. Augustine's, Ramsgate, Kent, 1845–6

Palace of Westminster and Jones's analysis of the decoration in the medieval palace in Spain. In both cases, patterns are formed by repeating a familiar word or phrase modified through changes to the background or alterations in the appearance of the quotation itself. In the palace of the Alhambra, the calligraphers varied the presentation of the familiar phrases "God is our refuge in every trouble" and "There is no conqueror but God" by presenting them in both regular and highly stylized Arabic scripts; in the Palace of Westminster, Pugin achieved variety by displaying the mottoes "God Save the Queen" and "God and My Right" in different languages.[77]

Once this concept is understood, it is easy to see that this method of design emphasizes the importance of associations stimulated by the visual presence and appearance of the text. Pugin introduced writing on the walls of his churches to inspire piety and establish bonds with the simple devotion and unadulterated liturgy of the preindustrialized world, blotting out the bare walls and revised thinking represented in the architecture of the Reformation. Likewise, by exhibiting inscriptions and heraldic emblems throughout the Palace of Westminster, he created an atmosphere redolent of a long and rich history of chivalry and tradition, investing the monarchy with the dignity and authority appropriate to ceremonies of state.

Finally, Pugin incorporated both religious scripture and heraldic emblems in the decorative schemes for his last home and the adjoining church of St. Augustine in Ramsgate, Kent (1846–51). The Ramsgate complex was intended to serve as residence, place of worship, and a place to introduce the architect's designs to prospective clients.[78] The unusual dining-room frieze, exhibiting the names of

important patrons and commissions (Fig. 1.31), may have been meant to impress clients by evoking associations with Shrewsbury and other notables and at the same time remind Pugin of his favorite clients and projects. Other ornamentation in Ramsgate also suggests the intention of representing status, particularly in the repeated use of martlets, Pugin's initials, and the phrase "En avant (Fig. 1.32)." En avant, meaning "forward," was adopted by Pugin's father as the family motto. Like many self-made Victorians, the elder Pugin suddenly "discovered" a family coat of arms that he subsequently displayed to mark his proud social standing.[79] The Pugin emblem also appropriately features the martlet: a footless bird known for haunting old cathedrals.[80]

Pugin produced these heraldic elements in a variety of patterns and materials, similar to the variation in the designs for the Palace of Westminster. Remnants of the wallpaper Pugin designed for Ramsgate have been revealed in recent restoration efforts showing a pattern composed of the martlet, the motto, and monogram, placed in diagonal bands against a background of foliage. Pugin ordered this pattern in red for the dining room, blue for the drawing room, and green for Mrs. Pugin's bedroom, saying that he felt the change of color would achieve sufficient variety to enable him to repeat the pattern in all of the principal rooms.[81]

Examination of schemes by Jones and Pugin indicates that the technique of changing colors and manipulating a few words or phrases to create new ornamentation was fundamental to their designs, enabling them to create hundreds of patterns for wallpaper, textiles, and carpets in a brief period (Fig. 1.34). They were the earliest nineteenth-century advocates and practitioners of the method outlined by Jones to create two-dimensional patterns, and both developed substantial businesses producing distinguished designs for a wide range of decorative arts items.

Jones and Pugin reformed British design through their method, their output, and their writing. Their texts articulated and shared many principles of design, including the tenet that "construction should be decorated; decoration should never be constructed."[82] Both played key roles in the Great Exhibition of 1851 and when Jones praised the superior design qualities of the Turkish carpets and other items exhibited by Islamic nations, Pugin agreed. They worked together until Pugin's death in 1852, selecting and purchasing objects displayed in the exhibition to form the nucleus of the decorative arts collection at the South Kensington Museum (now the Victoria and Albert Museum). Their writing and thoughts on many points were so close that a strong case can be made for collaboration, or for either of them as author, of the first catalogue of the South Kensington Museum; the catalogue explains the objects they purchased for display and for instruction. They also participated in John Weale's Quarterly Papers on Architecture, an early scholarly publication on architecture.

Although Jones was dedicated to developing architecture reflecting nineteenth-century technology and culture and Pugin was devoted to reviving a medieval past, they shared many fundamental beliefs in theory and design. One sequence of events suggests that their intellectual relationship began in the 1830s, when both established their reputations by making exceptional comparisons of prevailing practice and past styles. In 1832, Pugin produced a drawing of three house facades, labeling the first two houses 1470 and 1532 and the third, a less satisfactory composition, 1832. Three years later (August 1835), he continued this comparison, beginning his book *Contrasts*, but put this work aside to take on projects for Charles Barry and Gillespie Graham.[83] As a result, records show that he was in London on the evening Jones delivered his "On the Influence of Religion upon Art" lecture to the Architectural Association and may have been in the audience. Phoebe Stanton indicates that he returned to Salisbury on December 5 with *Contrasts* on his mind and prepared a text for the book, which he submitted for publication in January 1836, completing the drawings between February 23 and March 5 and finalizing the manuscript between May 2 and May 30.[84] Despite the interlude, this text seems to respond to the remarks made by Jones in the lecture delivered to the Architectural Society in the previous December.

In that lecture, Jones emphasized that the architecture of the Egyptians was "fully capable of handing down to posterity a complete chronicle of the manners, customs, and *feelings* of a people" and found this practice in marked contrast to the "inexpressive styles" prevailing in contemporary English architecture. Pugin repeated the idea of the importance of feelings as a generator of architectural form in the title of his first chapter in *Contrasts*: "On the Feelings Which Produced the Great Edifices of the Middle Ages." Pugin also agreed that there had been a decline in architecture during the last three centuries and said that the causes of this "mighty change" would form the subject of his text. He continued by proposing "that the great test of Architectural beauty is the fitness of the design to the purpose for which it is intended, and that the style of a building should so correspond with its use that the spectator may at once perceive the purpose for which it was erected." This concept parallels Jones's censure of the contemporary practice of appropriating the temple form as the style for a "Christian church, a theatre of pleasure, or an hospital for the sick." Pugin repeats another position expressed by Jones, saying that the "different nations have given birth to so many various styles of Architecture, each suited to their climate, customs, and religion; and as it is among edifices of this latter class that we look for the most splendid and lasting monuments, there can be little doubt that the religious ideas and ceremonies of these different people had by far the greatest influence in the formation of their various styles of Architecture." He continues to reflect the ideas of

Jones by affirming that the elements used by the Egyptians "were not mere fanciful Architectural combinations and ornaments, but emblems of the philosophy and mythology of that nation" and expands this idea of "Architecture resulting from religious belief" to embrace all societies.[85]

Both men extolled the superiority of Christianity and praised the buildings it inspired during the medieval period.[86] Both men also alluded to the contemporary practice of disparaging Christian faith as "superstition." Jones refers to pre-Reformation belief as "that unity of action of faith, now called superstition, which caused our forefathers to erect such splendid piles," and Pugin notes that he is "well aware that modern writers have attributed the numerous churches erected during the middle ages to the effects of superstition."[87] Numerous examples, like this, of analogous terminology and logic, abound in these two works; what separates them is Jones's decision to desist from developing a discussion of medieval architecture, which he explains by saying that the "sympathy which exists between the Gothic cathedral and the Christian religion" was "too powerfully felt by all to need comment." Pugin's text, on the other hand, focuses on the symbolism in the plans, structure, and decoration of medieval buildings.

Stanton notes that Pugin's text "seems to have been secondary to the trenchant message of the illustrations . . . and seems weak only because of the strength and assertiveness of

Fig. 1.34. J. G. Crace for A.W.N. Pugin, trial ceiling designs for the House of Lords, 1846

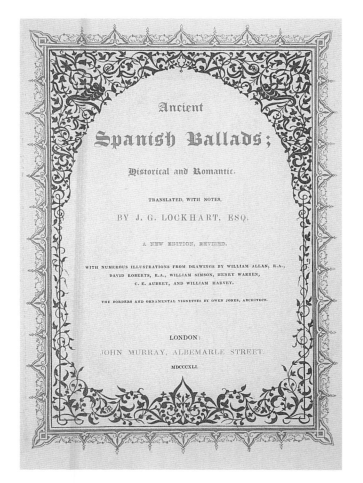

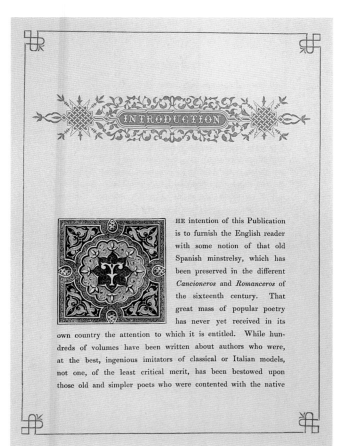

the plates."[88] There can be no doubt that the plates are more cutting than the text and that both exceed the criticism expressed by Jones. Where Jones generically scolded his countrymen for building churches "with every attention paid to the comforts of the creature and so little to the glory of the Creator in whose dwelling-place he is supposed to be," Pugin's illustrations attacked the work of specific architects and society as a whole.[89] Pugin juxtaposed images of the Inwoods' St. Mary Somerstown with Bishop Skirlaugh's chapel at Skirlaugh to demonstrate the poverty of modern buildings in relation to those raised four centuries earlier. No publisher was interested in producing Pugin's attack on the profession and modern society, so he produced the book himself in August 1836. Sales exceeded his expectations and brought him notoriety. Some praised his "pungency and wit" and "boldness and freedom," while others charged that his work was the outpouring of a "fearfully diseased mind" and accused him of "Jesuitically distorting facts."[90] He responded, in 1837, with *An Apology for a Work Entitled Contrasts; Being a Defense of the Assertions Advanced in That Publication, against the Various Attacks Lately Made upon It.*[91] This text offered ideas more extreme than those expressed in the earlier publication and stressed that a "return to the ancient faith is the only means by which a restoration of the long-lost feelings for art of every description can be achieved." Although some of his ideas continued to concur with those expressed by Jones in statements such as "Architecture is a noble science, resulting from moral principles" and "There is a forcible association between all works of genius and *religion*," he differs from Jones in statements indicating that "It is the broad principle of erecting the most glorious temples to the worship of God, and consecrating the highest efforts of art to his honour, for which I am contending. These are feelings which I assert belong exclusively to Catholicism, and they have entirely disappeared wherever Protestantism has been established . . ."[92]

The religious differences aside, the two-dimensional patterns, use of inscriptions, similar principles, and method of design adopted by Jones and Pugin, testifies to their mutual respect and influence on many levels. Jones introduced stylistic analysis into English architecture studies with the *Alhambra* publication, was the first to emphasize the influence of religion upon architecture, and to introduce the perception of architecture history as cultural history. The fact that *Contrasts* repeats and addresses the same ideas, although using them to recommend a different direction for architecture, is significant and suggests the influence of Jones's analysis and ideas on Pugin's work.

It is obvious that Jones and Pugin shared an appreciation of text demonstrated through their publications and in their use of inscriptions in architecture. Each of them was a bold innovator in theory and design, resolute in informing clients, the public, and the architecture profession about his convictions, and each appreciated inscriptions as a valuable tool in this effort. Although emblematic text does not appear as the chief symbolic and decorative element in every one of their commissions, the examples cited above indicate numerous comprehensive schemes, which they devised to communicate their beliefs, and those of their clients, through the use of emblematic texts. In addition, their decorative schemes reflect the range and characteristics of the use of inscriptions exclusive to Islamic art and architecture.

Irving and Pugin were not alone in studying Jones's text. The list of original subscribers includes an interesting mix of architects in Germany, Scotland, and the United States, as well as royalty and institutions of higher learning in Prussia, Spain, and Ireland. This list also contains the names of prominent English architects, engineers, and builders, such as: A. Bartholomew; I. K. Brunel; R. C. Carpenter; the Cubitts; Messrs. Grissell and Peto; Phillip Hardwicke; Lewis Vuillamy; T. H. Wyatt; and manufacturers such as Minton.

The beauty and content of the text inspired enthusiastic reviews. Joseph Gwilt, in his own highly commended 1842 edition of *The Encyclopedia of Architecture*, listed *Alhambra* as a study of ancient architecture essential for every student and practitioner.[93] The *Athenaeum* concurred, saying: "There has rarely, if ever, appeared a more magnificent work for the benefit of the architect or of the decorator" and described the text as "the most perfectly illustrated architectural work" they had ever seen.[94] Another article in the *Athenaeum* stated "The engravings can scarcely be surpassed, nor have any been before attempted on so large a scale, and of so laborious a character. The details, which are numerous, are drawn on stone, and printed in gold and colours by Mr. O. Jones himself, and we need no further warrant for their truth and perfection."[95]

Alhambra also received extraordinary praise and comprehensive coverage in of the French publication *Revue Générale de l'Architecture* (Vols. V and VI, 1844 and 1845).[96] César Daly, editor of the *Revue*, prepared a twenty-seven-page summary of Jones's text, including reproductions of twenty-five of the plates. Daly endorsed Jones's conclusions, echoing the belief that religion was the most dominant influence on architecture and explaining the construction of stalactite domes and other elements according to Jones's findings.[97]

Jones had experimented with chromolithography in order to represent the contemporary and restored colors of the Alhambra accurately. His use of strong, gouachelike, primaries differed markedly from the imitations of watercolors previously introduced into book publishing by Charles Hullmandel (1789–1850) and opened up new possibilities for rich color in all types of publications. Jones recognized the opportunity and followed his technical success in *Alhambra* by applying his colored printing techniques to produce plates for architecture and other subjects. He worked with several publishers, including John Murray and Longman, Green and Longman and the printer/publishers De la Rue and Day and Son. (See Appendix A for a listing of Jones's publications.)

Fig. 1.37. *Title page from* Fruits from the Garden and Field, *1850*

Fig. 1.38. *"Grapes" page from* Fruits from the Garden and the Field, *1850*

Figs. 1.39 and 1.40. Front and back covers of Winged Thoughts, *1851*

His technical refinement and visual sensibility contributed substantial value to the expansion of publishing in Britain in response to the demands created by a growing literate public. This growth becomes evident when the 850 new book titles produced annually before 1830 are compared to the 2530 new titles introduced annually by 1853. New periodicals appeared as well, including *Punch* (1841), the *Illustrated London News* (1842), and the *News of the World* (1843). Dickens, Thackeray, and other authors dramatically increased their readership by serial publication in periodicals. Drawings added to their texts reflect the growing importance of book illustration.

The integration of illustration, decoration, and printing reached high standards by the mid-1840s.[98] Jones and the publisher John Murray pioneered this synthesis in 1841 with a new edition of J. G. Lockhart's *Ancient Spanish Ballads*. The text, printed by Vizetelly of Fleet Street, contained handsome woodblock prints by recognized artists such as William Allan, David Roberts, William Simson, Henry Warren, C. E. Aubrey, and William Harvey, but the real innovations were in Jones's design of the book cover, title pages, vignettes, and borders (Figs. 1.35 and 1.36). These designs gave unprecedented artistic unity and distinction to the work and established a new direction in book publishing.

Jones recognized the potential of this approach and assured Murray that the book would immortalize both of them.[99] He was right. The press declared the book's embellishment to be the most beautiful ever produced and said the "exquisite" volume represented a luxury previously unknown in Britain. Over two thousand copies of the first edition were sold within the first year and a second edition was issued the following year.[100]

Jones followed this success by designing an array of new "illuminated" texts that raised color printing to a fine art. Previously the illustration of gift books, intended for visual gratification, had involved elaborate titles and head- and tailpieces, but did not include the artistic enhancements Jones provided on each page.

Some of the texts contained literary excerpts or quotations from the Bible set within delicate geometric or nature-inspired borders. Religious selections, appealing to the Victorian penchant for moralizing and for the public display of piety, included the *Sermon on the Mount* (1844, 1845), *The Song of Songs* (1849), and the *History of Joseph and His Brethren: Genesis Chapters XXXVII, XXXVIII, XL* (1862). Literary texts included Thomas Moore's immensely popular poem, *Paradise and the Peri* (1860), William Shakespeare's *Scenes from the Winter's Tale* (1866), and Dean Milman's *The Works of Quintus Horatius Flaccus* (1849). All of his texts appealed to the Victorian proclivity for amassing collections of objects as symbols of educated taste and financial status.[101]

The sentimentality of the age and the expertise of Jones's illuminations are evident in books of poetry, such as *Flowers* and Their Kindred Thoughts (1847), Fruits from the Garden and Field (1850; 1.37 and 1.38), and Winged Thoughts (1851; Figs. 1.39–1.42). These books, published by Longmans, alternated pages of poetry by Mary Anne Bacon with Jones's colored images. Jones advanced the state of chromolithography by using fine lines of color in the plates for these texts producing remarkable halftones and gradations in the depictions of the flowers, fruits, and birds.

Jones also produced plates and borders for other authors. These include Wilkinson's *Manners and Customs of the Ancient Egyptians* (1836), J. O. Westwood's *Palaeographia Sacra Pictora* (1843–5), William Henry Fox Talbot's *Pencil of Nature* (1844–6), and Henry Noel Humphreys's *Illuminated Books of the Middle Ages* (1849).[102] These texts presented serious research by experts in diverse areas.

Jones expanded his publishing experiments to include various techniques for producing book covers (Figs. 1.39, 1.40, and 1.43; Pls. 1.11–1.14, 1.23 and 1.24). The most unique cover involved impressing his design for *The Preacher* (1848) into wood. The heated, deeply reliefed metal plates used to incise the pattern usually burned the wood, increasing the resemblance to medieval wooden bindings. Jones also used "relievo-leather" bindings to suggest carved wood (Figs. 1.39, 1.40, and Pls. 1.11–1.14).[103] The leather added a pleasing visual and tactile quality to the binding and also facilitated the embossing of Jones's designs from the texts. The understated elegance of these covers has earned Jones lasting recognition as the creator of exceptional book covers.[104]

In addition to *Alhambra*, he is also recognized for producing several masterworks in publishing, including *The Grammar of Ornament* (1856; see Chapter Two for an indepth discussion) and *The Victorian Psalter* (1861; Pls. 1.13, 1.14, 1.17 and 1.18). The color plates in these texts, and those he prepared for the works of other authors, represent the modern equivalent of the ornament and calligraphy produced by Islamic and medieval scribes. Jones succeeded in harnessing the machine to reduce the manual labor and cost of these luxury items, making them available to wider dissemination and a new type of consumer. The details and borders in each of these books serve as a primer on ornament and the layouts serve as lessons in harmonious design. Jones's proficiency in color printing and book design constituted an important contribution to the visual culture of Victorian Britain. The sophistication of his patterns and aesthetic is consistent with his architectural purpose of integrating all elements into a cohesive scheme to enchant the visual perception and the imagination of the viewer.

Originally the term "illumination" referred to the use of red ink to distinguish portions of writing in a text of black ink. Later, when decorations and inks in other colors were added, the meaning of the term expanded to encompass all forms of ornamental writing. Jones's books revived the form of black lettering used in the medieval period and contributed to the growing interest in calligraphy. He also

Fig. 1.41. Title page from Winged Thoughts, 1851

Fig. 1.42. Chromolithography for "The Swallow" page from Winged Thoughts, 1851

prepared large commemorative inscriptions on vellum in a stylized thirteenth-century script (Pl. 1.25). Celebrated recipients of these special inscriptions included the mayor of London, Charles Dickens, and the architect C. R. Cockerell. Cockerell received his inscription upon retiring from the Royal Institute of British Architects. Dickens prominently displayed the inscription by Jones on the first landing at Gad's Hill Place (Pl. 1.26). The occasion for the presentation of the certificate is unknown, but suggests an interesting insight into the relationship between the prominent author and the architect. The text celebrates the location of Dickens's home on the summit of Shakespeare's Gad's Hill and quotes a passage from *Henry IV*: "But my lads, my lads, tomorrow morning by four o'clock, early at Gad's Hill! There are pilgirms going to Canterbury with rich offerings, and traders riding to London with fat purses; I have vizards for you all; you have horses for yourselves." The misspelling of "pilgrims" as "pilgirms" was probably intentional and served as a joke by Jones in response to Dickens's criticism of the mechanical perfection in Jones's designs.[105] Jones and Dickens served on committees together at the Society for the Encouragement of Arts and Manufactures and had mutual friends, including G. H. Lewes and George Eliot.

In Tom Stoppard's play *India Ink*, the character Anish delights in discovering a portrait painted by his father reproduced on the dust jacket of a poet's biography. The poet's sister observes that Anish's father would probably have preferred to see his painting in an art gallery, but the son responds: "Perhaps not. I'm sure my father never had a single one of his paintings reproduced, and that is an extraordinary pleasure for an artist . . . But replication! *That* is popularity! Put us on book jackets-calendars-biscuit tins! Oh, he would have been quite proud!"[106]

In designing for the prestigious printing firm of De la Rue, Jones achieved the ubiquitous replication Anish admired, producing the designs for stationery items (Fig. 1.46), diaries (Fig. 1.44), almanacs, postage stamps, currency and, yes, even the calendars and biscuit-tin labels (for Huntley & Palmer, Fig. 1.45). These designs gave De la Rue products a distinctive signature style. Thomas De la Rue (1793–1866), the founder of the firm, moved to London from Guernsey at the age of twenty-five to open a straw-hat business. By 1829, he was experimenting with printing, producing an edition of the New Testament in gold. In 1832, he registered a patent for printing playing cards from relief woodblocks in quick-drying oily inks. He revolutionized the design and production of playing cards with this patented process and with the designs for the backs of playing cards he commissioned from Jones (Pls. 1.27–1.30 and 1.32–1.34). Jones produced more than two hundred designs for playing-card backs, introducing colorful artistry to a huge industry that had previously focused on the faces of playing cards, not the backs. De la Rue dominated the European playing-card market with Jones's designs, and Lawrence and Cohen adopted Jones's patterns for playing cards distributed in the United States. When the North American sales are considered along with De la Rue's production of a half million packs per year, it becomes obvious that Jones's designs were literally in the hands of millions.

Jones designed special playing cards for the De la Rue display in the Great Exhibition of 1851. These included a pack of playing cards for Queen Victoria with the Royal Arms on the back in pure gold (Pl. 1.31) and a set of four packs with an individual pattern and monogram of four members of the royal family.[107] Dickens praised the floral patterns on these cards.[108] Priced at 2 guineas for the set, these cards were expensive then and still command high prices among collectors.

De la Rue's exhibit in the Great Exhibition highlighted other designs by Jones, including four hundred tools for bookbinding patterns. The collaboration of Jones and the House of De la Rue spanned three generations, and epitomizes the concept of total design, since Jones's consulting and design extended from the firm's products to domestic interiors for members of the family and even the founder's tombstone. Jones's designs enhanced the products and reputation of De la Rue and the wide distribution of those products gave Jones a vehicle for educating and refining the taste of the public, by "habituating all who used these articles to variety of form and colour in ornaments which, probably, scarcely any other field of operation would have

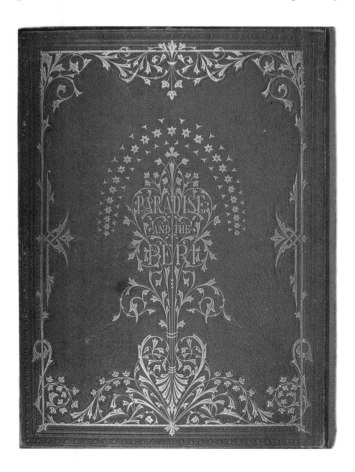

Fig. 1.43. Back cover of Paradise and the Peri, *1860*

Fig. 1.45. Designs for Huntley & Palmer labels for De la Rue, 1870s

Fig. 1.44. Design for a pocket diary for De la Rue, 1860s

opened so widely and so rapidly." Contemporaries credited much of the development in public taste to the influence of De la Rue's products under Jones's aesthetic guidance.[109]

The ubiquity and originality of Jones's designs and the boldness of his theory were remarkable. His comprehension of the relationship between culture and architecture became fundamental to nineteenth-century theory, informing the positions of Pugin, Ruskin, and others, and introducing the concept of morality into architectural debate. Jones initiated the call for a new style appropriate to the age and demonstrated methods for attaining a new style by experimenting with color, ornamental motifs, and materials. He improved architectural education with his analyses, scholarly texts, and chromolithography, and contributed to the artistic education of the public through his gift books and the products manufactured by the House of De la Rue. During the remainder of his career, Jones espoused the same philosophy and continued his efforts to reform architecture and the decorative arts through better education and good design.

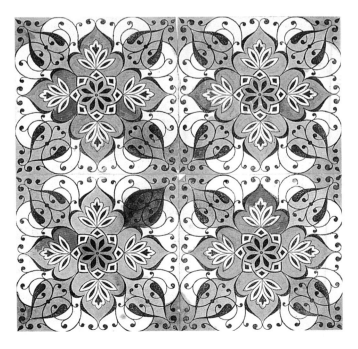

Fig. 1.46. Stationery design for De la Rue, 1867

Pl. 1.1. Section of the Yeni Valide Camii, Istanbul, *1833. Ink and color wash on paper, 20 x 28 in.*

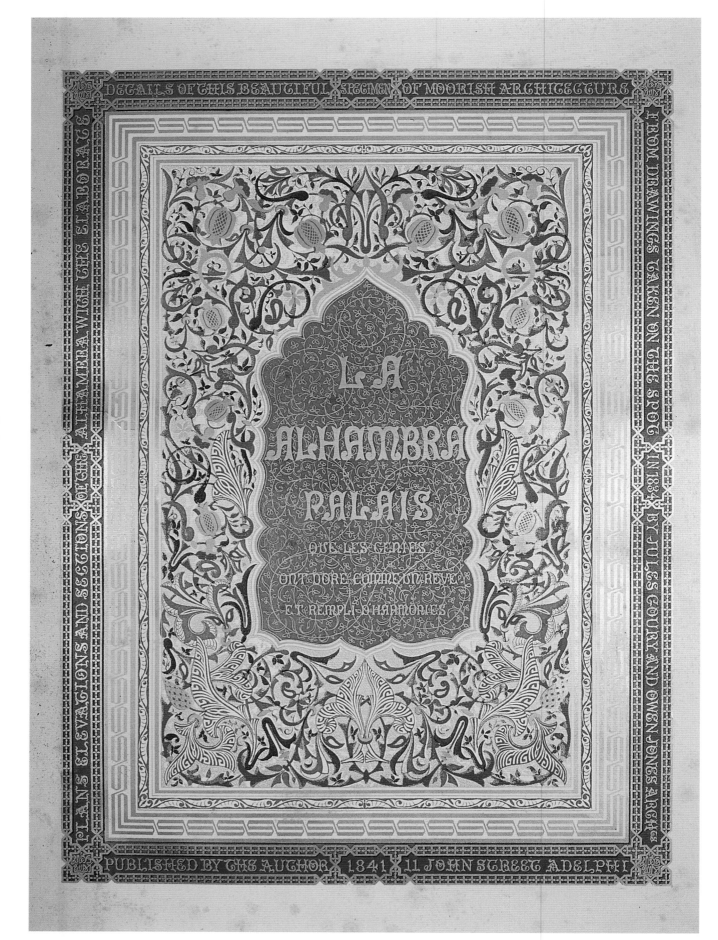

Pl. 1.2. Title page from Plans, Sections, Elevations, and Details of the Alhambra, *vol. I, 1841*

Pl. 1.3. "Ornaments Painted on the Pendants in the Hall of the Bark," Pl. XII from Plans, Elevations, Sections, and Details of the Alhambra, *vol. I, 1842*

Pl. 1.4. "Details of an Arch: Portico of the Court of Lions," Pl. XXVIII from Plans, Sections, Elevations, and Details of the Alhambra, *vol. I, 1842*

DETAILS OF AN ARCH.

PORTICO OF THE COURT OF LIONS.

$\frac{1}{10}$th Scale.

Details d'un Arc.

Portique de la cour des Lions

Ech. de 0.10 P.M.

PLAN ATA.

PLAN OF THE ARCH.

Drawn Lith.ᵈ Printed in Colours & Published by Owen Jones Luxton, 1842.

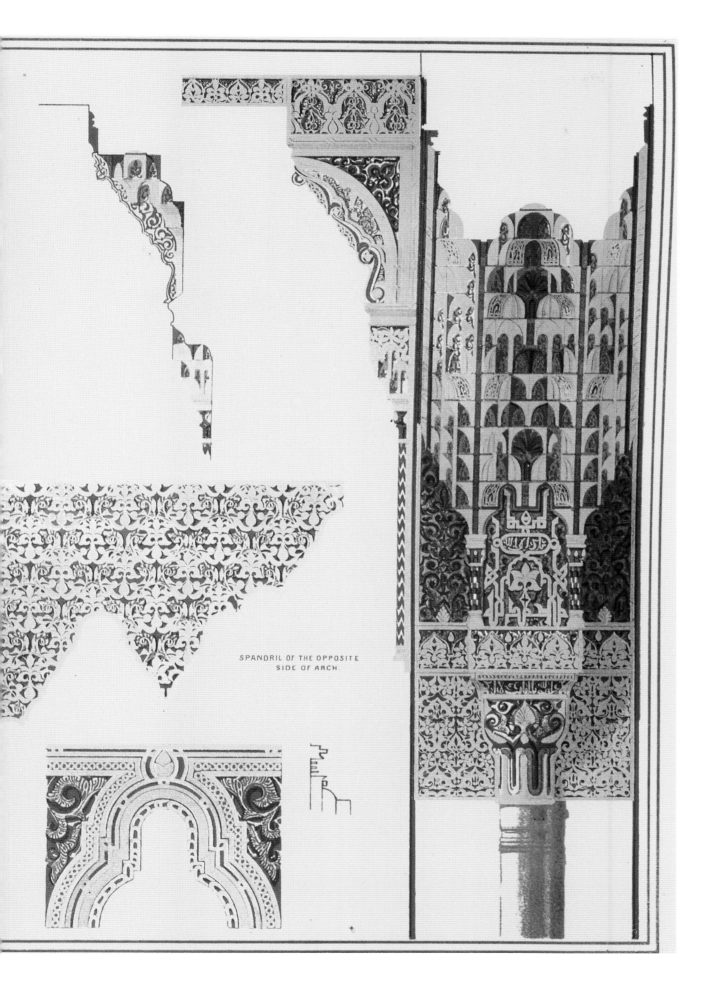

SPANDRIL OF THE OPPOSITE
SIDE OF ARCH.

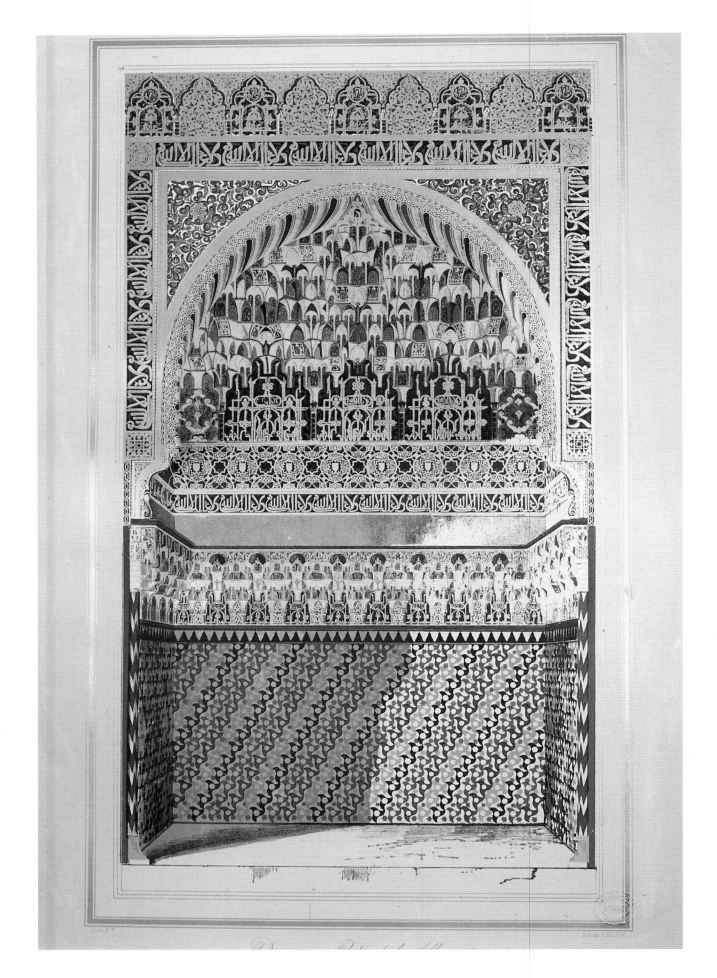

Pl. 1.5. "Divan, Court of the Fish-pond," Pl. IX from Plans, Elevations, Sections, and Details of the Alhambra, *vol. I, 1842*

Pl. 1.6. "Detail of Mosaic in the Divan, Court of the Fish-pond," Pl. XLIX from Plans, Elevations, Sections, and Details of the Alhambra, *vol. II, 1845*

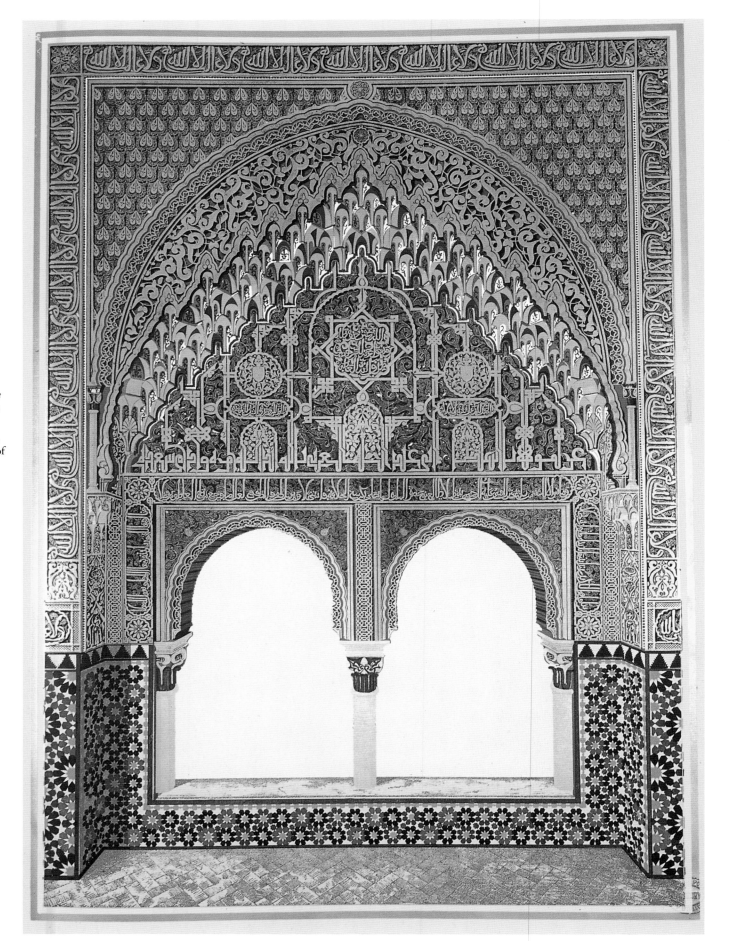

Pl. 1.7. "Window in the Alcove of the Hall of the Two Sisters," Pl. XXI from Plans, Elevations, Sections, and Details of the Alhambra, *vol. I, 1842*

Pl. 1.8. "Actual State of the Colors," *Pl. XXXVIII from* Plans, Elevations, Sections, and Details of the Alhambra, *vol. I, 1842*

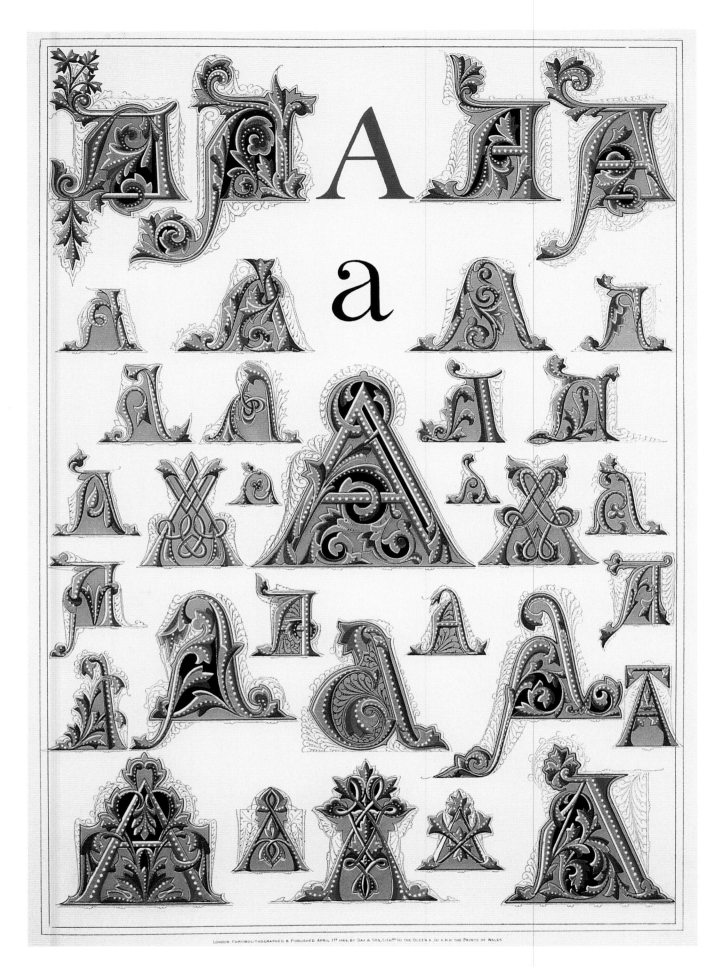

Pls. 1.9 and 1.10. Pages from One Thousand and One Initial Letters Designed and Illuminated by Owen Jones, *1864*

LONDON CHROMOLITHOGRAPHED & PUBLISHED APRIL 1ST 1864 BY DAY & SON, LITHRS TO THE QUEEN & TO H.R.H. THE PRINCE OF WALES

Pls. 1.11 and 1.12.
Front cover and back cover
of The Song of Songs,
1849

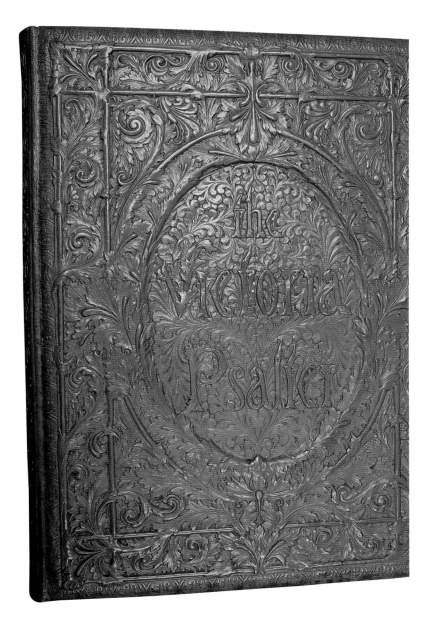

Pls. 1.13 and 1.14.
Front and back covers of
The Victorian Psalter,
1861

Pl. 1.15. Frontispiece and
first page of The Song of
Songs, 1849

Pl. 1.16. Chromo-lithography and design for two pages from The Song of Songs, *1849*

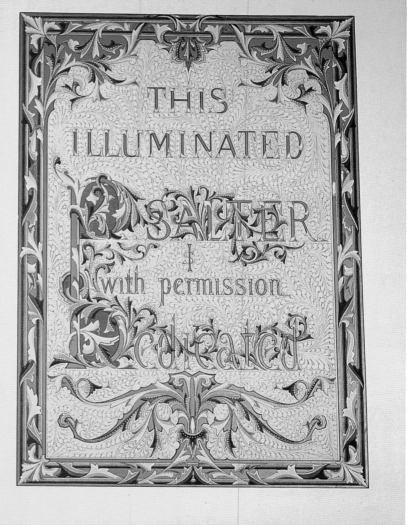

Pl. 1.17. Frontispiece and title page from The Victorian Psalter, *1861*

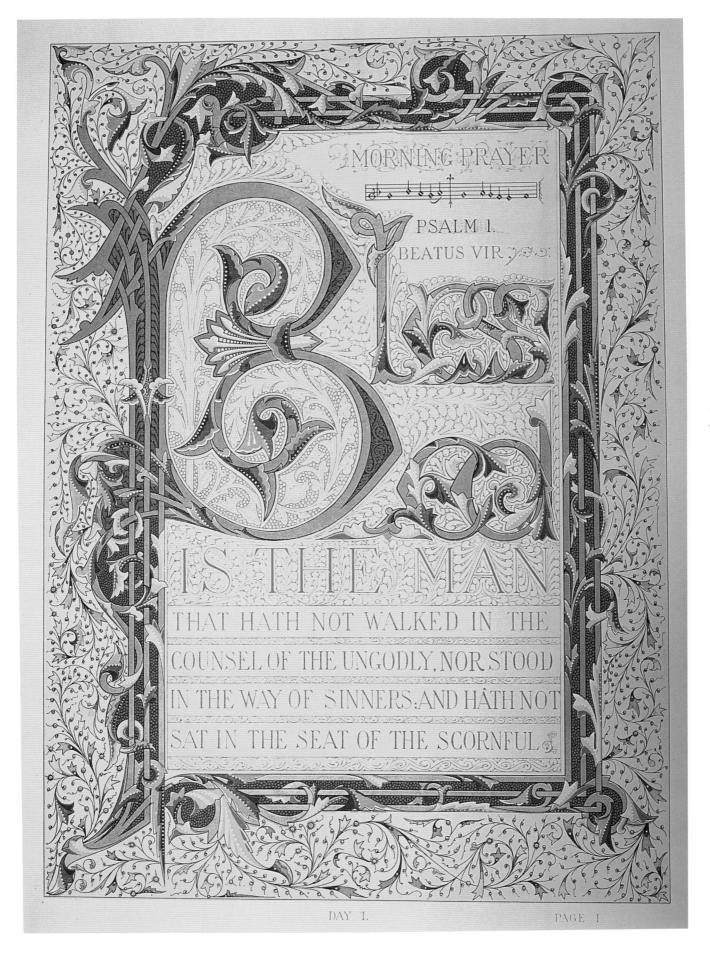

Pl. 1.18. Chromolithography and design for a page from The Victorian Psalter, 1861

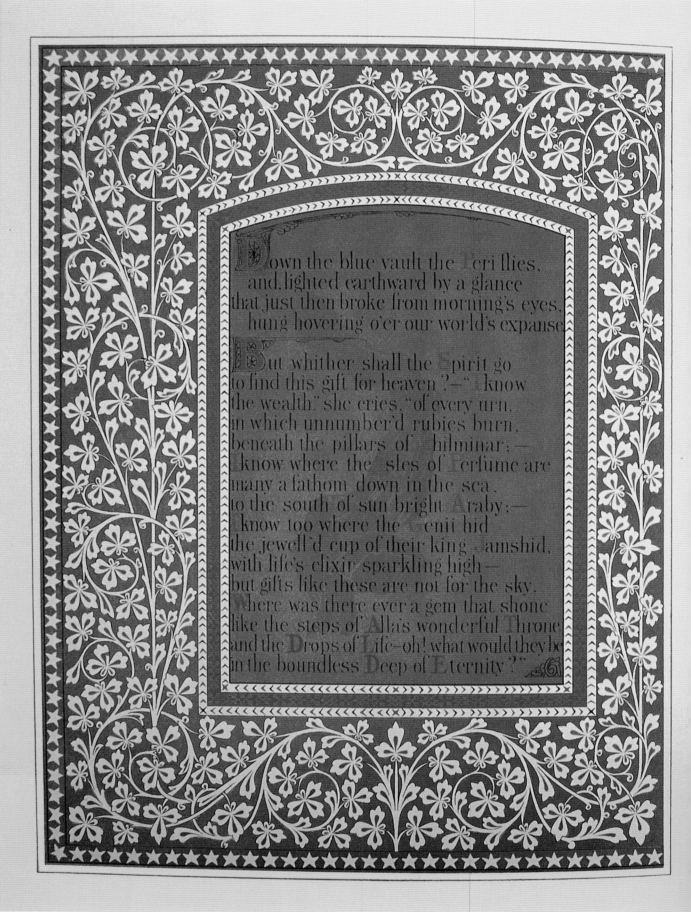

Pl. 1.19. Chromo-lithography and design for two pages from Paradise and the Peri, *1860*

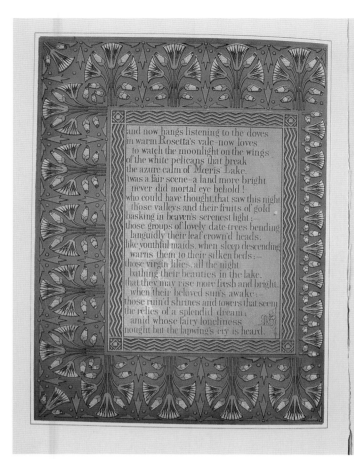

Pls. 1.20–1.22. Chromolithography and design for pages from Paradise and the Peri, *1860*

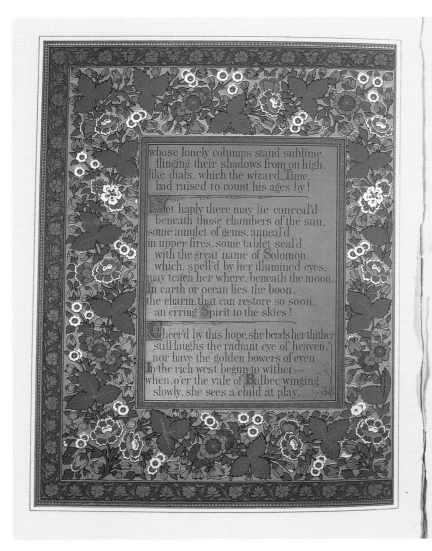

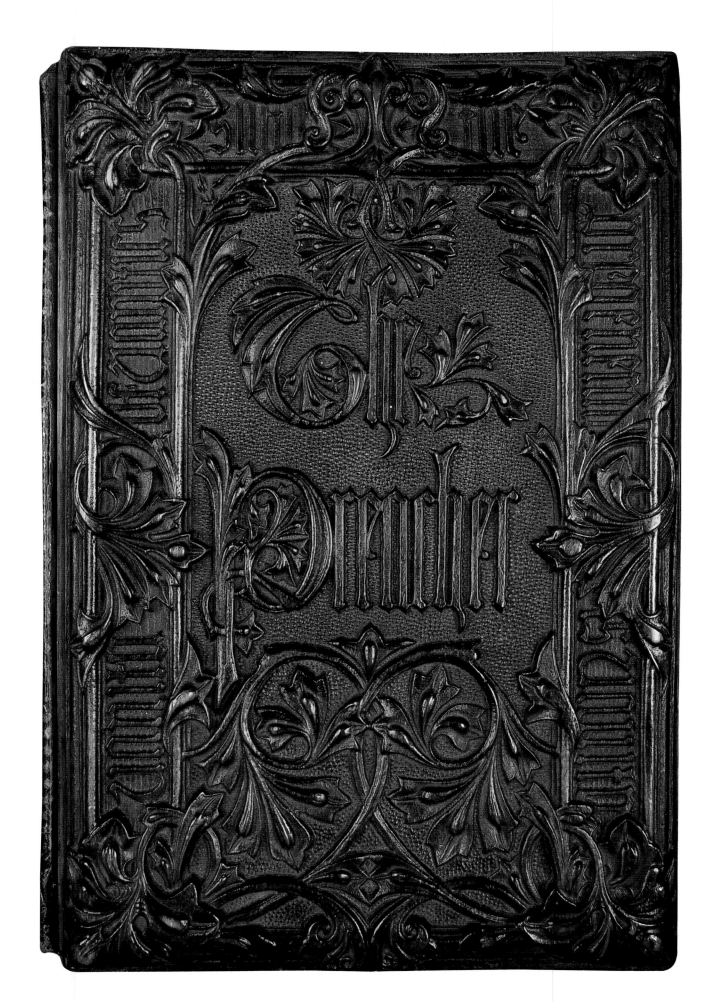

Pl. 1.23. Front cover of
The Preacher, *1849*

Pl. 1.24. Back cover and spine of The Preacher, *1849*

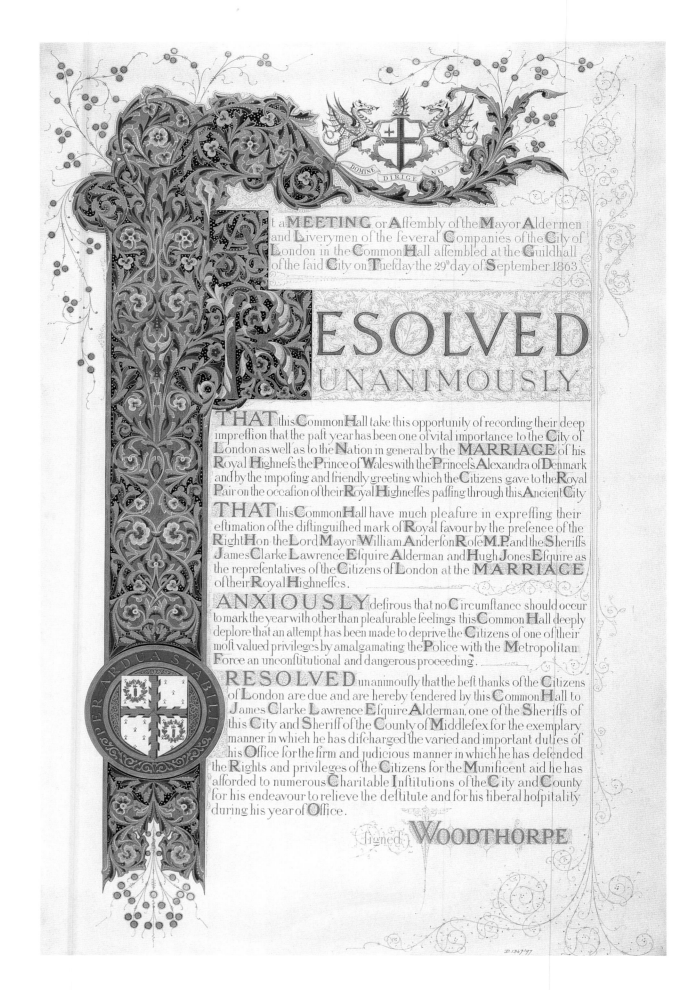

Pl. 1.25. Inscription for mayor of London

THIS HOUSE
GAD'S HILL PLACE
STANDS ON THE SUMMIT
OF
Shakspeare's
Gadshill

Ever memorable for its affociation in his noble fancy
with
SIR IOHN FALSTAFF

But, my lads, my lads, to morrow morning, by four o'clock, early
at Gadfhill. There are pilgirms going to Canterbury with rich
offerings, and traders riding to London with fat purfes:
I have vifors for all, you have horfes for yourfelves,

Pl. 1.26. Inscription for Charles Dickens

Pls. 1.27–1.30. Playing-card backs for De la Rue, n.d.

FAR LEFT *Pl. 1.31. Playing-card back for Queen Victoria for De la Rue, c. 1850*

Pl. 1.32–1.34. Playing-card backs for De la Rue, n.d.

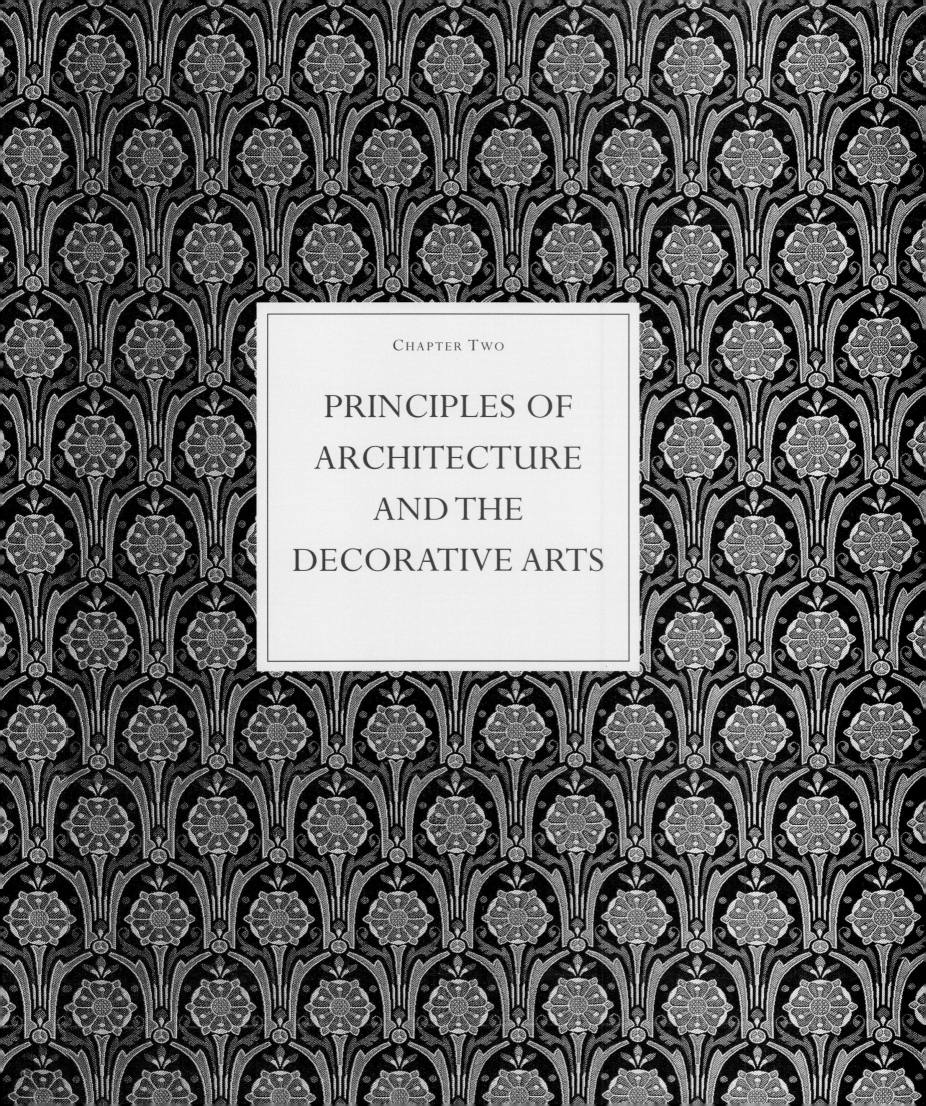

CHAPTER TWO

PRINCIPLES OF
ARCHITECTURE
AND THE
DECORATIVE ARTS

PRECEDING PAGES
*"Sutherland" textile design
in woven silk for Warner,
Sillett & Ramm, c. 1871*

The results of the Industrial Revolution had effected extraordinary social, economic, and political changes in England by the time Victoria ascended to the throne in 1837. The very appearance of countryside and towns was altered by the demands of dramatic increases in population, advances in transportation and technology, and the accumulation of wealth by new middle-class entrepreneurs (Fig. 2.3). Construction initiatives involving new types of structures included railway stations, suspension bridges, and concert halls, as well as traditional buildings at a much larger scale. Yet the apprentice system provided inadequate preparation for the complex engineering and new materials being developed; as a result, the majority of architects continued producing traditional designs, content to leave innovation to the engineers.[1] The architects focused on ornament rather than structure, choosing styles to satisfy client preferences or associations with particular types of buildings. Archaeological discoveries, stylistic revivals, and the force of tradition encouraged designers to repeat past conventions rather than develop new responses to changing circumstances. The resulting "Battle of the Styles" was widely criticized by architects, but few were willing to risk the uncertain reception and results of originality.

The state of the decorative arts was even worse, since the demand for ornamented goods coincided with the development of machines capable of carving ornament quicker and cheaper than hand production; the result was the manufacture of profusely decorated items. The desire for these overwrought products can be attributed to several factors. First, increased prosperity and the creation of the middle class produced a culture of consumers anxious to prove their status through the accumulation of goods for luxury and comfort. This group equated copiously ornamented goods with affluence, since decorated items

previously made by hand had been expensive.[2] The advent of inexpensive machine carving, what Jones called the "fatal facility" of industrialization, aided the production of objects laden with meaningless decoration. The manufacturers defended this extravagance as the fulfillment of consumer desires and denied any responsibility for trying to improve public taste.

In the 1830s, campaigns to battle these conditions resulted in the establishment of government-sponsored schools to train students to become designers for industry. The poor showing of British products displayed in the Great Exhibition of 1851 prompted a Parliamentary inquiry to determine why the schools had failed to improve industrial design. The excesses in the displayed items strengthened the resolve of Jones and the Great Exhibition organizers for design reform. Their aspirations gained momentum with Henry Cole's appointment as general superintendent of the School of Design in 1852. Cole took immediate steps to enlarge the faculty and change the focus of the curriculum from figure drawing and fine arts to practical instruction. Prince Albert assisted by donating Marlborough House for a museum of ornamental art where exhibits and lectures could foster the education of designers and the public. Items purchased from the Great Exhibition by Jones, Pugin, Cole, and Redgrave formed the nucleus of the museum's collection and their philosophy of design was communicated in the catalogue of museum objects.

Although Jones refused a position on the faculty of the appropriately renamed School of Practical Art, his contributions to the school's curriculum and philosophy directly influenced the English Reform Movement. He summarized his design theory in principles explained in lectures to the profession and the public, posted in the classrooms of the design schools and given to the students to study.

Fig. 2.1. "Motif #2, Greek No. 2," Pl. XVI *from* The Grammar of Ornament, *1856*

Fig. 2.2. "Motif #11, Greek No. 2," Pl. XVI *from* The Grammar of Ornament, *1856*

Design theory replaced the eighteenth-century emphasis on taste as the standard for architecture and the decorative arts in the nineteenth century. In *Pattern: A Study of Ornament in Western Europe, 1180–1900*, Linda Evans concludes: "Every nineteenth-century thinker concerned himself with the idea of the beautiful . . . as a theorist."[3] Evans described the period as "the present age, when theory is everything, when volume after volume issues from the press replete with the most subtle analysis of principles which are to guide us in our estimate of the beautiful." However, none of the treatises produced gained the recognition and acceptance of the thirty-seven propositions outlined by Jones in *The Grammar of Ornament* (1856). This chapter reviews the principles (or "propositions," as Jones referred to them) and examines their content within the context of Jones's lectures and written work.

THE GRAMMAR OF ORNAMENT

This extraordinary volume was published as an imperial folio containing a preface, Jones's propositions, twenty essays on particular styles, and one hundred chromolithographed plates illustrating one thousand examples of ornament. In the preface, Jones explains his intention to publish his philosophy for ornamental design to assist students and design practitioners in comprehending the fundamental principles essential to good architecture and the decorative arts and to provide examples of ornament to demonstrate general laws of composition."[4] He expressed the hope that the examples would not facilitate copying, but would inspire originality.

Proposition One, "The Decorative Arts arise from, and should properly be attendant upon, Architecture," reflects Jones's belief that architecture is "the great parent of all ornamentation" and that the decorative arts should enhance, and not compete with, architecture. This proposition introduces the idea of unified design fundamental to Jones's philosophy, reminding us of his observations of ancient cultures where every object "from the grandest monument to the simplest utensil" reflected the same design principles and motifs (Pls. 2.3 and 5.1). He contrasted the culturally rich common aesthetics of ancient societies with the meaningless historicism characteristic of British design in the nineteenth century. He chastised architects and manufacturers for acting independently and striving to produce novelty without beauty or beauty without intelligence.[5]

Jones rebuked his colleagues for abdicating the responsibility of decorating the interiors of their buildings and allowing "inferior and unguided hands" to produce places of discord and incongruity.[6] He addressed this condition in the first proposition by assigning the accountability for the decorative arts to the architect. Earlier architects, such as Robert Adam (1728–1792), created harmonious interiors by designing all of the elements in a room. Jones followed this model throughout his career, creating complete schemes for all types of interiors, from grand concert halls to private apartments. His comprehensive arrangements included innovations in lighting and ventilation; new motifs for furniture, moldings, and textiles; and designs for utilitarian items such as coal shuttles and bidets.

Proposition Two defines architecture as "the material expression of the wants, the faculties, and the sentiments of the age in which it is created" and style as "the particular form that expression takes under the influence of climate and materials at command." Jones believed that "the history of Architecture is the history of the world" and that architecture is in a constant state of evolution due to changes in local conditions and institutions. He agreed with the cycle of birth, maturity, and decline in art identified by Winckelmann and Seroux D'Agincourt, and his chronology of this cycle in Christian architecture agreed with Pugin. Jones and Pugin admired the unity of art and science in the Gothic period and blamed the disruptive force of the Reformation for reducing faith and destroying the integrity of architecture and Christian belief. Both designers condemned contemporary Christian churches for adopting the forms and symbols of pagan temples.[7]

This interpretation of the ill effects of the Reformation had been widely accepted among leading thinkers for some time. Victor Hugo provides one example in *The Hunchback of Notre Dame* (1831). In a chapter called *"Ceci tuera cela"* ("This Will Kill That" or "The One Will Kill the Other"), Hugo reasoned that printing would supplant architecture.

Fig. 2.3. Henry Alken, Past and Present, *1841*

He observed that while architecture had functioned as the primary record of civilization up to the fifteenth century, displaying the thoughts and experiences of humanity in stone, the printed word would prove more enduring. He pointed to the devastating impact of printing on religion, arguing that "without the invention of printing, the Reformation would have been but a schism; the invention of printing made it a revolution."[8]

Although Jones and Pugin admired pre-Reformation Christian architecture, they disagreed on the appropriateness of reviving Gothic architecture. Pugin saw the reinstitution of Gothic as an inspiration to piety. Jones saw it as adopting a "galvanized corpse," inappropriate for changed conditions and capabilities.

Propositions Three, Four, Six, Seven, Nine, and Ten identify the essential elements for good design in architecture and the decorative arts. Proposition Three states that all works of architecture and the decorative arts should possess fitness (or should be functional), proportion, and har-

mony to produce a sense of repose. This concept echoes the *"firmitas," "utilitas,"* and *"venustas"* identified by the Roman architect Vitruvius (c. 90 B.C.–c. 20 B.C.), restated as "firmness, commodity, and delight" by the English architect Sir Henry Wooton. John Claudius Loudon (1783–1843) also identified utility and fitness as key elements in architecture and criticized his peers for basing their designs on "the accidental associations of classical, historical, and imitative beauty" instead of recognizing utility and fitness as primary conditions for beauty.[9] Jones launched a similar attack on his peers, criticizing specific elements, such as inaccessible decorative porticoes that obstructed daylight and the inappropriate use of temple fronts on shops, churches, and gin palaces. He also condemned almshouses resembling mansions and railway stations imitating colleges. He rejected iron fashioned to look like stone and wood treated to resemble marble. He also charged that designers, manufacturers, and the public didn't consider the purpose of the articles they made or purchased and he blamed manufacturers for pursuing novelty and disregarding fitness.

Proposition Nine focuses on proportion in architecture and the decorative arts, maintaining that "every assemblage of forms should be arranged on certain definite proportions; the whole and each particular member should be a multiple of some simple unit." Jones drew an analogy between sound and sight, alleging that the ear and the eye find mathematical proportions pleasurable. He observed that each musical note occurs at one point on the string of a violin and that movement away from that point produces either a sharp or flat sound; he compared this phenomenon to the harmony experienced in viewing ratios of five to eight parts, as opposed to five to seven and three-quarters or eight and a quarter. He recommended that designers refine their schemes by adopting satisfying proportions, in the way that a musician composes a melody by inspiration and then corrects the counterpoint, or the poet drafts a verse and then improves the meter and grammatical construction.[10]

Propositions Four and Six discuss beauty in a manner consistent with the Renaissance theory of Leon Battista Alberti (1404–1472).[11] Proposition Four states that "True beauty results from that repose which the mind feels when the eye, the intellect, and the affections, are satisfied from the absence of any want." Proposition Six adds: "Beauty of form is produced by lines growing out from the other in gradual undulations: there are no excrescences; nothing could be removed and leave the design equally good or better." Jones used an illustration to show that "there can be no beauty of form, no perfect proportions or harmonious arrangement of lines, which do not produce repose," saying "All transitions of curved lines from curved, or of curved from straight, must be gradual. Thus the transition would cease to be agreeable if the break were too deep in proportion to the curves." He explained that when curves are separated by a break, they must run parallel to an imaginary

Fig. 2.4. *"Egyptian No. 3," Pl. VI from* The Grammar of Ornament, *1856*

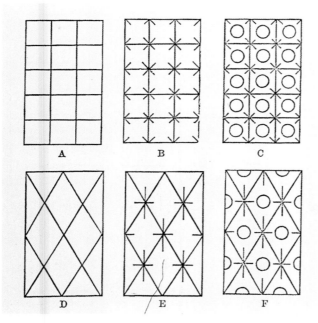

Fig. 2.5. Pattern development

line with the curves tangential to each other; when this practice is ignored the eye does not follow the curve but is diverted and repose is destroyed. He praised Greek moldings and ornament for exhibiting this type of refinement.

In *The Sense of Order*, E. H. Gombrich cites this explanation as an example of Jones's introduction of the psychology of perception into nineteenth-century architecture theory, well before the empirical experiments of Gestalt psychology.[12] Gombrich distinguishes a huge "gulf" between Jones's perceptual approach and Ruskin's "graphological expressionism." "Beauty," "perfection," "repose," and "harmony" were synonymous for Jones and his chief objective. In contrast, Ruskin hated the "perfection" Jones advocated and denounced Jones's principles and techniques as inhibiting to the artist.

Proposition Ten recommends creating harmony through "the proper balancing, and contrast of, the straight, the angular, and the curved." This proposition echoes theorist George Field's idea that the line, angle, and curve comprise the three primary figures and perfect harmony cannot be achieved if any of these elements is absent.[13] Jones praised Greek and Gothic architecture for the best balance of straight, angular, and curved elements, citing the capping of Gothic buttresses to counteract the verticality of walls and the placement of gables over windows to offset pointed arches and perpendicular mullions.

Jones demonstrated the balance of the three elements in a series of illustrations, showing: (A) the monotony of a grid, (B) the increased interest achieved by adding diagonal lines, (C) the harmony of the three elements, and (D) similar results achieved with a diaper pattern composed of equilateral triangles (Fig. 2.5).[14] Gombrich recognized these illustrations as further evidence of Jones's understanding of the psychology of perception, presaging Birkhoff's observation that "pleasure in perception derives from the right

mean between monotony on the one side and confusion on the other."[15]

The fifth proposition concerns a point of major debate and basic doctrine in nineteenth-century architecture theory: the appropriate use of ornament. Jones articulated the reformers' position: "Construction should be decorated. Decoration should never be purposely constructed." Jones agreed with Pugin that "all ornament should consist of enrichment of the essential construction of the building."[16]

Jones introduced an analogy to explain his position, saying that if two horses are used to draw a carriage when only one is necessary, a sense of luxury and an excess of power is experienced. But, if the second horse simply runs alongside the first without helping to draw the carriage, a disagreeable reaction occurs, derived from the perception of an abuse of means. He argued that, in the same way, ornament, however beautiful, that has nothing to do with construction or utility is disagreeable. He echoed Pugin saying "every object, to afford perfect pleasure, must be fit for the purpose and true to its construction."[17] He cited abuses of decorated construction in objects giving a false appearance of support, and noted successful examples in the Indian Collection at Marlborough House and in the enrichment of the Alhambra.

Jones's rules for ornamental design begin with Proposition Seven: "The general forms being first cared for; these should be subdivided and ornamented by general lines; the interstices may then be filled in with ornament, which may again be subdivided and enriched for closer inspection." This process allows ornament to conform to the shape of the object being decorated and eliminates the popular, but inappropriate, selection of human forms, animals, and realistic imitations of natural phenomena as decorative motifs. Again, Jones recommended the use of grids, composed of squares and diagonals, to create patterns of movement to delight, but not fatigue, the eye and to achieve a sense of repose through the continuity and predictability of the arrangement.

Propositions Eleven and Twelve continue the discussion of the construction of ornament. Jones illustrated Proposition Eleven ("In surface decoration all lines should flow out of a parent stem. Every ornament, however distant, should be traced to its branch and root.") with examples of distribution and radiation found in nature (Fig. 2.6). His first diagram shows a pattern corresponding to the dis-

Fig. 2.6. Examples of distribution and radiation found in nature

tribution of sap through a vine leaf, with a dominant line similar to a main artery supplying the sap to smaller veins. The second diagram illustrates the concept of radiation with a pattern similar to the distribution of fingers on the human hand or the veins in a chestnut leaf. Jones identified differences in the plant motifs of the Greeks and the Arabs, noting that the Greeks preferred cactus-type plants, where each new leaf grows out from the previous leaf to produce a continuous line, while Arab foliation (arabesque) emerges from a continuous stem.

Although arabesques are found in Byzantine and other early styles, the dominant use of the parent stem and flowing branches in Arabic and Islamic art lead to the "arabesque" label. Some scholars consider the motif to be the ideal exploitation of line. Others regard the arabesque as an abstraction transcending representation, producing endless repetition in form that enables the viewer to escape the constraints of time and facilitates meditation. In Islamic designs, verses from the Koran are often woven into the pattern, symbolizing the unbounded nature of the divine in the infinite pattern.

Proposition Twelve says "All junctions of curved lines with curved, or of curved with straight should be tangential to each other." Jones called this proposition "the melody of form" and likened his discussion of satisfying curves to the perception of proportions, indicating that compositions of curves are most agreeable when the technique of their production is least apparent. The creation of satisfying curves was important to Jones, like Hogarth, who believed that eyes traveled along the lines in the work. The nature of the line could produce either harmony or chaos.

Jones studied curves common to Greek, Gothic, and Islamic architecture, noting that the farther the line created moved away from the union of two circles, the more graceful the curve became (Fig. 2.7). Jones observed that

Fig. 2.8. "Sutherland" textile design in woven silk for Warner, Sillett & Ramm, c. 1871

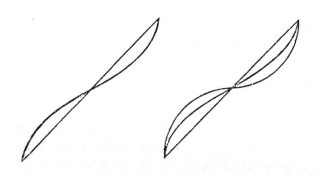

moldings and ornaments formed from curves of the highest order, such as conic sections, were produced in periods of high art, while curves developed from circles and compasswork appeared in periods of decline. Penrose's research on Greek architecture confirmed this idea, indicating that the curves and moldings of the Parthenon were of a very high order and that segments of circles were rarely used.[18]

Proposition Thirteen was critical to Jones's theory and distinguished him from other theorists on the subject of ornament. The proposition reads: "Flowers or other natural objects should not be used as ornament, but conventional representations founded upon them sufficiently suggestive to convey the intended image to the mind, without destroying the unity of the object they are employed to decorate" (Pages 70–1). This proposition rejects the direct imitation of nature pervasive in Victorian decoration, since Jones believed that "all ornamentation was ennobled by the ideal; never by a faithful representation of Nature."[19] Ruskin argued the opposite, saying that man could not "advance in the invention of beauty, without directly imitating natural form."[20] In Ruskin's hierarchy of ornament, the imitation of natural forms was considered the most advanced type of ornament.[21]

An understanding of color was also essential to Jones, and he followed the thirteen propositions concerning form and ornament with twenty-one propositions dealing with color. In his designs, Jones integrated grids, conventionalized motifs, and colors to create luminous patterns. The balanced elements combined to produce the appearance of texture and movement in complex but ordered arrangements.

The patterns present intriguing puzzles capable of engaging the eye and the mind in several ways. First, the

Fig. 2.7. Comparison of curved lines

Fig. 2.9. Decorative scheme for the apse, Christ Church, Streatham, London, 1851

repetition of elements establishes the structure of the arrangement and suggests the designer's input, a critical aspect to Jones. Second, the integration of color and pattern becomes apparent. The pattern might show a motif against a contrasting background, or a conventionalized flower might have stems in one color, leaves in a second, and the background in still another color. Third, the perception of color and pattern varies with distance. Viewed from a distance, the lines of the pattern are indistinguishable and merge into a single color. When properly balanced, the colors blend into a lively, yet subdued, arrangement (Jones's "neutralized bloom"). Viewed nearer, the largest elements are perceptible, and, at close proximity, the smallest details and interstices are visible. Achieving the correct balance between pattern and color to enhance form was critical to Jones.

As discussed earlier, Jones demonstrated a strong interest in color, traveling to the major ancient architecture sites associated with color, such as the Alhambra where he analyzed the pigments, and experimenting with chromolithography. He also introduced color in his early architecture commissions, a bold and unconventional move for a fledgling architect in nineteenth-century Britain. One such project was described by Cesar Daly, editor of the *Revue Générale*, after his visit to one of Jones's London interiors in

1845.[22] Daly praised the attractiveness of the hierarchical scheme, observing that the white walls and undecorated relief of the entry and passage served as a prelude to the colorful ceiling decoration and cornices of the main living room. Jones placed color and ornament high in a room to minimize competition with the appearance of the inhabitants. Daly claimed that Jones had succeeded in replacing the cold and dampness of London with the warmth and brilliance of another latitude.

Other critics praised Jones's decoration of Lewis Vuillamy's All Saints, Ennismore Gardens, Knightsbridge (1846–9), and James W. Wild's (1814–1892) Christ Church, Streatham (1840–2). These churches represented a new style based on Byzantine architecture and Middle Eastern motifs.[23] The plans resembled the church of San Zeno Maggiore in Verona (c. 1123), an unusual precedent in a period dominated by the strictures of the Cambridge Camden Society. Henry-Russell Hitchcock points out that when the *Ecclesiologist* reviewed All Saints in 1849, Vuillamy was forgiven for departing from the preferred English Norman or Gothic for two reasons: first, the 1837 design predated the science of ecclesiology and second, the success of Jones's nontraditional interior decoration.[24] The reviewer praised Jones's decoration of the semidomed apse as "proof of the triumph of the principle of decorative

78 *Chapter Two*

colour." The ceiling was painted blue and decorated with stars in the pattern of a large cross. The Arts and Crafts architect Heywood Summer replaced Jones's work at All Saints in 1892 but some idea of Jones's decoration is still evident in Christ Church (Figs. 2.9 and 2.10).

Jones also colored and gilded the facade of the Fleet Street offices of the *Pictorial Times*.[25] The colored exterior must have presented a sharp contrast to its soot-blackened neighbors in monochromatic brick and stucco. The polychromatic scheme may have served as a visual metaphor for the illuminated publication's intrusion into the world of black-and-white print media. The exterior could have also suggested the periodical's attentiveness to contemporary debates, since the question of color in architecture remained a topic of controversy.

THE BUILDING FOR THE GREAT EXHIBITION OF 1851: THE CRYSTAL PALACE

Jones followed these early examples of polychromy, color in architecture, with a *tour de force*: his color scheme for the decoration of the Exhibition Building for the Great Exhibition of the Works of Industry of All Nations of 1851, more commonly known as the Crystal Palace. Since the Great Exhibition is considered by many to be *the* defining moment of nineteenth-century Britain, and since Jones played a critical role in the success of the enterprise, it is important to expand the discussion of his involvement beyond the color scheme, since most accounts of the Great Exhibition focus on other individuals, on the design and construction of the building, or describe the items displayed, without acknowledging the significance of Jones's contributions.

During the 1840s, Henry Cole, the future organizer of the Great Exhibition, asked Jones to design a cover for one of Cole's publications.[26] Their relationship quickly evolved to the point where the young architect showed Cole completed commissions and Cole encouraged Jones to join the Society for the Encouragement of Arts, Manufactures, and Commerce. Jones joined in 1847, the year Prince Albert assumed the presidency of the organization.[27]

The society's concern for the standards and success of British industrial design and manufactures fostered exhibitions of British goods in 1847, 1848, and 1849. Growing interest in these displays encouraged the organization to envision an exhibition of national design and manufacture to be held in London in 1851. To prepare, Cole, Francis Fuller, and M. Digby Wyatt visited the 1849 exposition in Paris to observe how the French managed their displays.[28] Cole noticed that the French included wares from their colonies along with their domestic manufactures, and this observation inspired the possibility of holding an international, rather than national, exhibition in 1851.

Prince Albert approved the idea and agreed to preside over a royal commission appointed to superintend the exhibition.[29] Members of the Royal Commission included Prime Minister Lord John Russell and the architect Charles Barry, among others.[30] An executive committee, responsible to the Royal Commission, included Robert Stephenson as chairman, M. Digby Wyatt as secretary, and George Drew, C. Wentworth Dilke, Francis Fuller, Henry Cole, and Lieutenant-Colonel William Reid, Royal Engineers, C.B.

A building committee, formed in January 1850, included the duke of Buccleugh and the earl of Ellesmere; the architects Charles Barry, R. C. Cockerell, and Professor Thomas Leverton Donaldson, plus the engineers Isambard Kingdom Brunel, Robert Stephenson, and William Cubitt. Lord John Russell acted as the secretary. On March 13, the

Fig. 2.10. Interior after restoration, Christ Church, Streatham, London, 1851

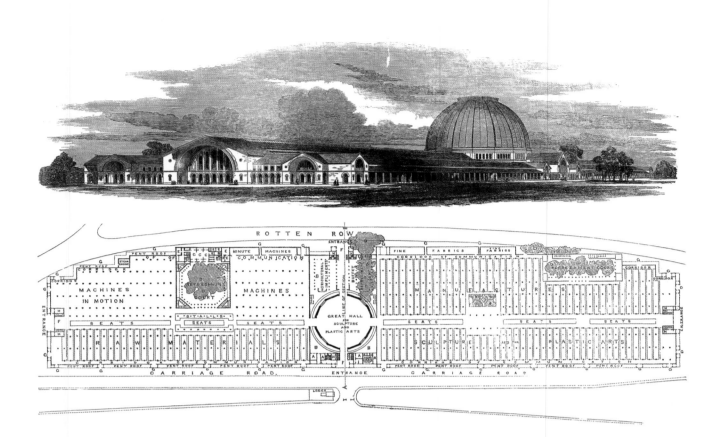

Fig. 2.11. Plan and elevation, the building committee's scheme for the Great Exhibition Building, 1850

committee announced an open competition to solicit ideas for the Exhibition Building. Although entrants had less than a month to prepare their designs, 245 plans were submitted. The committee awarded sixty-five of these projects an "honourable and favorable mention, on account of architectural merit, ingenious construction, or disposition, or graceful arrangement of plan" and eighteen received "further higher honorary distinctions, on account of their designs of distinguished merit, showing very noble qualities of construction, disposition, and taste."[31] Of these eighteen, particular attention was paid to the designs and models submitted by Hector Horeau of Paris and Richard Turner of Dublin. Horeau, designer of a winter garden in Lyons, proposed an iron-and-glass structure covered with a simple gabled roof. Turner, designer of the Palm House at Kew (1844), the conservatory in the Regent's Park Botanical Garden (c. 1840), and the second train shed of Lime Street Station, Liverpool (1849–51), also envisioned an iron-and-glass structure.

Although applauded, neither design was approved, and the committee announced plans to prepare its own scheme.[32] On May 16, 1850, Digby Wyatt proposed that he, Jones, and Charles Wild be employed to assist in the development of the design and construction supervision for the building. Salaries of 500 pounds for Jones and Wild were approved and Wyatt retained his previously approved

700 pounds in annual compensation.[33] The *Builder* opposed the choices, calling Wyatt "an excellent draughtsman and ornamentalist, but [one] who does not profess, so far as we know, any practical experience as an architect." Wyatt's inexperience was assumed to be the reason for the young engineer Wild's selection.[34] Jones was described as deserving of the praise he had received for his book on the Alhambra, but criticized for not knowing about construction.[35]

No documentation has been found giving the reasons for their selection, but it seems logical that Cole would have promoted his colleagues Wyatt and Jones, and Stephenson would have supported Wild, his former assistant. Wild had distinguished himself with the design and flotation of the tubes for the construction of the Britannia Bridge and with an article entitled "The Deflection and Relative Strains in Single and Continuous Beams" published in *Britannia and Conway Tubular Bridges* by Edwin Clarke (1850). The real issue is not why these gentlemen were chosen but the fact that the selection was brilliant. Each brought unique capabilities important to the exhibition's success.

Wild assisted Brunel on the plans for the huge dome (200 feet wide and 150 feet high) to crown the building.[36] The structure was to be 450 feet wide, 2,300 feet long, and 60 feet high, enclosing an area of approximately 900,000 square feet. This vast space, described by Hitchcock as "a sort of *Rundbogenstil* super-railway-station" was to be covered with an iron roof spanning 48 feet, supported by hollow iron columns on brick piers.[37] The principal entrance was centered on the south front with three other entrances on the north.

The committee considered the provisional nature of the building and aimed at producing a design capable of adaptation to other purposes without costly expenditures for labor and materials. They recognized the need for simplicity due to the short construction schedule and attempted to fulfill the desired objectives of economy and to provide facilities for the display of goods, the circulation of visitors, and for grand points for viewing the exhibition.

Jones is thought to be the delineator of the building committee's scheme published in the *Illustrated London News* on June 22, 1850 (Fig. 2.11).[38] This illustration was followed by Joseph Paxton's scheme on July 6, 1850. The acceptance of Paxton's scheme has overshadowed the fact that the building committee, composed of three of the nation's leading architects and two of history's most respected engineers, proposed an advanced and ambitious building. Brunel's daring dome, incorporating modern techniques and materials, would have surpassed the domes of St. Paul's Cathedral, London, and St. Peter's in Rome. Further, the committee's scheme combining iron construction with traditional building materials had been proven, while Paxton's plan for an iron-and-glass structure four times the size of St. Paul's Cathedral had not. Fears that England might "make an 'exhibition'" of herself may have convinced the committee that an attainable result was preferable to the risk of an experiment.[39]

The public saw it differently; they derided the committee's scheme and embraced Paxton's layout. Paxton's design was ultimately accepted; Fox and Henderson were selected as contractors and the responsibilities of Wyatt, Jones, and Wild shifted. Wyatt continued as secretary to the executive committee, while Jones and Wild were named superintendents of the works. Wild was responsible for checking the specifications and calculations of the building and testing the structural members during construction; Jones was responsible for devising "an elaborate system of decoration, extending internally and externally over eighteen acres of ground; the entire filling up of that vast space with stalls, tables, cases, &c.; the preparation of walks and avenues, ornamented with statues, fountains, and other objects of artistic beauty; [and] the entire arrangement of the countless number of articles brought forward to be exhibited."[40] Wyatt later described Jones in this capacity, as going "carefully over every form in the building susceptible of harmonious combination."[41]

Hitchcock was the first to note that Jones deserves major credit "for most of the surface decorative aspects of the Palace" including the color and other refinements.[42] One of the examples of these enhancements is the unique clock Jones created for the transept of the exhibition building

(Fig. 2.12). At 24 feet across, the clock dial was the largest in England, surpassing the 17 feet of St. Paul's and the 23 feet proposed for the Palace of Westminster. Jones incorporated the latest technology to move the hands electrically, eliminating the extensive weights and space previously required, and reducing the essential workings of this new type of timepiece to a compact unit capable of being mounted directly on the frame of the transept. Jones used the spokes of the transept's lunette for the face of the clock, placing the number six at each end of the semicircle and number twelve at the center of the arc. Two hands completed this unique timepiece.[43]

Hitchcock attributes many of the refinements of the building to Jones, including the scrolls beneath the spandrels and the roof cresting, and observes that these decorative elements introduce a new type of ornament, not dependent on the traditional preoccupations of the architect but created out of a thorough comprehension of the processes of manufacturing and the best methods of assembling and disassembling the components used.[44] Jones had

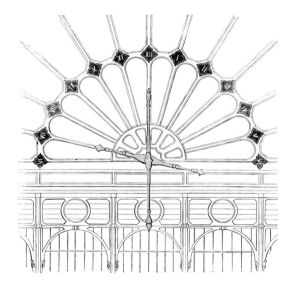

Fig. 2.12. Clock for the Great Exhibition Building, Hyde Park, London, 1851

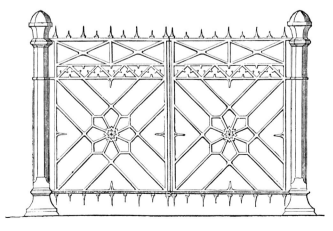

Fig. 2.13. Fence for the exterior of the Great Exhibition Building, Hyde Park, London, 1851

designed acclaimed works using cast iron and sophisticated engineering techniques prior to his connection with the Crystal Palace. Wild, who was Jones's brother-in-law, assisted him on these earlier projects and they shared a close relationship. Wild had also been the head of Fox and Henderson's drawing office. These relationships may explain the impressive coordination that enabled every element of the building to be designed and problems solved in an astonishingly brief period.[45]

Jones also designed many practical elements, including the 6 1/2-foot high fence surrounding the building at a distance of 8 feet to keep the public away from the building during construction (Fig. 2.13). The railing drew praise in the *Times* and in the *Illustrated London News*.[46] The *News* printed a drawing of the iron fencing and commended the way the railing repeated some of the key constructional elements of the building, such as the columns and trellis girders.

Jones made changes to Paxton's plan, altering the exits and replacing the glass at the lowest levels with wooden louvered panels.[47] He also planned the arrangement of the eight miles of items to be exhibited. The *Times* praised his plan for allaying the "jealousy and dissatisfaction" of foreign nations and observed that the arrangement provided each country with a distinct display space to prevent comparisons and give each nation a center of attraction. The proposed organization of Britain's products was well received; the least attractive items, such as machinery, raw materials, and produce were to be placed along the sides of the building, reserving the prominent central area for more attractive fine-art objects and manufactured goods. The *Times* summarized Jones's plan, saying the "brilliancy and splendour of colour and form will thus be shown off to the greatest advantage, and the effect will be still further increased by the adoption of a geographical arrangement which places the showy productions of tropical regions nearest to the transept, and removes to the extremities the less gaudy but more useful industry of colder climates."[48]

Jones's most noticeable contribution and greatest political challenge, however, was the building's decoration. The construction of the building was progressing rapidly by November 1850, but nothing had been decided on the decoration. Fox and Henderson's contract stipulated that the building was to be painted white, but no funds had been approved for further embellishment. Fox wanted a committee of taste to be appointed to decide the decoration.[49] Meanwhile, Jones solicited ideas from twenty architects, but since no two agreed, he felt free to present his own ideas on the application of color to enhance both the structure and the visual impact of the space enclosed. He outlined his proposal in a letter to Prince Albert, estimating that the painting would require an additional 2000 pounds.[50] Since avoidance of expense was paramount, this was a risky undertaking. Cubitt supported Jones's proposal and petitioned Lord Granville for the expenditure.

Fig. 2.14. Design for the interior decoration of the Great Exhibition Building, Hyde Park, London, 1851

Granville quipped that even if Raphael himself designed the decoration, 2000 pounds was not likely to be approved.[51]

Jones organized a paint trial to assist the commissioners in evaluating his proposal. A portion of the facade was painted according to his idea and three different schemes were displayed on the interior to show the changes experienced when the iron columns were painted either a neutral color, dark red, or with blue, yellow, and white stripes. Carpets were suspended behind the columns and damask was hung from the girders to simulate items to be displayed in the exhibition.[52] Jones also prepared two watercolors to represent the impression of his multi-colored (or parti-colored, as it was referred to at the time) scheme (Fig. 2.14).[53]

Jones believed the canvas intended for the roof and south side of the building would minimize light and shade on the interior and reduce the structure to an indistinct mass, resembling a dull cloud overhead. Likewise, if the iron was painted white, stone color, or in a solid dark tone, the relief of the columns would not be discernible and each column and girder would present a flat silhouette. To correct this problem, Jones suggested a multicolored arrangement, applying the primary colors in the proportions of eight parts blue to five parts red and three parts yellow. In these quantities, the colors would neutralize each other and no color would dominate or fatigue the eye. These ideas were derived from the color theory of the Field.[54] By adopting Field's ratios, Jones would attempt an experiment on a vast scale to achieve neutrality, or white light, to create the illusion of increased light within the building. The distribution of colors would imitate the effect of light and shade, since blue, which recedes, would be placed on concave surfaces; yellow, which advances, on the convex and red, the color of the middle distance, on the horizontal planes.

The Royal Commissioners viewed the paint trial in their first meeting in the building on December 5, 1850. As Jones predicted, the red and green columns were indistinct, but the multicolored column was clearly visible. A committee of Prince Albert, Sir Richard Westmacott, and Sir Charles Eastlake accepted Jones's proposal with minor modifications, including changing the undersides of the sash bars from red to white, painting the ridge piece of the roof blue and white, and recommending a lighter shade of red. They rejected Jones's proposal to suspend textiles displaying the insignias of participating nations below the roof to counteract the flatness of the 1848-foot nave.

Although Jones had the approval to proceed, reports indicate that Prince Albert was aghast at both the coloring and the daring originality of the scheme and argued with Jones on a daily basis over the proposed decoration.[55] Others were opposed as well; in fact, the condemnation of Jones's prismatic scheme reached such a level of intensity that the *Builder* began printing articles entitled "The Great Paint Question Covering the Controversy."[56] The *Art*

Journal proclaimed that covering the slender columns with alternating stripes of vivid color would "produce a mass of confusion to the eye, and totally destroy that harmony and simplicity which will give grandeur to the interior."[57] Other reporters agreed, predicting that the decoration would be painful, unsightly, and vulgar and that the scheme would compromise the colors of the goods displayed. The articles printed in the *Expositor: A Weekly Illustrated Recorder of Inventions, Designs and Art-Manufacturers* were particularly brutal, attacking Jones's scheme by saying: "Never was there seen such palpable disfigurement, such unmistakably abominable taste, such a hideous glare of colours, such manifest unfitness to the purpose of a show of coloured goods."[58] The writer continued describing the decoration as "geegaw motley" and suggested imprisoning Jones until after the exhibition opened to prevent the building becoming the world's laughing-stock. The popular press also printed the negative reactions of readers and alternative proposals for the decoration, including C. Bruce Allen's plan to paint the columns white and each of the seven aisles a different color of the solar spectrum.[59]

The intensity of the criticism prompted Jones to address the Royal Institute of British Architects to refute his detractors. On December 16, he faced an exceptionally crowded meeting of his peers to explain how he planned to enhance the grandeur of the structure by marking every line in the building, increasing the perception of the height, length, and bulk of the building. He supported his ideas by citing historic examples of the use of the primary colors in Egyptian, Byzantine, and medieval decoration, and explained the contemporary experiments with color carried out by Field. He concluded with the explanation that although it was difficult for someone trained in the arts to conceive of his arrangement and to estimate the harmony in his scheme, it was virtually impossible for the "uninstructed spectator, who, from the experimental decoration of a *single* column, draws a premature, and, necessarily, fallacious inference as to the collective effect of the whole." For his own part, he "had confident hope—grounded on the experience of years devoted to this particular branch of art, that the principles and plans" he proposed "for the decoration of this magnificent structure" would not disappoint the public or be unworthy of the great occasion for which they were produced.[60] The *Times* and other daily papers reprinted Jones's speech the following day. Other major periodicals, including the *Illustrated London News*, the *Builder*, the *Athenaeum* and the *Civil Engineer and Architect's Journal* included the text in their next issues.[61] The result was increased invective printed in the popular periodicals.

Decorators used the opportunity to enhance their reputations by forwarding proposals. John G. Crace, a member of the distinguished family of royal decorators, approached Paxton with his scheme and then submitted the plan to the *Builder*.[62] Crace called Jones's idea of painting the columns

Fig. 2.15. Transept for the Great Exhibition Building, Hyde Park, London, 1851

yellow, white, and blue appropriate for wood but not for metal. Instead, he advocated painting the flat sides of the columns a pale bronze green and the circular parts the maroon red of anticorrosive paint. He adopted Jones's method of separating the colors selected, but chose a subdued gold as the "mediator" color.

Likewise, the decorative painter Frederick Sang wanted to emphasize the metallic composition of the structure, suggesting a pale bronze color for the columns and walls in "a cheerful neutral tint." He rejected Jones's use of primary colors by insisting that just as no artist would enclose a painting in a gaudily painted frame, the exhibition should not insult the products displayed by placing them in a gaudily painted building. Ironically, he followed this assertion with a proposal for a multicolored roof to rival the stained glass of York and Cologne cathedrals. These remarks provoked immediate criticism for their obvious inconsistencies. Others were quick to point out that the idea of truth to material did not permit painting one metal to look like another and, further, that the effect of sun streaming through colored glass would produce an even stronger and less controlled use of color than the plan proposed by Jones.[63]

A painter named E. V. Rippingill accused Jones of being incorrect on the matter of color and of devising a plan without a foundation in science or common sense. Rippingill argued that weak colors would serve the purpose of decoration, since strong colors attacking the eye would be highly prejudicial to the effect; instead, he recommended pinks and tender greens with a little orange to produce a warm, neutral gray to show the displayed items to the best advantage.[64] A clergyman suggested embossed tablets with the message "Glory be to God in the Highest and on Earth Peace, Goodwill toward Men" for the ribs and other building supports. Others recommended inscriptions addressing "the noble and universal purposes of the Exhibition."[65] The number and variety of attacks and the superficiality of the proposed alternatives demonstrates a pervasive ignorance about the use of color in architecture. Throughout the maelstrom, Jones remained calm, steadfastly directing the decoration according to his original plan.[66] As the work advanced, opinion began to change. The first indication of this shift appeared in the press on January 15, 1851, when the *Times* incorrectly reported that "a small portion of the transept roof has been painted in the colours decided upon by the commissioners, who it will be recollected, modified the more objectionable features of Mr. Owen Jones's design. The effect promises well, the brilliant blue especially looking extremely cool and refreshing."[67]

On January 25, the *Illustrated London News* reported an agreeable result from the painting of the transept.[68] By January 30, the *Times* commended Jones's choice of blue and white for the exterior, saying "whatever difference of opinion there may be as to the taste displayed by that gentleman in his contemplated mode of painting the interior,

the praise of a happy selection of colours for the outside of the building will not be denied to him" and continued "if any doubt remained on the subject, it would be dissipated by the view of a small portion of the north front, where a specimen of Mr. Jones's plan is exhibited side by side with the suggestions of others."[69] As for the interior, the reporter conceded that "the effect of the small portion of painting already executed is not so unfavorable as from the experimental specimen might have been anticipated," but maintained "the style of decoration is not what it ought to be." He continued with the equivocation "when a man of Mr. Jones' eminence as a decorator is intrusted with a work of this kind, it is only fair that he should be allowed, both by the public who criticize, and by the commissioners who employ him, considerable license in the execution of his designs," but he should "not perversely adhere to his own preconceived ideas of a certain decorative style to be adopted, when both the commissioners and the public have urged on him the propriety of some modifications." He challenged the architect with the warning "We put it to him whether an obstinate adherence to his own views on the subject is likely to conciliate approbation" and argued that "it would be mortifying, after having entirely succeeded in the execution of a building suited to receive the choicest specimens of the world's industry, if we did not do full justice to it in the style of embellishment." The February 3 report in the *Times* stated only "Mr. Owen Jones says there will be no difficulty about the decorations."[70]

The painting was progressing rapidly, since iron straps suspending wooden platforms enabled about five hundred workmen to paint simultaneously. As the work continued, opinion shifted further. Members of the press rationalized their reactions by either charging that the placement of the original paint test had interfered with a correct impression of the intended scheme, or, falsely, that Jones had muted the colors in the final execution.[71] Some tried to distance themselves from the initial skepticism and condemnation. The *Journal* took this approach, maintaining that: "The *Times* and some of its correspondents were very hostile at first to MR. OWEN JONES'S proposed decorations as being too rich in colour. We always maintained the contrary, contending that with such narrow stripes of colour, amid so much light and in so large a space, strong colours only would be visible," and the *Journal* was glad to see the *Times* had come around to the same opinion. The report continued by quoting an authority who championed Jones's plan and refuted the other schemes proffered. This expert observed that the English were "afraid of vulgarity except in black, snuff brown, bottle green, or some such dismal hue, and perhaps this bent of the general taste helped to swell the disapproval of Mr. Jones's plan when first propounded." Whatever the reason for the initial disapproval, the speaker felt that two points were now certain: "The first is, that his [Jones's] system of internal decoration is the best that has yet been suggested; and the second, that the most gaudy colours will be toned down to such an extent that the eye cannot be disagreeably affected by them." The speaker explained that this toning down would result from the canvas's reduction of light, the infusion of color from the mass of manufactured goods, and from the proportional combination of colors producing the colorless light Jones predicted.

On the same day, the *Times* reported that Jones intended to cover the stalls with red cloth to hide the unsightly woodwork and add warm coloring to the interior. The reporter speculated that the combination of the cloth "with the great mass of blue overhead and the yellow stripes on the columns, will produce a most harmonious and brilliant effect."[72] The roof, painted in blue and white and the columns, in blue, white, and yellow, would distinguish the building's components at the same time that they were unified through the effects of perspective and parallax. The Turkish red cloth on the stalls, and hangings, would provide a uniform background for the displays and complete the chromatic proportions.

As preparations neared completion, Jones's success was assured. Lord Granville wrote to Colonel Grey saying that "The Building will look better than His Royal Highness or any of us expected" and the press described the progress as follows:

As to the calico covering, the effect of it upon the internal decorations will in a remarkable manner verify the accuracy of the anticipative sketches which Mr. Owen Jones months ago laid before the commissioners. In gloomy dark days, the brilliant appearance of the structure will be somewhat impaired, but when the weather is fine the shade will prove refreshing and agreeable. A considerable portion of the Turkey red cloth used in the lining of stalls, and as a back ground for the gallery railings, has been placed, and this, combined with the masses of brilliant colours beginning to show all over the area of the building tells with the best effect upon the general aspect of the interior. It now gradually expands, and warms into a perfect picture, the tints of which are most harmoniously blended, and the *coup d'oeil* surprisingly beautiful.[73]

On opening day, reaction from the poets, the press, and the public was unrestrained in extolling Jones's scheme and in applauding "his superior taste and skill." This time, descriptions of his originality and accomplishments in creating a "very fairy land of beauty and wonder," and "a palace of the Arabian nights evolved by magic on England's sober soil" were intended as tributes, not accusations.[74] Donaldson called the Crystal Palace "the most successful edifice of modern times."[75] The best reporting and assessment appeared in the *Illustrated London News*. The report printed on May 1, 1851, is important in trying to gauge

the effect of Jones's scheme upon the visitor (Figs. 2.15 and 2.16); the periodical reported:

On entering the South transept a spectacle is afforded which fills the mind with wonder and produces an overwhelming effect upon the senses from the novelty, the grandeur and beauty. The surpassing beauty is in great measure owing to the lights and shadows and colors with which the objects are presented to view, and which have rendered the building the most attractive in the World. The transept is the most brilliantly lighted in as much as the noble arched roof is left open to the sky and not covered with calico like the remainder of the building. Passing from this central spot the light becomes more subdued in every direction; and, as the eye wanders up the vistas, the three primitive colors

of Sir D. Brewster [the scientist David Brewster], red, yellow, and blue, strike the eye by the intensity of their brightness in the foreground; but by blending in the distance, by the effect of parallax and diminished visual angle, the whole as in nature disappears into a neutral gray. To appreciate the genius of Owen Jones, the visitor must take his stand at the extremity of the building—looking up the nave, with its endless rows of pillars, the scene vanished from extreme brightness to the hazy indistinctness which Turner alone can paint.[76]

Ruskin called the building "a cucumber frame" and two years later, wrote in *The Stones of Venice* that he had "never yet seen a painted building, ancient or modern, which seemed . . . quite right" to him.[77] In the same text, Ruskin said that columns should never be painted with vertical stripes. Most observers of Jones's scheme, however, echoed the sense of awe-inspiring beauty described in the quotation above. The novelty of Paxton's structure and Jones's

Fig. 2.16. Henry Courney Selous, Opening of the Great Exhibition by Queen Victoria on 1st May 1851, *1851–2. Oil on canvas, 67¾ x 97¾ in.*

decoration elicited emotions of pride and pleasure. Viewers agreed with the *Westminster Review's* reporter who wrote: "Nothing can be more beautiful than the sky-blue tint of the roof of the nave. Before the external cloth was on, the spectator might have imagined it a carven sky. The effect also on looking diagonally amongst the columns from the gallery, is very fine in its geometrical effect."[78]

The art critic Mrs. Merrifield provided a similar description to the *Art Journal Catalogue*; she maintained that the interior perspective, softened under the miles of calico veil covering the glazed roof:

appears to be enveloped in a blue haze, as if it were open to the air, the warm tint of the canvas roof contrasts with the light blue colour of the girders into which it is insensibly lost, and harmonizing with the blue sky above the transept [which had no canvas veil outside], produces an appearance so pleasing, and at the time so natural, that it is difficult to distinguish where art begins and nature finishes.[79]

Lothar Bucher, a friend of Gottfried Semper, described the effect of the color as follows:

If we let our gaze slowly move downwards again, it encounters the filigreed girders, painted blue, far apart from each other at first, then moving ever closer, then superimposed on each other, then interrupted by a dazzling band of light [the crossing of the unveiled crystal transept], then finally dissolving in a remote background in which everything corporeal, even the lines themselves, disappear and only the colour remains. I had the impression that the coarse matter with which architecture works was completely dissolved in colour. The building was not decorated with colour, but built up of it.[80]

The triumph of Jones's scheme is more remarkable when the circumstances are considered. Jones had to anticipate unfamiliar visual effects in an unprecedented structure to be filled with unpredictable contents. The size of the building and the comprehensiveness of Jones's scheme would be the most extensive use of color in the history of architecture.[81] Fortunately, Jones's observations of the effects produced in the vast structures of ancient architecture and his interest in the latest optical studies on color and sensation enabled him to envision and unite the effects produced by the building and its contents into one harmonious unity. He accomplished this objective by placing brilliant colors closest to the viewer to visually "anchor" the building and give concordance to the disparate objects on display. Once this grounding in the familiar was achieved, he was free to use color to imitate infinity by accenting the inevitable dematerialization of the structure and creating a "general lightness and fairy-like brilliance never before dreamed of." As David Van Zanten, expert on architectural polychromy, has observed, "Jones transformed the idea of coloured decoration from an applied covering into a glowing aura expressive of the cultural soil in which the structure had grown and in harmony with the light and air of its surroundings."[82]

Many contemporaries, such as C. R. Cockerell, realized that "Without his [Jones's] assistance the Crystal Palace would have been but an overgrown greenhouse."[83] The success of the decoration confirmed Jones's authority on color and design and brought him national recognition.[84] He used his celebrity status to campaign for three objectives: architectural reform, improved design education, and the elevation of public taste. Within a month following the opening of the exhibition, he began writing a series of articles published in the *Journal of Design* entitled "Gleanings from the Great Exhibition of 1851." These articles discussed items on display in relation to theoretical issues in architecture and the decorative arts. Readers could visit the exhibition to study the examples Jones cited and reflect upon his ideas.

The first article repeated the concept of the bond between architecture and culture and emphasized objects in the exhibition to prove his argument, contrasting the overwrought, tasteless manufactures of the Western nations with the contributions from India and the countries of the Middle East. Jones repeated these observations and his principles in two lectures "An Attempt to Define the Principles which Should Regulate the Employment of Colour in the Decorative Arts" delivered at the Society of Arts on April 28, 1852 and a series of four lectures entitled "On the True and False in the Decorative Arts" delivered at the Marlborough House in June 1852.

While Jones accepted the latest scientific theory on color expressed by George Field and Michel-Eugène Chevreul and was influenced by the use of colors in ancient architecture, he derived his first and second propositions on color from observing nature, noting that: "Colour is used to assist in the development of form, and to distinguish objects or parts of objects from one another." Echoing Field, Jones explained that if all objects were the same color, they would be undifferentiated and that color was used to distinguish species, materials, and natural phenomena. He concluded that the ancients understood natural phenomena and adopted the use of color to define architecture. He cited examples of color used in the horizontal architraves of the ancients to emphasize the length, strength, and unity of structures that would have appeared weaker with disruptive vertical striations. He noted the way the ancients used color to distinguish architectural elements, such as capitals, shafts, and bases of columns and the way medieval builders emphasized the height of columns with spiral lines. In his paper "An Attempt to Define the Principles Which Should Regulate the Employment of Colour in the Decorative Arts," he refuted Ruskin's assertion that color should be independent from form, saying that Ruskin's position sanctioned the "violent instances of bad taste" evident in contemporary fashion, such as dresses fashioned with concentric rings of color and the broad-checked trousers of fast men that "cut the leg into slices."[85]

The second proposition continues the discussion of color

and form: "Colour is used to assist light and shade, helping the undulations of form by the proper distribution of the several colours." Jones explained that without light and shade, the forms of objects are indistinct, a globe becomes a circle without illumination on the exposed surface and shadow on the receding side. Jones used his painting of the Crystal Palace as an example of this proposition, saying he adopted the primary colors to produce the illusion of light and shade, enhancing the impression of the building and making it appear longer and taller than the actual dimensions.

The third and fourth propositions address the correct distribution of color. In the third proposition, Jones recommends the use of the primary colors in small quantities in limited areas balanced by secondary and tertiary colors on the larger masses. Jones recognized that some of his contemporaries dismissed the primary colors as vulgar, but he insisted that the primary colors are not vulgar or discordant when properly applied. He recalled the use of the primaries in the early periods of art in Egypt, Greece, Nineveh, Central America, and in Eastern cultures, noting that secondary colors were preferred later.

He observed that primitive societies combined observations of nature to devise new patterns and apply colors, while mature and declining societies repeated exhausted conventions and useless caprices. He suggested two explanations for the shift: an innate desire for change and the possibility that in periods of decline in art, artists lacked the capacity to balance the primary colors and sought refuge in the secondaries and tertiaries.

He continued discussing primary colors in the fourth proposition, saying they should be used on the upper portions of objects, and the secondary and tertiary colors in lower areas. This principle was followed in ancient architecture, with the exception of the Egyptians' use of green to symbolize the lotus leaf in the upper portion of their temples. The color scheme and location of color in the Crystal Palace can be used to show how Jones applied his theories to achieve different visual effects. The first involved the atmospheric effect realized with the blending of the primaries in the roof. This ethereal effect was destroyed when the canvas was removed at the close of the exhibition and the sun bleached out the red and yellow elements, leaving only the blue of the sky and the girders visible. The aerial perspective disappeared and the girders at the ends of the building became a blue mass, reducing the appearance of the nave by 200 to 300 feet, since the eye could no longer measure the distance. The objective of Proposition Four was realized when the primaries in the roof were balanced by the multicolored contents of the building below to achieve total harmony.

Propositions Five, Six, and Seven repeat the definitions and chromatic proportions published by Field. The fifth proposition outlines Field's "Theory of Chromatic Equivalents," indicating that equal intensities of the primaries harmonize or neutralize each other in the proportions of three parts yellow, five parts red, and eight parts blue. The secondaries harmonize in the proportions of eight orange, thirteen purple, eleven green. The tertiaries' proportions are nineteen parts citrine, twenty-one russet, and twenty-four olive. The secondaries, as compounds of two primaries, are neutralized by the remaining primary in the same proportions, or, eight of orange by eight of blue, eleven of green by five of red, and thirteen of purple by three of yellow. Each tertiary, a binary compound of two secondaries, is neutralized by the remaining secondary: twenty-four of olive by eight of orange, twenty-one of russet by eleven of green, and nineteen of citrine by thirteen of purple.

Proposition Six describes the variety of tones produced when colors are mixed with white and the shades produced when the colors are mixed with gray or black. Likewise, Proposition Seven introduces the concept of the hues created when one color is mixed with another; for example, when yellow is mixed with red or orange, an orange-yellow is produced and the combination of yellow with blue or green produces a lemon yellow. The same type of variation occurs when other tones, shades, and colors are combined. Proposition Seven describes the technique for achieving balance in mixing colors by advocating that when a primary tinged with another primary is contrasted with a secondary, the secondary must have a hue of the third primary.

Jones argued that although no mechanical means of balancing the infinite variety of tones, shades, and hues had been developed, the study and application of colors according to the proportions advanced by scientists would produce more successful arrangements than those based on instinct. He pointed to the East Indian collection of textiles in the Great Exhibition as an example of the perfect application and balance of color and recommended that those interested in learning about the balance of color study the Indian fabrics.

Jones also admired the way Eastern styles embodied the religious belief intrinsic in every thought and action of the people. He compared this unity to the disorder and skepticism in contemporary Christian art and predicted that the latter carried through subsequent generations would produce correspondingly weaker results. In an uncharacteristic passionate outburst in his paper "An Attempt to Define the Principles which Should Regulate the Employment of Colour in the Decorative Arts," he charged that:

Children born in an age of ugliness cannot hope to have their instincts quickened for the beautiful; but, on the contrary, the natural instinct will be extinguished, and will no longer be born with them. I can conceive a paternal and wise government visiting with punishment all those who produce abortions in

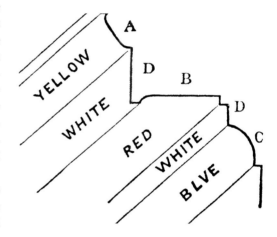

Fig. 2.17. *Diagram of molding with colors indicated, 1852*

art, as justly as those who lower the tone of the morals of the society; in either case they rob the rising generation of their birthright.[86]

He continued: "If it be true, as Field says, 'that whatever refines the taste, improves the morals, enhances the powers, and promotes the happiness of the people,' the converse is true also. That which corrupts their taste debases their morals, destroys their powers, and promotes their misery."[87] This statement shows that Jones, like his contemporary reformers, believed in the moral value of art and its potential to elevate the spirit and ethical level of society. He differed from Pugin, Morris, and others by endorsing the goal of universal betterment through art rather than adopting a more prescriptive approach.

Fig. 2.18. "Sultan," textile design of silk tissue woven by Warner's September 20, 1870

Jones used the color scheme of the Crystal Palace to explain Proposition Eight: "In using the primary colours on moulded surfaces, we should place blue, which retires, on the concave surfaces; yellow, which advances, on the convex; and red, the intermediate colour, on the undersides; separating the colours by white on the vertical planes." He showed diagrams of moldings to illustrate the proposition, labeling each surface with the recommended color (Fig. 2.17). He applied yellow at A to emphasize the relief of the molding and blue at C to assist in the impression of concavity. Red was applied at B, since Jones preferred to see red in shadow. He recalled the alarm caused by his proposal to paint the undersides of the girders of the Crystal Palace red but concluded that they could not have been any other color. He ended by painting the fillets, or vertical planes, at D white to separate the colors and prevent a harsh contrast.

Proposition Nine presents a critical concept in the color theory of Field and Jones: "the various colours should be so blended that the objects coloured, when viewed at a distance, should present a neutralised bloom . . . no one colour should attract the eye to the exclusion of the others" and "when viewed at a distance they should melt into one another." Jones could have cited his use of the primaries in the Crystal Palace to articulate the structural elements at close range but neutralize each other at a distance, blending into a vibrant bloom of color, but chose, instead, to discuss the "Oriental" practice of adding fragments of color to large gold ornaments placed on colored grounds. The colored elements established balance by reducing the impact of the gold. Although scientists knew about the neutralization of colors for almost a century, Jones was unique in translating their theory into brilliant arrangements and extraordinary effects.[88]

In Proposition Ten, Jones states that "No composition can ever be perfect in which any one of the three primary colours is wanting, either in its natural state or in combination." He explains that combinations of blue and yellow, red and yellow, or red and blue produce discords; as do combinations of green and yellow, purple and blue, or orange and red. He notes that these discords can be resolved by adding either white or black, since these two neutrals contain all the other colors.

Propositions Eleven through Fourteen derive from Chevreul's law of simultaneous contrasts. This law involves the changes in perception experienced when various colors are juxtaposed. Chevreul discovered that the appearance of colors is modified by adjacent colors, since each pigment simultaneously reflects the rays appropriate to its color, white rays, and the rays of its complementary color. Jones gave examples to describe this phenomenon outlined in Proposition Eleven, where he says "When two tones of the same colour are juxtaposed, the light colour will appear lighter, and the dark colour darker." He used two sheets of colored paper, one light (A) and one dark (B). The papers were cut in half and displayed on a white background in three combinations: 1) half of the light colored sheet (A) alone on the left; 2) the other half of A placed in the center abutting one-half of the darker sheet (B), and 3) the remaining half of B placed alone on the right. The half of A on the left appeared darker than the half adjacent to B. Jones points out that the effect is strongest where the two colors meet and diminishes with increased distance from the center.

Proposition Twelve continues the discussion of contrast: "When two different colours are juxtaposed they receive a double modification—first, as to their tone (the light colour appearing lighter and the dark colour appearing darker); secondly, as to their hue, each will become tinged with the complementary colour of the other." This time, when two half-sheets of pale red and two half-sheets of dark blue are arranged as in the earlier experiment, the red seems paler and tinged with orange, while the blue appears darker with a slight tinge of green.

The next two propositions concern the effect of the juxtaposition of colors. In Proposition Thirteen, Jones says, "Colours on white grounds appear darker; on black grounds, lighter." He maintains that this phenomenon is experienced because the white rays in a color become subdued or overpowered by a white background but black reflects few white rays, resulting in colors appearing lighter in contrast to black.

Contrasts of colors with black are noted in Proposition Fourteen also: "black grounds suffer when opposed to colours which give a luminous complementary." Jones explains this phenomenon, observing that the dark complements of light colors increase the brilliancy of black and, conversely, light complements diminish the intensity of the black. These conditions are apparent by comparing the change in the appearance of black viewed next to orange and blue examples; in the first instance, the complementary of the orange ground adds blue to the black, making it appear darker or more intense; but when blue is placed on a black ground, the orange complementary lightens the appearance of the black, diminishing its brilliancy.

Jones realized that the appearance of any color could be subdued or heightened through juxtaposition and introduced several propositions indicating techniques to increase the harmonious effects of juxtaposed color based upon his studies of "Oriental" works and the textile fabrics of the Indian collection purchased by the government. Proposition Fifteen is the first of these principles: "When ornaments in a colour are on a ground of contrasting colour, the ornament should be separated from the ground by an edging of lighter colour—as a red flower on a green ground should have an edging of lighter red" (Fig. 2.18). This proposition is based upon a phenomenon discussed earlier under the law of simultaneous contrast and involves the area of indistinctness perceived when two complementary colors are placed contiguously. Jones developed several propositions outlining ways to create a boundary at the edge of the elements within a pattern to confine the eye and control the perception of color preventing the indistinctness created by juxtaposition. In Proposition Fifteen, definition of form is achieved by outlining each element in a lighter color; in Proposition Sixteen, an edging of a darker color is advocated for colored ornaments placed on a gold ground, since the darker edge reduces the invasion of the gold onto the colored ornament. Proposition Seventeen continues the use of a black outline, this time for gold ornaments on any colored ground (Figs. 2.19 and 2.20). Proposition Eighteen further advances the division of pattern and ground by asserting that "ornaments in any colour, or in gold, may be separated from grounds or any other colour by edgings of white, gold, or black."

Proposition Nineteen discusses the need for the background color for the desired pattern-ground distinction:

Fig. 2.19. Textile design number 28 in silk tissue first woven by Warner's April 1870

Fig. 2.20. Detail, design number 28 (above)

Fig. 2.21. Photograph of M. Digby Wyatt (left) and Owen Jones (right) at the Crystal Palace, Sydenham, n.d.

"Ornaments in any colour, or in gold, may be used on white or black grounds, without outline or edging." In this case, the intensity of the white ground, reflecting all rays, overpowers the rays reflected in the colored elements and assists in defining the form. Likewise, the figure on a black background is scarcely modified since the rays are absorbed and not reflected and the figure is easily distinguishable.

Proposition Twenty states that when tones or shades of the same color or hue are used, a light tint on a dark ground may be used without outline, but a dark ornament on a light ground needs outlining in an even darker tint. This proposition resulted from studies indicating that the light tint advanced, separating itself from the ground, but the dark tint appeared to "pierce through" the ground if not arrested by a darker edging. Jones believed ornaments in relief or metallic materials did not require an outline of color, since natural light created definition through the contrast of light on one side and shadow on the other.

All of these principles, or propositions, were fundamental to Jones's design philosophy and practice. His theory and understanding of color facilitated and enhanced his two-dimensional patterns for textiles and wallpapers. The outline of individual elements within a pattern to prevent the simultaneous contrast of colors and the elimination of the grading associated with light and shadow replaced three-dimensional realism with a flat motif.

The choice of gilding, light colors, and white in the place of shading added a luminous quality to Jones's designs as well as a sense of texture and movement. Jones layered colors, in the manner of the Persians, by applying lighter hues of the figure color and white as accents. This technique adds interest and complexity very different from the gradation of colors experienced in three-dimensional configurations. The added colors contribute to the unity of the design in several ways. First, each hue appears in the same place throughout the design—for example, at the edge or the center of a motif. Second, the added fragments of color reinforce the palette of the pattern without introducing contrast or confusion. Third, the added colors increase the vibrancy of the design. The repetition and placement of the colors adds interest to the pattern and provides the type of predictability conducive to repose.

Jones's facility with complements and values and his understanding of the ghosting of afterimages add the psychology of color to his unique designs. His decoration of the Crystal Palace at Sydenham provides a good example of how he developed a new scheme for each situation. The success of the decoration of the Crystal Palace in Hyde Park would have prompted many designers to repeat the arrangement in the permanent facility at Sydenham (1852–4), but Jones recommended a different scheme for the new structure. When this was announced, the press claimed "as far as colour is concerned, we are perfectly secure, seeing that the whole of this department is under the management of Mr. Owen Jones."[89] In developing the new scheme, the architect followed the same reasoning and rules observed in the first Crystal Palace but altered the coloration to conform to the changed size and conditions of the new building. Unlike the enormous display of manufactured goods in Hyde Park, the nave of the new structure was to be filled with plants and trees from every climate in a resplendent green oasis and promenade. To provide proportional contrast and substantiality in this setting, Jones painted the columns red with molding accents in blue and yellow. The horizontal trusses, roof ribs, and exterior of the building repeated the Hyde Park scheme (Pl. 2.21).

The painting was completed in April 1854 and drew immediate praise. Digby Wyatt admired the way the exterior colors captured the sunlight and gave the structure an ethereal appearance. The *Builder* described the interior as "very charming" and said the combination of red columns and green foliage was refreshing and invigorating to the eye.[90] The reporter observed that the new building did not seem as long as the original due to the changed form of the roof and the rearrangement of the columns, but the altered effect should be attributed, in part, to Jones's revised coloration.

Another major difference occurred in the items displayed. Industrial items were assembled in the southern half of the Great Transept but the principal attractions were the Fine Arts courts in the northern section, displaying plaster casts of architecture and sculpture. Jones designed the Egyptian, Greek, Roman, Alhambra, and Modern Sculpture courts (Pls. 2.22–2.25); Digby Wyatt created the Italian, Renaissance, Medieval, and Byzantine courts and the historian James Fergusson completed the Assyrian Court.[91] Jones and Digby Wyatt visited European and Middle Eastern collections to obtain the casts of important works.[92]

Jones's treatment of the Alhambra Court received the greatest praise, but his experiments with color in the Greek Court proved controversial.[93] Although discussions about polychromy in ancient architecture had taken place for more than two decades and color was recognized as an important element in the Gothic Revival, Jones's depiction of various painting theories in the Greek Court was "hotly disputed."[94] The focus of this contention concerned the painting of a representation of the Parthenon frieze. Jones divided the frieze into three sections and painted each section according to a different color theory; the result varied from all-white ornament and ground to white ornament on a blue ground and finally, to a multicolored arrangement. He explained and defended his experiment in "An Apology for the Colouring of the Greek Court." In the text, he acknowledged the debate over polychromy and said he hoped to eliminate some of the prejudice surrounding the question by painting a reconstruction of a Greek monu-

ment at Sydenham. He recognized the theories of Goury, Semper, Hittorff, and Penrose and concluded that "an examination of the facts recorded by these various authorities will convince anyone that the question is now narrowed to one of degree only—To *what extent* were white marble temples painted and ornamented?"[95] He maintained "they were *entirely* so; that neither the colour of the marble nor even its surface was preserved."[96]

To demonstrate his point, he said the representation of the Panathenaic Frieze at Sydenham was only 16 feet to the center of the bas-relief, while the Athens original was 40 feet above the ground; however, even at 16 feet the details in the all-white section were barely discernible while the details in the multicolored section were fully comprehensible. Jones argued that the quality of Phidias's sculpture gave further evidence, since Phidias had been forced to take great pains with the sculpture knowing that later coloration would emphasize any mistakes or inferiority in his work.

Jones said his experiment was not an attempt to rival the achievement of the Greeks but to replicate what might have existed. He acknowledged the limitations of the experiment, saying the coloration could not be fairly assessed until tried on marble under conditions similar to the original but in the meantime, he felt his effort would succeed if it generated unbiased research into the question of polychromy. Jones appended an extract from Semper's *The Four Elements of Architecture* entitled "On the Origin of Polychromy in Architecture" to the "Apology."[97]

Despite the negative reactions of some, Jones's painting of the Greek Court drew the interest and admiration of many critics and visitors including Queen Victoria and the talented photographer and delineator Philip H. Delamotte. In his *Photographic Views of the Progress of the Crystal Palace Sydenham*, Delamotte described the painting of the trabeated ceiling in the Greek Court as "one of the triumphs of Mr. Owen Jones."[98] Delamotte noted that "the ornaments of this ceiling have for the most part been copied from existing patterns—but the manner of their juxtaposition, and the intermediate tints by which they are kept in due proportion and harmony, are entirely due to the taste and skill of that gentleman."[99]

Jones's reputation as an eminent colorist and the extent of his international reputation and esteem is revealed in the numerous attempts to incorporate his ideas in buildings at home and abroad. He devised the color scheme for the exhibition building in Oporto, Portugal (1865) and influenced the decoration for the New York Crystal Palace in 1853. Reports on planning the decoration mirror his philosophy in aiming at producing "a style of decoration pleasing from its novelty and from the harmony arising from the use of colour in accordance with the laws of science and the practice of the best masters" and in the stated propositions, including: "Decoration should in all cases be subordinate to construction." The reports also repeat his observations that

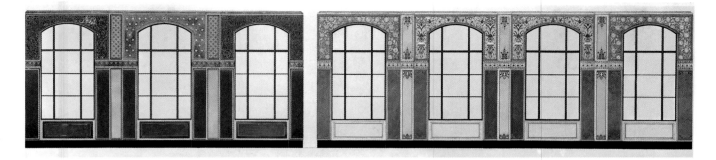

Fig. 2.22. Decoration of the Oriental courts, South Kensington Museum, 1863

ornamental patterns should be abstract and beauty should result from the harmony achieved through good proportions and geometry rather than elaborate detail.[100] It is not surprising that the adoption of Jones's coloring yielded effects similar to those previously experienced in the Crystal Palace in Hyde Park; for example, when a section of blue painting in the roof was compared to an unpainted section, the painted section seemed double in height, although the two sections were the same dimension.[101]

Although Jones's ideas were celebrated and emulated in exhibitions all over the world, he was not asked to design the decoration for Britain's second international exhibition in

Fig. 2.23. Detail, wall decoration of the Oriental courts, South Kensington Museum

1862. Members of the profession and the public called for his selection, declaring that he knew "more about colour than all the officials of South Kensington put together" but Henry Cole was unmoved. The fact that Jones's close friend Digby Wyatt wrote a letter to Cole recommending Jones as the best person to handle the task suggests that the famous colorist wanted the job, but the officials in South Kensington responded by saying that the colors of the first Crystal Palace had shown off the building better than its contents and that the much greater areas of solid roof and walling (in the 1862 structure) needed a more diversified approach. Some attribute the reason that Jones was not invited to the strain in Jones's relationship with Cole, since Jones rejected Cole's offers of a faculty position and the opportunity to participate in the development of the museums in South Kensington in order to design the Fine Arts courts at the Crystal Palace at Sydenham.[102] While this argument has merit, it does not address the fact that Jones produced *The Grammar of Ornament* at Cole's urging and decorated the museum's Indian, Chinese, and Japanese courts in 1863, referred to collectively as the Oriental courts (Figs. 2.22 and 2.23).

Ironically, the man selected to devise the 1862 scheme, John G. Crace, had been one of the detractors trying to discredit and unseat Jones in 1851. Given the chance in 1862, Crace ignored his predecessor's lessons on structural decoration and introduced an elaborate scheme of stenciling, gilding, and variegated patterns aimed at producing a warm glow in the building with a scheme of gray window trim and cream, red, and gray piping for the roof trusses. The ribs received alternate bands and patterns of red and blue with black-and-white chevrons on the edges and black circles at the intersections of each joint. Gold stars and scrolls added further accents. Red and gold panels between the ribs displayed scrolls and rosettes.

A variety of colors and patterns reigned below as well; the iron columns of the nave were painted pale bronze, with vertical gold fillets and gilded capitals on alternate grounds of red and blue. The gallery railings were painted with gilt and a light bronze color and backed by a patterned red cloth combining rose, shamrock, and thistle motifs. The courts beneath the galleries were maroon with gray ceilings. In addition to the wide range of colors and variety of motifs used, the decoration was made more complex through the numerous media employed, including stencils, inscriptions, large medallions painted by art-school students, and sunbursts at the center of each of Fowke's domes. The ornate scheme and profusion of patterns was considerably more mid-Victorian than Jones's 1851 scheme.

Although reviews were satisfactory, many critics said the individual elements employed by Crace were unsuccessful on a large scale. The decorator proved incapable of conceiving the cumulative effects of the decoration vertically and horizontally and unlike Jones, who was confident of his scheme before the first brushstroke, complained of the difficulty of carrying out the decoration since the scaffolding obscured his view of the structure.[103]

The *Critic* printed the most damaging review, predicting that Crace's pale bronze would be called "dirty green streaked with dirtier yellow" and characterizing the roof ribs as "painted 'with a perfect harlequinade of crosses, dots, chequers, scrolls, and nondescripts, touching every note on the gamut of colour from black to white, with all the cruelty of a handsome pianist with a prodigious hand and no ear for music.'"

The organization of the items displayed was also judged to be inferior to Jones's layout. The arrangements were not complete by the May 1 opening and the exhibits in place were criticized for yielding such a "conglomeration of telescopes, organs, lighthouses, fountains, obelisks, pickles, furs, stuffs, porcelain, dolls, rocking-horses, alabasters, stearine, and Lady Godiva" that the nave was reduced "to a striking similitude of a traveller's description of Hog Lane, Canton." Worse, critics maintained that the combination of the decoration and layout tended to "harass and weary" visitors in contrast to the uplifting experience reported in 1851. Within one week, "an eminent London physician had three cases of persons attacked with apoplexy just after they had quitted the building and attributed the attacks to the Exhibition." Among those reacting negatively, the noted Russian author Dostoyevski reported being struck with fear at the aspect and compared the experience to witnessing Babylon or the Apocalypse.[104]

The London Exhibition of 1862 failed to make a profit and acrimonious debates arose over the future of both the building and the site. Most people agreed with Macaulay that the year 1851 was "long to be remembered as a singularly happy year of peace, plenty, good feeling, innocent pleasure, and national glory" due in most part to the successful efforts of Prince Albert, Cole, Paxton, and Jones; the year 1862 would be as the reverse.[105] The negative impression lingered, and as late as July of the following year the *Building News* continued to express the belief that Jones would have done a better job.[106]

Although Jones was not involved with the decoration of the building, his designs and theory were well represented. He displayed his designs for book covers and architectural drawings for his decorations at Christ Church, Streatham; the Manchester Exhibition Building, the Crystal Palace at Sydenham and Hyde Park; his proposals for the Palace of the People, Muswell Hill; the ceiling of Hancock's show-

rooms, designs for St. James's Hall; and designs for other decorative schemes.[107] He also designed display cases for several British manufacturers. Some of these firms, such as Osler's, had their own design studios, but turned to Jones for masterworks. For the 1862 exhibition, he produced a platform display with "tasteful decoration" for Chappell's musical instruments and impressive colored cast-iron gates for Kinnaird. He designed a pair of 20-foot-high candelabras to reveal Osler's precision glass cutting (Fig. 2.24). These colossal fixtures were prominently displayed on either side of the exhibition's grand staircase. Jones also created a much-admired stand for Osler's to display smaller crystal pieces (Fig. 2.25).[108]

The success of the Osler commissions was matched in Jones's design of a structure to house four pieces of statuary: the *Tinted Venus* (1851–6) and two other tinted statues (*Cupid* and *Pandora*) by the leading Neoclassical sculptor John Gibson, and *Zenobia* by his American pupil Harriet Hosmar (Pls. 2.26 and 2.27).[109] Jones's polychromatic temple and Gibson's colored sculptures marked a bold foray into the continuing debate on the use of color by the ancients. The tinted statues represented Gibson's belief that the Greeks had painted their sculpture and Jones's decoration of the temple reflected his conviction that the architecture was painted as well.

Their convictions were emphasized in the Latin quotations painted on the front and sides of the structure. On the front, the message of the frieze read: "IN TEMPLO IOVIS

Fig. 2.24. Candelabra for Osler's, 1862

COLORIBUS ARDET LUX IPSA DIVERSIS" ("In the temple of Jupiter light itself burns with various colors.") The text surrounding the niche behind the statue was "LUCRETIUS LIBER V. / V.M.ILL.VII. / FORMAE DIGNITAS BONITATE COLORIS TUENDA EST" ("Lucretius, Book 5 / the worthiness of the shape must [or will] be protected by the goodness of color.") On the side, the frieze read: "FORMAS RERVM OBSCVRAS ILLVSTRAT CONFVSAS DISTINGVIT OMNES ORNAT COLORVM DIVRSITAS SVAVIS" ("The sweet variety of colors illuminates the dark shapes of things and separates them all [that were once] mingled.") The text above the niche stated: "NEC VITA NEC SANITAS NEC PVLCRITVDO NEC SINE COLORE JUVENTUS" ("Neither life nor health nor beauty nor youth without color.")[110]

The *Tinted Venus* and its shelter were one of the exhibition's chief attractions and were later published as Plate 101 in J. B. Waring's *Masterpieces of Industrial Art and Sculpture at the International Exhibition* (1863). Critics found the ensemble to be most convincing, observing that Hosmar's uncolored statue appeared harsh against the temple structure, while Gibson's tinted statues blended harmoniously and were enhanced by the beauty and simplicity of the structure.[111] Jones's commitment to the continuing debate on color is underscored by the fact that he waived his design commission and paid Jackson and Graham to build the temple.

Even more significant than these prestigious commissions testifying to Jones's talent and stature is the acceptance of his theory, revealed in the texts written about the exhibition and in the items displayed. Products in the 1862 exhibition eliminated the naturalistic excesses characteristic of British goods in 1851. Judges approved this change and gave some awards to English manufacturers. Although it is difficult to prove that Jones was responsible for this shift, the reiteration of his theory in two of the major texts written about the 1862 exhibition cannot be disputed. In discussing wallpapers in *Masterpieces of Industrial Art and Sculpture at the International Exhibition*, Waring said "No one has done more in the country to place decorative art on right principles, and extend its influence" than Jones. Waring continued by quoting Jones's discussion of the conventionalized surface decoration evident in Oriental patterns.[112] Recognized designer Christopher Dresser went much further in *The Development of Ornamental Art in the International Exhibition* (discussed in Chapter Five).

Jones had already presented the thirty-one propositions in *The Grammar of Ornament* in the inaugural lecture series for the Museum of Ornamental Art (1852). They were published at the same time as an appendix to the *Catalogue for the Museum of Ornamental Art*. The propositions were also quoted in Lindley's lectures titled "The Symmetry of Vegetation" given at Marlborough House in November 1852 and published in 1854 as *The Symmetry of Vegetation; an Outline of the Principles to be Observed in the Delineation of Plants*.

Jones's propositions gained increased attention through the controversial False Principles in Design exhibit mounted at Marlborough House (1852). Cole asked Jones to prepare the exhibit, but no documents survive indicating who the curator was. Richard Redgrave wrote the catalogue, emphasizing the direct imitation of nature as the worst sin in decoration. To prove the point, the exhibit showed numerous items ornamented with realistic plants and animals. Wallpapers with realistic scenes proliferated, depicting images of military battles, perspective views of the Crystal Palace, and other commemorations. Patterns repeated objects in isolation illogically, including horses in mid-air and bouquets tied with swirling ribbons (Figs. 2.26 and 2.27).

The display drew deeply divided reviews, with positive support weighed against the offense some felt at the organizer's heavy-handed approach. Some critics ridiculed the exhibit and the attitude of the reformers. The best example survives from a story published in Dickens's *Household Words* on December 4, 1852. In the tale called "A House Full of Horrors," a Mr. Crumpet, whose "cheerfulness was like a bird at tea," visited the Museum of Ornamental Art and acquired Correct Principles of Taste. He described the exhibit as a Chamber of Horrors hung with frightful objects in curtains, carpets, clothes, lamps, and what not . . . " and confessed his shame at finding the pattern of his trousers on display. Worse, he was unable to wipe the perspiration from his forehead for fear that someone would see the wreath of coral on his handkerchief. When he returned home, his misery deepened as he realized he lived among horrors, such as the paper in his parlor showing four kinds of birds of paradise, plus bridges and pagodas.

Dickens included another satire of the "false principles" in *Hard Times*, a novel serialized in *Household Words* in the summer of 1854. This time a caricature of Henry Cole was presented, as a school inspector addressing a group of students. When the class did not recognize the absurdity of wallpapers with horses or carpets with flowers, the inspector erupts:

You are not to have, in any object of use or ornament, what would be a contradiction in fact. You don't find that foreign birds and butterflies come and perch on your crockery. You never meet the quadrupeds going up and down the walls . . . you must use, for all purposes, combinations and modifications (in primary colours) of mathematical figures which are susceptible of proof and demonstration. This is the new discovery. This is fact. This is taste. What is called taste is another name for fact.[113]

Although *The Civil Engineer and Architect's Journal* thought the exhibit valuable and "well carried out," some manufacturers of the products displayed and members of the public took offense at the stigmatization of the items in the exhibit. One response was a pamphlet entitled "A Mild Remonstrance against the Taste-Censorship at Marlborough House In Reference to Manufacturing Ornamentation and Decorative Design." The text attacked Redgrave, Jones, and Cole, describing them as the "Triumvirate of Taste—the Great Trinity!" The writer, Argus, mocked the implication that Englishmen know nothing of taste, beauty, refinement, or fine art and, in a statement probably directed at Jones, said that "a few exalted spirits in the land of rain, and fog, and semi-darkness—a travelled few—who have become conscious, we may almost say proudly conscious, of the fact."[114]

He criticized Jones for being "Half Moor, and more than half a Mussulman . . . in his mode of thinking on taste." He objected to the amount of money spent on purchasing Indian objects from the 1851 exhibition and to their prominence in the museum's collection. The author challenged Jones's principles and submitted his own: "Ultimate principle—Human Progress and Enlightenment. This demands Art and deprecates Conventionalism. Immediate Principle—Commerce. This demands the Complex in Ornamentation in preference to the simple.'" The False Principles exhibit was removed from Marlborough House, but the "Triumvirate of Taste" remained steadfast in the promotion of Jones's principles in the curriculum in the School of Practical Art.

The collection contributed to their campaign for the education of the design profession and the public about architecture and the decorative arts, but it was not their only objective. They also wanted to create a book containing "all the best acknowledged examples of ornamental design" for use in the schools. The governments of Germany and Austria had commissioned works of this nature in 1830 and 1831, respectively. In Britain, Ludwig Gruner (1801–1882), art advisor to Prince Albert, prepared *Specimens of Ornamental Art Selected from the Best Models of the Classical Epochs* (1850), but the faculty in the schools of design rejected Gruner's text since he illustrated Pompeian, Roman, medieval, and *cinquecento* designs. The

FACING PAGE
Fig. 2.25. Display stand for Osler's, 1862

Fig. 2.26. English textile, c. 1850, featured in False Principles in Design exhibition in the "Direct Imitation of Nature" section, 1852

faculty considered Pompeian ornament representative of a period of degenerate morality and, therefore, inappropriate for their students.[115]

Cole asked Jones to produce a book of historical examples consistent with the principles advocated by Jones and the schools of design. Jones presented preliminary information to Cole on February 18, 1852, but must have put the book aside during his travels and decoration of the Crystal Palace at Sydenham. Jones's early outline for *The Grammar of Ornament* lists styles omitted from the published version, including the "Yucatan" and the "Venetian." Jones scholar J. Kresten Jespersen explains that the death of Frederick Catherwood, the expert on the Maya and on Yucatan architecture, accounts for the elimination of the South American material and the rivalry between Jones and Ruskin, a Venetian authority, probably led to the elimination of Venetian ornament.[116] Three styles, not on the preliminary outline, were added to the published text. These include the chapters on primitive, Assyrian, and Indian ornament.

Fig. 2.27. English textile, c. 1850, featured in False Principles in Design exhibition in the "Direct Imitation of Nature" section, 1852

The Grammar of Ornament also contained the principles developed in Jones's earlier lectures and writings, plus six new propositions (Propositions Eight, Twenty-One, Twenty-Eight, Thirty-Five, Thirty-Six, and Thirty-Seven). Geometry was fundamental to Jones's understanding of proportion, distribution, and the conventionalization of natural foliage and flora. He published hundreds of examples of frets, diapers, chevrons, and rosettes in *The Grammar of Ornament* and adopted geometrical configurations in his designs (Page 6 and fig. 4.6).

Three of the new propositions concerned color. The first of these, Proposition Twenty-One repeats the rationale of the Crystal Palace scheme: "In using the primary colours on moulded surfaces, we should place blue, which retires, on the concave surfaces; yellow, which advances, on the convex; and red, the intermediate colour, on the undersides; separating the colours by white on the vertical planes." This principle used color to define structure in direct oppo-

sition to Ruskin's assertion that color should be applied independent of structure. Likewise, another new principle related to color may have been a further response to Ruskin. This principle, Proposition Twenty-Eight, stipulates that: "Colours should never be allowed to impinge upon each other." This tenet warns against simultaneous contrast in opposition to Ruskin's rule advocating the gradation of color.

Another new principle, Proposition Thirty-Five, explains Jones's position on the subject of imitation of materials, a topic of considerable controversy. Pugin had argued for truth to materials and both Jones and Ruskin called the painting of one material to represent another deceitful.[117] Jones allowed exceptions based on logic saying, "Imitations, such as the graining of woods, and of the various coloured marbles, [are] allowable only, when the employment of the thing imitated would not have been inconsistent." He explained that graining an inexpensive door to look like oak was permissible, since an oak door was appropriate, but painting or graining that introduced illogical combinations, such as doors resembling marble, should be avoided. He also discouraged the use of imitations to suggest materials beyond the means of the inhabitants or the character of the house being decorated, citing marbleized halls and staircases as an obvious sham, and, therefore, unsuitable.[118]

Proposition Thirty-Six is aimed at Ruskin and all other advocates of historicism. Jones maintains that "The principles discoverable in the works of the past belong to us; not so the results. It is taking the ends for the means." Jones believed that attempting to create a new style of ornament or architecture without heeding the lessons of the past would be folly, but he also believed that it was equally inappropriate to adopt the style of another age and climate, since no earlier style could accurately reflect current culture and conditions. He considered revival styles to be affectations that might demonstrate a nation's greatness or resources but that were incapable of gaining universal sympathy since they were inconsistent with contemporary thought and institutions. Jones declared "Architecture is progressive, and must keep pace with the developement of the wants, the faculties, and sentiments of mankind."[119]

The last principle, Proposition Thirty-Seven, also addresses the contemporary situation: "No improvement can take place in the Art of the present generation until all classes, Artists, Manufacturers, and the Public, are better educated in Art, and the existence of general principles is more fully recognised." Again, Jones and Ruskin are at odds, since Jones believed that principles could be taught to designers and the public, but Ruskin rejected the type of formal training offered by the English reformers.

Jones believed that the development of ornament preceded every other form of art and resulted from man's innate desire to produce the forms of beauty evident in the works of nature. To prove his argument, he expanded the

98　*Chapter Two*

study of ornament to include the designs of "savages" (the Maori in New Zealand). His recognition of the merit of their ornamental designs and his insistence that these were the result of instincts and aims common to all mankind was highly unusual in Victorian Britain where the peoples of the nonindustrialized world were considered backward and uncivilized (Pl. 2.28).[120]

Although he considered tattooing a barbarous practice, he published a drawing of a head from a New Zealand Maori as an example of the highest principles in ornamental art, where every line was best adapted to develop the natural features of the face (Fig. 2.28).[121] He also published a sample of cloth from Tongatabu (Pl. 2.29, top center) concluding that: "Nothing can be more judicious than the general arrangement of the four squares and the four red spots. Without the red spots on the yellow ground there would have been a great want of repose in the general arrangement; without the red lines round the red spots to carry the red through the yellow, it would have been still imperfect." He said directing the points of the small red triangles inward produced repose and noted that turning them outward would have destroyed the harmony of the design. He said the triangles and leaves of the pattern showed that basic elements and simple tools in the hands of even the most uncultivated, would lead to the creation of all the known geometrical arrangements of form, if the native was guided by an instinctive observation of the way forms are arranged in Nature. He said the most complicated patterns of Byzantine, Arabian, and Moresque mosaics were generated by the same means and concluded that successful ornament resulted from the creation of general effect by the repetition of a few simple elements. Variety should be introduced in the arrangement of the elements of a design rather than by adding multiple unrelated forms and motifs.

Jones found the ornament of the savage "always true to its purpose" in contrast to the overworked decoration of developed nations where instead of developing the most appropriate form and then adding beauty, beauty was destroyed by the addition of ornament to ill-contrived form. To correct this practice, he recommended replacing artificial styles with a return to fitness (function) and the natural instinct that had been destroyed over time by the abuse of ornament, making it necessary to create a body of rules to educate designers in universal principles of good design. Jones developed and expressed these rules in his lectures and, again, in a paper read to the Royal Institute of British Architects on December 15, 1856. Excerpts from this lecture entitled, "On the Leading Principles in the Composition of Ornament in Every Period" were printed in the next two issues of the *Builder*, and the propositions were repeated in *The Grammar of Ornament*.[122]

Although Ruskin dismissed Jones's rules as the "dregs of corrupted knowledge," Jones's axioms and text gained enthusiastic recognition in England and abroad. Volume XV of the *Revue Générale* printed the principles in 1857; the same year, he received the gold medal of the Royal Institute of British Architects, the award of the Order of St. Maurice and St. Lazare by the king of Italy, and the Order of King Leopold of the Belgians. The architect Prosper Mérimée recommended Jones for the French government's Legion of Honor, but politics prevented the award from being granted.[123]

Another tribute came from Jones's friend, the popular novelist George Eliot, who was inspired to write a review of *The Grammar*, one of her few pieces of nonfiction.[124] She began her assessment by discussing the potential benefits improved surroundings offered to the mental and physical well-being of society and noted that the quickest and easiest way to accomplish improvement was through the redecoration of existing interiors. She noted that "Fine taste in the decoration of interiors is a benefit that spreads from the palace to the clerk's house with one parlor." She continued, proclaiming: "All honour, then, to the architect who zealously vindicated the claim of internal ornamentation to be a part of the architect's function, and has laboured to rescue that form of art which is most closely connected with the sanctities and pleasures of our hearths from the hands of uncultured tradesmen." She concluded: "All the nation ought at present to know that this effort is peculiarly associated with the name of Mr. Owen Jones" and that "one monument of his effort . . . is his 'Grammar of Ornament.'"

The popularization of Jones's ideas through the success of his prolific designs and the adoption of *The Grammar* in schools of design and architecture all over the globe meant that Jones's principles had an extraordinary distribution and reception. Study of his book contributed to the influence of Jones's color and design theory on the work of later architects as celebrated as Frank Lloyd Wright and Le Corbusier. Jones's patterns and philosophy directly influenced individual designers, including Christopher Dresser and William Morris and contributed indirectly to the Arts and Crafts, Art Nouveau, and Aesthetic movements. This legacy is discussed in Chapter Five.

Fig. 2.28. Female head from New Zealand from the chapter "Ornament of Savage Tribes" in The Grammar of Ornament, *1856*

Pl. 2.1. Title page from The Grammar of Ornament, *1856*

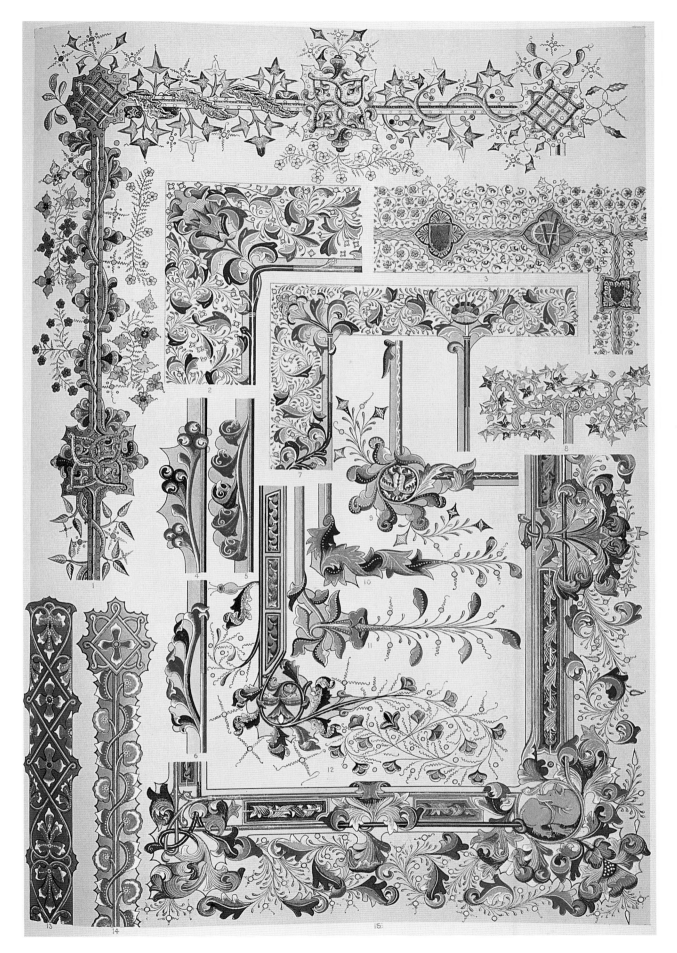

Pl. 2.2. *"Illuminated Mss. No. 2," Pl. LXXII from* The Grammar of Ornament, *1856*

Pl. 2.3. "Greek No. 8,"
Pl. XXII from The
Grammar of Ornament,
1856

Pl. 2.4. "Nineveh &
Persia No. 1," Pl. XII
from The Grammar of
Ornament, *1856*

Pl. 2.5. "Pompeian No. 2," Pl. XXIV from The Grammar of Ornament, 1856

Pl. 2.6. "Byzantine No. 2," Pl. XXIX from The Grammar of Ornament, *1856*

Pl. 2.7. "Arabian No. 4," Pl. XXXIV from The Grammar of Ornament, *1856*

Pl. 2.8. "Moresque No. 1," Pl. XXXIX from The Grammar of Ornament, *1856*

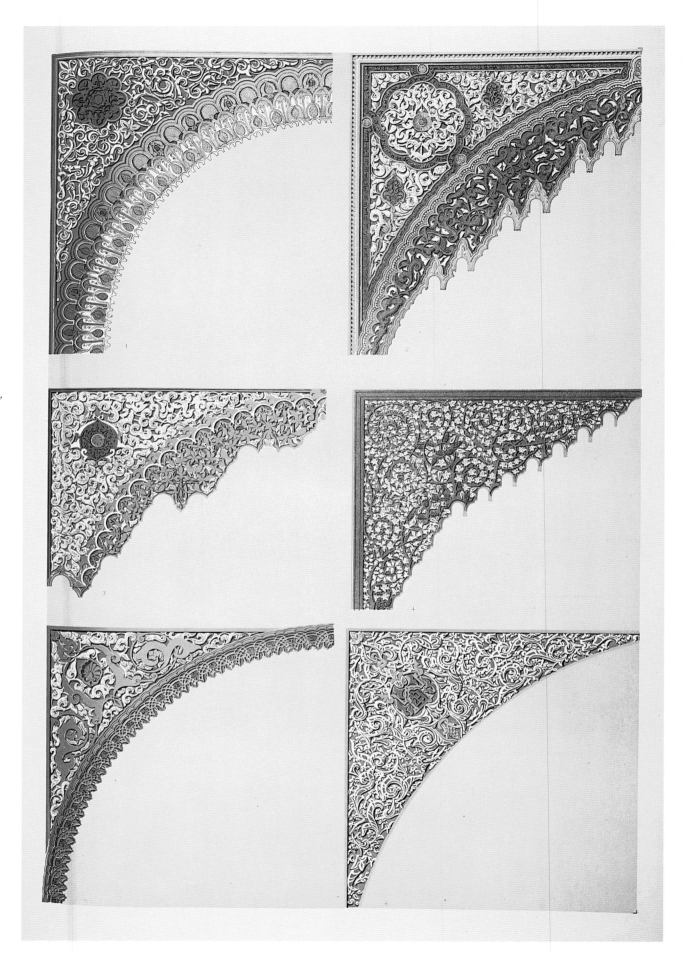

Pl. 2.9. *"Moresque No. 2,"*
Pl. XL *from*
The Grammar of
Ornament, *1856*

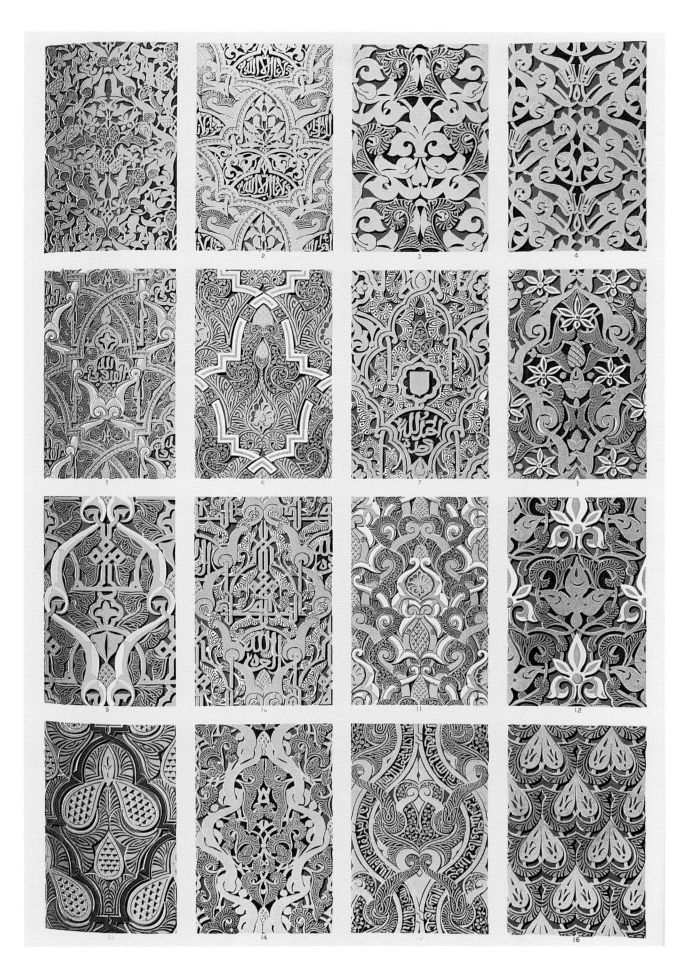

Pl. 2.10. "Moresque No. 3," Pl. XLI from The Grammar of Ornament, *1856*

Pl. 2.11. "Persian No. 1," Pl. XLIV from The Grammar of Ornament, *1856*

Pl. 2.12. "Persian No. 2," Pl. XLV from The Grammar of Ornament, 1856

Pl. 2.13. *"Celtic No. 2,"*
Pl. LXIV *from*
The Grammar of
Ornament, *1856*

Pl. 2.14. *"Stained Glass," Pl. LXIX from* The Grammar of Ornament, *1856*

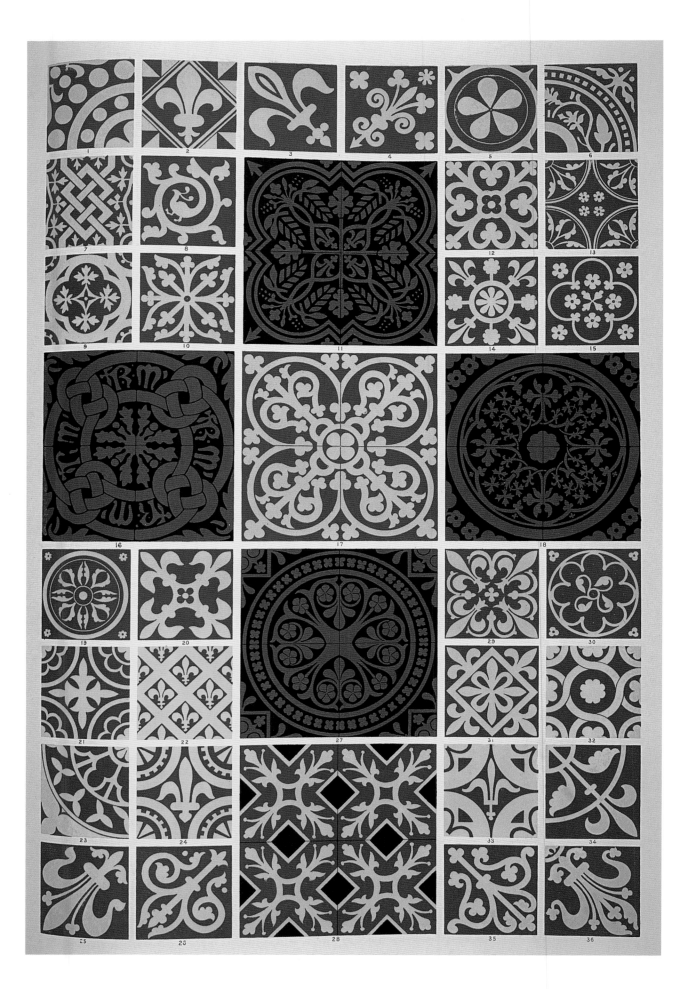

Pl. 2.15. *"Middle Ages No. 5," Pl. LXX from* The Grammar of Ornament, *1856*

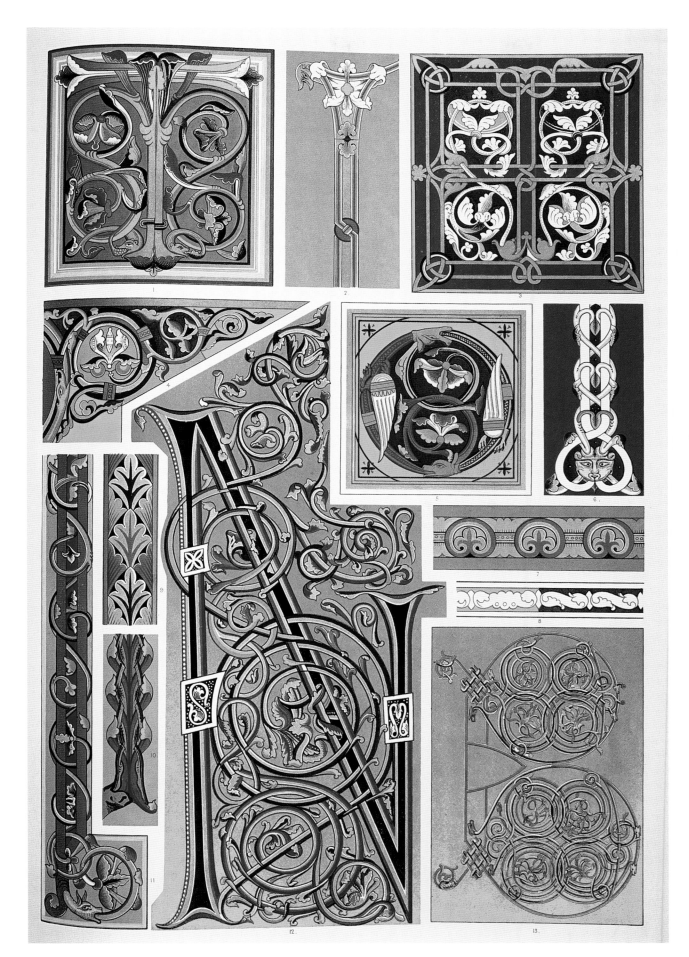

Pl. 2.16. "Illuminated Mss. No. 1," Pl. LXXI from The Grammar of Ornament, *1856*

Pl. 2.17. *"Italian No. 2," Pl. LXXXVII from* The Grammar of Ornament, *1856*

Pl. 2.18. "Renaissance No. 5," Pl. LXXVIII from The Grammar of Ornament, *1856*

Pl. 2.19. "Leaves from Nature No. 5," Pl. XCV from The Grammar of Ornament, 1856

No I.

No 2.

No 3.

No 4.

No 5

Pl. 2.20. "Leaves from Nature No. 7," *Pl. XCVII from* The Grammar of Ornament, *1856*

Pl. 2.21. Joseph Nash, Opening of the Crystal Palace, Sydenham, by Queen Victoria, June 10th, 1854, *1854–5. Watercolor, 23⅛ x 29⅞ in.*

Pl. 2.22. M. Digby Wyatt, illustration of the Egyptian Court from Views of the Crystal Palace and Park, Sydenham, 1854

Pl. 2.23. M. Digby Wyatt, illustration of the Greek Court from Views of the Crystal Palace and Park, Sydenham, 1854

Pl. 2.24. M. Digby Wyatt, illustration of the Roman Court from Views of the Crystal Palace and Park, Sydenham, *1854*

Pl. 2.25. M. Digby Wyatt, illustration of the Alhambra Court from Views of the Crystal Palace and Park, Sydenham, *1854*

Pl. 2.26. Front elevation,
Sculpture Pavilion for the
London Exhibition of
1862

FORMAS RERVM OBSCVRAS ILLVSTRAT CONFVSAS DISTINGVIT OMNES ORNAT COLORVM DIVRSITAS SVAVIS

NEC VITA NEC SANITAS NEC PVLCRITVDO NEC SINE COLORE IVVENTVS

Pl. 2.27. Side elevation, Sculpture Pavilion for the London Exhibition of 1862

Principles of Architecture and the Decorative Arts   125

Pl. 2.28. "Savage Tribes
No. 3," Pl. III from
The Grammar of
Ornament, 1856

Pl. 2.29. "Savage Tribes
No. 1," Pl. I from
The Grammar of
Ornament, 1856

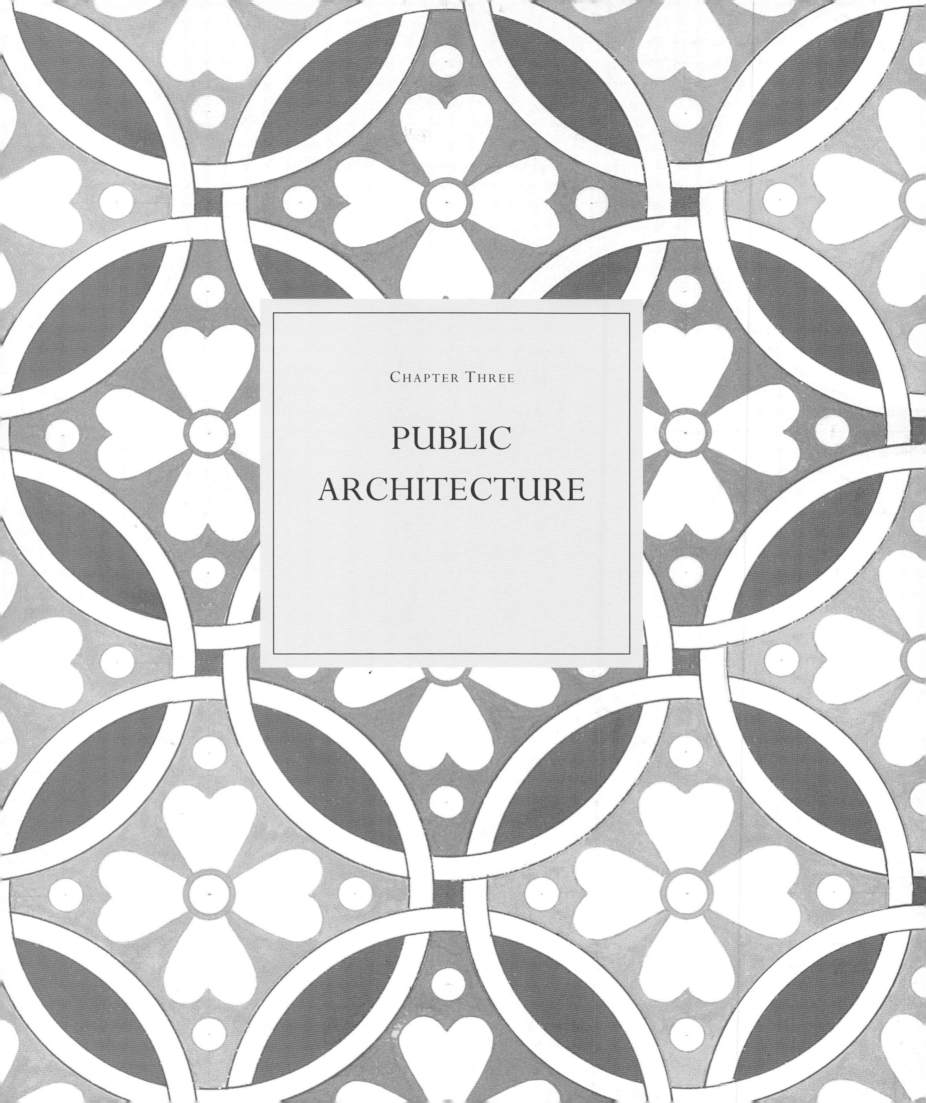

CHAPTER THREE

PUBLIC
ARCHITECTURE

In his essay "On the Influence of Religion upon Art" Jones recognized the growing chasm between architecture and engineering and urged his peers to gain greater understanding of the structural and artistic possibilities offered through the use of new materials and building techniques. The ways in which Jones followed this objective to achieve public buildings both functional and beautiful are discussed in this chapter. He addressed the demands and challenges of the age, providing new types of buildings and traditional building types at a larger scale. He introduced innovations in lighting, ventilation, and circulation as well as a new aesthetic. While his progressive ideas and artistic taste sometimes proved too new and too daring for widespread adoption, his buildings and projects made valuable contributions to the situation and understanding of architecture and won the respect of his peers and the admiration of the public.

After returning from Spain, Jones became well known through his talk "On the Influence of Religion Upon Art" to the Architectural Society, his various publications, and his entries into architecture competitions and the biennial exhibitions at the Royal Academy. In the 1830s, the Royal Academy was the official institution for all of the arts in England, but was more interested in other disciplines besides architecture. The exhibitions reflected this imbalance by relegating the architecture submissions to a room off the main exhibition area.[1] The drawings and models received little attention from the public or press until the quality of Jones's work drew the attention of the media.

Critics praised his exceptional skill in rendering the scenes from his travels on view, including the ruins of the Great Temple at Karnak (1835) and illustrations of the Alhambra (1835, 1838, 1839, and 1840). A writer in the *Athenaeum* called his *View of the Alcove at the Upper End of the Hall of the Two Sisters in the Alhambra* "one of the most mag-

nificent displays of gorgeous colour and elaborate tracing we never saw."[2] The *Civil Engineer and Architect's Journal* concurred, saying that Jones's drawing reduced all of the other interiors to second rank.[3] After this rendering was displayed in 1839, the *Athenaeum* regularly reported on the architecture submissions to the academy, generally praising the work of Jones but disparaging many of the other entries.

A typical example reviews his rendering in *La Sala del Tribunal* (Hall of Judgment) shown in 1840 and described: "As a picture, the effect is powerful and harmonious; and, as an architectural illustration, we cannot sufficiently admire the patient enthusiasm which alone could have supported the artist in his laborious exertions faithfully and minutely to delineate the most intricate details of this gorgeous edifice."[4] The *Gentleman's Magazine* agreed, declaring that "*La Sala del Tribunal* may have been the most elaborate drawing" they had ever seen and described it by saying: "The splendid decorations are most brilliantly coloured after the original, giving a dazzling effect to the drawings and conveying the idea of an edifice which, but for these illustrations, we should have imagined only to have existed in the pages of fiction."[5]

Jones's designs for projects and commissions received positive recognition as well. These entries include praise in the *Athenaeum* and in the *Gentleman's Magazine* for the originality of his competition schemes for the Birmingham Town Hall (1831), for St. George's Hall, Liverpool (1841), and for commissions including a villa in Kensington Palace Gardens (1845), a dairy for J. J. Morrison (1845), the interiors of Osler's Gallery (1860) and for Hancock's of Bruton Street (1861).[6] The following comment on the dairy is typical of the positive reviews of his inventiveness: "Though the design is of unusual character there is nothing extravagant or forced about it, nothing of an exotic look; the com-

position is simple but effective and picturesque, the two portions well grouped together, the little terrace quite alluring, in short, we cannot better express our opinion of it than by terming it a pleasing architectural Anacreonatic."[7]

Jones's exhibition entries were significant opportunities for the presentation of his ideas and for gaining media coverage for architecture. At this time, architecture periodicals and the popular press began reporting on the competitions being held for the new public buildings being erected throughout Britain.[8] Competitions were an important aspect of nineteenth-century architecture. The *Builder* reported over twenty-five hundred competitions between 1843 and 1900, approximately forty-four contests a year for fifty-seven years.[9] These contests indicate the demand for new buildings and the shift of financial and economic power away from aristocratic patrons and/or privileged clergy to committees of businessmen or parishioners. Unfortunately, the profession was too weak to regulate or affect these contests and the results were often unfair and inappropriate.[10] Frequent problems arose as a result of incomplete or ambiguous instructions and changes made midway through a contest. Serious infractions involved unethical actions by committees who reversed previously announced decisions or gave commissions to unsuccessful candidates instead of the competition winner. Frequently, committees selected ideas from several entries and then commissioned their own architect to combine these elements into a new design.

Submitting a competition entry generally involved uncompensated expenses for the time and cost of design preparation. The winners generally received tokens of recognition or the first installment of the commission fee, but that was often all they received. Competitions did provide exposure for new and unknown architects, however,

and the dissemination of new ideas through the publication of contest announcements and results in the new architecture journals and in the popular press.[11]

Jones participated in a variety of open and invitational competitions throughout his career and his designs were usually singled out for the talent, effort, and originality they exhibited. Unfortunately, his early schemes for the Birmingham Town Hall and St. George's Hall, Liverpool, have not been located, but reactions to the scheme for St. George's Hall survive. The competition involved a new type of building, a large public concert hall to house the city's triennial music festivals. The unusually lucrative awards of 250 guineas for the best design and 150 guineas for the second best attracted over eighty entries. Harvey Lonsdale Elmes won first place and George Alexander received second place.[12]

Jones's design for a heavily corniced oblong structure displaying a prominent decorative frieze inscribed FREEDOM OF DEBATE, POLITICAL, SCIENTIFIC, AND MORAL drew mixed reviews.[13] The *Athenaeum* admired the entry as an attempt to design according to "higher principles" and noted that although those principles had been "imperfectly carried out," the scheme showed originality superior to the second-place winner.[14] The reporter for the *Gentleman's Magazine* also praised the exterior of Jones's building, but found the rich decoration of the interior "too fantastic for execution" and manifesting too much of the architect's love of the Alhambra.[15] The *Civil Engineer and Architect's Journal* concurred.[16] Critics of Jones's entry in the 1844 competition held to propose designs and materials for the interiors of the new Palace of Westminster voiced the same concern and it was a remonstrance that would reappear throughout his career.[17]

As mentioned in Chapter One, for the Palace of Westminster, Jones submitted an ambitious plan for all of the principal floors in the palace and provided samples of the encaustic tiles and British marbles to be used in implementing his scheme.[18] The *Athenaeum* commended the plan, saying it was the only submission providing any valuable assistance on what ought to be done in the building.[19] (For a more detailed discussion of this project, see Chapter One.)

Jones's next competition involved plans and estimates for the first public baths to be built in London.[20] The twenty-two proposals submitted projected costs between 6,800 and 20,000 pounds. Jones's estimate of 16,500 pounds was the third highest and considerably above the average estimate of 11,957 pounds and the winner's 11,700-pound projection.[21]

The committee for the competition was criticized for retaining the drawings and for refusing to allow the participating architects and the public to inspect the proposals. Protest over this decision caused the committee to reverse their decision and to arrange an exhibition of the submissions. Unfortunately, Jones's work was not singled out for comment apart from the notation that he and two other firms (Lee and Burnett and William Brooks and Son) each submitted two completely different schemes.[22]

Commissions for another building type, the prestigious private London club, received substantial press coverage. The competition for the Army and Navy Club was thought to be particularly significant since the project offered "great scope for embellishment" and an adequate budget for decoration. Jones, Anthony Salvin (winner of the 1844 contest for the Carlton Club's alterations), Lewis Vuillamy, G. G. Scott, and sixty-five others produced designs that the *Builder* applauded for "evidence of considerable advance in architectural taste."[23] Unfortunately, club members untrained in architecture formed the selection committee and the *Builder* said it was obvious they were incapable of understanding the architectural drawings submitted.

The entries were unsigned and only identified through mottoes such as "Incognito" or "Pro Patria Semper," or visual symbols such as a "gilt crown" or a "Triangle within a circle." Jones chose the following quotation from Shakespeare to accompany his entry:

> When we mean to build
> We first survey the plot, then draw the model,
> And when we see the figure of the house
> Then must we rate the cost of the erection.[24]

His choice may have been intended as a humorous comment on competitions, since *Henry IV, Part II*, involves intrigue and conspiracy. The selection may also have been prophetic, since several architects compromised the contest by revealing their identities and soliciting votes for their entries.[25]

The committee's final choice invoked scorn. The *Athenaeum* contended that after this decision no architect needed to be proud of winning a competition and observed that the committee's actions exemplified the assertion that often the worst design was chosen in a competition.[26] The committee received further criticism for rejecting all of the submissions and inviting six of the participants to provide new designs to satisfy new criteria (a larger site and an increased budget).[27]

Jones proposed a considerably smaller structure than most of the other entries and his projected cost of 27,624 pounds was one of the lowest estimates. Reduced scale and economy are not characteristics associated with his work and this scheme suggests that he was trying to present a design capable of being realized within the committee's 30,000-pound budget. The designs of many of the other presenters seemed to have been prepared without considering the cost.

Although Jones did not win any of the competitions he entered in the 1830s and 1840s, his designs indicate that he was an emerging architect unafraid to tackle larger structures and new types of buildings. The number of competitions he entered while producing his publication on the Alhambra, other book designs, and private commissions, attests to the high level of energy and commitment that prompted him to submit a plan for all of the floors in the Palace of Westminster when the design of only one floor would have sufficed, as well as two schemes in the baths-and-wash-houses competition.

The question of style presented a significant problem in his early competition submissions. The choice of an appropriate style was a major concern to committees charged with expressing the importance and progress of their institutions and local areas. Choices were usually conservative to avoid unnecessary risk and ridicule. Most committees, thinking like Ruskin, wanted "no new style of architecture" and favored familiar classical motifs invested with the prestige and status of history. And, indeed, the winning styles in Jones's early competitions were classical: Corinthian for the Birmingham Town Hall and St. George's Hall, Liverpool, and Italian Renaissance for the Army and Navy Club.[28] Jones was capable of creating praiseworthy classical designs, but chose instead to submit work that moved away from classical precedents. His originality may have been one cause of his rejections.

His bold ideas and unconventional elements may have challenged conservative committees at the same time that his exceptional artistic talent may have intimidated them.[29] In *Masterpieces of Architectural Drawing*, Helen Powell and David Leatherbarrow discuss the phenomenon of nineteenth-century competition juries rejecting stylish and exaggerated perspectives as unfair, since the judges felt that elaborate rendering techniques could attract jurors by the artistry of the presentation rather than the merits of the design.[30] As a result, some committees specified black-and-white drawings to eliminate the influence of color upon the judges. Consequently, the large perspective drawings in color (following the French tradition) that Jones and Vuillamy introduced into England may have hurt Jones's chances in contention, together with his exceptional proficiency in color renderings. Although his designs and drawings were singled out for praise in the architecture magazines, his work may have been too new, too "fantastic," and too sophisticated to reassure and satisfy the jurists in the contests he entered.

The reason why designs such as Jones's failed to win competitions was perhaps best understood by Frank Lloyd Wright, who refused to enter competitions contending that:

The world has gained no building worth having by competition: (1) The jury itself is necessarily a hand-picked average. Some constituency must agree upon the jury. (2) Therefore the first thing this average does as a jury, when picked, is to go through all the designs and throw out the best ones and the worst ones. This is necessary in order that the average may average upon something average. (3) Therefore any architectural competition will be an average upon an average by averages in behalf of the average. (4) The net result is a building well behind the times before it is begun.[31]

Because Jones's unconventional ideas set him apart from the average, they may have been responsible for bringing him to the attention of the French entrepreneur Pierre-Paul-Antenor Joly. Joly, a hero of the 1830 revolution, was editor of *Vert-Vert* and founder of the Théâtre de la Renaissance in Paris. Although the theater was a success and was popular with Victor Hugo, Alexander Dumas, Hector Berlioz, and many others, the French government considered the material being presented subversive and closed the theater in 1841.

Joly was confident that he had devised a "system" for managing public entertainment and traveled to London in 1843 to promote a project for a complex to include theaters, a library, an exhibition hall, and a gymnastics center with heated swimming baths and areas for pistol shooting and fencing. The entertainment complex would also offer a café and shops selling flowers, pastries, and ice cream. The activities would be housed under an iron-and-glass roof in a site in Leicester Square. Jones was to design this winter garden.[32] Although the project did not materialize, Jones's selection as *premier architecte* attests to his reputation and credibility for undertaking such an extraordinary venture.

His involvement in the design of an entertainment complex introduced one new building type in which Jones excelled his peers. His progressive ferrovitreous buildings of the 1850s and '60s satisfied the Victorian veneration of social congregation and display at the same time that they demonstrated Jones's command of architecture and the latest developments in engineering and materials. Consequently, these unprecedented palaces-of-the-people differed substantially from other contemporary architecture in functional, structural, and aesthetic intentions.

Jones's first ferrovitreous design, his competition entry for the 1857 Manchester Art Treasures Exhibition Building, shows innovation in form. The roof and walls were to be united in a single arch springing from ground level (Pl. 3.1). This pure geometric configuration showed the same confidence, sublime magnitude, and refined simplicity found in the visionary projects of the eighteenth-century French architect Etienne-Louis Boullée, but with one major difference: Jones's design was capable of being executed in a timely and affordable manner.

On June 14, 1856, the *Illustrated London News* reported that Jones had won the competition with a novel, graceful, and desirable scheme. The competition committee rescinded their decision, however, and named a local architect, Edward Salomans, for the project. The particulars of this situation bear repeating as another example of the notorious practices associated with nineteenth-century competitions.

Fig. 3.3. Henry Wyndham Phillips, Portrait of Owen Jones, *1856*

The *Builder* published the following report of "The Manchester Exhibition Building Competition":

In answer to the advert of the executive committee for conducting the "Exhibition of the Art Treasures of the United Kingdom in 1857," twenty-five designs were submitted; and in addition, we are told, the committee had before them a design by a firm of operative engineering, sent in before the competition was invited. Our esteemed contemporary, the *Illustrated News*, was premature when it announced last week that the building had been entrusted to Mr. Owen Jones. Mr. Jones had submitted a design, and after receiving a visit from Mr. Deane, the manager, and giving explanations, was taken down to Manchester, and attended the committee. No question of moment, as we understand, was raised, except that of cost; and after some negotiations, the architect set this at rest, as he thought, by the production of a tender from Mr. Kennard, to carry out the design for the sum named by the committee, viz. 25,000£ and Mr. Jones returned to his hotel to await the minute of the committee confirming the selection. The minute came but it was to say that after anxious consideration it was found that his design could not be made to suit their wants; but it was hoped that they might have his assistance for the *decoration* of the building, which would be erected, probably, on the plans of the committee, rather than on one of those submitted![33]

The *Builder* criticized the committee for issuing vague competition particulars and for abusing the trust of the architects. The next issue reported that the committee had chosen the iron founders who approached the committee outside of the competition to solicit the opportunity to construct the building. The magazine announced and ridiculed these contractors, Messrs. C. D. Young & Co., as "the perpetuators of the abomination with which the land of the '51 Exhibition Commissioners is now disfigured—the Brompton Boilers."[34] Three weeks later, it described the new design as "a repetition of the three steam-boilers, side by side, with which Brompton is disfigured, with an ornamentation brick 'front' attached to one end."[35]

On July 5, 1856, the *Builder* took the unusual step of printing a letter by Jones directed to the publication's readers:

As a warning to my professional brethren, who might be tempted to engage in competitions where the terms are as ill defined as they have been in the late Manchester competition, I enclose you a letter I have had the honour to receive from the chairman of the executive committee.

I need hardly say that I have declined the proffered gift.

OWEN JONES

Sir—At the last meeting of the general council of this exhibition, it was resolved to acknowledge with some mark of the council's approbation such of the designs for the exhibition building as, either from the genius of their conception, their artistic merit, or their approach to meet the full requirements of the contemplated art treasure display, should, in the opinion of the executive committee, merit such a distinction.

It is gratifying to me to inform you that the design submitted by you was amongst the limited number so selected; and in tendering the enclosed draft as a slight compensation for the labour and expense which have been bestowed on your plans, the committee trust that you receive their acknowledgement of the ability displayed in your suggestions, and their thanks for the interest you have evinced in the success of the undertaking.

I am, sir, &c.

(Signed)   THOS. FAIRBAIRN
Chairman of the Executive Committee[36]

The draft enclosed was for 21 pounds. Jones returned the money and refused to participate in the decoration of the building, and the decorating firm of Crace replaced him.[37]

Jones exhibited the Manchester design at the Royal Academy the following year. The critic for the *Civil Engineer and Architect's Journal* found the design "novel, but not prepossessing" and the *Builder's* reporter saw no art in the scheme and felt it was uncharacteristic of Jones.[38] Ironically, fifteen years later, M. Digby Wyatt cited Jones's Manchester competition entry as one of the only successful designs for an exhibition building ever produced and suggested that it should serve as the model for future.[39] In the exhibition of Jones's work held the following year after his death, the *Building News* praised the "boldness and originality" of the Manchester scheme and noted that at a time when "iron and glass were new and untried materials of which our architects and decorators were almost afraid, in the hands of the late Mr. Jones these rich products of our country's mineral wealth were transformed into sparkling forms irradiated with the varied hues of the rainbow."[40]

At the same time Jones was producing his Manchester competition entry, he was preparing plans for another type of entertainment complex introduced in the nineteenth century: the large concert hall. The growing importance and popularity of indoor performances of music began early in the nineteenth century, prompting the construction of concert halls to accommodate the larger orchestras and choruses required to perform the works of Wagner and other contemporary composers and also to provide room for the huge crowds attending commemorations of Handel, Beethoven, Mozart, and other famous composers.[41] By mid-century, large concert facilities had been built in Birmingham, Liverpool, Manchester, Bradford, and Leeds, but nothing had been done in London.[42] In 1856, the music publishers William Chappell and Thomas Frederick Beale, the conductor (Sir) Julius Benedict, and the violinist John Ella formed

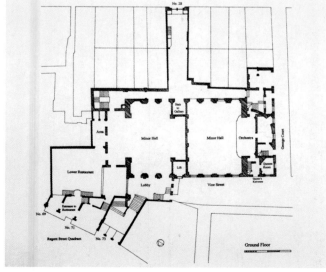

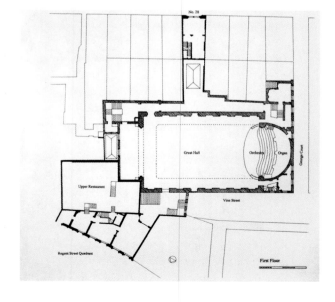

Fig. 3.4. Ground-floor plan of St. James's Hall, London, 1856; redrawn by Alix Ogilvie

Fig. 3.5. First-floor plan of St. James's Hall, London, 1856; redrawn by Alix Ogilvie

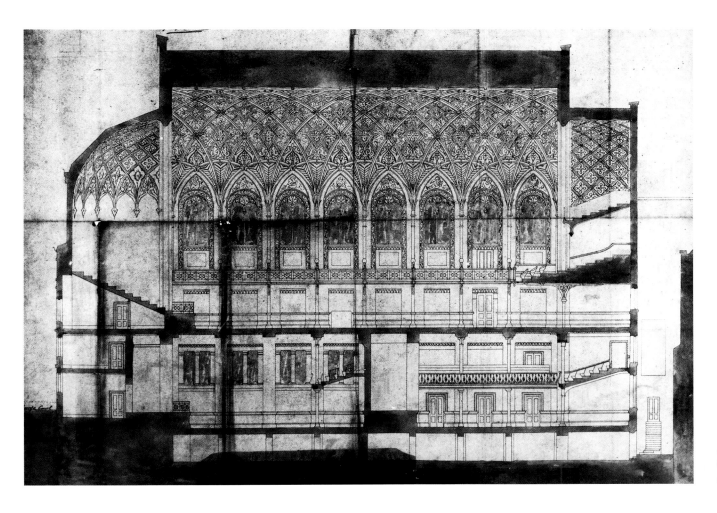

Fig. 3.6. Section of the Great Hall, St. James's Hall, London, 1856

the Provisional Committee for the St. James's Hall Company, a limited corporation to finance the construction of a concert facility to hold audiences of twenty-five hundred people in the West End of London.[43] Jones's selection as architect is not surprising, since he had long associations with Chappell and others involved with music.[44]

Jones's designs for St. James's Hall (1858–1905; Figs. 3.4–3.8) were executed and St. James's remained London's principal concert chamber for nearly half a century.[45] The Royal Society of Music gave its annual performance of the *Messiah* there, and William Chappell launched the "Monday Popular Concerts" of classical chamber music in St. James's Hall in February 1859. The success of the Monday, and later Monday evening and Saturday afternoon, series became the center of musical life in the metropolis.[46] The concerts have been immortalized by W. S. Gilbert in *The Mikado* (1885) as the "Classical Monday Pops" and are considered "among the most influential events of the 19th century in their popularization of many musical genres."[47] In addition, the most distinguished international artists and *virtuosi* performed in the hall, including Anton Rubinstein, Liszt, and Paderewski. Dvorak, Grieg, and Tchaikovsky appeared as guest conductors."[48] St. James's Hall also functioned successfully as host to countless banquets, social benefits, and as home to the large audiences

who attended the weekly public readings given by Charles Dickens, and the lively musical performances of the popular black-faced Christy Minstrels.[49]

The unusual site, in the rear of buildings lining the southern side of the Regent Street Quadrant and those on the northern side of Piccadilly Street, denied Jones the opportunity for a dramatic exterior and limited his design to a rectangular building of 140 feet long by 75 feet wide, plus appendages for the public entrances and rehearsal and storage facilities. Two public rooms on the ground floor, measuring 60 by 60 by 24 feet, and 60 by 55 by 24 feet, were intended to function as spaces for small concerts, banquets, and meetings. The eastern room was cruciform, with galleries located in its eastern, northern, and southern arms. The rectangular western room accommodated an orchestra. The premier concert space, measuring 60 by 136 by 60 feet, occupied the level above. This room had 38-foot arches at either end, creating room for the back stalls, and a gallery in the eastern end and space for an orchestra, choir seating, and a huge organ in the western apse.[50] Gallery seating was provided along the walls.

A shop at 73 Regent Street and a house at 28 Piccadilly were demolished to accommodate the public entrances for the concert facility. Concern for adequate ingress and egress was high, due to the recent death of six people and the

Fig. 3.7. Section toward the organ of the Great Hall, St. James's Hall, London, 1856

injury of many others in a panic in the Surrey Music Hall and the deaths and injuries occurring in other public buildings with insufficient exits and poorly designed stairs and corridors.[51] The *Illustrated London News* praised the "unequalled facilities for visitors arriving and leaving the hall" provided in the four entrances and five exits that Jones designed and said the stairs and corridors suggested the idea of safety through their spaciousness.[52] The *Art Journal* agreed and gave "unqualified approbation" and proposed that the arrangements for access in St. James's Hall serve as a model for other public structures.[53] The main staircase was approximately 24 by 16 feet and contained landings covered with six-inch slabs of Yorkshire stone from the Park Spring quarries. The steps were also covered with Yorkshire stone, and, like the landings, received support from the exterior walls and from internal wrought-iron girders.[54]

The site presented another major problem, since the soil contained quicksand. The ground was stabilized by pouring a concrete foundation composed of blue lias cement mixed with gravel from the site. The foundation was 5 feet deep and 8 feet wide under the exterior walls.[55] The unanticipated expense of the foundation increased the project's cost to 50,000 pounds.[56]

The Crown's ownership of the property created another problem, since the plans had to be approved by James Pennethorne and the Crown Commissioners. Jones submitted the plans and sections for the concert facility on November 5, 1855, but the approval was withheld until February 1857. Pennethorne praised the handsome internal decorations of the building but objected to the proposed height, saying that it would be "detrimental to all the neighborhood." He insisted that "the top of the parapet should be reduced to a level not exceeding sixty-three feet above the level of the foot pavement in Vine Street." Disagreement over this alteration continued until July 1856 when the company "at last agreed to the height being reduced." The contractors, the Messrs. Lucas of Belvedere Road, Lambeth, who were also building the Italian Opera House, began preparing for construction as soon as the plans received approval from the House of Lords on January 9, 1857.[57] On February 27, 1857, the *Building News* informed its readers that "the greater portion of the western side of George Court, and a part of the southern side of Little Vine Street have been pulled down, and the debris is being cleared away in preparation for putting in the foundation."[58]

On November 6, 1857, the *Building News* identified St. James's Hall as one of the largest facilities under construction in the West End and pointed to several important constructive features in Jones's design as worthy of careful consideration.[59] These included the spacious vaults under the structure and Jones's innovative use of wrought iron for structural support throughout the building. Jones used 2-foot-by-5-inch wrought-iron girders supported by eight cast-iron columns to brace the floor of the great hall. Smaller girders and trimming 12 inches deep joined the principal girders diagonally to form the horizontal truss under the floor. In addition, wrought-iron cantilevers and stanchions supported the staircases and the galleries that projected 8 feet at a height of 10 feet above the base of each stanchion. The ironwork was executed by Messrs. Kennard.

The semicircular roof was also formed from wrought-iron ribs placed 11 feet 9 inches apart (Fig. 3.8). These ribs measured 2 feet 9 inches in depth at the crown of each arch and narrowed to 20 inches at the springing. Diagonal braces of T iron (6 by 4 inches) and longitudinal ties of T iron were used to stiffen the ribs. The stanchions to support the principal ribs were built into the walls and stretched from 2 feet below the floor of the great hall to the springing of the iron ribs. The stanchions were secured to bases of York stones with bolts, plates, and T-iron struts.

The article listed other materials, including the half-inch layer of asphalt applied to the walls to prevent dampness from rising above the ground and the more than 1½ million bricks projected for the construction. These included the yellow brick walls and red brick window surrounds already showing favorably on the exterior, as well as the equally successful stringcourses formed with yellow brick dentils on a background of red bricks below a strip of red bricks. Pillars between the windows were topped with projected bands of Portland stone.

Construction progressed rapidly, with most of the roof in place and the entrance in Piccadilly almost complete by January 1, 1858 (Fig. 3.9). On March 1, the *Art Journal* remarked on the rapid pace of construction of the building and described the structure as one "which cannot fail to command admiration as well as to excite surprise."[60] Twelve days later, the *Builder* also printed a positive review and confirmed the *Building News'* opinion that the innovative construction deserved attention and offered the potential for changing contemporary methods of construction.[61] They praised the pioneering use of iron as the main structural support of the building and the iron connections and braces that gave integrity and strength to the fabrication. They observed that the iron ribs eliminated the need for an elaborate truss to span the 60-foot-wide hall. They discussed other elements, such as the development of straight lintels over the windows, replacing traditional rounded arches. The lintels were formed from four courses of vertical bricks set in cement and reinforced with hoop iron.

Jones used models of the building to conduct experiments with ventilation. His final arrangement consisted of four pairs of zinc airshafts that linked apertures in the roof

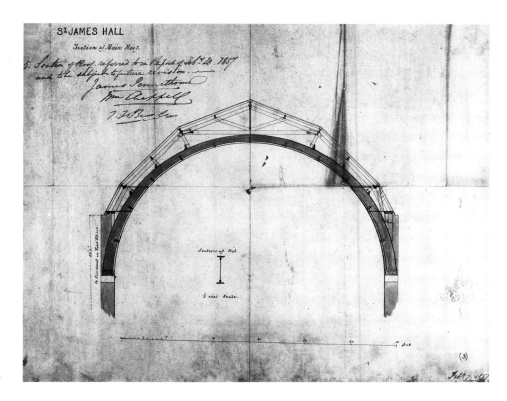

Fig. 3.8. Section of the iron ribs and roof of St. James's Hall, London, 1856

Fig. 3.9. Elevation of the Piccadilly entrance of St. James's Hall, London, 1856

Fig. 3.10. Interior of the Great Hall, St. James's Hall, London, 1856; published in 1858

to openings in the ceiling of the concert hall. Outside air descended through 33-inch-diameter zinc tubes, and entered the great hall through panels of ornamental fretwork. At the same time, the interior heated air rose through the perforated panels and escaped up the tubes. Reports on the pleasant coolness of the concert facility are probably indebted to this system.[62] The success of this system is supported by the fact that Jones used similar procedures for ventilation in later buildings.[63]

He also experimented with a new concept for lighting the hall. Instead of the traditional massive chandeliers normally used to illuminate large spaces, Jones designed smaller, star-shaped gasoliers (Fig. 3.10). Light was diffused uniformly throughout the hall and the ceiling decoration was shown to advantage by suspending the "starburners" on slender tubes from the ceiling ribs. The gilding on the ceiling reflected the artificial light, creating an effect of unaccustomed beauty and brilliance. The starburners gained immediate popularity with other architects and the public.[64]

When St. James's Hall opened on March 25, 1858, reviews praised both the construction and decoration of the building. The *Builder* compared the new facility to the larger Exeter Hall and the Music Hall in Surrey Gardens and praised Jones's work for achieving a loftiness that fostered a "grand and imposing aspect" lacking in both its predecessors.[65] The *Illustrated London News* also remarked on the interior volume, crediting the height of the facility for the superior ventilation and pleasant temperature of the hall. The *News* proclaimed the new concert forum as the most superb music hall in the city, saying: "Nothing can exceed the beauty of the decorations; they are at once rich, chaste, and delicate. A pale blue is the prevalent colour, and its effect is to give the light which streams from innumerable burners hung from the vaulted roof, the clearness and mildness of the light of day."[66]

The *Building News* continued the praise, noting the success of the innovative construction comprised of 350 tons of iron instead of conventional buttresses and horizontal floor bracings. The magazine also lauded the success of the decoration of the grand hall and applauded the way the ornamentation had been accomplished by simple means, without excessive expenditure."[67] The *Builder* echoed this observation, celebrating both the beauty of the ceiling and the reasonable cost.[68]

The economical ornamentation of the hall was achieved through the use of Desachy's fibrous plaster and Martin's cement. Both products were lightweight, nonflammable,

138 *Chapter Three*

and capable of being painted shortly after installation. Martin's cement could be painted within twenty hours of being applied to old brickwork or twelve hours when applied on lathed work; Desachy's plaster could be painted immediately.[69] Jones's extensive use of Desachy's plaster, at St. James's and in other buildings, popularized the material.

Jones also relied on the same dependable craftsmen for his projects. These artisans included the sculptor Raffaelle Monti and the decorative painter James Skeate. Jones had employed these men to execute the decorations for the Crystal Palace at Sydenham before hiring them to decorate the concert hall in Piccadilly. Monti modeled the sculptural forms for the interior and exterior of St. James's and Skeate completed the ceiling painting in less than a month.

The damp climate of Britain created problems for decoration. Many buildings, especially churches, were left unpainted for several years after construction to reduce problems from moisture. When immediate decoration was desired, Jones, Pugin, and other architects sometimes resorted to painting their designs on paper and pasting them in place.[70] Jones used this procedure for the ceiling of St. James's Hall. Skeate stenciled the pattern in oil for a quick and economical alternative to painted plaster.[71] It continued to "command admiration as well as to excite surprise."[72]

The ceiling was the focal point of the decoration in the grand concert room. Fibrous-plaster ribs divided the semicircular vault diagonally, intersecting each other to form eighty lozenge-shaped coffers (Fig. 3.11). These coffers were further subdivided by smaller ribs in the same shape. The effect was described as a "moulded roof of great beauty, even without the aid of colour"; however, Jones, once again, proved himself a master of pattern and polychromy by producing "a rich glow of contrasted colour and gilding." Jones confined the color scheme to his preferred primaries, painting the ground within the large lozenges blue and adding a "complex and beautiful design, of subdued white." Some of the smaller panels, placed on top of the larger forms, "were filled with peculiarly Alhambran enrichment in high relief, gilded on a red ground."[73] The other panels contained the perforated openings for the ventilation system. As usual, Jones substituted gold for yellow, gilding the decorative elements in relief and the most prominent rib moldings. The combination of the moldings, the coloration, and the gilding created an effect that some said was "well beyond what could have been anticipated"[74] and others described as a "fairy-like webbing of colour, that produces a most charming effect . . . and a perfect harmony."[75]

The principal ceiling ribs joined palmette-topped colonettes on the side walls to form eight bays. Each bay contained putti holding scrolls inscribed with the names of eminent composers, including Mozart, Handel, Beethoven,

Haydn, and Purcell. Each bay also held a window crowned with gilded foliated ornament praised by the *Builder* for exceptional beauty.[76]

Structural elements contributed to the decoration in the form of the slender colonettes that stretched from the ceiling to the floor and the slim wrought-iron supports for the galleries cantilevered from the colonettes. In addition, a gilded iron railing in a simple geometric pattern formed the front of the galleries. The rail was backed with red cloth corresponding to the cloth-backed railings Jones designed for the Hyde Park Crystal Palace. Some viewers thought the railing too plain and regretted that Jones had not applied more "art" in its execution, but most accounts were positive. Even *Punch* expressed admiration of the facility, noting that St. James's opened "by several doors, having been provided with ample means of ingress and egress, so that the public will be enabled to walk into it with ease, and to escape from it with expedition in case it should ever catch fire. That this new music-hall should be burnt down, however, would be lamentable; for it is really a magnificent one; vast in dimensions, elegant in proportions, splendid in decoration."[77] *Punch* also observed that the opening night audience included the Prince Consort, a large number of aristocrats and members of the upper classes.

Musicians and critics praised the "beautiful acoustics of the great hall" and the "unique atmosphere of intimacy and charm, [that gave] a warmth of welcome to those who came there to make music and to listen to it."[78] The *Building News* also reported that musicians considered the hall "a very successful effort towards an acoustical building, and one of the finest-proportioned music-halls in Europe."[79] Audiences occasionally complained, however, of hearing strains from the banjo-playing Christy Minstrels downstairs.[80] Jones had improved the acoustics by covering the walls of the concert hall with pitch before plastering and placing a layer of felt between the subfloor of three-quarter-inch deal and the finished pine surface.[81]

Jones's innovation of locating a first-class restaurant adjacent to the concert hall on Regent Street met with mixed reviews. The convenience of full dining service, catering, and light refreshments before and after performances was applauded by some, but others complained of noticing cooking odors during concerts.[82] Since the Victorians seemed to take particular exception to the smell of cooking, it is difficult to know if a problem of consequence existed.

Despite these complaints, most agreed with Christopher Dresser, who said "When in St. James's Hall we appear transported to some fairer world—art is here."[83] Audiences of over two thousand people filled the hall until it closed in 1905 to be replaced by the Piccadilly Hotel (now the Meridien Hotel).[84] At that time many, including the conductor Sir George Henschel, mourned the loss of "dear old St. James's Hall."[85]

Fig. 3.11. Interior of the
Great Hall, St. James's
Hall, London, 1856

Ruskin remained unusually quiet, although Jones had produced a thoroughly modern building in flagrant violation of Ruskin's "principles of architecture." Jones transgressed Ruskin's rules by using iron for structural support, placing the facility outside the realm of architecture, according to Ruskin. Further, he used Desachy's cast plaster instead of wooden beams to save expense, time, and labor; this substitution of materials represented deception to Ruskin, and worse, exemplified the problem he identified at the very core of modern architecture: the desire "to produce the largest results at the least cost." The ceiling decoration of the hall defied Ruskin's Lamp (or spirit), of Sacrifice, which involved choosing the costlier of two equally beautiful marbles, simply because the one selected was more expensive. Similarly, Jones's simple gallery railing breached Ruskin's dictum on elaboration where the choice between two equally beautiful items would be settled by selecting the more elaborate decoration to represent "more cost and more thought."[86]

With the completion of St. James's Hall, Jones turned his attention to plans for an even more modern, and complex, public entertainment facility. The Palace of the People, Muswell Hill, Hornsey, conceived as the "twin brother" of the Sydenham Crystal Palace, to give North Londoners the same advantages enjoyed by their South London counterparts.[87] Jones described his ideas for the complex in a pamphlet and exhibited eighteen drawings showing elevations and sections of the proposed building in St. James's Hall in December 1858, and later showed some of the drawings and the model at the architecture exhibition at 9 Conduit Street, at Colnaghi's, and at Legatt's.[88]

The 450-acre site was ideal, since the land abutted a major line of the Great Northern Railway and main thoroughfares out of London.[89] One hundred and fifty acres were reserved for the building and terraces, plus gardens "to be laid out in the Early English, Italian, Dutch, French, and modern English styles." This arrangement included a thirty-acre lake, plus facilities for archery, cricket, tennis, horseback riding, and other physical recreations. A Mr. Spencer, the director of the marquis of Lansdowne's gardens, was approved to manage the grounds and conduct experiments on the scientific cultivation of flowers and plants.[90] The remaining three hundred acres were divided into two parts, with thirty acres to be set aside for the use of "benevolent institutions connected with art, science, literature, music, horticulture, and the railway interest," and the remaining 270 acres were to be developed with suburban villas.[91]

Jones located the building at the center of the site and planned glazed eating areas at each end of the facility to allow patrons to enjoy views of the gardens and the surrounding countryside of Hornsey, Kent, Surrey, and Middlesex.[92] He used the drop of the land to advantage, locating the building at the highest point, 200 feet above the railway, allowing him to provide a railway connection on the north side of the building at the lowest level with a covered carriage entrance above.[93] This direct covered access to the building was a considerable improvement over the arrangement in the Crystal Palace at Sydenham (Fig. 3.12).

The profile of the structure was markedly different as well. Jones replaced the arched transepts of Sydenham with eight glass towers and a large central dome. He added diaphanous apses (the refreshment rooms) at both ends of the building and a two-tiered theatre on the northern side.

Like the earlier Crystal Palaces, the interior was symmetrical, but Muswell Hill offered distinct advantages.

Fig. 3.12. Elevation of the Palace of the People, Muswell Hill, 1859

Fig. 3.13. Side elevation of the Palace of the People, Muswell Hill, 1859

The first improvement was evident in the creation of a large winter garden at the center of the building. This interior garden was crowned with a dome 200 feet in diameter and 144 feet in height (Figs. 3.13–3.15). Thirty-six-foot-high masonry walls supported the dome.[94] The press observed that this conservatory would "surpass anything which has yet been attempted in this country."[95] By reserving this space for an arboretum, Jones accomplished several objectives. The masonry arcades separated the area from the rest of the facility, providing a temperature- and humidity-controlled zone for the growth of tropical plants without adversely impacting the rest of the facility, solving a problem experienced at Sydenham.[96] Openings in the arcades would be glazed, enabling views into the conservatory from all areas of the building and views of the rest of the building from inside the winter garden. The *Building News* thought the arcades enhanced the architectural effect of the building by providing "an appearance of structural solidity" and "large surfaces for colour to contrast with the comparatively minute surfaces of the iron tracery of the dome."[97]

The central exhibition spaces were located in 336-by-260-foot naves placed on either side of the winter garden. Each nave contained a 120-foot-wide display area flanked with 70-foot-wide side aisles. Forty-eight foot wide galleries circled the dome, the naves, and the ends of the building. The area to the west of the winter garden was reserved for the display of industrial and commercial objects. Moving machinery, agricultural equipment, and raw products were assigned the central space, and manufactured goods were to be displayed in the galleries above. The eastern end of the building was dedicated to the arts and sciences. Artwork and school exhibits were located on the ground level, with illustrations from mathematics, geography, geology, astronomy, physics, biology, and sociology occupying the galleries above.

Greater emphasis was to be placed on the education of the public in this institution than in its predecessors. A large lecture hall, 216 feet in diameter, on the north side of the building would enable speakers to discuss pieces from the collection. Spacious 24-foot corridors connected the lecture hall to all three levels of the building. As a result, patrons could access their seats comfortably and quickly and could be evacuated in five to ten minutes, if necessary.[98] The apsidal arrangement was adopted so that each of the ten thousand people in the audience would be able to hear and see distinctly.[99] Construction of the theatre followed the same principle as the dome and the other roof struc-

Fig. 3.14. Winter Garden of the Palace of the People, Muswell Hill, 1859

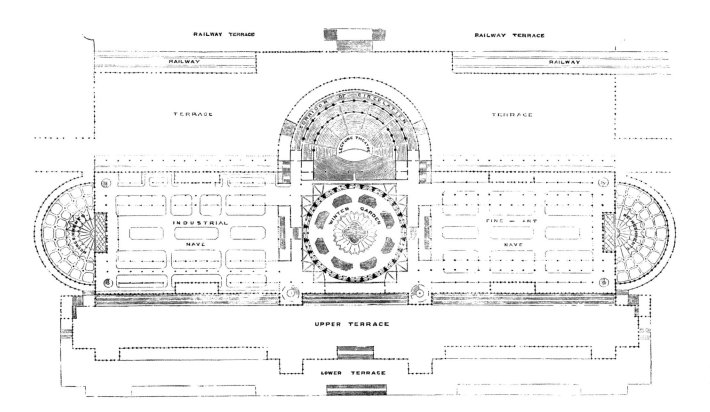

Fig. 3.15. Plan of the Palace of the People, Muswell Hill, 1859

Fig. 3.16. Interior of the Crystal Palace Bazaar, London, 1857; demolished 1890

tures, with curved ribs springing from columns; in the dome and lecture theater, the ribs met in a circle at the top, through which the interiors were lit.[100]

Members of the press reporting for the *Building News*, the *Builder*, the *Illustrated London News*, the *Athenaeum*, and the *Art Journal* were enthusiastic in their praise of the designs for the Muswell Hill complex.[101] The *Art Journal* celebrated Jones's "higher grade of architectural genius" and the "fertility of his artistic resources."[102] The *Athenaeum* also lauded Jones's variety, effectiveness, and originality in working in iron and glass to produce one of the new buildings suited to the age.[103]

The endorsement by the press, members of the architecture profession, and the confirmation of the cost estimates by Fox and other contractors were not enough to secure the necessary funding, however, and the venture collapsed in 1860. Three years later, the Alexandra Park Co. Ltd. was formed to purchase the land and erect a "People's Palace" built of material salvaged from the 1862 Exhibition Building. Jones was not involved.[104]

Jones's last exhibition building responded to requests for a permanent facility to be erected in St. Cloud, France. Jones developed several schemes for this project and documented them in photos. The first design entitled *Palais de Cristal de Saint-Cloud, Exposition Permanente de l'Industrie Française, Jardin d'Hiver et Parc de Plaisance* dated October 4, 1860, resembled the People's Palace at Muswell Hill (Pl. 3.2); however, the French scheme showed a more prominent and

graceful dome and more advanced construction. At Muswell Hill, the curved iron ribs met in the center, forming a simple, radiating frame; at St. Cloud, the ribs form pointed arches in a radical departure from the earlier work of both Jones and Paxton. Delicate iron pendentives transferred the weight of the framework to four corner posts. The appearance of St. Cloud received further refinement from Jones's addition of two-tiered apses on the ends of the building, gradually reducing the height of the structure to meet the ground. Other changes involved the substitution of plants for exhibits in the main nave areas and the placement of long pools of water on each side of the building.

The second design introduced a quieter profile and a more uniform arrangement. The towers were eliminated and the dome was moved to the center of one side, with two smaller domes at either end of the nave. An arrangement of gables, fan-shaped transepts, and three-story recessed arches created an impressive trio of entries on the opposite side.[105] Streamlining became the dominant element in Jones's third design, where the building presents a smooth rounded silhouette under a large dome (Pls. 3.3 and 3.4). The simplicity of this structure seemed as futuristic in its nineteenth-century context as the visionary drawings of Boullée. Although a century apart, Boullée and Jones shared the ability to envision sublime structures capable of transforming architecture. Unfortunately, their grandest schemes were never realized, and their brilliance is only surmised through their impressive perspectives.

Jones's exhibition structures demonstrate his originality, proficiency, and willingness to embrace new materials, technology, and typology. They also show that he understood the Victorian desire for public improvement and the concern for practical issues of safety, comfort, and convenience. At the same time, he recognized his contemporaries' love of spectacle and social promenade. He addressed all of these issues in structures that were sublime, yet comfortable, functional, and beautiful.

In *Crystal Palace: Joseph Paxton and Charles Fox*, John McKean describes the spectacle and promenade afforded in the Crystal Palace in Hyde Park and argues that this new type of voyeurism spread directly from the Crystal Palace to the department store. Walter Benjamin also associated consumerism with the international exhibitions. Benjamin described the international displays as sites of pilgrimages to the "commodity fetish," glorifying the exchange value of merchandise. At the same time, Benjamin concluded, the exhibits were not the only objects on display; the visitors were also elevated to the level of commodities, submitting to being manipulated and enjoying their alienation from themselves and others.[106]

Although the pleasure derived from viewing consumer goods and the leisurely amusement of shopping inspired the seventeenth-century exchanges and the elite shopping avenues introduced in eighteenth-century London, it was the theatricality and spectacle of the bazaars, with numerous stalls selling a variety of items under one roof, which captured the same type of "enthronement of merchandise, with the aura of amusement surrounding it . . ." that drew the public to the international exhibitions.[107] In *English Shops and Shopping*, Kathryn Morrison describes the bazaars introduced in early and mid-nineteenth-century London as the "most architecturally adventurous retail establishments of the early to mid-nineteenth century" and Jones's London Crystal Palace (1858) as "the most architecturally innovative."[108]

The site for the Crystal Palace Bazaar had the advantage of being on London's most crowded thoroughfare, but the disadvantage of being another irregular plot squeezed behind buildings fronting Oxford Street and Regent Street.[109] As at St. James's Hall, Jones was forced to lay out a new building with multiple entrances on different streets and fit a structure within the limitations posed by preexisting buildings. The resulting irregular interior measured 250 feet from east to west and 140 feet from north to south. The structure measured 33 feet at its narrowest point.[110]

The interior presented a spacious hall covered with an impressive vault 36 feet high. The vault was formed from wrought-iron ribs and flitch beams (structural timbers bolted together). Two tiers of cast-iron columns, placed 12 feet apart, supported the ribs (Fig. 3.16).[111] Eight-foot-by-six-foot sales counters divided the center of the floor into two main avenues with wide passages. Additional merchandise was displayed and sold in stalls located under the galleries on the north, south, and western walls.[112]

The principal entrance on John Street presented an unusual facade of colored glass in a large arch under a gabled roof. Another unusual feature was the amenities provided. These included a spacious dining room, lavatories and support facilities for the exhibitors, plus refreshment and rest rooms for the public.[113] The Crystal Palace Bazaar was the first retail establishment in the West End to provide lavatories for customers. Jones was aware of the need for public facilities, particularly for women, having served on a committee for the Royal Society for the Encouragement of Arts formed to study the problem in the early 1850s. The committee, composed of Jones, G. H. Lewes, Charles Dickens, Thomas Carlyle, Richard Redgrave, and (Sirs) Henry Cole, Charles Barry, and M. Digby Wyatt, recommended the establishment of public water closets and urinals in central London but decades passed before the Ladies Lavatory Company opened in Oxford Circus.[114]

The Oxford Street entrance was a standard doorway fronting a corridor to the central display area and it was the originality and beauty of this display area that won immediate acclaim. The decoration centered on the color and patterns of the vaulted ceiling. The arched roof was divided into diamond-shape sections containing star-shape patterns formed with a ruby star at the center surrounded by six blue stars and an outer circle of six amber stars. The colored stars were surrounded with panes of clear glass.

Jones took care to prevent reflections and shadows from altering the appearance of the items on display by installing a roof of opaque Hartley glass about 1 foot above the arched ceiling. In addition, the configurations of red, yellow, and blue stars followed the proportions recommended by Field to achieve neutralized or white light. The experiment succeeded, creating a luminous interior. Natural light enlivened the polychrome ceiling during the day and the reflected light from star-shape gas fixtures suspended from the ceiling accentuated the gilding and painted decorations of the vault at night.

Jones used different schemes to paint the upper and lower tiers of the iron columns supporting the structure, contrasting the light blue, white, and red of the upper columns with dark maroon, light blue, and white below. The gilding on the abacus of each column was repeated in molding at the same height encircling the interior. The gallery railing was gilded as well.[115]

Previously, Jones drew the attention of the press by skillfully repairing and redesigning the facade of the premises of Chappell's on Bond Street. Jones and his brother-in-law Charles H. Wild replaced the original beam with an iron

Fig. 3.17. Exterior details of Chappell's showroom, Bond Street, London, 1850

Fig. 3.18. Interior of Osler's Showroom, London, 1858; demolished 1926

plate-girder. The *Journal of Design* commended the "ingenious construction" and Jones's decision to leave the girder exposed, rather than making the "frequent mistake of appearing to support a whole facade upon sheets of plate-glass and a few sash-bars."[116] The critic praised Jones for wisely recessing the shop-front a few feet and adding "extremely elegant" iron decoration (Fig. 3.17). The writer concluded that the talent indicated in this scheme, if duplicated throughout London "would materially elevate the style of our now anything but admirable street architecture." The facade was altered, however, several decades later when the premises were enlarged.

Little is known of two other retail schemes completed by Jones in 1856. These were for the prestigious Regent Street shops occupied by Houbigant, the French perfumer and glover, and Jay's, the famous mourning emporium. Both interiors were well received and Jones's decoration for Houbigant was described as one of the most significant attempts to improve the artistic character of a retail space.[117]

Fortunately, the London showroom Jones designed for Abraham Follett and Thomas Osler is documented (Fig. 3.18). The *Building News* cited Osler's as "one of the most important structures recently erected in the metropolis" and applauded Jones for significantly improving the architecture of Oxford Street.[118] No record of the facade has been found, but contemporary accounts remark on the unique and effective decoration, consisting of slightly projecting stringcourses terminating in chamfers at the ends of the facade and simple incising in cement "equal in effect to the elaborate mouldings which architects of less merit would have pressed into the work." The magazine reported that although there was not much ornament, the decoration provided was "striking from the evidence it bears from a master mind having been engaged upon it." The ground-floor windows were also unusual. Jones replaced the typical mass of plate glass with three windows and recessed arches on the sides. The magazine praised this arrangement for enhancing the display of goods and recommended that other retailers adopt this configuration.[119]

Osler began making glass toys in Birmingham in 1807. Upon his death, the business passed to his sons, Abraham and Thomas; they expanded the product line and opened a London showroom in 1845.[120] Jones worked with members of the firm in the 1850s, making arrangements for the famous fountain Osler's displayed in the Great Exhibition of 1851 and reinstalled in the Crystal Palace at Sydenham. When the firm renewed their lease on 44 Oxford Street in 1858 and acquired the lease for 45 Oxford Street, they received permission to destroy the existing buildings and asked Jones to design a new facility. The novelty of the new interior quickly became one of the famous "sights of London" and another example of Jones's ability to produce "highly effective" arrangements through "inexpensive means."[121]

Double doors on Oxford Street opened into a lobby paved with Minton tiles in geometric patterns. Shoppers passed through this lobby and an adjoining vestibule into the main showroom where Jones produced "an almost infinitesimal perspective, and a wonderful effect of extended space" by placing fourteen elliptically headed mirrors directly opposite each other on both sides of the room. He created the illusion of an area larger than 106 by 24 by 25 feet 4 inches high by placing a large mirror (24 feet 9 inches high and 12 feet wide) on the northern wall. The cumulative effect of the reflections of the glass tables loaded with crystal was described as a "fairyland of crystal fascinations."

As in Jones's other work, the "elaborately and beautifully decorated roof" formed the focus of the decoration. Molded ribs of Desachy's plaster divided the ceiling into fourteen sections to correspond with the fourteen mirrors below. These compartments were further subdivided to create a ceiling of 1,456 glazed panels. The groundwork of the molding was painted white and accented in blue, red, and gilding. Red paper, of a "small and appropriate pattern," appeared between the mirrors, and paneled mahogany counters 2 feet 9 inches high projected 3 feet 6 inches from the walls. Jones also designed showcases for small items. The showcases were considered "worthy of note as a combination of artistic colouring by the first master of the art of colour of his day."[122] Gas sun-burners, similar to the fixtures he had used previously, were installed for night illumination.

Jones increased his retail commissions in the 1860s. In 1862, he added a wing to Osler's showroom. The *Art Journal* described this new space as more appropriate and beautiful than the original gallery. A year earlier, he exhibited a ceiling design for Hancock's of Bruton Street at the Royal Academy. The design, to be executed in "patent canvas plaster," received an enthusiastic reception. The *Building News* said "Nothing can exceed it either in design or colour." The ceiling contained a central panel with circular ends, and the graduation of the ornament away from the center was described as "marvelous." The *Building News* reviewer was confused about Jones's style, but conceded that "it matters little what the style is because it is so thoroughly harmonious . . . there is not a feeble or false line in the whole work" and praised Jones's coloration of white, blue, and red with a little gilding as "exceedingly chaste and elegant. The centre, as with the line ornament, is the richest portion, but the whole work is linked most skilfully together, and it is only after attentive examination that one is enabled to detect the secret of its success, or to realize its full value as a work of art."[123]

Hancock's had been established at 39 Bruton Street in 1848 and the firm expanded rapidly. They opened other premises at 152 New Bond Street and 4 Little Bruton Street that Jones may also have designed, since exhibit number four for "Plans and Elevation of Shops and Cottages. Designed for Mr. Hancock," and number 150, "Plan and Elevation of Shop Designed for Mr. Hancock," were included along with number 123, "Ceiling of Mr. Hancock's Showroom, Bruton Street," in the 1874 exhibi-

Fig. 3.19. Exterior of Jackson and Graham showroom, 36–38 Oxford Street, London, 1869

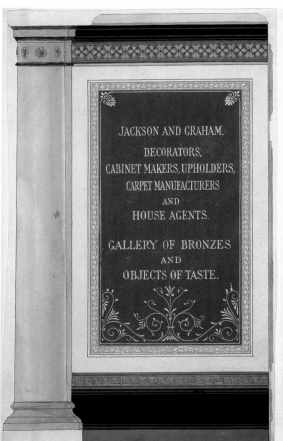

Fig. 3.20. Detail of exterior of Jackson and Graham showroom, London

tion of Jones's works. Typically, Jones also produced designs for his client's products; in this case, he collaborated with the sculptor Monti on designs for silver trophies Hancock's executed in 1867 and 1868.[124]

In 1862, he redecorated premises in Grosvenor Street, Grosvenor Square, for Collard and Collard, the esteemed piano manufacturers. They had acquired the spacious town residence of the late duke of Rutland and commissioned Jones to transform this urban mansion into showrooms and a concert facility. The *Illustrated London News* praised Jones's restoration of the ceilings, originally designed by the celebrated Adam brothers, and his perfect arrangements for light and ventilation.[125] Pevsner described Jones's alteration of the Georgian exterior as "very simple and restrained."[126]

Jones designed other exteriors, including the front of 36–38 Oxford Street, the premises of Jackson and Graham, the renowned decorators and manufacturers who produced furniture, carpets, and other furnishings for Jones and other leading designers (Figs. 3.19 and 3.20). Jones's designs for retail establishments provide another example of his ability to devise original and effective schemes to satisfy new social and functional requirements. Purveyors of luxury items recognized Jones's ability to create first-class environments capable of enticing visitors into their showrooms and promoting the goods for sale. Jones designed many of the products sold in these establishments, including crystal items for Osler's, silver trophies for Hancock's, pianos for Collard and Chappell, and all types of decorative furnishings for Jackson and Graham. His design activity extended to personal commissions for several of these clients, including cottages for Hancock, a country house for Charles Lukey Collard, interiors for De la Rue, and even the tombstones of De la Rue, Collard, and Chappell (Fig. 3.21).

The talent for creating large-scale sumptuous interiors at a modest cost made Jones the obvious choice to provide interesting decors for the Langham and Charing Cross hotels, two of the modern luxury hotels being built in London during the early 1860s. The Langham was one of the earliest and most important.[127] The decision to build a large hotel at the junction of Portland and Langham Places was bold, since most new hotels were sited adjacent to railway stations. A design competition was held and, in typical Victorian fashion, the winning architect, John Giles, was persuaded to join with James Murray, another competitor, who had produced the interiors preferred by the committee. The earl of Shrewsbury, chairman of the company of shareholders, laid the foundation stone in July 1863, and the hotel was opened, without being fully furnished, two years later.[128]

The six-story, three-hundred-room hotel cost approximately 300,000 pounds to construct and furnish and represented one of the largest buildings in London. The Portland Place facade was 200 feet long and 120 feet high. The internal organization followed the American precedent of providing both single rooms and suites, plus large public rooms and the latest amenities, including elevators and convenient facilities for hygiene and bathing: 36 bathrooms and 100 lavatories.[129] The public spaces included an enormous dining room 100 feet long and 50 feet wide, three coffee rooms (one nearly 50 feet square), an ambassador's audience room, a board room, plus several smoking and billiard rooms. The style, described by the *Building News* as "bold and picturesque," followed the eclecticism that noted historian Robert Thorne describes as "a reconciliation of existing styles . . . using basic classical forms but invigorating them by bolder modelling and the introduction of Gothic decoration."[130]

Jones's decorations drew mixed approval. The *Building News* described most of the polychromatic decorations as "very successful in colour" and as being composed of "diapers of that late Mooresque character which Mr. Owen Jones . . . especially affects in his ornament. The appearance of the rooms thus decorated is very novel and striking, and their affect is further enhanced by a judicious assortments of tints in the various carpets, which have evidently also been designed expressly for the situation."[131] The *Times* objected to the scheme for the dining room, criticizing "the miserable ill taste which has disfigured the room with rows of massive chocolate covered columns."[132] No visual evidence of this commission remains.

Jones continued the use of dark colors in the refreshment room for E. M. Barry's Charing Cross Hotel (1863–4). The walls were divided into upper and lower sections with wallpaper and piers above and plinths and moldings below. The piers and wallpapers on the top sections were Indian red with ocher trim. The plinths below were black and received praise in the *Builder* for their good design and for "the precision and delicacy of workmanship which Mr. Owen Jones is so well able to secure." The ceiling was divided into nine square compartments filled with diapered patterns. The beams were painted in a crimson and blue pattern typical of Jones.[133]

In *British Railway Hotels 1838–1983*, Oliver Carter reports that both Jones and E. M. Barry were responsible for the decoration of the dining room.[134] This design featured dark piers and columns, light moldings, and a grand ceiling with a shallow coffered saucer dome and rich architectural embellishment. This work was carried out by Jackson and Graham, the firm commissioned to make the decorations and furnishings for the property.

In 1865, Jones participated in the invitational competition for the design of the station buildings and hotel for the Midland Railway's London terminus, St. Pancras Station. The other participants were G. G. Scott (winner), Somers Clarke (200-pound prize), Barry (100-pound

Fig. 3.21. Tombstone of Wm. Chappell, Kensal Green Cemetery, London, 1860

Fig. 3.22. Elevation of St. Pancras Station competition entry, 1865

prize), T. C. Sorby (50-pound prize), and C. P. Cockerell, among others.[135] This was the only competition held to select the design for a railway building of importance in London and was not without problems and criticism. The controversy focused on the fact that Scott's winning design substantially exceeded the instructions, resulting in an unfair comparison. Somers Clarke exposed this situation in a letter to the *Builder*, saying that the addition of two extra stories of bedrooms gave Scott's proposed building the dignity and importance denied to the other proposals for shorter structures. Scott's entry also exceeded the second-highest estimate by 50,000 pounds.[136] Since Scott was later forced to make modifications, including the elimination of one floor of the hotel and two floors of the station's offices to reduce expenses, the criticism that Scott had overstated the project to win the competition seems appropriate.

Another disparity is the fact that the competition instructions stipulated that the hotel should be located on the western side of the site and that the vast roof of the terminus should be introduced on the central and eastern sides of the site. Jones was the only entrant who made the hotel subsidiary to the train shed (Fig. 3.22); the others hid the roof of the station and created uniform compositions concealing the functions of the buildings. The *Builder* praised Jones for boldly grappling with Barlow's design of the shed and making the vast span of the roof the most prominent feature on the facade. The writer concluded that by avoiding the opportunity to treat the great railway roof architecturally, the other architects had made a great mistake.[137]

Also during 1865, Jones began the redecoration of Fishmonger's Hall in London. The Greek Revival building on the entrance to London Bridge was completed in 1834

to the designs of Henry Roberts (1803–1876) and his assistant, the young George Gilbert Scott. Jones replaced the original ivory, tawny, and gilt scheme on the interior with bold primary colors and Greek motifs appropriate to the existing architecture and gas lighting. Descriptions of Jones's ceilings remark upon the "peculiar blue" he used in this scheme and in others, a light but intense color, achieved by adding small areas of white to the overall color. The ceiling was bordered with gilding, delicately flecked with blue and red. The carpet designs reflected the patterns of Roberts' original ceilings, a technique popularized by the architect Robert Adam in the late eighteenth century. The *Daily News* praised the integrated treatment of the cornices and the Corinthian capitals capping the pilasters in the great hall achieved by painting the recesses crimson and gilding the projections. A honeysuckle motif was stenciled in a frieze below the molded entablature. The walls were green. In the court dining room, Jones retained the original oak doors and dadoes and painted the walls ivory with "luminous blue" panels. "A delicious sense of coolness" was experienced in the corner drawing room with the carpets and furnishings in green and blue offset by a white marble and yellow scagliola chimneypiece. During a banquet held January 18, 1866 to honor the new decoration, the company took credit for allowing Jones to "exercise his discretion." In responding to a toast on his behalf, Jones explained that the original Greek Revival building exemplified the style popular when the hall was erected and in carrying out his redecoration, he did not create anything new, but added color to bring the building to life and to demonstrate his theory of color in Greek art. At an earlier banquet in the hall, Jones described his intended scheme with the often-repeated phrase "form without colour is like a body without a soul." Fortunately, surviving drawings in the Victoria and Albert Museum show the colors and designs Jones used to enhance the original building (Pls. 4.16 and 4.17), since Jones's scheme was replaced in 1894 by the Gothic Revival architect, G. F. Bodley. Bodley's decoration was replaced in 1929 by H. S. Goodhart Rendel. Extensive damage suffered in air raids during World War II led to repairs and redecoration by Austen Hall in 1952. Hall's work is closer to the efforts of Roberts and Jones and fosters some understanding of the scale and impact of the rooms decorated by Jones.[138]

Two years later in 1867, Jones was one of the twelve architects invited to compete in a new design for the National Gallery. The invitees who participated included Banks & Barry; Barry; Brodrick; G. S. Clarke; Cockerell; Jones; J. Murray; Penrose; G. E. Street, and Digby Wyatt. G. G. Scott and S. Smirk were invited but chose not to participate.

Parliament had authorized funds to purchase the adjoining land north of the National Gallery in 1865 and the First Commissioner of Works William Cowper (1811–1888) felt a competition was necessary to arrive at a design since "special difficulties" in the project required "the assistance of several of the most eminent and experienced architects" to suggest alternative solutions.[139] Each architect was to receive 200 pounds for the expenses of submitting two proposals: the first for an entirely new building and the second for a remodeling of Wilkins's existing building (1832–8).[140]

The program began by identifying the need "to design an architecturally distinguished building fit for 'the finest site in Europe' . . . adapted for the exhibition of pictures," but then followed with vague and contradictory instructions. For example, the building had to accommodate crowds of holidaymakers, and, at the same time, provide for the repose and concentration necessary for the study of art. The architects were given site measurements and information on the space required for administrative tasks and for receiving, cleaning, and storing pictures, but were also told that the size and number of rooms was up to their judgment. Likewise, they were told to use top lighting and later told that the method of lighting was up to them."[141]

The appointed judges objected to the ambiguous instructions and appealed to the First Commissioner, Lord John Manners, for guidance; he responded that their primary concerns should be the suitability of the proposals and elevations submitted.[142] He told them to ignore the issue of cost and to feel free "to refrain from recommending any one of the competing designs for adoption." They complied, declaring no winner based on the fact that the late commissioner of works had drawn up such an impossible set of conditions, that the judges were bound to declare the competition unacceptable.[143]

The contestants sent a letter of protest to Manners, but he maintained there had been no promise of a selection and

supported the judges' decision. On February 28, 1867, the judges announced that although they were not prepared to recommend any of the designs for adoption, they found Barry's design for a new gallery and Murray's design for adapting the existing gallery "as exhibiting the greatest amount of architectural merit." The protest continued for a year and finally, on June 16, 1868, the Office of Works chose Barry to design the new National Gallery, but the project was never completed.

Jones submitted the two required designs, estimating the cost for Design A (an entirely new building) at 375,000 pounds and Design B (an addition to the existing building) at 95,500 pounds. His Design A submission included plans for the ground and first floors, plus an elevation of each exterior. He also provided transverse sections through the center of the proposed building, longitudinal sections through the courts and the galleries, and a comparison of Design A with the existing National Gallery. He added photographs to assist in communicating his proposal. The first showed the existing gallery in Trafalgar Square and the second exhibited his scheme superimposed on the existing building. Reception to this technique was not favorable; the *Times* remarked that "Judging by the photographs, we cannot help asking why should we pull down the old building of Wilkins to make way for the new one of Mr. Jones?" The *Building News* and the *Athenaeum* criticized the incorrect scale depicted in the photos, since Jones's proposed building appeared smaller than the existing structure.[144]

Since the instructions specified only black-and-white illustrations, Jones was unable to render his intention of using colored marble and terra-cotta on the south and east fronts of the building. His scheme divided the main facade into seven sections. Three of these sections projected forward, the two on either side of the central pavilion recessed, and the remaining sections terminated the structure. Jones capped the center section with a rotunda and hipped the remaining roof. Reviews were mixed; One critic objected to the uniform height of both roofs, while another critic praised the exterior ornament. The reporter for the *Athenaeum* disagreed, finding "nothing in its exterior striking for itself or proper to a picture gallery."[145]

Jones stressed simplicity, function, and circulation. His scheme was capable of being built in stages, a good strategy for a large commission dependent upon funding appropriations and long construction schedules. All of the new service and support facilities could be built while the existing gallery was still intact and the absence of hierarchical order to the construction meant that either the exhibition spaces or administrative and services spaces could be built first, another budgetary advantage.

At the ground level, circulation was roundabout, returning visitors to the entrance hall to access the stairs to the galleries above. Administrative facilities were located in the northwest section of the structure in a block measuring 95 by 51 feet, with utilities in the basement below.

A keeper's residence was provided in the center of the north front and places for police and attendants were provided in the corners of the interior courts.

Jones emphasized side lighting for the display spaces on the ground floor as the keynote of his design, explaining that a facade without windows would be like a human face without eyes and would result in an expressionless building. He contended that side lighting offered improved display space, since pictures could be exhibited on screens placed at right angles to the windows and the number and spacing of screens could be changed as required.

In Design B, the addition to the existing building, he left Wilkins's original design as "a record of the state of the art of architecture at the time of its creation," believing that it was as difficult for one architect to alter the work of another as it is to forge handwriting. He followed the same principles in the addition as he had in Design A.[146] Jones confided to his old friend Joseph Bonomi that he had made "a splendid design for the National Gallery," but the critics did not agree.[147]

The critics were impressed, however, with his designs in cast and wrought iron. These include his cast-iron facade for the premises of J. and G. Haywood (cast-iron manufacturers), in Derby in 1865 (Figs. 3.23 and 3.24), and other structures. The Haywood facade, manufactured by James Haywood of the Phoenix Iron Works in Derby, is believed to be the first cast-iron facade erected in Britain.[148] The cost for the materials and the patterns for all of the parts reached 900 pounds. The patterns were capable of being reused to produce fifty or sixty additional facades and, if that happened, the cost would have been averaged over all of the fronts manufactured. Contemporary publications hailed the design as a success and it was published in the *Architect*, but no evidence has been found to show if the facade was reproduced.[149] This scheme was published as an important example of Victorian architecture in J. Mordaunt Crook's *Victorian Architecture: A Visual Anthology*.[150]

Jones designed another unusual work in cast iron manufactured in Derby: an 80-foot long, 40-foot wide and 42-foot high kiosk weighing 180 tons. R. M. Ordish and W. H. Le Feuvre worked out the engineering details and Messrs. Handyside & Company produced the iron work. The patterns cost 550 pounds, but the cost of the iron was only 13 pounds per ton. The total cost of the structure was 3000 pounds and Handyside quoted the ability to deliver its duplicate, ready for erection, to any English port for 2800 pounds. The *Builder* and the *Building News* printed engravings of this "great masterpiece of prefabrication" and agreed that the kiosk was "the most remarkable specimen of ornamental ironwork yet erected" (Fig. 3.25).

Both publications remarked on the bedplates extending 10 feet under the flooring to provide adequate resistance to the strain from the weight of the diagonal lattice roof. The roof was supported on peripheral columns, pro-

Fig. 3.25. Iron kiosk, 1866

viding an open interior. The ribs of the roof sprang diagonally from the top of the columns. The *Builder* noted that the design was not only capable of being reproduced but the 10-foot module permitted new structures of increased size. The *Builder's* reporter praised the ingenious and unprecedented dovetailing of the ribs and said the open arabesque work showed what could be done when cast iron was well executed.[151] When the Indian client who ordered the pavilion defaulted, the structure was erected on the grounds of the Royal Horticultural Society at South Kensington and later offered at auction; the whereabouts today are unknown.

In the cast-iron kiosk the decorative pattern was integral to the structural support, presenting a pure example of decorated construction. Cast iron was used more frequently in conservatories and Jones is known to have designed several for clients, including one for James Mason at Eynsham Hall (considered in the Chapter Four). Jones was able to achieve elegant forms in iron. This may be best demonstrated in a pair of gates manufactured by Andrew Handyside & Co. The carriage gates were 12 feet high and 12 feet wide, with side panels 10 feet high and 6 feet wide (Fig. 3.26). The sensuous foliate curves presage the lyrical forms of Art Nouveau and offer evidence of a new type of graceful ornament inspired by nature.

Jones's experiments with new materials and building techniques resulted in unprecedented structures glowing with light and color. The interiors of his public buildings

offered Londoners, beleaguered by polluted fogs and damp weather, rich environments of grandeur and drama. At the same time, he renounced the meaningless excesses and overwrought embellishments promoted by manufacturers and offered simple and economic solutions atypical of the period. In a time dominated by radical change and uncertainty, Jones created order, beauty, and a new style of architecture.

Fig. 3.26. Iron gates cast by Andrew Handyside & Co., 1867

Pl. 3.1. Design for the Manchester Art Treasures Exhibition Building, 1867. Watercolor, 23¾ x 47½ in.

Pl. 3.2. Elevation, section, and plan of design number 1 for St. Cloud Exhibition Building, Paris, 1860

FOLLOWING PAGES
*Pl. 3.3. Design number 3
for St. Cloud Exhibition
Building, Paris, 1860*

*Pl. 3.4. Interior of design
number 3 for St. Cloud
Exhibition Building,
Paris, 1860*

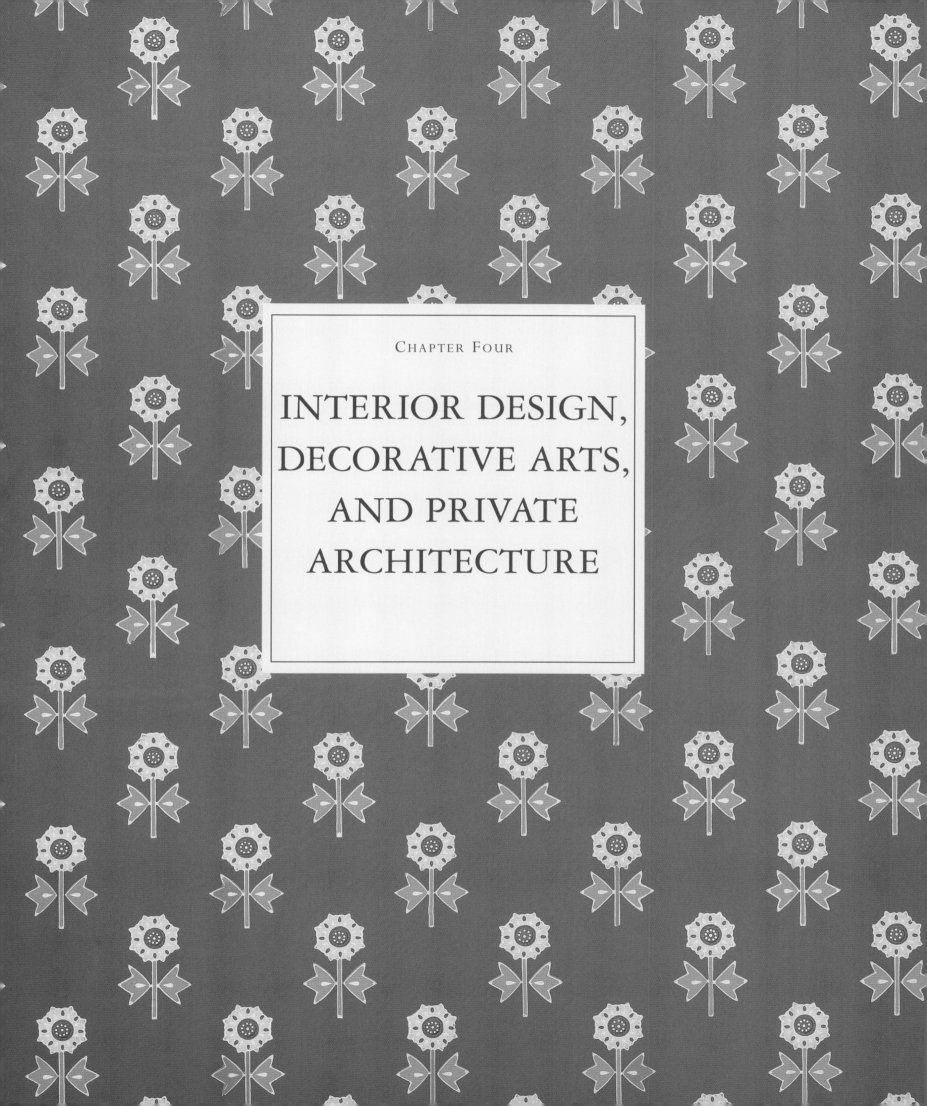

CHAPTER FOUR

INTERIOR DESIGN, DECORATIVE ARTS, AND PRIVATE ARCHITECTURE

Although few records exist for Jones's interior schemes, sufficient drawings and contemporary descriptions remain to demonstrate his method of design and the effects he realized. He outlined his rules to refine taste and improve interior decoration in his lectures in the Museum of Ornamental Art in 1852 and published these lectures as "On the True and False in the Decorative Arts" in 1863. The lectures were addressed to designers, manufacturers, and the public, since Jones understood that the commitment of all three groups was necessary to correct current thinking and introduce art in industrial design. In this chapter, Jones's recommendations are reviewed and examples are included to show his ability to translate his theory into practice.

Since Jones's primary goal was the creation of harmony in the classical sense, he applied the same techniques and principles used in designing textiles and wallpapers to the decoration of interiors. He began by considering the physical properties and intended functions of each space along with the income and status of the client. Even though his clients were prestigious and prosperous, the logic of his recommendations was appropriate for any income level. This was due to the fact that he envisioned the various conditions and treatments of particular spaces and developed rational solutions to achieve the best results. He evaluated materials, colors, and patterns, singly and in combination, and anticipated the viewer's response to the total ensemble. His analysis included advice on wallpapers, textiles, carpets, furniture, and architectural elements.

ELEMENTS OF A DECORATIVE SCHEME:
Wallpaper, Textiles, Furnishings, Carpets, and Curtains

Jones's ideas about wallpaper design were bold and introduced at a time of major change in the production, availability, and patterns of papers. Wallpaper had been used in the seventeenth and eighteenth centuries as an alternative to more expensive tapestries and other textile hangings. Papers had been hand printed in distemper from carved wooden blocks, a slow and laborious process. They were considered, and taxed, as expensive luxury goods, and it became fashionable to install papers in grand houses and public buildings in Europe and America.[1] The invention of machine printing in the nineteenth century introduced several important changes. First, mass production dramatically increased the quantity of wallpapers available and expanded the range of papers, including some lower-priced products. Second, oil paints and other treatments were developed, improving the durability of the papers. Some manufacturers were even able to produce washable or "sanitary" papers. Third, machine production fostered changes in the level of detail and type of designs produced. Greater realism and complexity were possible with engraved metal rollers than with carved wooden blocks. The more affordable papers appealed to a new, prosperous middle class anxious to acquire symbols of status.

The manufacturers offered a wide range of subjects, including historical styles, particularly eighteenth-century Rococo and Gothic, and sixteenth-century strapwork and arabesques. Realistic papers depicting flowers such as cabbage roses or trompe l'oeil imitations of marble or stone were popular. Commemorative and pictorial papers were also available, illustrating political and military events, arts, or amusements, such as sports, or animals and ballet dancers (Fig. 4.3).[2]

Jones rejected these themes, arguing that wall decorations should appear flat, respecting the nature and structure of the wall. He argued that popular perspectives of the Crystal Palace, animals, or fruits were inappropriate, since the realism was illogical: horses did not stand on top of one another and strawberries did not grow on walls. Second, he recommended unobtrusive, two-dimensional patterns as backgrounds for the artwork customarily hung on walls. He thought diapers and conventionalized motifs were best,

Fig. 4.1. "Nipon" textile design in silk tissue for Warner's, 1873

Fig. 4.2. Damask tablecloth woven by Erkskine Beveridge, c. 1851

since they added color, "texture" and vitality through repetitive patterns and the blending of colors to produce a neutralized bloom.

These revolutionary ideas defied the naturalism and eclectic historicism that dominated wallpapers and textiles in the first half of the nineteenth century; the geometric and conventionalized patterns created by Jones and A.W.N. Pugin were the exceptions.[3] Jones's designs differed from Pugin's in color and motif. Pugin represented Christian symbols as a visual stimulus to piety or introduced heraldic emblems to identify a patron or establish a sense of tradition in the Palace of Westminster. In contrast, the morality of Jones's patterns was subtler. He ignored symbolism, creating motifs to produce a rhythmic or decorative effect. His wallpapers contributed one element within a coordinated decorative scheme intended to achieve the repose Jones believed would refine and improve the morality of society; consequently, he stressed replacing the senseless designs typically installed in children's rooms with patterns derived from his principles to begin educating the eye and fostering refined taste at an early age.

Jones and Pugin used primary colors with different objectives. Pugin was reviving the medieval palette and Christian symbolism associated with specific colors (Figs. 4.4 and 4.5). He contrasted figures and grounds to distinguish each emblem; conversely, Jones balanced colors to create neutralized fields of undemonstrative pattern (Pages 70–1).[4] Jones praised the distribution of color in Pugin's designs and in Persian textiles, saying the principles common to both could contribute to a new style of ornamentation. As an initial subscriber to *The Plans, Sections, Elevations, and Details of the Alhambra*, Pugin was exposed to Jones's analysis of color and pattern in the Moorish palace before beginning to design wallpapers.

Jones advocated colors to establish the character and aspect of each room. For example, he recommended green for entrance halls and stairways as a relief for eyes fatigued by the sun's glare and diapers or flocks in dull reds or greens as backgrounds for artwork in studies and dining rooms. Drawing rooms could be any color and could be accented with gilding. The main consideration was the blending of the colors and patterns to achieve a balance.

Jones recognized the futility of trying to banish floral papers in bedrooms and tried to persuade the public to shift to quieter patterns and colors as backgrounds to artwork rather bold displays of realism.

Jones designed papers for Jeffrey & Co.; Townsend, Parker & Co.; and John Trumble & Company. He created a wide variety of patterns with geometrical, conventionalized, and stylized curvilinear motifs. The designs show him to be both a stylistic pioneer and a scholar of ornament, producing original designs as well as timeless frets, rosettes, and arabesques. His diapers of triangles, stars, and geometric shapes must have shocked consumers accustomed to heavy Rococo curves and recognizable images. His abstracted flowers must have been equally disconcerting (Pls. 4.1 and 4.2).[5]

His method of design was also unusual. Jones used gouachelike, flat colors, often applying them in the manner of ancient Persian textile designers. This involved applying small areas of white or gilding to add vibrancy without compromising the flatness of the image. The eye mixes the white with the color beneath and perceives depth without mimicking three dimensions. In the same way, areas of darker color, applied as dots, lines, or outlines, add further interest without modifying the form. In addition, various shades of color enliven some of the images. The patches of color perform two functions. First, they reduce the intensity of a solid color and second, they establish new layers or networks of color and pattern without compromising the flatness of the image (Fig. 4.10).

Jones's abstract patterns and their imitations proliferated by the mid-1850s in both hand- and machine-printed papers.[6] The change in taste was obvious at the London Exhibition of 1862. The realistic excesses of the 1851 wallpapers had disappeared and English firms won most of the prizes.[7]

Fig. 4.3. Unknown English designer, wallpaper illustrating the Crystal Palace, c. 1853–5

Fig. 4.4. A.W.N. Pugin,
Drummond Chapel,
Albury Park, 1846–7

Fig. 4.5. A.W.N. Pugin,
Blessed Sacrament Chapel,
St. Giles, Cheadle, 1846

Manufacturers such as John Trumble & Company were proud to link the name of their firms with Jones. In 1859 Trumble announced they were the "Sole Manufacturers of Mr. Owen Jones's New Designs for 1859."[8] This advertisement marked a significant commercial development: the promotion of a firm's products through association with a major designer. Metford Warner, director of Jeffrey & Co., also began hiring major designers, including Jones, Walter Crane, E. W. Godwin, and others to design wallpaper as art.[9] The designers of the mid-1860s, such as Jones, Christopher Dresser, and William Morris planned their designs to conform to the limitations of wallpaper production; later designers, such as Walter Crane, simply submitted sketches and the manufacturer adapted the design to machine production.

In the 1860s, Jeffrey & Co. printed fifteen sets of paper, including coordinated dadoes, friezes, and filling papers, designed by Jones for the khedive's (viceroy) palace in Cairo. Jones worked over eighteen hours a day for three months designing the patterns, moldings, and furniture for fifteen rooms in the palace built to house the royalty of Europe when they arrived for the opening of the Suez Canal. The manufacturer printed a special a catalogue of the papers for this prestigious commission, but no copy of the catalogue is known today.[10] Jeffrey & Co. also chose a pilaster decoration, by Jones, as the focus of their display in the International Exhibition in Paris in 1867.[11]

By the 1870s, the adoption of geometric designs and flat, abstract patterns was pervasive, and art papers were gaining recognition.[12] Metford Warner even succeeded in convincing the organizers of the London Annual Exhibition of Fine Arts to admit the wallpapers of Bruce J. Talbert, Godwin, Jones, and others as examples of art.[13] The Building News published designs by these architects on October 11, 1872 and May 8, 1874 (Fig. 4.6). The examples show the fashionable tripartite division with complementary patterns for the dado, filling, and frieze.[14] The accompanying article praised Jones for giving impetus to the improvement in wallpaper design and for creating "highly chaste" patterns based on a study of nature. The article also endorsed Jones's position, maintaining that wallpapers should be unobtrusive in design and color and are best in monochrome shades as a backdrop to artwork.

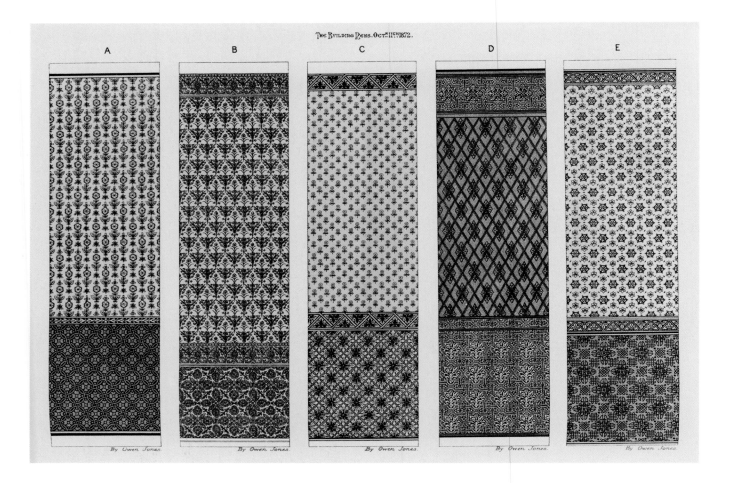

THE BUILDING NEWS. OCT. 11TH 1872.

A   B   C   D   E

By Owen Jones.   By Owen Jones.   By Owen Jones.   By Owen Jones.   By Owen Jones.

Fig. 4.6. Wallpaper designs published in the Building News*, 1872*

Two years later, the *Furniture Gazette* echoed that opinion, crediting Jones for infusing "pure and good taste" into wallpaper design, as with so many other improvements in ornamental art, and found him the person most responsible for positive change.[15] The writer said he had "almost invented a style of paper of his own, in which purely natural forms were entirely discarded." His patterns were "based upon principles of natural growths but totally devoid of imitative character" and "showed great subtlety, ingenuity, and refinement of line; and they kept strictly within the bounds proper to mechanically produced ornament" (Figs. 4.7 and 4.9). The writer noted the extensive printing of Jones's designs in both the best class and in the cheaper papers.

However, the popularity and widespread adoption of Jones's principles did not eliminate wallpaper with naturalistic or commemorative patterns. Leslie Hoskins suggests that one reason for the continued commercial success of realistic papers was economic, since designs by Jones and other reformers were usually handblocked and, therefore, too expensive for most consumers. Hoskins sees the design reformers' greatest contribution as theoretical, rather than practical, but observes that the generation of designers after Jones sought freedom from the restrictive covenants in more organic styles.[16]

Nevertheless, patterns by Jones have been reproduced many times and some are still produced by Cole & Son and Sanderson & Co. Some of the later papers recreate the scale and colors of the original designs, but many were altered to appeal to changes in taste. For example, when Sanderson & Co. acquired the designs of Wm. Woollams & Co., they reproduced Jones's designs in "updated colors."

Textiles

Though Jones's wallpaper designs were exemplary, like C.F.A. Voysey and Morris, Jones preferred textiles to wallpaper. Jones applied the same principles and color philosophy to textile design that he used for wallpapers. Nikolaus Pevsner published a chintz by Jones in *Pioneers of Modern Design* (1936) to illustrate the principles of the English reformers. The reformers obviously agreed, since cuttings of the chintz had been glued in the November 1851 issues of the *Journal of Design and Manufactures* as exemplars of good taste (see page 6).

The *Journal*, begun by Henry Cole in 1849, contained articles on what Pevsner described as the "programme of remarkably sound aesthetics," developed by Cole, Jones, M. Digby Wyatt, and Richard Redgrave. Pevsner noted that

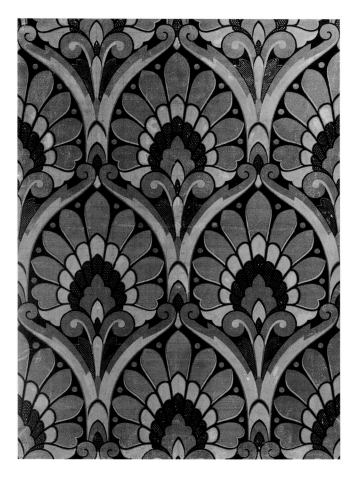

Jones's designs exhibited the principles of the movement, but those of Cole and the other reformers did not. Pevsner quoted the *Journal's* description of the chintz, and it is worth repeating:

The design is, as it ought to be, of a perfectly *flat* unshadowed character. Secondly, the quantities and lines are equally distributed, so as to produce at a distance the appearance of *levelness*. Thirdly, the colours [they are black and maroon on white] produce a neutral tint. And lastly . . . it is quite unobtrusive, which a *covering* of handsomer stuffs [the material was presumably for loose covers of chairs] ought to be. The lines and forms are graceful too, when examined closely.[17]

Documentation shows that Jones designed this chintz as part of the furnishings for 84 Westbourne Terrace, an address in one of the newly fashionable speculative developments in London. Jones's avant-garde chintz would have presented an attractive alternative to the brown calico coverings typically used over upholstery.

The extent of Jones's textile designs is not known and, again, the extensive copying of his style makes it difficult to identify his designs from those of his followers. Records and samples of his designs for hand-woven silks produced by Daniel Walter & Sons, Charles Norris & Co., and Warner & Sons are housed within the Warner Archive.[18] Mary Schoeser,

Fig. 4.10. "Stanhope" textile design in silk tissue, September 1872

Fig. 4.11. "Etruscan" textile design in woven silk for Daniel Walters & Sons, 1870–4

former archivist for the Warner Archive, has published the best research on Jones's silks. Like Pevsner, Schoeser appreciates the textiles as examples of Jones's principles. Schoeser explains that Jones's designs do not copy patterns in *Alhambra* or *The Grammar of Ornament* directly, but express the same principles, particularly with regard to color. Schoeser studied the color instructions and loom samples for each weaving and found that the textiles woven up to Jones's death, and many woven after, conform to his color theory. Schoeser also observed that Jones combined his knowledge of color with an understanding of weaving. Schoeser explained that in a design called "Stanhope" (1872; Fig. 4.10) Jones specified two versions of the design based upon different colorways: one with a black background and the other with a rose ground. The design is produced by blending two colors within one weave structure, indicating that Jones used the weaving process in the creation of patterns and colors (Fig. 4.11). Sue Kerry, another former archivist of the Warner collection, agrees. Kerry says that Jones's designs show his understanding of weaving, since the weaves are integral to his patterns (Figs. 4.11 and 4.12).[19]

A letter from Frank Warner in the Victoria and Albert Museum reports on Jones's painstaking effort to extend one of his designs onto ruled paper and to color in each square. Schoeser explains this process as the crucial technical stage for Jacquard weaving, involving the transfer of the design to grid paper to create a pattern to instruct the Jacquard card cutter (Figs. 4.13 and 4.16). Each square represents the color of the thread to be used on the loom (hand or machine). The design transfer requires a tremendous increase in scale; for example, one 28-inch design by Jones required ruled paper measuring 16 feet by 9 feet 3 inches and containing 5,587,000 squares. Jones and his assistants spent three months transferring the design of "Sunflower" to be woven at the London International Exhibition of 1873.[20]

The Warner Archive contains twenty-six of Jones's silk patterns. Originally, Daniel Walter & Sons produced three of the patterns; Charles Norris & Co. produced at least one called "Floral Spray"; Warner's produced the rest. Some of these designs have been produced in wallpapers and textiles.[21] Other patterns for textiles and wallpapers show similarity, but are not identical: for example, the textile

170 *Chapter Four*

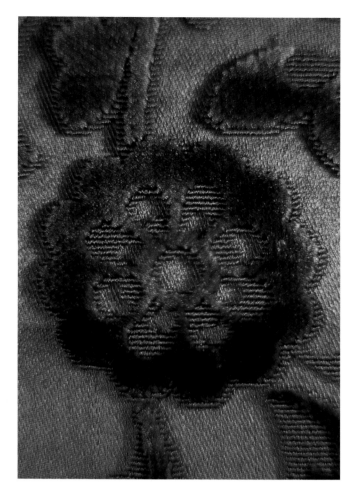 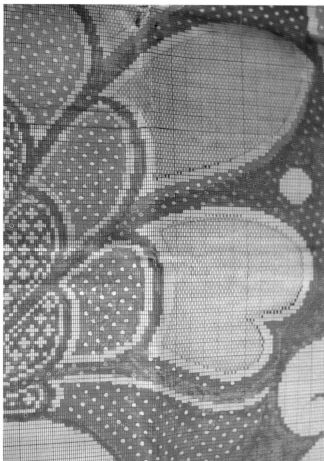

FOLLOWING PAGES

Fig. 4.12. Detail of "Baveno" textile design in silk terry and velvet, c. 1870; woven in 1879 by Warner & Ramm

Fig. 4.13. Grid paper for "Sicily" textile design in silk tissue; first woven by Warner's in 1877

Fig. 4.14. Billiard room for Eynsham Hall (originally believed to be for James Gurney)

"Sicily" resembles a wallpaper pattern in the archives of Sanderson & Co. and Cole & Sons (Figs. 4.7 and 4.13).[22]

Variations in textile production expand the twenty-six known designs in the Warner Archive considerably. These variations include production of one design in different weaves or materials; for example, "Clive" and "Stanhope" have been woven as silk damasks and as silk tissues and "Madras" has been produced in silk and cotton. Another variation occurs when the same pattern is produced in large- and small-scale formats: "Clive," "Italian," and "Marlboro" have been woven in different sizes. Weaving the same pattern in different colors produces another variation, and most of the patterns were woven in several colors (Figs. 2.8, 2.18, pages 70–1, and Pl. 4.8). Variations in color allowed Jones and other designers to keep the pattern consistent in a commission while varying the color to suit the character or purpose of a particular room. An example of this occurs in Jones's decorations for James Gurney, 43 York Terrace, Regent's Park in 1871.[23] Warner's account books show that Jones chose "Sultan" in blue for the billiards room and ordered "Sultan" in black, gold, and orange for the curtains and walls of the drawing room.

The records for the Gurney commission are unusual, since documentation is sparse on the installation of particular patterns. A 1930s photograph shows an 1850s silk by Jones in situ in Sherborne Castle, Dorset, but there is no evidence to indicate Jones's participation in the decoration and no documentation to show when the particular silk was woven or hung. This is not unusual, since many designers specified Jones's patterns, as in the case of Waller & Sons, who chose "Nizam" for the walls of Clarence House, the home of the duke of Edinburgh, four years after Jones's death (Fig. 4.15).[24]

Many of Jones's designs remained popular and some, previously unwoven, were introduced after his death. Benjamin Warner succeeded in producing one of the patterns ("Baveno"; Fig. 4.12 and Pl. 4.6) and, as a result, revived the difficult artistic production of figured velvet. The ruled pattern was finished on February 17, 1879, and the first successful piece was produced two months later.[25] There are still two of Jones's textile designs in the Warner Archive that have never been woven (Pl. 4.5).

The Warner account books prove the continued popularity of his designs. Eleven hundred yards of hand-woven

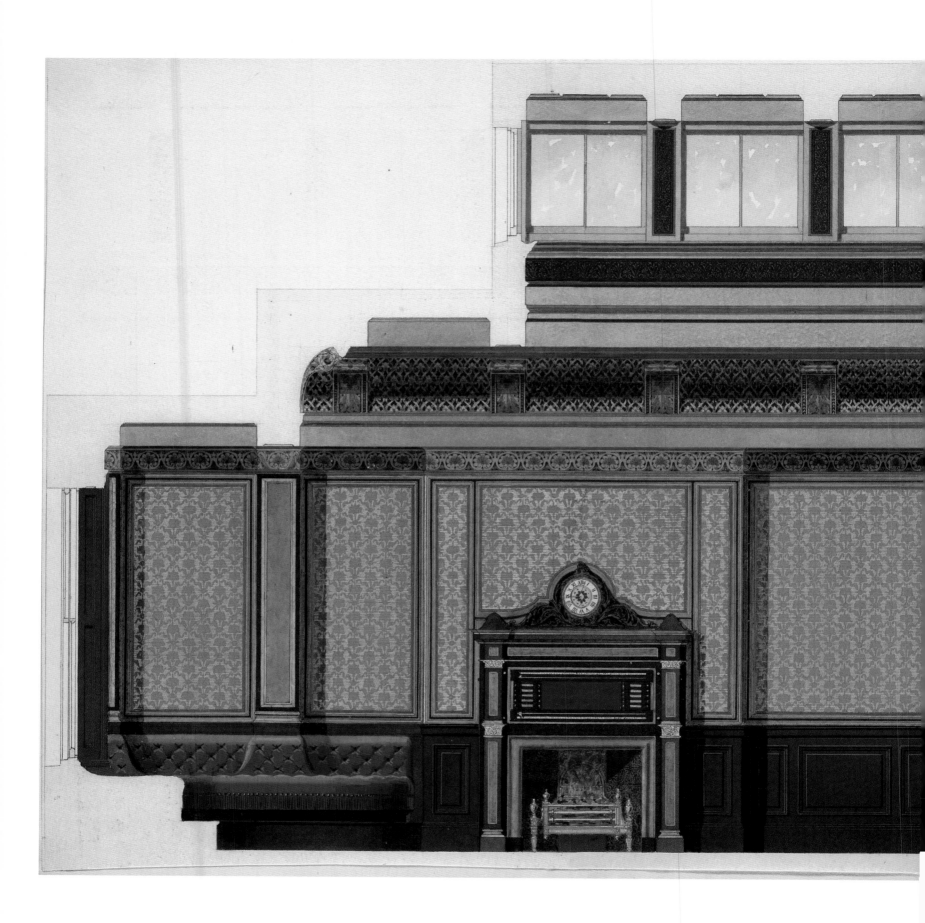

Fig. 4.15. "Nizam" textile design in silk damasquette, August 15, 1870

Fig. 4.16. "Rajah" textile design in silk tissue, August 15, 1870

silks in Jones's patterns were sold in the last three months of 1876, two years after Jones's death. Over 2500 yards were sold in 1877 and over 1100 yards in 1878. The most popular patterns were "Nizam," "Peri," "Culross," and "Sunflower" in 1876; "Argyle," "Nizam," "Sunflower," and "Marlboro" in 1877; and "Sunflower," "Argyle," "Nizam," and "Italian" in 1878.

From 1877 to 1884, over ninety firms placed orders for patterns by Jones and over a third of these firms ordered several times. Purchasers included the major decorating firms of Marsh, Jones & Cribb, Jackson and Graham, Holland and Son, and James Lamb. Prestigious retailers such as Morrison & Co. and Liberty & Co., placed orders as well. Although orders declined over the years, as styles changed, Warner's has produced Jones's patterns (by hand and power weaves, and as prints) for most of the last one hundred and thirty years.[26]

When Jones's works were displayed in his memorial exhibition mounted in 1874, Warner's lent fifteen silks and Jackson and Graham displayed twenty-five. Samples of Jones's wallpapers were also exhibited. The display of these items led one critic normally unsympathetic to Jones's work to recognize "the peculiar excellence" of Jones in designing purely ornamental work for flat surfaces such as walls and ceilings. The critic said Jones revived the taste for, and then supplied, flat conventional ornament, "introducing nothing out of keeping with the material employed, or the use to which it was to be put" and was the person chiefly responsible for dispelling sprawling, realistic patterns and introducing the "superior beauty and fitness of smaller and more geometrically constructed designs."[27]

The design motifs vary, but most of the patterns combine abstracted flowers or foliation with elegant scrolls. Good examples of conventionalized flowers and foliation occur in "Athens," "Baveno," "Italian," "Sunflower," and "Sutherland." Examples of elegant scrolls, reminiscent of Italian Renaissance patterns appear in "Stanhope," "Rajah" (Fig. 4.16), "Cynose," and "Cleopatra." Several patterns, such as "Clive," "Delhi," and "Nipon" offer small diapers. Examination of the patterns again reveals Jones's technique of reusing the same motif but varying the design in scale, level of detail, background, or color, to produce a new pattern.

Jones also designed table linens for Erkskine Beveridge & Co. of Dunfermline, Scotland, but little documentation of the work survives. A history of the firm published in 1928 stressed the importance of Jones's designs to the company. Beveridge displayed at least three damask tablecloths woven to Jones's designs in the Great Exhibition of 1851.[28] Digby Wyatt published another of Jones's designs executed by Beveridge's in *Industrial Arts of the Nineteenth Century*. Each of the patterns shows a central motif and a corresponding border. The motifs include the same type of abstracted foliage and arabesques found in Jones's designs in other media.

Jones followed his remarks on wallhangings in "On the True and False in the Decorative Arts" with guidelines for furniture, window coverings, and carpets. His first rule maintained that furniture should be appropriate to its function and place. He said "that which is appropriate in a mansion would be misplaced in a cottage"; likewise, furniture designed for a gentleman's study would not suit a lady's drawing room.

Although it would be several decades before the famous phrase "form follows function" was articulated, Jones anticipated the idea with the words "the use [of furniture], in all cases, should define the form." He rejected capricious or superfluous ornament. If carving was desired, light-colored woods should be chosen, since he believed dark woods were shown to best advantage through form and outline.[29] He counseled that furniture should be selected with an eye to the future. The buyer should consider how long each piece would continue to have appeal and not become tedious through over-elaboration.

Jones praised a bookcase by Pugin as a good example of furniture designed according to correct principles. Although Jones disapproved of the Gothic motifs, he approved of the way the ornament was used to enhance the construction of the piece and the way each element, including locks and hinges, contributed to the overall scheme. Jones also showed drawings of ancient Greek, Assyrian, and Egyptian furniture in his lectures to show that the pieces had been designed according to function.

Jones followed the same principles in designing furniture for Alfred Morrison, a major nineteenth-century collector and patron of the decorative arts. Jones's first commission for Morrison was an addition to Fonthill House, Wiltshire, built by James Morrison, Alfred's father, on the site of Beckford's Fonthill Splendens. After Alfred inherited Fonthill, Jones designed new staircases, a drawing room, and an addition to the country estate to accommodate Morrison's collection of Chinese porcelain and enamels. Jones designed ebony-veneered cases with glass doors at the top to display the objects (Fig. 4.17). He decorated the panel doors at the bottom with a stylized monogram. The conventionalized foliage surrounding the initials "A. M." (Fig. 4.18) and the delicate inlay of the cabinets were repeated in the 11-foot-high and 6-foot-8-inch-wide fireplace surround. The intricate details were incised into the ebonized wood and then blocks of ivory were inserted and shaped by hand. Both pieces demonstrate Jones's method of combining classical elements with stylized foliate inlay to produce a new style of ornament. The use of ebonized wood, straight lines, and slender turned supports are typical characteristics of the art furniture introduced in the 1860s by Jones and other designers intent on counteracting ill-conceived mass-production. Some of the designers of art furniture, such as T. E. Colcutt, incorporated painted

Fig. 4.17. Upright case of ebony inlaid with ivory for Alfred Morrison's Fonthill House; fabricated by Jackson & Graham, 1863

Fig. 4.18. Detail of Alfred Morrison monogram inlaid in ivory in ebony case (above), 1863

Fig. 4.19. Marquetry on fireplace in Alfred Morrison's residence at 16 Carlton House Terrace, 1865

Fig. 4.20. Detail of chair for Alfred Morrison's residence at 16 Carlton House Terrace, 1865

panels in their work, but Jones preferred contrasting woods and inlaid patterns. At Fonthill, Preston Hall, and other commissions, Jones set ivory inlay in ebonized wood; in other instances, he contrasted ebony with lighter colored woods (Figs. 4.25 and 4.26). (Jones remodeled the hall, dining room, and drawing room of Preston Hall, Aylesford, Kent, for Henry Arthur Brassey, third son of Thomas Brassey, the railroad magnate.)

Jackson and Graham, the prestigious London decorators and full-service firm, made the pieces for Fonthill and Jones's other furniture. The firm is significant in British decorative arts for innovations in the design and quality of furniture manufacture. They were the first high-style cabinetmakers to employ in-house designers and hired skilled craftsmen and designers from all over Europe, including the Frenchman Eugène Prignot, whose design for a large cabinet won an award for the company at the Paris Exhibition of 1855. They were also first in installing steam-powered saws and other machinery to prepare woods for assembly and hand finishing. By the 1860s, their workforce fluctuated between six hundred and one thousand employees.

Jackson and Graham produced furniture from designs by Dresser, Bruce Talbert, and Charles Eastlake. Their most significant collaboration, however, was with Jones. Several facts underscore the importance of their relationship. First, the firm paid their chief designer about 700 pounds per year in the 1870s, but paid Jones commissions of 1000–1500 pounds. Second, one of the partners, Philip

Graham, chief designer in the 1860s and 1870s, worked closely with Jones on major commissions.[30] Third, the firm exhibited Jones's designs in numerous international and regional exhibitions and, finally, Jones redesigned the firm's Oxford Street premises in 1869, a clear and public statement of their association (Figs. 3.19 and 3.20).

The ability to supply all household items, in addition to high-quality furniture, was important to Jones. His commissions were total artistic schemes with every element emanating from his designs. He worked closely with manufacturers and often supervised installations. Surviving furniture designed for Morrison for his residence at 16 Carlton House Terrace, London, and for James Mason for Eynsham Hall, indicates the level of excellence achieved through Jones's collaboration with Jackson and Graham.

Alfred Morrison increased an inheritance worth several million pounds through his management of Morrison and Dillon, the first department store in London. Morrison spent some of his wealth amassing major collections of Roman glass and Chinese artifacts, including "many of the finest objects from the Summer Palace at Pekin."[31] He was also an important contemporary patron, commissioning works from the best artisans to rival the achievements of the past and dispel the notion that the ability to produce great art and craft had been lost. His choice of Jones and Jackson and Graham to create the interiors for his London townhouse and country estate underscores their superior artistry. Others agreed; Jackson and Graham entered an

Fig. 4.21. Half-tester bed, 1860

upright case and other furnishings from Fonthill in the Paris Exhibition of 1867, London in 1871, and in Vienna in 1873.[32] These submissions won awards for the firm's craftsmanship and gold medals to Jones for design in 1867 and 1873.[33]

Jones also designed furniture for Morrison's London townhouse at 16 Carlton House Terrace (1865–9). Morrison's furniture was dispersed after his death, but a table and two chairs have been linked to this commission since the woods and inlays of the furniture match the woodwork at the house (Figs. 4.19, 4.20, and Pls. 4.9–4.11) and fit descriptions printed in the nineteenth century. These descriptions reveal disagreements over the merits of the pieces. While the *Furniture Gazette* extolled the chairs' "determinate and well-considered adaptation to *use*," Dresser criticized the "over elaborate inlay" and said the furniture appeared "to have been designed for the inlay, and not first constructed, and then the constructed wood decorated."[34] Another critic agreed, saying the chairs and cabinets were "beautiful specimens of workmanship," but the inlay obscured and weakened the constructive lines of the pieces. A third critic disagreed, maintaining that each chair was as philosophical as it was beautifully constructed.[35]

The *Journal of the Society of Arts* gave the best review, saying the furniture "marks a bold departure from conventional forms . . . . It is here amply demonstrated that a bedstead need not be a hideous object; and the quaint form of the chairs and

Fig. 4.22. Table for Eynsham Hall, 1870s

their superb inlaying work amply prove that this age might—if it really were as strong as it pretends to be—initiate, as other ages have done, a clear and distinctive style of decoration entirely and completely its own"[36] (see Fig. 4.21).

When the Morrison pieces are compared with the furniture for Eynsham Hall, variations in form and decoration reveal Jones's intent to design for the character and status of each patron. The table for Morrison, the art patron, is a masterwork with (Pls. 4.10–4.12) inlays of contrasting woods in circular bands and a conventionalized foliate pattern in the center; in contrast, the table for the scientist

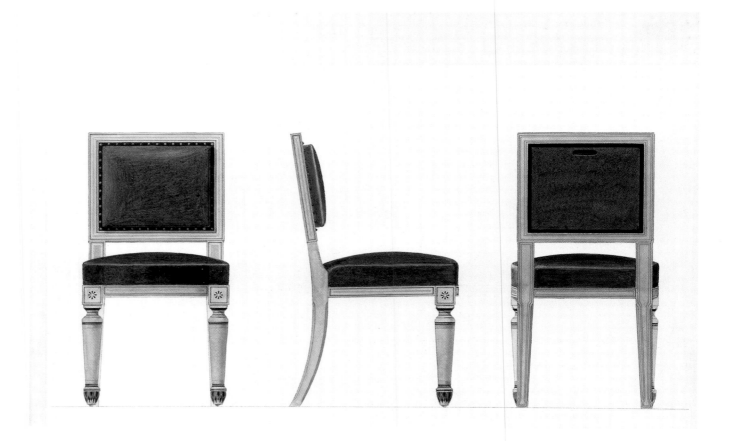

James Mason (Fig. 4.22), is simpler and is distinguished by the appeal of fine wood, expert craftsmanship, and a streamlined design highlighted with inlays in various woods and colors.

A comparison of the chairs for these commissions presents the same differences. The Morrison chairs establish a sophisticated André-Charles Boulle-like (1642–1732) reverse of pattern and materials. The detailed marquetry patterns are replaced in the Eynsham chairs with contrasting woods inlaid to emphasize the streamlined forms of the pieces. Other furniture from Eynsham shows simple, functional pieces, with the beauty of the wood providing the decoration (Figs. 4.24). These pieces look forward to the plain lines and natural woods of Arts-and-Crafts and modern furniture, rather than conforming to the overwrought forms of contemporary High Victorian models. While the Eynsham pieces look forward, Jones's formal pieces follow the severe architectural forms in the tradition of Boulle, George Bullock, and Pugin (Figs. 4.23, 4.25, and 4.26).[37] Critics observed a classic chasteness and reserve in the form, construction, and ornamentation of Jones's pieces. This style and spirit continues in the artistic furniture of the Aesthetic Movement represented in works by James Lamb.

Although few pieces of Jones's furniture are known today, critics writing at the time of his death described his furniture pieces as "too numerous to mention, but show the eagerness with which the artist's designs were sought."

They praised his designs and collaboration with Jackson & Graham for producing perfect specimens of decoration and manufacture. The furniture for Morrison and Mason exhibited after his death was recommended for study for anyone interested in producing superior work.[38]

Carpets represented another opportunity for decoration, and Jones offered guidelines on the color, pattern, and construction of carpets. He recommended dark colors to provide a background for furniture. He condemned machine-printed carpets in realistic patterns as the proliferation of evil and countered with designs showing great variety in color and pattern. Again, he produced centralized schemes and evenly distributed patterns framed with borders in the colors of the central motif or field of pattern (Pl. 4.18).

Dresser praised the neutrality of Jones's carpets, describing their background nature and all-over surfaces as "almost perfect." As with the ceilings, he said the carpets contained characteristics common to Indian, Persian, and Moorish qualities, but the patterns were original to Jones. He praised Jones for having the ability to add his own creativity to his extensive knowledge of the works of other nations and produce new designs.[39]

Jones prepared full-scale drawings of each design, indicating the position of each color. Manufacturers who wove the designs included Jackson and Graham, Woodward, Grosvenor & Co., and Templeton's. Several of these firms entered carpets designed by Jones in major exhibitions; for

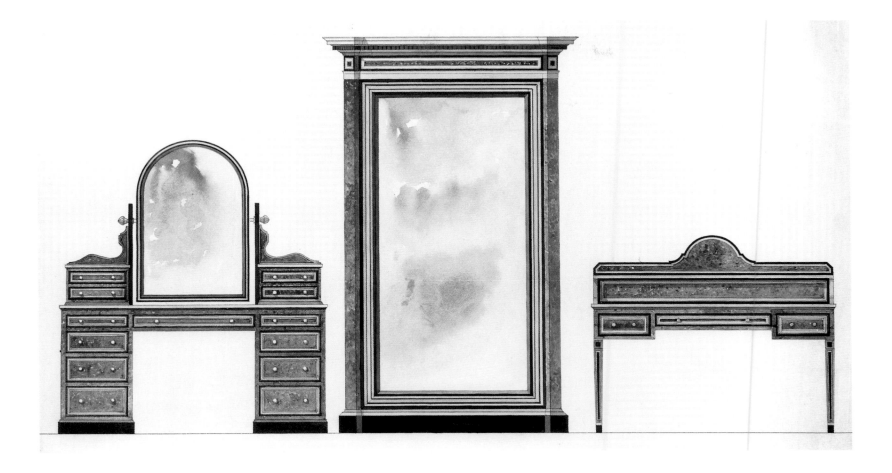

example, a carpet for Fonthill was displayed in the 1867 Paris Exhibition. The carpet was described as "a work of rare excellence" and "the finest specimen of that fabric [Axminster] ever manufactured," involving 256 points [or separate tufts of wool] per inch.[40]

Jackson and Graham, Woodward, and Grosvenor & Co. displayed six carpets by Jones in the 1871 exhibition. The types of carpet varied; there were two Brussels, one Patent Axminster, two velvet piles, and two Tournay velvets.

Curtains and Furniture Coverings

In "The True and False in the Decorative Arts," Jones continued by discussing the relationship of furniture to curtains and furniture coverings. In a surprising statement, he said the curtains were the most important feature in a room, since they contributed the greatest breadth to the general effect of a room. He believed the choice of color was critical, since the mass of color in the curtains gave tone to the color scheme.

He explained that it was acceptable for the curtains to match the color of the walls or provide a complete contrast. He observed that the common practice of matching the color of the curtains to the furniture was not advisable, when the amount of color provided by the curtains and furniture would be excessive. He recommended furniture cov-

erings darker than the curtains, for several reasons: the curtains were seen against the light and their color was deepened in the shades of the folds. In contrast, the furniture was lit directly and, therefore, light colors gave too much prominence to furniture.

He maintained that curtains should always be treated simply, but when the wall treatment was subdued, the curtains could be richer. He cautioned that the effect of patterns needed to be considered with the fabric hanging in folds, and extended. Shaded patterns, strong horizontals, and bouquets of natural flowers would appear broken by the folds and should be avoided. He condemned the fashion of using flowered chintz for curtains and bed linens, another chintz for the walls, and a floral carpet. While some people thought this arrangement harmonious, he found it wearisome and monotonous. He explained that harmony was not the repetition of one note, but an orderly combination of three different notes. He recommended diaper patterns or, with velvets, plain colors to hang in rich folds (Pl. 4.13).

He also recommended borders to give the curtains a finished appearance. For plain fabrics, a second border or trim could be added. Few drawings exist to show Jones's curtains; one, however, survives from a display in the 1876 Centennial Exhibition (Pl. 4.14).[41] Jones believed curtains were best suspended on rings from brass poles, since this typified his "law of decorating the useful" and allowed

Fig. 4.24. Designs for a suite of burr-wood bedroom furniture, n.d

Fig. 4.25. Ebony-and-ivory cabinet attributed to Owen Jones, 1870s

light to reach the ceiling. He rejected elaborate cornices and drapery treatments as ugly dust catchers and a waste of money. In the same way, he rejected valances of fringe and said any valances should be kept simple.

He believed furniture coverings should be the most subdued color and furnishing in a room. He preferred small diapers in damask for pattern and insisted that dark colors be used with dark woods, lighter fabrics with light-color woods. When chintz coverings were used to protect formal fabrics, the pattern chosen should produce a quiet neutral tint to complement the repose of the room.

DECORATIVE SCHEMES AND PRIVATE ARCHITECTURE COMMISSIONS

Jones also offered guidelines on how to bring all of the furnishings together to achieve character and harmony in a decorative scheme. When this was successful, a visitor would gain an immediate impression of the station, taste, and nature of the owner. Interest would grow from one room to the next through gradual transitions in color and pattern, not dramatic shifts in style.

He advised that halls and staircases should be cool and refreshing. He warned against simulations of marble and other attempts at grandeur beyond the owner's finances. He maintained that dining rooms, considered part of the male province, should be formal and restrained. The furniture should be simple, chosen for functionality and convenience, rather than grandeur. Likewise, the walls were to be quiet and subdued, with full curtains in heavy materials such as Utrecht velvet. Dining rooms should not double as picture galleries and if any pictures were displayed, "they should be very few and very good." The best picture should be placed above the fireplace mantel, with the chimneypiece below simply carved in dark marble. The decoration of the ceiling was an allowable exception, since guests could enjoy the decoration while seated at the table.

Drawing rooms were different; infinite variety was possible, depending on the purse of the patron and the physical characteristics of the room. Jones rejected the elaborate panel-papers, white-and-gold woodwork, and painted walls fashionable at the time and recommended elegant diapers in textiles or paper instead. He repeated his earlier points on the importance of flatness in wall treatments and the blending of colors to achieve a neutralized bloom. He strongly objected to overloading drawing rooms with furniture and ornaments. He argued that furniture should be restricted to necessary pieces and ornaments should be "few and precious."[42]

The most elaborate decoration in the room was placed on the ceiling. Jones designed two types of ceiling decoration framed with borders; these include centralized schemes and all-over patterns. The first type focuses attention on the cen-

Fig. 4.26. Detail of ebony-and-ivory cabinet (facing page)

tral motif with secondary motifs in the corners and, often, in the center of the sides (Pl. 4.15). Many of these designs were rendered in pale blue with details accented in red or gilding. These delicate schemes are reminiscent of geometrical motifs found in the Middle East and in classical arrangements. The same style of graceful decoration is found in Jones's carpets, stationery items, and illuminated texts.

The second type displays an evenly distributed pattern. These arrangements were effective in large spaces where a centralized pattern with borders would have left large blank areas in the ceiling. Jones also introduced all-over patterns when he desired a particularly rich decorative effect. He sometimes introduced decorative coffers to subdivide the space and designed ventilating panels as functional and decorative, but unobtrusive, elements within the scheme. These techniques provided the drama and innovative lighting schemes for Osler's, the Crystal Palace Bazaar, and St. James's Hall. The distributed ceiling designs appear in the designs for 16 Carlton House Terrace, Preston Hall, and Eynsham Hall.

It is important to note that Jones popularized ceiling decoration in Britain. When he introduced his ceiling elaboration in the 1840s, there was opposition, but Dresser tells us that by 1874 many embraced it. Dresser emphasized the originality of Jones's designs. He said the designs demonstrated Jones's knowledge of Moorish art in new patterns. Other critics contrasted the delicate coloring in Jones's schemes to the heavy-handed coloring of other designers.

In his third Marlborough House lecture Jones asked his audience to remember the shock experienced when a wallpaper or carpet selected from a small sample was installed in quantity or how incongruous their home appeared when all of their purchases were assembled. He explained that these problems were eliminated when the consumer developed the ability to envision general effects, but this talent of "seeing with the mind," required extensive study. Jones acknowledged that a few people exhibited good "taste" based on instinct and repeated observations of refined design, but their taste was limited if they did not also have the ability to delineate form. Jones explained that drawing facilitated the detection of pertinent details and the capacity to understand and evaluate observed elements. Without this skill, the public was inexperienced at observation and unable to differentiate between good and bad design, but if the public were to become educated in design, artists and manufacturers would respond to the improved change in taste.

It's important to note that Jones's residential clients do not reflect the general public; instead, they present an interesting group of Victorians successful in science, business, and the arts. Most demonstrated unusual intellect, an intense work ethic, and progressive ideals. These attributes gave them the ability to appreciate the genius of Jones and the confidence to choose an avant-garde architect whose work met the same high standards they set for themselves. In return, Jones created individualized interiors reflective

Fig. 4.27. North entrance of Kensington Palace Gardens, London, 1845

of their interests and personalities. Each commission was a total artistic environment reflecting his principles.

22 Arlington Street, Piccadilly

Newspaper reports and personal descriptions provide the only access to Jones's early schemes. Fortunately, the originality and quality of his designs, and the prestige of many of his clients, often attracted the interest of the press. This is the case with his work for John H. Somerset, seventh duke of Beaufort, a patron of the arts and member of the House of Lords. Beaufort purchased 22 Arlington Street, Piccadilly, in 1840 and engaged Jones to redecorate the interior. The townhouse had been designed a century earlier (1740) by William Kent for Prime Minister Henry Pelham.

Jones developed an unusually varied scheme, adopting a different style to provide a unique character for each room. He chose formal Renaissance-derived motifs, appropriate for the townhouse of a statesman, for the entrance hall. Pompeian decoration made a colorful display in the banqueting room. Edward Latilla painted these rooms with his own invention, a silica-based fresco paint called "encaustic." One critic praised the decoration, particularly the "most gorgeous character" of the Henry IV–style drawing room with its bright blue walls displaying fleur de lis and the story of Mary, Queen of Scots in gold and silver.[43]

Later Jones would condemn interiors composed of different styles in each room. Before then, the subsequent owner of Beaufort House, the eleventh duke of Hamilton, replaced Jones's scheme with decoration modeled on Kent's work at 44 Berkeley Square. As a result, the twentieth-century historians Nikolaus Pevsner and E. Beresford Chancellor who describe Jones's work in 22 Arlington Street are incorrect, since none of his work survived.[44]

Kensington Palace Gardens

While the seventh duke of Beaufort chose historic Arlington Street for his town residence, many wealthy Londoners were moving to the new suburbs and terraced housing being built in the West End. These developments were a by-product of the astonishing growth in industry and trade that resulted in more individuals gaining wealth and status from earned income than from inheritance. Many of the nouveaux riches wanted to enjoy their elevated status but were uncomfortable about moving into areas previously reserved for the aristocracy.[45] Speculators recognized this situation as an opportunity to make a profit by developing single-class residential areas to accommodate the new middle and upper classes. By mid-century, the proliferation and stratification of these developments meant that a person's street address communicated economic and social standing along with geographical location. Jones produced designs for several of the residential developments, including one of the most ambitious projects in Kensington Palace Gardens.

The idea for this scheme originated in 1838 when a committee appointed to review the management of the royal gardens recommended replacing several kitchen gardens with one large plot at Frogmore and financing the development of this land and other gardens by leasing the former grounds as building lots; the kitchen gardens at Kensington Palace were to be part of this scheme. The plan transformed the original gardens, part of the "wilderness" laid out by Queen Anne, and some undeveloped land near Kensington Palace, into thirty-three generous lots of approximately an acre, aligned along a private road. The new road, 70 feet wide and over one-half-mile long would be named the Queen's Road (now Kensington Palace Gardens) and would connect Bayswater Road on the north with Kensington High Street on the south (Figs. 4.27 and 4.28).

The joint surveyors to the Land Revenue Office Department, James Pennethorne and Thomas Chawner, submitted the final plan in January 1842. The scheme established the "select and private" character of the area by placing gates and lodges with liveried attendants at both entrances to the new road.[46] The concept of an exclusive neighborhood adjacent to the palace appealed to the commissioners, who thought the cloister would appeal to "the cream of would-be purchasers and produce something above the normal villa average" in revenues.[47]

A difficult economy and depressed building market may have contributed to the fact that only three lots had been leased by September 1843, when John Marriott Blashfield of Upper Stamford Street, Blackfriars, made a liberal offer to lease at least twenty of the lots at a rent not to exceed 1870 pounds per year. Blashfield was a partner in the large firm of Wyatt and Parker, manufacturers of cement, scagliola, and mosaic pavements. He had no experience as a developer but Chawner and Pennethorne recommended acceptance of his offer, since they feared that it would take at least three years to let the plots individually and the rents received would not surpass the graduated scale proposed by Blashfield. In addition, Blashfield's offer exceeded the minimum rental desired on the twenty plots by more than 200 pounds per year.

Blashfield agreed to build twenty-one houses at a cost of over 63,000 pounds during the next five years. He also agreed that six houses would be roofed within the first year and a total of thirteen houses would be built within the first three years. The exteriors were to be faced with cement colored and jointed to imitate stone or with bricks dressed with stone or cement.[48] In addition, each of the plots had to be landscaped and surrounded by a short wall topped with an iron railing and accessed through iron gates. Finally, all designs had to be submitted to the commissioners for approval. In exchange, Blashfield could sell the gravel he excavated in building the foundations and would only pay "a peppercorn" in rent the first year.

Blashfield hired Owen Jones as architect-agent for the project and accepted designs for the projected houses by Jones and others. Six houses were started in 1844 and an additional six lots were sold in 1845. On January 31, 1846, the *Illustrated London News* described the progress as a "Metropolitan Improvement," observing that:

The quaint red barracks at Kensington have been recently removed, together with Grapes public-house, to complete the new and magnificent road now forming from Bayswater to High Street, Kensington. The houses building upon this site, and which overlook Kensington Gardens, are in the first style of architecture. Two mansions are already finished; one in the Byzantine character [Jones's design for number 8], which, although novel to this country, appears to be more particularly suited to our climate and domestic comforts than most others. There are likewise four magnificent stone buildings of Italian character, one of which stands upon a space of an acre and a half of ground. A lodge in the same correct style as that at the north end is to be erected at the Bayswater entrance; and there seems to be a general feeling that this road, from its great breadth, imposing aspect, and the correct taste displayed throughout, bids fair to become a most aristocratic neighborhood. It has, likewise, a very beautiful appearance at night, from the large size of the gas lamps, and their close approximation to each other.[49]

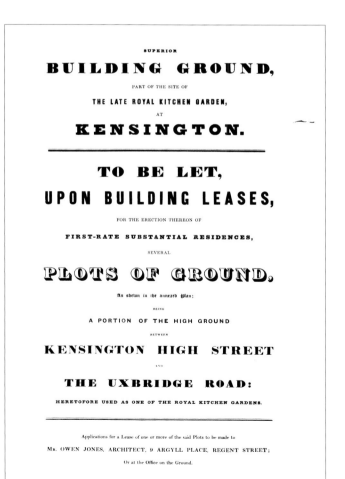

Fig. 4.28. Advertisement for Kensington Palace Gardens, London, c. 1844

Fig. 4.29. Garden facade of 8 Kensington Palace Gardens, London, 1843; demolished 1961

The cost and location of the new properties and the acute economic situation reduced the number of potential buyers so that by 1847, only one house sold. This house, 24 Kensington Palace Gardens, cost 9000 pounds to build but sold well below its estimated value at a price of 3400 pounds.

Jones's first design in Kensington Palace Gardens was number 8, a substantial three-story, five-bay Italianate villa with a four-story tower on the garden facade (Fig. 4.29). The symmetrical front elevation (Fig. 4.30) embodied two projecting bays flanking a three-bay entrance loggia. The roof of the loggia served as a first-floor balcony and combined with the other first-floor balconies to create a horizontal emphasis. The garden facade repeated the recessed bay and balcony combination. Jones chose the round-headed windows, popularized by Charles Barry, for the entrance, loggia, first-floor openings and the third- and fourth-story tower windows. He added a small cusp above the side arches and decorated the spandrels in the central arcade. The third story had new double-sash windows. A frieze, cornice, pierced parapet, and two extraordinarily tall chimneys completed the front facade. A terrace extended the full length of the garden facade, providing a gracious outdoor space and access to the garden.

While the form of the house is based upon the plan of an Italian villa, the ornament derives from several sources, showing Jones's distinctive technique of blending various motifs to form a unique style of decoration. The geometrically patterned parapets and cusps suggest Middle Eastern influence, while the cornice, pilasters, obelisks, urns, and acanthus leaves are classical. Italianate elements are evident in the brackets and the corbels of the stringcourse and tower. In addition, stylized natural elements are introduced around the windows, on the arcade, and in the frieze.

On October 13, 1843, Chawner and Pennethorne reviewed the plans and informed the commissioners that:

. . . the design will probably produce an appearance equal to that originally intended for this site and we do not feel that we ought to object to the peculiarity of the proposed Moresque enrichments though hitherto not much adopted in this country.[50]

The commissioners forwarded these observations to Blashfield who responded:

The Moresque ornament of the windows might be removed (probably with advantage) by a stroke of the pencil the design would then be strictly Italian and as *I wish*. The chimney stack at the angle of the tower does not at all please me and I object-

Fig. 4.30. Front facade of 8 Kensington Palace Gardens, London, showing later addition on the right

ed to it at first but Mr. Owen Jones feared having a tower without the chimney so managed we should have all the rooms smokey or require trine tunnels to them as they have at Trentham Hall where Mr. Barry has erected a similar tower.[51]

The fact that the tower and the cusps were not changed to please the commissioners and the developer was probably, as Mark Girouard surmises, the result of Jones's determination.[52]

The commissioners described Jones's designs for the entrance gates, lamps, and palisading, as having been:

. . . designed in the Moresque style to correspond with the house and shews as if intended for four plots. We understand Mr. Blashfield wishes to apply it to all the plots let to him on both sides of the Queen's Road intending to produce an effect by its extent, massiveness, and its peculiarity of design. We think the effect will be good of making the iron railing altogether of one pattern, and the design submitted cannot fail to produce a rich effect though . . . not altogether in accordance with hitherto approved models.[53]

The iron railing was not built; a design by Wyatt and Brandon was erected instead.

While the removal of cusps over the windows and the substitution of balustrades for pierced pararpets would have easily converted the exterior into a classical arrangement, the interior was a different matter. The ground floor's decoration was lavish and clearly derived from Jones's appreciation and study of the Alhambra. Brightly colored tiles appeared in the dadoes and floor of the entrance hall, the central stairs, and on the exterior terrace. The installation of tiles on the terrace was unusual, but won praise for presenting a lively and pleasing effect.[54] A large skylight over the central stair filled with multicolored glass panes created another unique and bright effect.[55] "Elaborate plaster work in Moorish designs" appeared on the walls and ceilings of some of the ground-floor rooms and one room in the basement. The ceilings were decorated with intricate and delicate designs (Fig. 4.31).

The ground-floor plan included a long vestibule, five large rooms and a conservatory. The conservatory, at the rear, joined an octagonal room with refined decoration. The octagonal area probably functioned as a morning room (Fig. 4.34). The room on the opposite corner was most likely a gentleman's study, since a corridor and outside entrance provided access enabling the owner to conduct business

Fig. 4.31. Ceiling of
8 Kensington Palace
Gardens, London, 1843

separate from the rest of the household. Presumably the other rooms served as a dining room, library, and drawing room and the finished room below the conservatory was a smoking or billiards room. After Prince Albert's introduction of smoking at court, smoking gained acceptance, but was generally restricted to specific rooms, frequently located in basements.[56] Jones is often credited with popularizing smoking and billiards rooms; this reputation may stem from this well-known commission.

The scheme for 24 Kensington Palace Gardens was submitted on August 26, 1845, and approved by Pennethorne two days later. Pennethorne thought the house would be "large, handsome, and well disposed," and he did not object to the picturesque Moresque style depicted.[57] The plans and elevations of number 24 differ from number 8 (Figs. 4.34 and 4.35). Number 24 adopts a palazzo arrangement of three stories over a basement. A portico provides the central focus and a balcony creates a strong horizontal emphasis on the symmetrical facade. Classical horizontality is also represented in the parapets, cornices, and stringcourses.

The ornament is eclectic, including orbs, blind arcades, geometric patterns, slightly pointed window surrounds, and onion domes, which are considered classical, Romanesque, Islamic, Gothic, and Moresque, respectively. Innovations occur in the floral patterns of the balcony brackets and the capitals of the second-floor pilasters that presage the fluidity of Art Nouveau. Michael Darby compares the capitals to those in the Alhambra:

Jones evolves his by bringing the archivolt to the top of the pilaster, and then turning it back on itself, at the same time splitting the end into three stylized leaves. Thus, the capital grows into the archivolt; similarly the brackets supporting the balcony seem to grow upwards, and the huge scale of the leaf-life forms which decorate them expresses this structural force. Jones's ornament is no longer a simple veneer as it had appeared at no. 8 where the pretty floral designs did no more than frame a detail, or break the monotony of a large expanse of wall, it now . . . helps to animate the composition by expressing the tensions within it.[58]

The interior is also markedly different from number 8. The wide vestibule across the front of number 8 is replaced by a long, narrow entry, separating the front rooms into two sections. The reception area joins a perpendicular corridor linking the exterior entrances on either side of the house and dividing the ground floor into front and rear sections. The front left quarter contained a study and adjoining room only accessible from this central passage. The exclusivity of this arrangement suggests an office for the owner to meet with tradesmen. The remainder of the ground floor is taken up with formal rooms for entertaining: the dining room and two large drawing rooms with terraces.

Jones set the scale, price range, and demeanor for the private enclave of Kensington Palace Gardens with his designs

for numbers 8 and 24. Prominent architects, including Phillip Hardwick, Sydney Smirke, and Barry, followed his lead, building "private mansions . . . laid out and finished up in a superior style."[59] Despite this approval, only slightly more than a third of the properties had been built on and occupied by 1851, when the situation changed dramatically; within three years, all of the houses were occupied and all of the sites were taken. Mark Girouard explains the changed circumstances, observing that in 1851 Kensington Palace Gardens was no longer out on a limb, geographically or financially. The surrounding area was being developed and the proximity of the Great Exhibition put Kensington Gardens prominently in the public eye. London was

Fig. 4.32. Skylight for 8 Kensington Palace Gardens, London, 1843

Fig. 4.33. Interior of 8 Kensington Palace Gardens, London, 1843

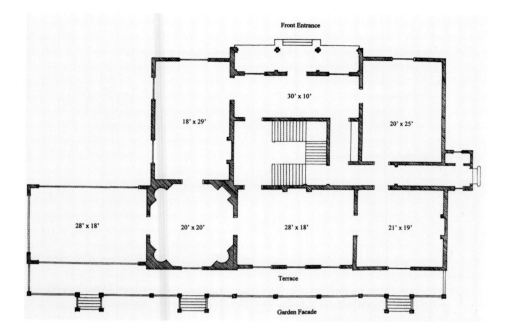

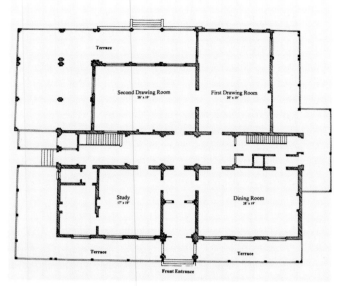

growing wealthier and larger, spawning increasing numbers of city residents and professional families able to afford large houses; these families began deserting Bloomsbury "for the big new stucco mansions of Kensington and Paddington." Girouard also cites the influence of the fifth earl of Harrington, who began building his house in Kensington Palace Gardens in 1851 and explains that "in the social climate of the 1850s to have an earl as a neighbor counted for a great deal."[60]

By the 1870s, the *Illustrated London News* called Kensington Palace Gardens "the most aristocratic London neighborhood " and among contemporary critics, Michael Jenner observes that the "Victorian suburban villa found its highest expression in the larger and more spaciously sited mansions of Kensington Palace Gardens, which also demonstrated a refreshingly playful individuality of style, ranging from Islamic domes and Perpendicular Gothic to the more common classical arrangement."[61] The area, now familiarly known as "Millionaire's Row,"[62] has retained its dignity and exclusivity into the twenty-first century and functions as the London location for many foreign ambassadors; for example, Jones's onion-domed number 24 is appropriately occupied by the Saudi Arabian ambassador.[63] Number 8 was used during World War II for the interrogation of German spies and was reported in poor condition in 1945. The Crown Estate Commissioners' plans to preserve the building were thwarted when the building was declared unsafe in 1955 and demolished in 1961.[64]

Although Henry-Russell Hitchcock described Jones's houses in Kensington Palace Gardens as being "more like oversized Georgian garden fabricks than serious Early Victorian Mansions," the two houses exemplify the stylistic evolution of the 1840s. Jones adopted the villa and palazzo forms of the Italianate Revival introduced by Charles Barry, evident in the astylistic facades and the prominent tower.

The round-headed windows and ornamental details such as the decorative frieze and elaborate window dressings, are further characteristics of Italian Revival. Other Early Victorian elements include larger, grouped windows, elaborate balconies and cornices, and the provision of iron and glass conservatories. In addition, Jones's interiors show the increased elaboration of the period and Jones's unique style shown in the introduction of stronger colors, tiles, and non-traditional ornament.[65]

Westbourne Terrace

Scant information exists on Jones's other residential works during this period. A list of his survives that records the building of four houses in Westbourne Terrace in 1840.[66] These structures would have been part of the "seventy-three first class Mansions" comprising the aristocratic Westbourne Terrace Tontine: a development promoted as "one of the finest ranges of Buildings in the Metropolis" featuring "very elegant and commodious interiors."[67] The four-story-over-daylight-basement mansions were arranged on either side of a spacious open center filled with wide boulevards, pedestrian walkways, and enclosed gardens. Uniform facades with rusticated ground floors displayed the new fashion for attention to window surrounds on the upper levels.[68]

Jones probably designed the interior layout and decoration of the four houses in the shells built by the developer-contractor. A centralized ceiling design survives from Jones's decoration of 12 Westbourne Street for the surgeon John George Perry. The design shows the red and blue of the main motif repeated in the lines of the border and in delicate motifs at the corners and center of each wall (Pl. 4.15).

A patterned chintz survives from Jones's decoration of 84 Westbourne Terrace (1850; page 6) for Thomas De la Rue.

As mentioned earlier, cuttings of the chintz were glued in the November 1851 issues of the *Journal of Design and Manufactures* to illustrate correct design principles, particularly the elimination of shadow, the *levelness* of the pattern at a distance, and the blending of the colors to produce a neutral tint. This chintz offered a handsome alternative to the brown holland typically used for furniture covers, without consideration of a room's color scheme.

Jones used related motifs from his textiles resembling stylized anthemia, fern fronds, or the familiar crochet hook, as endpapers and decorative patterns in his contemporary illuminated texts, including *The Song of Songs* and *The Preacher*.[69] He introduced similar motifs in his designs for wallpapers. The repetition of similar motifs in different media established a new style appropriate for many applications.

21 Northbank, Regent's Park:
The Home of George Elliot and George Henry Lewes

Jones's record of carrying out several commissions for the same clients and friends indicates their loyalty and their desire to seek his counsel in all areas of design. This type of appreciation is evident in Jones's relationship with the writers George Eliot (Mary Anne Evans) and George Henry Lewes.[70] Lewes, author of the two-volume *Life of Goethe*, plus articles and books on philosophy, promoted Positivism, declaring "all inquiry is limited to such objects as admit of verification in one way or another."[71] Lewes, Eliot, and Jones shared a long and close friendship that most probably evolved out of the intellectual compatibility and sympathy between the writers and the architect, who urged his peers to shun historicism and adopt science.

In 1863, Lewes and Eliot purchased a forty-nine-year lease on the Priory, 21 Northbank, Regent's Park, for 2000 pounds. This was a considerable risk for two writers with unpredictable incomes and significant financial commitments. Lewes provided for his sons and for his estranged wife, Agnes, and Eliot supported a widowed relative. The couple's worries over money were tempered somewhat by the growing popularity of Eliot's work. The prospect of increased prosperity from her writing was one motivation for the move to Regent's Park.

Another motivation was the hope that the move would help foster the social acceptance and admission to intellectual circles Eliot desired, but that had been denied them because Lewes was still married to Agnes. A residence in London would allow Eliot to host dinners for noteworthy figures and to hold salons on Sundays. Interiors by Jones would help to create the best impression in both situations, since Jones was a respected scholar as well as the city's most prominent architectural decorator. Eliot enthused to a friend that Jones would create exceptional interiors for the couple, enabling them to admire what they had without expressing vanity.[72]

The redecoration proved daunting at first, since Lewes and Eliot had to move to temporary lodgings while the alterations were completed. This inconvenience was compounded by their concern over the 500-pound cost of the job. Lewes's journal entry of November 1, 1863, reports that "Owen Jones kindly undertook to decorate the drawing room and dining room for us, and has made a very exquisite thing of it; only in the pursuit of artistic effect, he has drawn us into serious expense, sacrificing our drawing room furniture, and causing new furniture to be bought." These concerns were further exacerbated when a mover stole Eliot's purse and the piano tuner inadvertently ruined the new wallpaper and carpet, requiring the printing of new paper. Eliot confided these problems to a friend, but concluded, "Still, in spite of annoyances, we are highly delighted with the house now we are in it."[73]

They were impressed with Jones's fastidious attention to details. Eliot wrote a friend that Jones had been unwearying on their behalf, staying two nights until after midnight to make sure every engraving was hung in the right place. Lewes even described Mary Anne at their housewarming as "splendid in grey moire antique—the consequence of a severe lecture from Owen Jones on her general neglect of personal adornment."

Although the renovated appearances of the house and the hostess proved to be a success, the coveted social acceptance was still elusive. At first, Jones, Thomas Carlyle, Anthony Trollope, and other notables came to dine, but their wives refused to accompany them. Mrs. Owen Jones had been the first to recognize that the popular, but unidentified, author George Eliot was Lewes's companion. With Eliot's continued rise in stature as a writer, some of the women began attending Eliot's salons and parties and offering female companionship. One of these women was Mrs. Alfred Morrison.

Lewes and Eliot hired Jones to undertake further renovations in the Priory in the 1870s, but nothing survives to describe this later work except a journal entry of Lewes's reporting that when he returned home that day, he found Mary Anne and Jones in "deep consultation," again, discussing her personal appearance.[74]

The Viceroy's Palace in Cairo

Unfortunately, no photographs or drawings of Jones's work in the Priory have been identified. The same is true for the commission Jones considered to be his most important: the decoration of fifteen rooms in the khedive (viceroy) of Egypt's palace at Gesch. Ismail Pacha (r. 1863–1879) became khedive upon the death of his father, Mohammed Said Pacha, and immediately initiated the ambitious building campaign that drove him into bankruptcy. As mentioned earlier, one of the most significant early commissions in this campaign was the palace at Gezeerah (Jazirah)

Fig. 4.36. Elevation of 24 Kensington Palace Gardens, London, 1845

intended to house the monarchs and dignitaries of Europe attending the events celebrating the opening of de Lesseps's Suez Canal in 1869. The German architect Julius Franz designed the building and another German, Franz Bey, constructed it. Jones and the German architect Carl von Diebitsch (1819–1869) designed the interior decorations.[75]

The guest palace was located across the Nile River from Cairo on an estate comprising the khedive's personal palace, extensive landscaped gardens, and a zoo. The khedive wanted to impress the European community with their surroundings and momentous events. Guests were regaled by the first performance of Verdi's *Aida* and a carriage tour through the estate and on to the pyramids of Giza. Contemporary guides informed travelers about the palace's "magnificently furnished and decorated reception-rooms" and the pieces of furniture described as "beautiful works of art."[76]

Ismail Pacha provoked a lively spirit of competition between the European architects (especially French, Italian, and German) anxious to secure his commissions. Jones probably met the prospective khedive while guiding foreign dignitaries around one of the Crystal Palaces. Their association was established by 1856, when the *Illustrated London News* printed a drawing of a carriage Jones designed for the future viceroy of Egypt.[77]

Records show that during the 1862 exhibition in London, von Diebitsch met members of the wealthy Egyptian aristocracy who invited him to Alexandria and Cairo. His acceptance resulted in several commissions. He designed furniture, draperies, and other items destined for Cairo. The manufactured items were transported from Berlin to Trieste by train, shipped to Alexandria by boat, and then loaded on trains for Cairo. When the khedive commissioned a room for the Jazirah palace from von Diebitsch in 1863, the viceroy promised the German architect that if the project were successful, he would receive a contract for another room. Eventually von Diebitsch designed all of the rooms in the north wing of the palace and the staterooms in the amazing garden kiosk, built from four hundred tons of cast iron prefabricated in the Lauchhammer foundry in Germany.[78]

It is not clear how Jones received the commission to decorate fifteen rooms in the palace, but he described the undertaking as the triumph of his life. He spent three months designing the decorations to be executed in London and assembled in Cairo. All of the designs for each room were developed from a module derived from the proportions of the room. Jeffrey & Co. produced the printed papers for the walls, dadoes, friezes, cornices, and ceilings, as well as the moldings for the dadoes, friezes, and cornices. Jackson and Graham manufactured the furniture and exhibited some of the pieces in the 1867 International Exposition held in Paris, where they drew acclaim for

Jones's "complete mastery of the principles and knowledge of the details of Arabic art."[79]

Jackson and Graham also displayed drawings for this project in the exhibition of Jones's works held after his death. Although the whereabouts of these drawings is unknown, two drawings for portions of friezes labeled "VPC" in the Victoria and Albert Museum could indicate the Viceroy's Palace in Cairo. Designs purchased from Catherine Jones, the architect's sister, and catalogued as being for the Viceroy's Palace, depict two schemes for a detached building with a central dome and elaborate plasterwork interiors. The buildings are surrounded by an open colonnade and set in a rectangular garden. The drawings are inscribed in French and dated August 1861 (Pls. 4.19 and 4.20).[80] These designs may have been part of Jones's proposals for the khedive's most ambitious state commission: the gardens of al-Jazirah. Efforts to determine if these designs were implemented have been unsuccessful.

16 Carlton House Terrace and Eynsham Hall

The absence of documentation on Jones's architecture leaves the recently restored rooms in 16 Carlton House Terrace, London, and the drawings for Eynsham Hall, Oxfordshire, as the best examples of his late residential commissions. Beside the work at Carlton House Terrace, Jones had designed other schemes for the Morrison family.[81] These include the ornamental cottage and dairy designs for James Morrison, Alfred's father, exhibited at the Royal Academy in 1845 and the addition and redecoration at Fonthill House.

Working with Morrison's collection at Fonthill introduced Jones to new ideas on color and changed his thinking about Chinese art so completely that he decided to produce *Examples of Chinese Ornament* (1867) to expand the information on Chinese design printed in *The Grammar of Ornament* over a decade earlier (Pls. 4.21 and 4.22).[82]

Alfred Morrison obtained the lease for 16 Carlton House Terrace from the Crown Commissioners in 1865.[83] Morton Peto built the premises between 1863 and 1866 to continue the Nash scheme of terraced houses completed thirty years before (Fig. 4.37). Morrison immediately hired Jones to design the ground- and first-floor furnishings. Many people considered the interiors of 16 Carlton House Terrace one of Jones's finest works and the commission is significant in this study as an important example of how Jones implemented his principles of design to achieve interiors of

Fig. 4.37. John Nash, exterior of Carlton House Terrace from the Mall, London, 1833

Fig. 4.38. First-floor drawing room (now board room) of 16 Carlton House Terrace, London, 1865

Fig. 4.39. Detail of ceiling of first-floor drawing room (now board room) of 16 Carlton House Terrace, London, 1865

great distinction and harmony.[84] Contemporary accounts of the decoration appear in *Travels in South Kensington with Notes on Decorative Art and Architecture in England* by Moncure Daniel Conway and *Beautiful Houses; Being a Description of Certain Well-Known Artistic Houses* by a Mrs. Haweis.

The decoration took four years to complete under the supervision of Foster Graham of Jackson and Graham. The coffered ceilings of painted decoration and fibrous plaster were described as reminiscent of the best Italian work carried out four centuries earlier. Some of the deep moldings formed star-shape patterns repeated in the carpets below. Throughout, Jones used his extensive knowledge of past styles to create new ornament, combining Greek anthemion, foliate patterns, and Arabic geometry in new configurations. Conway said the effect was a testament to Jones's ability, since the antique objects and fine metalwork pieces in Morrison's collection executed by the best Spanish, Italian, and Viennese workmen had a recognizable relationship with Jones's decoration.[85]

The walls were covered with changeable silks, made in Lyons, to designs by Jones. The intense colors (red, blue, yellow, and pink) complemented the marquetry of finely grained woods that ornamented the moldings, doors, and much of the furniture (Figs. 4.38, 4.40, and 4.41). Although Jones varied the pattern in each room, the natural woods used for the doors, moldings, and dadoes contributed to the

Fig. 4.40. Ground-floor drawing room (now reception room) of 16 Carlton House Terrace, London, 1865

Fig. 4.41. Moldings in board room of 16 Carlton House Terrace, London, 1865

harmony of the overall scheme as well as to the beauty of each room. The superior level of craftsmanship was another contributing factor. The extensive replication of flawlessly executed decoration produced the sense of repose and harmony Jones promoted. While each pattern is interesting individually and in combination with the other elements in a particular room, the regular reoccurrence of elements and materials creates a predictable and therefore calming background, leaving center stage for the inhabitants.

The Crown Estate, owners of the property, adapted the premises and numbers 13–16 Carlton House Terrace for their use in 1989. Much of Jones's original work survived; for example, six of the original seven ceiling designs were intact, showing how Jones developed an octagonal star into different patterns and used color and gilding to modify light conditions. Jones used relief and gilding in the ground-floor reception room and the room above, since these rooms receive no direct sunlight and are often in shadow. Gilding highlights the red and blue star motifs and ribbed domes of the ceilings in these rooms. In contrast, the rooms facing the Mall have entirely different characters and patterns, with little or no gilding (Figs. 4.39, 4.42–4.45).

Victorian scholar John Cornforth lauded both Jones's extraordinary sensitivity to the tone and grain of wood and his ability to emphasize the color and details of the material with black and gold. Cornforth compared Jones's mar-

quetry to the same attention to detail associated with Robert Adam, but noted that Adam relied on paint where Jones was capable of designing for wood inlay.[86] Adam combined the Neoclassical motifs, observed on his travels, in unconventional arrangements to produce a new style of ornament; likewise, Jones drew on the geometric, Arabic, and Neoclassical motifs observed during his travels to create new decorative motifs and schemes.

The renovation of 16 Carlton House Terrace involved some alterations to Jones's scheme and the addition of elements, including friezes in some rooms that are not original. Folding doors have been installed in the first-floor drawing room to create a large board room and smaller conference room, when necessary, and a large sideboard has been moved from the ground floor to serve as a partition on the first floor. In addition, new entrances have been created into some rooms.[87] Although these changes prevent the renovation from being considered a total restoration of Jones's work, enough of the original work survives to present a good illustration of Jones's ideas regarding pattern and ornament and the effect achieved in situ.

Fortunately, extensive plans and drawings survive to illustrate Jones's last domestic commission: the renovation of Eynsham Hall for James Mason. The original manor house built for James Lacy in 1763 was enlarged by Charles Barry between 1843 and 1845 for a later owner, the fifth earl of Maccelsfield, Thomas Parker. Mason purchased the Eynsham

FOLLOWING PAGES
All from 16 Carlton House Terrace, London, 1865

CLOCKWISE FROM UPPER LEFT
Fig. 4.42. Ceiling of ground-floor drawing room (now reception room)

Fig. 4.43. Detail of ceiling of first-floor drawing room (now board room)

Fig. 4.44. Detail of ceiling of commissioners' room

Fig. 4.45. Detail of ceiling of ground-floor drawing room (now reception room)

PAGE 195
Fig. 4.46. Detail of ceiling of library

194   *Chapter Four*

Fig. 4.47. Entrance facade of Eynsham Hall, after additions by Owen Jones in 1872; demolished 1904

Fig. 4.48. Garden facade of Eynsham Hall, after additions by Owen Jones in 1872; demolished 1904

Park estate in 1866, at the height of country-house building, and commissioned Jones to plan a major expansion and renovation. The work was finished shortly before Jones's death in 1874 and demonstrates a scheme reflecting the highly specialized rooms popular in Victorian country houses, arranged according to Jones's design principles.[88]

Jones almost doubled the footprint of Eynsham adding wings on the east and west of the central block and placing a new fourth floor on the one-hundred-year-old structure

(Figs. 4.47, 4.48, and Pl. 4.23). In this intrepid renovation and expansion, Jones introduced the latest concepts in country-house design arranged with unusual sympathy for the existing structure. The typical Victorian expansion would have stretched the footprint of the building with long corridors and wings off the earlier building to effect an accretion of architectural elements conveying the wealth and status of the estate owner through the unwieldy mass of his mansion composition; in contrast, Jones created a

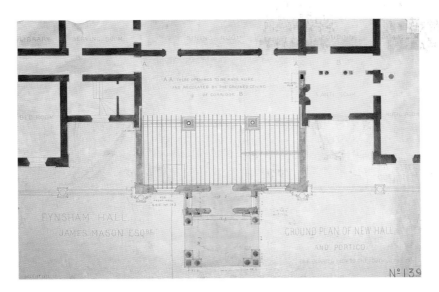

Fig. 4.49. *Drawing number 139 for ground plan of the new hall and portico of Eynsham Hall, December 17, 1872*

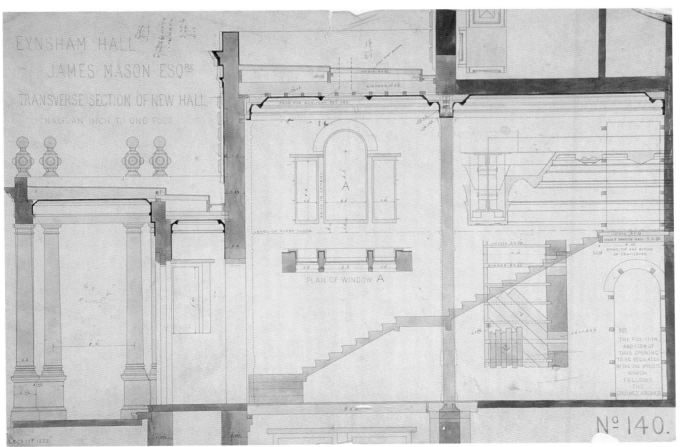

Fig. 4.50. *Drawing number 140 for transverse section of the new hall of Eynsham Hall, December 17, 1872*

tightly controlled arrangement with balanced vertical and horizontal lines.

Jones doubled the size of the entry hall and added a two-story entrance. The columned portico visually united the additions by mitigating the height of the new fourth story and created a stabilizing horizontal plane by repeating the height of the east- and west-wing additions. By restating elements from Barry's scheme and establishing a new central focus, Jones ignored contemporary fashion and pro-

duced a composition more in keeping with his objective of harmonious "repose" than the exuberant, accretive "piles" of his contemporaries.

The portico and vestibule established a formal entry sequence into the expanded entrance hall (Figs. 4.49 and 4.50). Jones wrapped a double staircase around three sides of the two-story space, creating both a useful and dramatic accent to the ceremonious arrivals and departures below. Paneled oak doors and dadoes provided a rich yet restrained

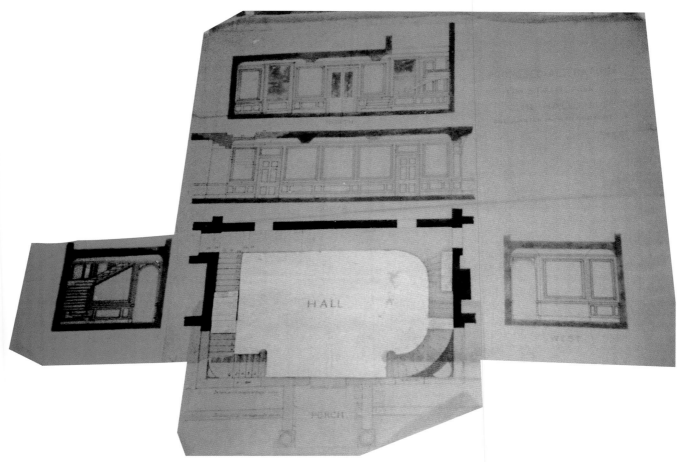

Fig. 4.51. Proposed alteration of staircase of the new hall of Eynsham Hall

Fig. 4.52. Drawing number 141 for longitudinal section of the new hall of Eynsham Hall, December 17, 1872

EYNSHAM HALL. JAMES MASON ESQ.RE   LONGITUDINAL SECTION OF NEW HALL.

NEW OAK DOOR AND ARCHITRAVE

NEW OAK ARCHITRAVE

No 141

198   *Chapter Four*

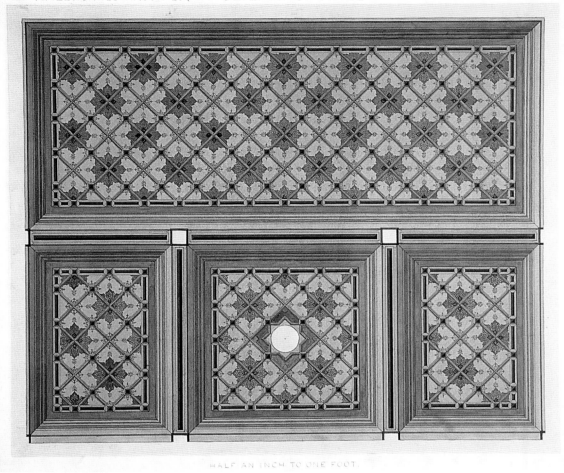

EYNSHAM HALL. JAMES MASON ESQ^{RE}   CEILING OF HALL

HALF AN INCH TO ONE FOOT.   N⁰ 223

Fig. 4.53. Drawing number 223 for ceiling of the new hall of Eynsham Hall

complement to the coffered ceiling (Figs. 4.51–4.53). This arrangement is consistent with Jones's characteristic practice of providing intricate ceiling patterns as the focus of a room's decoration, adding vitality and beauty to the interior without detracting from, or competing with, the inhabitants of the space below.

It is interesting to note that although cast iron had been popular as a support for entry stairs in country houses since the early nineteenth century and Jones had been designing praiseworthy iron staircases and railings for over two decades, he chose wood for the entrance hall stairs for both Eynsham Hall and 16 Carlton House Terrace. Unlike his peers' practice, the woods were not used to imitate a Jacobean or Elizabethan theme, but were selected to express the beauty of the unadorned material.[89] A substantial amount of iron was used in this space, however, but not exposed; two-story iron columns placed within the walls braced massive iron beams added to bear the load of the new fourth story.

Drawings show the provision for gas lighting installed as part of the Eynsham remodeling (Fig. 4.54). Jones designed the light fixtures and ventilation panels to accommodate the gas illumination. He also redesigned

Fig. 4.54. Light fixture (believed to be for Eynsham Hall)

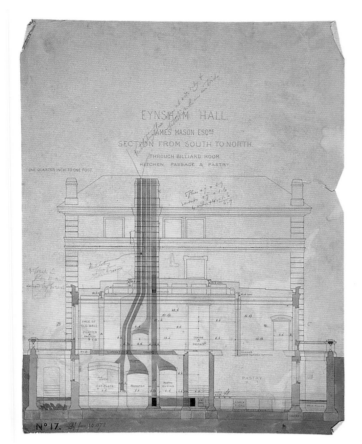

Fig. 4.55. *Drawing number 17 for section from south to north through billiard room, kitchen, passage, and pantry of Eynsham Hall, January 24, 1872*

each of the existing fireplaces, converting them from wood burning to coal and provided subterranean entrances and spaces for the delivery and storage of coal. Other service arrangements created in the lower level included a tradesmen's entrance, staff offices, and boiler rooms, plus enlarged kitchens outfitted with the colossal warming, baking, and roaster ovens required for the grand-scale hospitality of the period (Fig. 4.55).[90]

The magnitude of this transformation fits the "golden age of Victorian country-house building" described by Girouard in *The Victorian Country House*. James Mason typifies the nineteenth-century entrepreneur who amassed a fortune (in this case, by mining copper in Portugal), and then sought social acceptance through the purchase of large land holdings and the renovation or erection of "a massive pile" for lavish entertaining and "appearance." The Eynsham Hall expansion is also characteristic of the Victorian penchant for compartmentalizing all aspects of life and associating specific functions and behavior with particular rooms reflecting either male or female society. Jones's plan, furnishings, and decorative schemes reflect this convention with deep colors, geometric patterns, and ebonized wood in the masculine spaces in contrast to the light-hearted pastel colors, gay floral patterns, and white furniture in the feminine arena.

Fig. 4.56. *Drawing number 83 for details of the new billiard room of Eynsham Hall*

200   *Chapter Four*

The rooms designed for the activities of James Mason were arranged to create what Girouard calls an "increasingly large and sacrosanct male domain (Fig. 4.59)." Girouard explains that, during this period, a billiards room placed next to the owner's study or business room, with an adjacent W. C. and washbasin, constituted a comfortable male sphere. Jones added a new east wing to provide for this arrangement with a 35-by-30-foot billiard room as the "nucleus of the male preserve." A dramatic setting for Mason and his guests was achieved by extending the height of the room to 34 feet under a glass lantern and a coffered ceiling (Figs. 4.57 and 4.58). Furnishings included a standard-sized billiard table for the men and a smaller version for the ladies, plus a large divan and seating near the fireplace.

The adjacent lavoratory contained the W. C. and two washbasins, plus an extraordinary feature, a fullsize bathtub. The 22-by-12-foot gunroom was another novelty beginning to make an occasional appearance in the 1870s. Girouard notes that the appearance of this specialized chamber "marks the progress from the relatively haphazard shooting of the early nineteenth century to the great organized beats of the 1890s, and the development of shooting from a recreation to a mystique."[91]

Pursuits particular to Mason are reflected in the construction of a 36-by-14-foot, glass-roofed fernery and an adjacent 22-by-16-foot laboratory (Figs. 4.80 and 4.88). In addition to mining, Mason carried out agricultural research and was named a fellow in the Royal Society of British scientists for his significant contribution in this area.

The creation of the male domain extended on the other side of the billiards room with the remodeling of rooms contained in the body of the original house. These rooms include Mason's study and a new library in maroon and turquoise with built-in bookcases of black-painted wood and matching furniture. The decorative scheme for the dining room, also considered part of the male sphere, continued the dark, imposing woods and coloration of the other masculine spaces with furniture and walls covered in silk in a pattern by Jones called "Sutherland" (Pages 70–1). Ceiling designs from several of these rooms, including the billiards room and dining room, were later praised and published in the *Furniture Gazette*.[92]

Spaces for feminine occupation included the new drawing room, a ballroom, and rooms for music, correspondence and card playing finished with paint and fabrics in lavender, blue, and white. The light and airy character of the drawing room was accomplished by alternating French doors and large mirrors trimmed in white against lavender walls (Fig. 4.26). A similar fresh and lively appearance was achieved in the new 40-by-30-foot ballroom where lavender walls capped by a delicate garland were covered by a bower of conventionalized flowers arranged in a trellis pattern on a white background. The fanciful garland motif of the frieze was repeated in the railing surrounding the raised orchestra in the center of the room (Pl. 4.27).

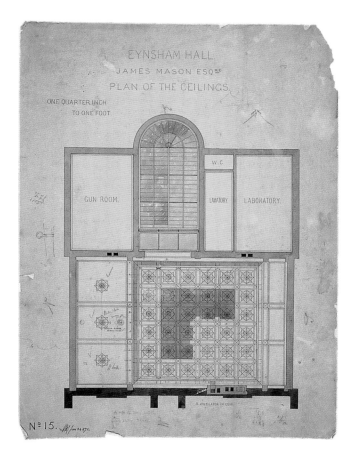

Fig. 4.57. Drawing number 15 for plan of ceilings of Eynsham Hall, January 24, 1872

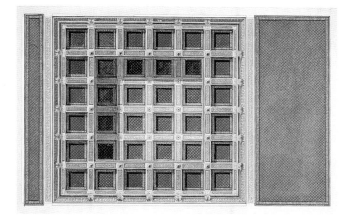

Fig. 4.58. Rendering of new billiard-room ceiling of Eynsham Hall

As in Jones's other commissions, the decoration throughout the house relied upon abstract and foliate patterns incorporated in textiles, ceilings, borders, and moldings. Each space had uniquely designed ornamentation, but the repetition of large borders, elaborate ceilings, and articulated woodwork produced a feeling of overall harmony and coordination in contrast to the fashion for differentiated, historicized chambers.

Jones added a popular Victorian amenity: the 24-by-50-foot conservatory. His attractive designs for the iron elements and framing of this light and airy space required no further decoration (Pl. 4.28).

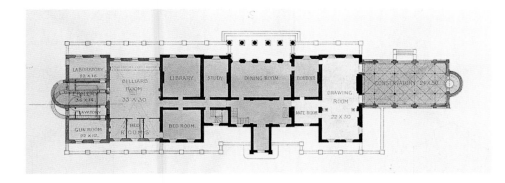

Fig. 4.59. *Plan of Eynsham Hall*

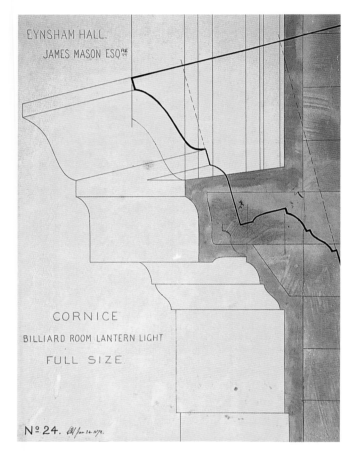

Fig. 4.60. *Drawing number 24 for cornice in billiard room of Eynsham Hall*

Jones's design extended into the landscape. He created two-tiered formal terraces (Pl. 4.29), flower beds, pools, fountains, and stone balustrades to complement Barry's classical facade. He retained Barry's portico and grand Ionic columns and kept the new modifications consistent with Barry's scheme. He reproduced Barry's quoins in the new chimneys, repeated the third-floor window treatment, and terminated the building with a parapet.[93]

This replication should not be interpreted as an abandonment of principles or the desire to create a new style of architecture, but should be interpreted as evidence that Jones preferred harmony over making a signature statement. The drawings for the Eynsham Hall renovation reveal that he was introducing the latest concepts in architecture under challenging conditions; for example, he had to devise ways to strengthen the foundation and walls of a century-old structure to support a new fourth story. In addition, he had to prepare clear instructions for the Oxfordshire workmen hired to carry out the alterations, fabricate the moldings and the other elements needed, and install the modern heating, lighting, and ventilation systems. His signed drawings cover every aspect of the job, from elevations and working plans to details of beams and gas lighting fixtures and full-scale illustrations of cornices and column capitals (Fig. 4.60).

The skill he exhibited in masterminding the renovation of Eynsham Hall confirms Jones's practice of the full range of architecture and establishes the fact that defining him as a decorator, colorist, or theorist, only tells part of the story. The interiors of Eynsham Hall, 16 Carlton House Terrace, and the other domestic commissions confirm Jones's consistent application of the design principles he advocated in "On the True and False in the Decorative Arts" and in his other lectures and writing. Further, the interiors demonstrate his ability to create a new aesthetic style appropriate to the taste and fashion of the period.

Unfortunately the terraces, balustrades, pools, and fountains are the only visible remains of Jones's comprehensive scheme at Eynsham Hall. The structure he enlarged was razed in 1903, when Mason's son inherited the property, and a new building, designed by Ernest George, was completed in 1908. Moldings designed by Jones for the earlier building were installed in two rooms in the new structure and Jones's silks were rehung in the new library and dining room.[94]

Jones's last domestic commissions demonstrated the same principles he had expressed in concluding the Marlborough House lectures two decades earlier. In those lectures, he also conveyed the plans and hopes of the group organizing the move of the Crystal Palace to Sydenham to house museums for art, sculpture, and architecture. He predicted that when the public had time to study the contents of these museums, they would accept his propositions, particularly the concept "that Architecture and the attendant arts have ever been, *and, therefore, ever should be,* the expression of the *wants,* the *faculties,* and the *sentiments* of the age in which they are created."

By studying and comparing the examples of every age exhibited before them, designers and the public would develop the ability to differentiate between good and bad design and to distinguish temporary fashions from eternal principles. With this understanding, no one would want to continue to copy from the past. Clients and manufacturers would abandon capriciousness and designers would introduce features or forms to accommodate new functions, in new materials, and with varied decoration. The result would be an architecture composed in Britain, in harmony with the climate, institutions, and habits of the people. Jones believed this architecture would be elegant, appropriate, and original, and would deserve to be called *"Our Own."*

Jones defined his philosophy of design as a movement and compared the importance of this movement to initiatives promoting knowledge, morality, and health. Citing examples of progress in philosophy, industry, and agriculture, he cautioned his audience that intellectual knowledge, power, and material greatness were not worth much without the refinement of Art and argued that the government should provide financial support to the Art movement. He acknowledged the government's funding of the Department of Practical Art, but insisted that a greater investment was necessary to support substantial change. He recommended generous funding, insisting that the money spent to form art museums would save greater expenditures for the construction of jails. He understood that evil would never be eradicated, but believed that giving the populace healthy pleasures and cultivating their mental and artistic sensibilities could reduce crime.

He argued that Britain should follow other governments and support art. He recommended beginning by appointing a special minister to foster art. He was optimistic about the chances for success, since a movement to foster and reform art would not have the interference of vested interests. The only opposition might come from taxpayers, but Jones thought citizens would be willing to pay a few shillings or

pounds a year, since the money would be returned tenfold in increased happiness for all generations.[95]

Jones said the people should hold their officials just as responsible for providing cultural resources as for protecting political rights and material advantages and advocated locating an art museum in every town and a drawing school in every village. Later, Gottfried Semper echoed this position.[96] Jones also wanted the government to establish a central art college and complete a code of laws and principles to govern every branch of art. He believed artists could be educated in masses according to these principles and, as a result, a new unity of expression would replace the discord of individualism.

He outlined the steps to be taken in educating the professors to manage the art schools to be established throughout the country. These professors would then train the faculties. Jones realized the scheme would take years to accomplish, but believed it would be worth the effort to produce a refined public, desirous of wares aesthetically superior to the goods of other nations. As a result, British industry, allying Art with Science and Industry, would take the lead internationally and Britain would become the envy and model of all the nations on earth.

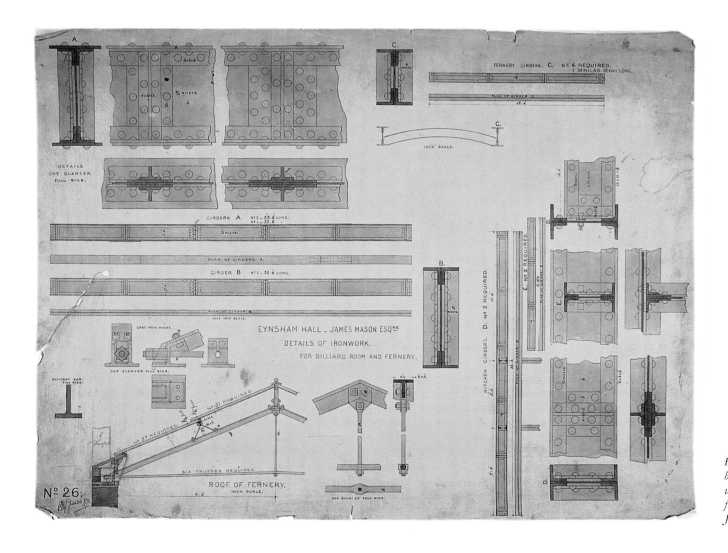

Fig. 4.61. Drawing number 26 for detail of ironwork for billiard room and fernery of Eynsham Hall, January 24, 1872

Pl. 4.1. Diaper design, c. 1860

Pl. 4.2. Wallpaper design,
c. 1860

Pl. 4.3. Wallpaper design, c. 1852–74

N.º 19

Pl. 4.4. Wallpaper design, 1860

Pl. 4.5. Unnamed textile design for Warner's, 1868

Pl. 4.6. "Baveno" textile design in silk terry woven posthumously by Benjamin Warner, 1879

Pl. 4.7. "Peri" textile design in silk tissue, c. 1870

Pl. 4.8. "Sultan" textile design in silk tissue, c. 1870

FACING PAGE
Pl. 4.9. Chairs for Alfred Morrison's residence at 16 Carlton House Terrace, c. 1865

Pl. 4.10. Table for Alfred Morrison's residence at 16 Carlton House Terrace, c. 1865

Pls. 4.11. Detail of table for Alfred Morrison's residence at 16 Carlton House Terrace, c. 1865

LEFT
Pl. 4.12. Detail of table for Alfred Morrison's residence at 16 Carlton House Terrace, c. 1865

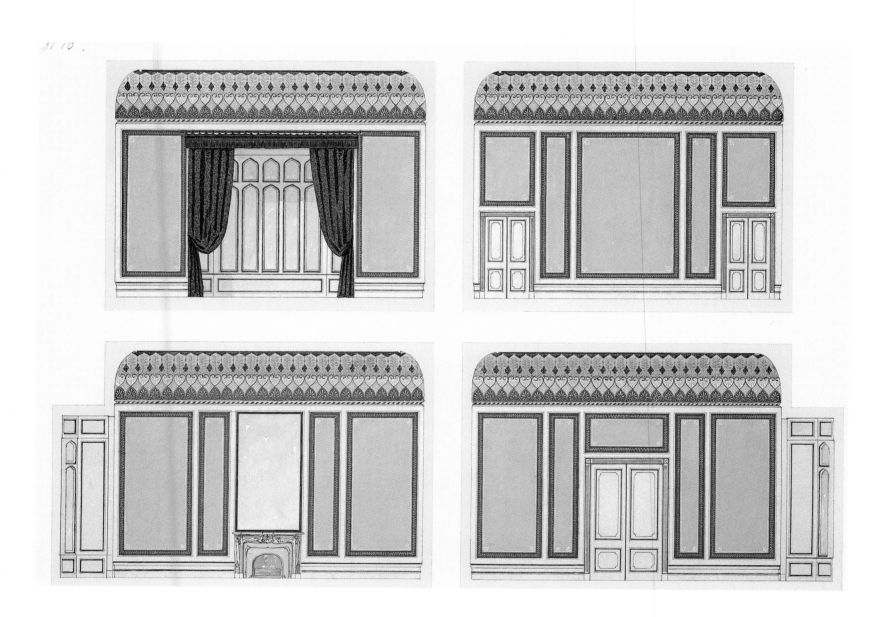

Pl. 4.13. Design for the
decoration of a music room,
1850s

Pl. 4.14. Page from Treasures of Art, Industry and Manufacture *represented in the American Centennial Exhibition, 1877, showing drapery by Owen Jones on the right*

Pl. 4.15. Centralized ceiling motif, c. 1865

FAACING PAGE
Pl. 4.16. Carpet design for Fishmonger's Hall, c. 1865

FISHMONGERS. HALL.

SKETCH FOR CARPET.

ANTI ROOM.

Scale two inches to five feet.

Pl. 4.17. Carpet design for Fishmonger's Hall, c. 1865

FACING PAGE
Pl. 4.18. Evenly distributed carpet design, c. 1865

PAGES 220–1
Pl. 4.19. Section of garden pavilion of the Viceroy's Palace, n.d.

PAGES 222–3
Pl. 4.20. Elevation of garden pavilion of Viceroy's Palace, n.d.

Pl. 4.21. "Copper bottle decoration," Pl. LIX from Examples of Chinese Ornament, *1867*

Pl. 4.22. "Bottle decoration," Pl. LIII from Examples of Chinese Ornament, 1867

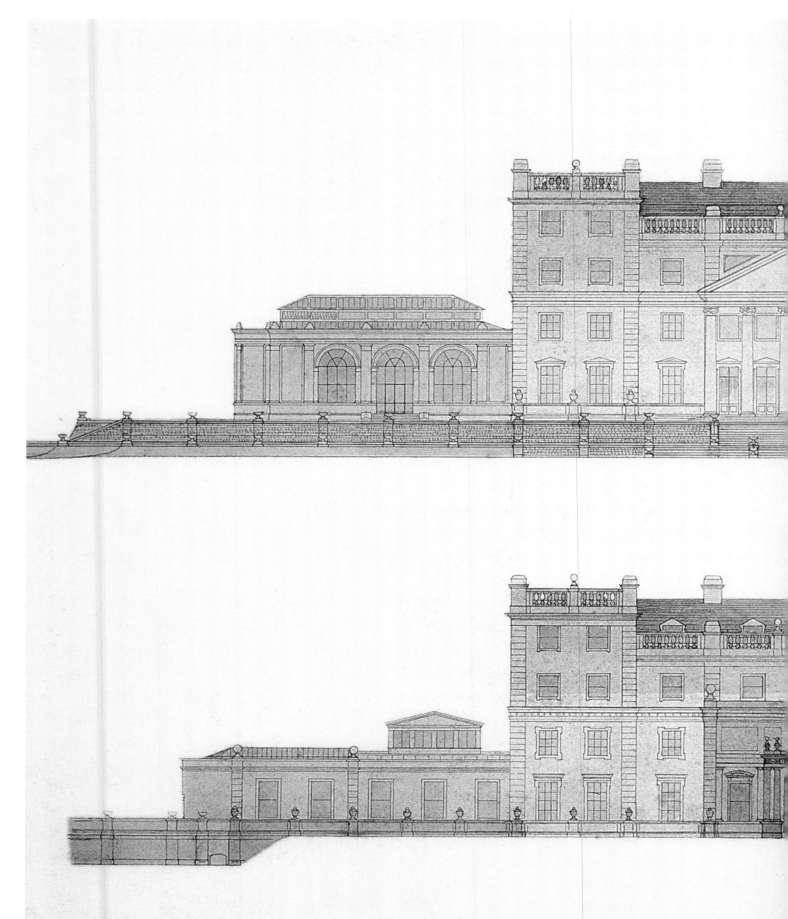

Pl. 4.23. Drawings of Eynsham Hall expansion; additions by Owen Jones shown in pink

EAST.

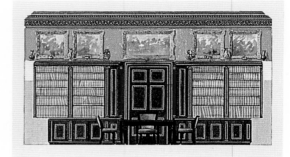

NORTH.

SOUTH.

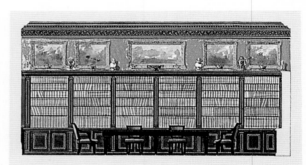

WEST.

EAST

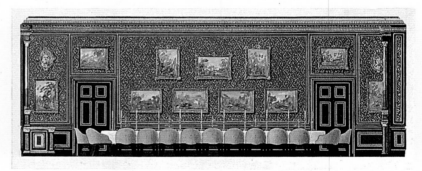

NORTH

SOUTH

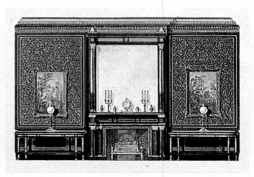

WEST

228   *Chapter Four*

FACING PAGE
*Pl. 4.24. Drawing
number 104 for design
of the furniture and
decoration for library of
Eynsham Hall, c. 1872*

*Pl. 4.25. Drawing
number 93 for design
of the furniture and
decoration of dining room
of Eynsham Hall, c. 1872*

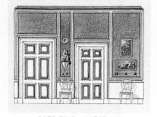
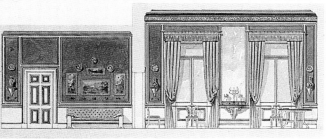
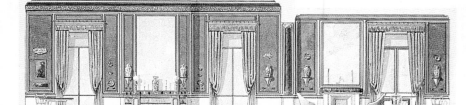
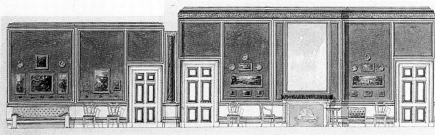
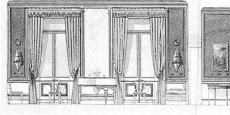
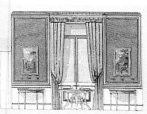

EYNSHAM HALL

JAMES MASON ESQRE

DESIGN FOR THE DECORATION & FURNISHING

OF THE

DRAWING ROOM, MUSIC ROOM

AND CARD ROOM

CARD ROOM — EAST WALL

CARD ROOM — WEST WALL

CARD ROOM. SOUTH WALL DRAWING ROOM

DRAWING ROOM. WEST WALL MUSIC ROOM.

MUSIC ROOM EAST WALL DRAWING ROOM.

DRAWING ROOM NORTH WALL CARD ROOM

*Pl. 4.26. Drawing
number 5 for design of
furniture and decoration
of the drawing, music, and
card rooms of Eynsham
Hall, c. 1872*

Interior Design, Decorative Arts, and Private Architecture 229

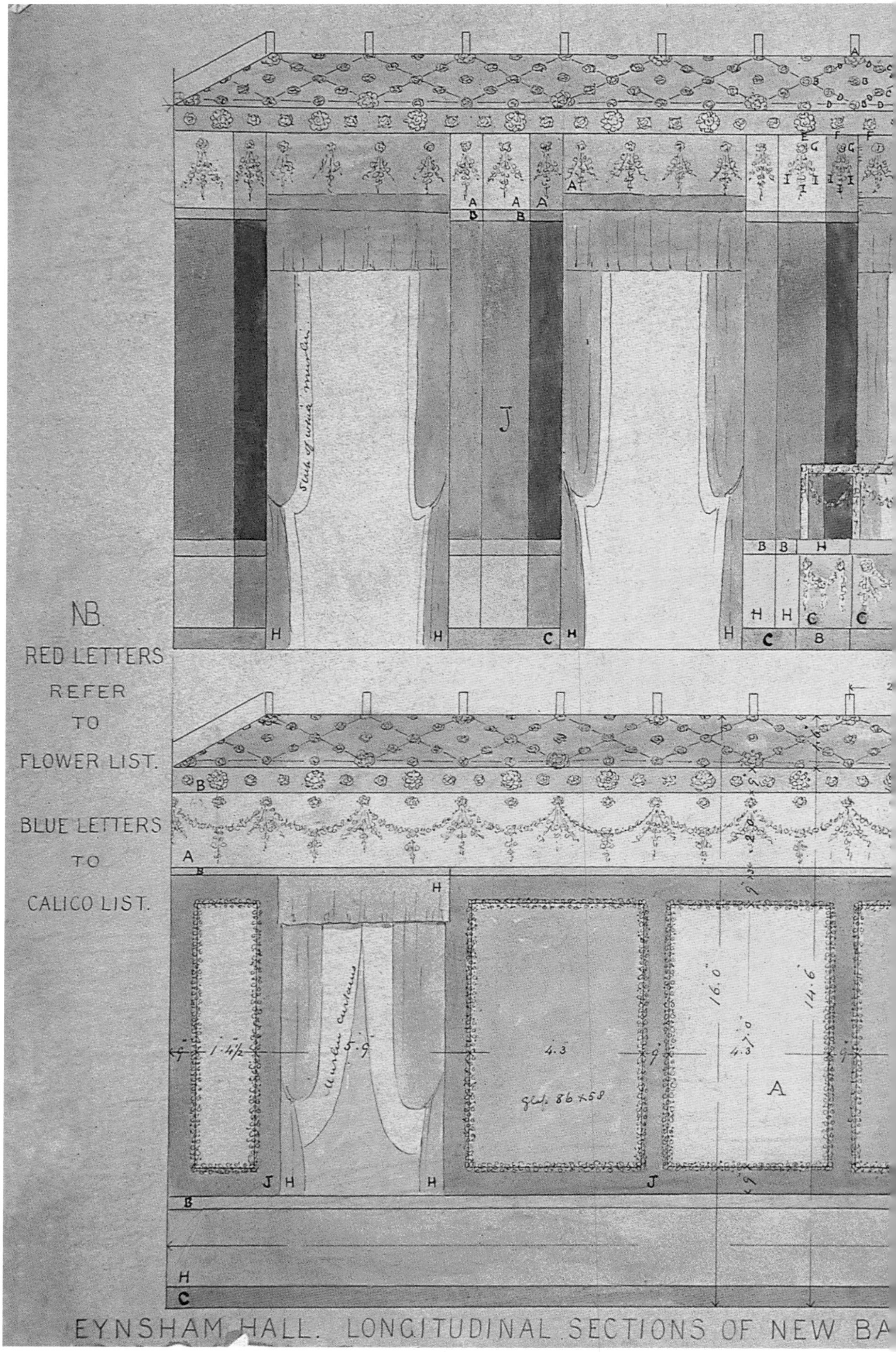

Pl. 4.27. Longitudinal
section of new ballroom of
Eynsham Hall, c. 1872

NB.
RED LETTERS
REFER
TO
FLOWER LIST.

BLUE LETTERS
TO
CALICO LIST.

EYNSHAM HALL. LONGITUDINAL SECTIONS OF NEW BA

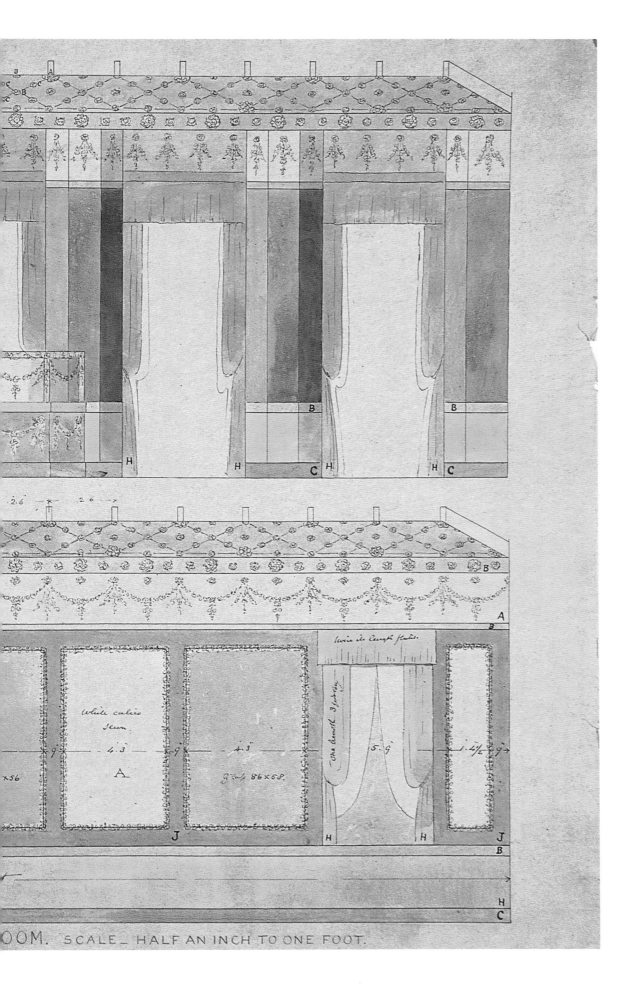

OOM. SCALE — HALF AN INCH TO ONE FOOT.

Pl. 4.28. Drawing number 10 for details of conservatory of Eynsham Hall, c. 1872

PLAN AT N.M. FULL SIZE.

EYNSHAM HALL.

JAMES MASON ESQ[RE]

DESIGN FOR THE TERR

FLOWE

V.A.M.

Nº 29. [signature] Jan 24 1872

Pl. 4.29. Drawing
number 29 for terrace
garden of Eynsham Hall,
January 24, 1872

234   Chapter Four

GARDEN. PLAN Nº2.

...STRIBUTED.

60   70   80   90   100 feet.

E.499-1952.

CHAPTER FIVE

THE LEGACY

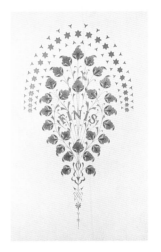

It is impossible to exaggerate the authority and stature of Owen Jones during the middle of the nineteenth century or to overestimate the influence of his theory and designs on his contemporaries and on subsequent generations. Millions were exposed to his color schemes in the London Crystal Palaces. Thousands more experienced St. James's Hall and the wallpapers, stationery, and other household items made to his designs. Generations of students and practitioners in Europe and the United States studied his principles and examples in *The Grammar of Ornament, Plans, Elevations, Sections, and Details of the Alhambra,* and in César Daly's lengthy excerpts from *Alhambra* in the *Revue Générale de l'architecture.* Finally, Jones's commissions were discussed in the *Builder,* the *Architectural Review,* the *Civic Engineer and Architect's Journal,* and other periodicals. The adoption of his principles and the imitation of his patterns made possible by this widespread exposure suggest that he may well have been the most influential designer of the nineteenth century. His advocacy of non-Western cultures and the rational design principles inherent in Moresque architecture in particular, were so well accepted by the 1870s that architects in Europe and America are said to have included Islamic elements in their work to indicate their modern approach to architecture.[1] Although the scope of his influence can only be suggested here, it is possible to gain some appreciation of his impact by discussing his ideas in relation to a small sample of other leading designers and theorists, including Christopher Dresser (1834–1904), William Morris (1834–1896), Eugène-Emmanuel Viollet-le-Duc (1814–1879), John Ruskin (1819–1900), Frank Lloyd Wright (1867–1959), and Le Corbusier (1887–1965).

Since each of these designers shared Jones's aspiration for the application of universal principles to generate original designs, a brief review of their ideas and design methods promotes a better understanding of Jones's level of contribution. Dresser, Wright, and Le Corbusier openly acknowledged a debt to Jones, but countless others adopted his methods of design and philosophy without acknowledging the source.

CHRISTOPHER DRESSER

Jones's impact on Christopher Dresser was the most direct and obvious. Dresser was a pupil in the School of Design at Marlborough House from 1847 through 1854. During his course of study, Dresser heard Jones's lectures and studied Jones's principles. Later, Dresser credited Jones for teaching him to think.

During his training Dresser also studied plant morphology and began applying his knowledge to creative design. He called his approach "artistic botany" and began teaching his methods in the Female School of Design in 1854. At the same time, he wrote two books on plant morphology. The University of Jena recognized the merit of these texts by awarding Dresser an honorary doctorate degree.

Dresser also wrote a series of articles for Cassell's *Technical Educator,* published in book format as *The Art of Decorative Design* (1862). The illustrations and appendices in the text show Dresser's extensive knowledge of plants, while the design theory expressed reveals a total dependence upon Jones's philosophy. Dresser praised the excellence of Jones's Greek and Alhambra courts in the Crystal Palace at Sydenham and lauded St. James's Hall, but failed to acknowledge Jones as the originator of the theory advocated. Tribute proved unnecessary, however, since Jones's principles were so familiar that critics for the *Athenaeum* and other publications immediately identified the source.

Today readers may recognize Jones's influence from some

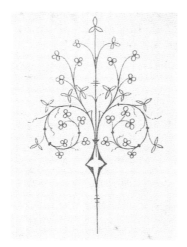

Fig. 5.1. Last page from Paradise and the Peri, *1860*

Fig. 5.2. Motif from The Book of Common Prayer, *1850*

excerpts of Dresser's beginning with his assertion that "a repetition of ancient forms is not appropriate; for ornament, like architecture, must express the sentiments of the age in which it is created."[2] This statement combines two of Jones's tenets: "Architecture is the material expression of the wants, the faculties, and the sentiments of the age in which it is created," and "Principles discoverable in the works of the past belong to us; not so the results."

Dresser's discussion of proportions provides another clear example. Dresser repeats Jones's observation and example that obvious proportions, such as 4:8, are not as appealing to the eye as subtler ratios, such as 5:8. Dresser also parrots Jones's dictum that "flowers and other natural objects should not be used as ornaments, but conventional representations founded upon them" and followed his teacher in condemning the realism in contemporary carpets and wallpapers. Like Jones, Dresser rejected the forms of pagan temples and medieval churches for places of Protestant worship and maintained that no new style of religious architecture could be achieved due to the disunity in Christian belief and institutions.

Dresser repeated and sometimes acknowledged Jones's philosophy in other writings, including *The Development of Ornamental Art in the International Exhibition* (1862), where he again promoted conventionalized pattern making, ornament appropriate to the spirit of the age, and adherence to Jones's color theory. Dresser also included many quotations from Jones, including: "Construction should be decorated. Decoration should never be purposely constructed"; "The useful is a vehicle for the beautiful"; "There should be no features about a building which are not necessary for convenience, construction, or propriety"; "All ornaments should consist of the enrichment of the essential construction of a building"; and "The decorative arts arise from architecture."

Fig. 5.3. Portrait of Owen Jones published in the Builder, *May 9, 1874*

Throughout the text, Dresser used Jones's principles as the standard for discussing and critiquing the products displayed in the London Exhibition of 1862. One obvious example occurs in the way he judged the wall decorations according to the flatness of their ornament. Jones had identified and discussed two-dimensional flat patterns in *Alhambra* and had advocated this method of pattern making to improve British design. By 1862 Dresser was able to recognize the substantial advance in British design resulting from the implementation of this technique. Dresser judged the "somewhat Moresque" wallpapers displayed by Jeffrey & Co. as the most successful entries displayed. He described the papers as "based upon true principles." This basis of design and the "somewhat Moresque" patterns suggest that the manufacturer had chosen to display designs by one of their leading designers, Owen Jones.

Dresser's review of the carpets exhibited included several references to Jones, beginning: "In these views we are not alone: indeed, they belong to a school which has a noble advocate and supporter in Mr. Owen Jones, whose skill as an ornamentist surpasses that of any other with whom we are acquainted, and has, as holders of its tenets, all who are skilled in the decorative arts." He quoted Jones's assertion that "The surface of a carpet, serving as a ground to support all objects, should be quiet and negative, without strong

PAGES 240–1
All illustrations from Christopher Dresser, Studies in Design, *1874*

Fig. 5.4. Frieze, Pl. XXXIV

Fig. 5.5. Frieze, Pl. III

contrast of either form or colour" and evaluated the carpets according to Jones's propositions. This is evident in his praise of a Jackson and Graham carpet, probably designed by Jones, for its "pleasing, neutral, and rich bloom."

Dresser referred to Jones directly when discussing bookbindings. Dresser judged bookbinding and the revival of the art of illuminating to be "two of the most favorable signs of the times in relation to the ornamental arts." He commended Luke Limner (the artist John Leighton) for improving bookbinding and extolled Jones's cover for *The Victorian Psalter* as "unquestionably one of the finest embossed covers ever produced." His appreciation of this cover was so strong that he recommended art students and all passersby to pay it careful consideration (Pls. 1.13 and 1.14).

Dresser thought that book illustrations should correspond to the sentiments expressed on each page and, again, credited Jones for providing the finest example in *Paradise and the Peri*, a Persian myth illuminated by Jones and Henry Warren. Dresser explained that every change in meaning in the text was enhanced by a variation in the ornamentation, such as the dominant use of blue to emphasize the text "Down the blue vault the Peri flies" (Pl. 1.19). Similarly, he notes the success and distinction of the Egyptian character of the ornamental borders on pages with references to Egypt and the Nile. Dresser also observed the contrast between the black grounds on pages dealing with death and sadness and the colorful flowers on pages concerned with youth or repentance. As a worthy disciple of Jones, Dresser paused to point out that "the flowers are not naturally treated, but are true floral ornaments founded upon a correct basis." He concluded by calling the *Paradise and the Peri, The Victorian Psalter,* and other texts illuminated by Jones works of art (Pls. 1.17, 1.18, and 1.20–1.22).

Clearly Dresser judged the products displayed in the London Exhibition of 1862 according to Jones's principles and commended the firms, such as Jeffrey & Co. and Jackson and Graham, who manufactured Jones's designs. He praised specific items by Jones and quoted the words of his "masterly mind." And Dresser repeated Jones's philosophy in other writings. For example, he paraphrased Jones's ideas on color in an article in the *Furniture Gazette* on April 18, 1874, and reprinted thirteen of Jones's principles in his first issue as art editor of the *Furniture Gazette* on January 3, 1880.

Studies in Design, published in twenty parts between 1874 and 1876, continues Dresser's earlier goals, including the education of art students in the creation of ornament consistent with Jones's principles. Dresser begins *Studies in Design* with Jones's assertion that the desire for decoration is natural to humans, as evidenced in the tattoos and decorated instruments of the "savage." In the second chapter, he again followed Jones, explaining that the process of creating ornament should depend upon scholarship and knowledge, not originality. Dresser explained how his own method of design conformed to this idea, beginning with the selection of a style of ornament and then study of the religion, government, climate, and habits of the people who produced the ornament of that style in order to comprehend their spirit. He said he tried to engage that spirit to allow him to create sympathetic patterns. This explanation is puzzling, since it suggests a divergence between his philosophy and Jones's, as Jones believed that scholarship was essential to identify the principles fundamental to all good design, and that once the student of art understood those principles, they would be used to produce new ornament appropriate to represent the spirit of the nineteenth century. Jones would have rejected reproducing ornament in the spirit of another age and culture. Further consideration indicates that Dresser did too; he recognized that "no past style of ornament is precisely suited to our wants" and was using knowledge of the past as a source of inspiration. Like Jones, he advised students to study the past, not as a copyist but to gain knowledge and seek out truths and broad principles.

Dresser emphasized Jones's belief that "The attainment of repose is the highest aim of art." He titled chapter six "On the Means by which Repose Is Attainable in Decoration" and restated Jones's axiom that "Repose is attained by the absence of any want." He then repeated Jones's principles of color, advising readers on the location, strength, and combination of colors to achieve repose. He continued this direction in later chapters, giving specifics on methods of achieving harmonious interior decoration, including appropriate colors and enrichment for walls, ceilings, and carpets. He agreed with Jones's assertion that surface embellishments should appear flat and described ideal decoration according to Jones's concepts for walls with a neutralized bloom, ceiling decorations as a focal point, and carpets set off by deep borders.

Dresser's writings present Jones's axioms in a clear and conversational manner, enabling the student, client, decorator, or manufacturer to adopt the principles with understanding and assurance. At times, Dresser refers to Jones directly; for example, he instructs students to study the ornament in Jones's *Preacher*, emphasizing "that page near the middle of the book, where the central strip of ornament is blue, and the words commence with 'Who knoweth the spirit of man?'" For most of the text, and in his other writings, Dresser restates Jones's axioms as his own ideas. As a result, Jones's ideas gained wider distribution, although often unacknowledged.

Dresser also demonstrated the application of Jones's theory in his designs, and it's interesting to compare patterns by Dresser and Jones to observe how the same philosophy engendered different results. The major difference is not in the method or technique of the two designers, but in their intentions. Jones wanted to achieve repose, while Dresser wanted to communicate a sense of energy; consequently, Jones combined straight, angular, and curved lines to

Fig. 5.6. Dado and wall patterns, Pl. XII

Fig. 5.7. Design for a wall or dado pattern, Pl. XVIII

achieve harmony, while Dresser emphasized diagonals, angular forms, and spiked motifs (Figs. 5.4 and 5.5). Figs. 4.15, 5.8, and 5.9 show how Dresser followed the format of Jones's centralized ceiling patterns, but transformed his teacher's ideas into bold new motifs and borders. Their diaper patterns show the same contrast of quieter patterns by Jones and more vigorous designs by Dresser.

Dresser owned a large collection of Jones's designs and many of Dresser's patterns show the inspiration of Jones.[3] For example, scholars Michael Darby and Stuart Durant note the reappearance of Jones's luxuriant scrolls from the cover and endpapers of *Winged Thoughts* (1851) as the central motif in Plate XXIV in Dresser's *The Art of Decorative Design* (1862; Figs. 5.10 and 5.11). Many of Dresser's designs are indistinguishable from those of Jones, but others for ceilings, wallpapers, and carpets lack the delicacy and refinement of his teacher (Figs. 5.8 and 5.9).

Dresser also developed a considerable body of unique patterns, but his philosophy, described by Nikolaus Pevsner as "sensible but not especially original," remained true to Jones's ideas. While Durant and other Dresser scholars make this distinction, many, unfamiliar with the work of Jones, do not recognize Jones's influence. Dresser's claim to be the most prolific and important designer for industrial production can be challenged on the basis that Jones's designs received greater praise and publication than Dresser's during the 1850s, '60s, and '70s, and Dresser was out of fashion by the 1880s.[4]

Fig. 5.8. Christopher Dresser, ceiling decorations, Pl. L from Studies in Design, *1874*

Although the writings and designs of Jones and Dresser clearly demonstrate their theoretical connection, the absence of archival material eliminates potential evidence of their personal or professional relationship. Their association with the School of Practical Art is well known and Dresser always recognized Jones's lectures in Marlborough House (1852) as the source of his best information and inspiration as a student. Jones invited Dresser to prepare Plate XCVIII for *The Grammar of Ornament* (Fig. 5.12). Durant points out that Dresser's plate is the only one signed in the text. Durant also observes that Dresser's association with someone of Jones's stature probably explains the unusual opportunity to write a series of articles for the well-established *Art Journal*. Other circumstances also sug-

gest Jones's role as a mentor. These include the fact that Dresser was hired to teach in the educational program at Sydenham, a project of importance to Jones, and that Dresser's early designs were produced by firms such as Jackson and Graham and other companies with which Jones was associated. While these benefits may have accrued from Dresser's association with Jones, Dresser must be credited for increasing Jones's influence by repeating his principles in lectures and writings aimed at a wide, popular audience. Dresser fleshed out Jones's principles, citing examples of the ideas and suggesting practical applications.

EUGÈNE-EMMANUEL VIOLLET-LE-DUC

While Jones's influence is clear in the quotations, acknowledgements, and paraphrases of Dresser, his impact on other nineteenth-century figures is not as obvious. In some cases, Jones's influence can only be implied by examples of parallel thinking, analogous arguments, and publication dates. This is the case with Eugène-Emmanuel Viollet-le-Duc. While records show that Jones gave the French architect and theorist a tour of the Crystal Palace and that the two architects owned copies of each other's books, records have not been found to indicate the nature or extent of their relationship.[5]

In *The Radiance of Chartres*, James Rosser Johnson notes a "curious similarity" between the theories of Viollet-le-Duc and the English writers on architecture and decoration, particularly Jones, George Field, and Jones's "friend and admirer," Sir John Wilkinson, author of *On Colour and on the Necessity for a General Diffusion of Taste among All Classes*. Johnson describes these men as "making their own rules, exciting their passion for order and authority by formulating rigid systems of laws and principles in which uncertainty was never allowed to intrude, least of all in the uncertain field of color."[6] He continues: "If they had any doubts, they did not express them. Rather, in reading their authoritative pronouncements, one is impressed by an unshakeable confidence in the correctness of their own ideas."[7]

Johnson observes that the color theories of Jones and Viollet-le-Duc differ in only one regard: the power of red in combination with other colors. He notes further that both believed in a rational basis for architecture and agreed that "construction should be decorated; decoration should never be constructed." The focus of Johnson's book is the stained glass of Chartres, so it is understandable that he does not pursue other concepts shared by Jones and his French colleague. If he had, he might have reported their conviction about the emotional power of architecture and the analogous relationship between architecture and music. Further, they both advanced the arguments that the ancient Greeks would have produced a completely different style of architecture if iron had been at their disposal, and that modern architects needed to seek a style based on the rational use of contemporary materials and technology or be usurped by the engineers.

Even though Viollet-le-Duc recommended the structural rationalism of thirteenth-century Gothic work as an appropriate model and Jones rejected any type of historicism, they both believed in analyzing the masterpieces of the past to identify the universal laws of good design and included historical explanations of architecture and ornament in their lectures and writings. In addition, their texts show that they shared an atypical appreciation for the quality of art produced by primitive societies and rejected unprincipled eclecticism. In practice, they were both daring in their use of iron, color, and abstract ornament. Viollet-le-Duc knew Jones and would have known *Alhambra* before writing the *Dictionairies* or *Entretiens*.[8] Hopefully, future scholars will discover documentation to explain their relationship; in the meantime, the agreement on so many points critical to their theories makes the influence of Jones an intriguing prospect.

JOHN RUSKIN RESPONDS

While Dresser and Viollet-le-Duc advocated principles in agreement with Jones, John Ruskin maintained a fierce opposition. The antipathy between Jones and Ruskin develops throughout their lectures and writings. In "The Poetry of Architecture" (1837–38) and *The Seven Lamps of Architecture* (1849), Ruskin responds indirectly to the fundamental ideas Jones introduced in "On the Influence of Religion upon Art" and *Alhambra*. Jones used the stature and attention gained from his decoration of the Crystal Palace to articulate his theory in "On the Decorations Proposed for the Exhibition Building in Hyde Park" (1850), "Gleanings from the Great Exhibition" (1851), "Attempt to Define the Principles which Should Regulate the Employment of Colour in the Decorative Arts" (1852), "On the True and False in the Decorative Arts" (1852), and "On the Necessity of an Architectural Education on the Part of the Public" (1852). Ruskin responded in *The Stones of Venice* (1853) and *The Opening of the Crystal Palace Considered in Some of its Relations to the Prospects of Art* (1854). Jones introduced new principles counter to Ruskin in *The Grammar of Ornament* (1856) and Ruskin tried to refute Jones's philosophy in "The Deteriorative Power of Conventional Art over Nations" (1858) and "The Unity of Art" (1858), later combined and published as *The Two Paths* (1859). Selections from the works above show the contrast in tone, method, and substance of these ideological adversaries.

One of their major points of disagreement involves race and their positions on Indian and Islamic design. In *Empire Building: Orientalism and Victorian Architecture*, Mark Crinson develops several points important to understanding the attitudes and motivations of Jones and Ruskin.[9] Crinson notes that although Ruskin never traveled to an Islamic country or saw an Islamic building, he discussed Islamic architecture in two significant ways: first, as part of his theory of geographic determinism, and second, in his campaign against Jones and the Schools of Practical Art.

Crinson notes that Ruskin was essentially positive about Islamic design in his early work. For example, in *The Stones of Venice*, Ruskin praised the spirituality and "exquisite refinement" of the work, describing the architecture as "fantastic" and exhibiting "excitement," "enchantment," and "evanescence." He also expressed appreciation for the seriousness and vibrancy of the work, but judged the ephemeral nature of the structures to be indicative of an inferior race.

Crinson contrasts this position with Jones's elevation of the consciousness and appreciation of Islamic architecture through the scope and scholarship of his study of the Alhambra. Crinson argues that since the Victorians equated the quality of architecture with its creators, architectural information contributed significantly to the perception of national character; consequently, by devoting the same level of scholarship to the Moors and Arabs previously exerted in studying Greek, Roman, and Egyptian architecture, Jones's contribution was extraordinary. Earlier architects, such as Cockerell and Freeman, had dismissed Islamic architecture as irrational and capricious; they felt it lacked laws of taste and consistency. Jones corrected and supplanted their impressions by identifying and explaining the logic fundamental to Islamic design, observable in the geometry of their patterns and their balance of color. Jones recognized universal principles in their buildings and recommended the adoption of these principles in contemporary practice.

Jones also understood the unity of religious belief and the memory of architectural origins elemental to Islamic culture and design. He explained that religious belief engendered the use of geometric patterns and inscriptions, rather than realistic depictions of saints or animals. He realized that quotations from the Koran served as visual clues

Fig. 5.9. Christopher Dresser, corner ornament for a ceiling, Pl. XLI from Studies in Design, *1874*

to spirituality and that many of the patterns recalled the tents hung with textiles in the Arabs' past.

Jones analyzed other non-Western cultures and was the first architect to consider the ornament of undeveloped nations worthy of study. He departed from convention by devoting one chapter in *The Grammar of Ornament* to Maori patterns and five to Islamic architecture, but only one to medieval architecture. Further, his revelation that the use of color in Islamic architecture was consistent with recent scientific studies and that the designs were based on rational geometry challenged conventional Western views. Finally, his tireless efforts to promote a new style of architecture based on the principles he observed in Islamic and other ancient architecture may have been among the things that provoked Ruskin to condemn Islamic and other non-Western architecture.

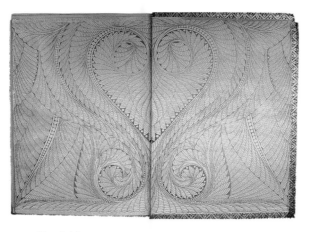

Ruskin cited the abstraction of non-Western ornament as one reason for his criticism. He argued that realistic recording of nature praised the work of God and ennobled the laborer, but conventionalized ornament deprived man of nature's moral guidance and would lead to the destruction of intellectual power and moral principle. He developed this stance in his later writings, contrasting the naturalism practiced in the North, inspiring virtue, with the conventionalism adopted in the South, leading to barbarism and cruelty. He explained this distinction in *The Two Paths* as:

All ornament of that lower kind [conventionalism] is pre-eminently the gift of cruel persons, of Indians, Saracens, Byzantines, and is the delight of the worst and cruelest nations, Moorish, Indian, Chinese, South Sea Islanders, and so on. I say it is their peculiar gift; not, observe, that they are only capable of doing this, while other nations are capable of doing more; but that they are capable of doing this in a way which civilised nations cannot equal. The fancy and delicacy of eye in interweaving lines and arranging colors—mere line and colour, observed

without natural form—seems to be somehow an inheritance of ignorance and cruelty, belonging to men as spots to the tiger or hues to the snake.[10]

Crinson argues that Ruskin's choice of cruel nations deliberately listed the groups Jones recognized in *The Grammar of Ornament*. Crinson goes further, arguing that the tempered racism of *The Stones of Venice* had become the main argument of *The Two Paths*, since Ruskin was trying to maintain Western culture against the onslaught of positivism and Jones's universal principles.

Ruskin did accept the relationship between culture and architecture introduced by Jones, but presented the concept as his own idea, saying: "Every form of noble architecture is in some sort the embodiment of the Polity, Life, History, and Religious Faith of nations." He recognized that "every age had its own unique vision and art corresponding to its peculiar ethical and social life," but, paradoxically, refused to extend that concept to the nineteenth century, insisting "We want no new style of architecture."[11] Instead, he advocated a return to the Pisan Romanesque, the early Gothic of the Western Italian Republics (pre-Giotto), Venetian Gothic, and the English earliest decorated.[12]

His ideas on structure and materials were illogical. He rejected iron for structural support, saying structural knowledge was based on the use of stone, clay, and wood and, therefore, the use of iron was inappropriate. He rejected "structural deceits," but opposed the principle of "decorated construction," saying sculpture, unrelated to the construction of building, was essential to architecture. Finally, he defined architecture as "the art which so disposes and adorns the edifices raised by man for whatsoever uses, that the sight of them contributes to his mental health, power, and pleasure."[13]

Without naming Jones, Ruskin denounced the fact that "A day never passes without our hearing our English architects called upon to be original, and to invent a new style."[14] He insisted that the "forms of architecture already known are good enough for us . . . and it will be time enough to think of changing them for better when we can use them as they are."[15] He continued his opposition to Jones by insisting that the architect should associate with the sculptor, not the engineer.

Ruskin implicitly attacked Jones's philosophy and that of the schools of design, saying, "We shall not manufacture art out of pottery and printed stuffs; we shall not reason out art by our philosophy; we shall not stumble upon art by our experiments."[16] Gombrich notes that Ruskin is doing precisely what he is attacking: reasoning art through philosophy.[17]

Another subject of dispute concerned the type, function, and appearance of architectural ornament. Jones believed that ornament was secondary to the form and function of a building and blamed the failure of contemporary architecture on the disregard for function. In contrast, Ruskin considered ornament "the principal part of architecture,"

TOP *Fig. 5.10. Christopher Dresser, "Knowledge is Power,"* Pl. XXIV *from* Art of Decorative Design, *1862*

ABOVE *Fig. 5.11. Endpapers from* Winged Thoughts, *1851*

impressing upon a building "certain characteristics venerable or beautiful, but otherwise unnecessary."[18] He saw ornament as "a source of aesthetic gratification, a mark of cultivation, and most of all . . .a status symbol, a way of broadcasting institutional or individual dignity and prosperity to the world."[19]

Jones praised the decoration of the Alhambra as an example of ornament used to emphasize and enhance construction. He explained that beauty of form had been achieved in Moorish designs by creating patterns where the lines within the patterns appeared to grow out from each other in gradual undulations with no excrescences.

In *The Seven Lamps of Architecture*, Ruskin condemned Islamic architecture as "impure" and dismissed Arabic ornament as mere line. Jones was not dissuaded, however; after the Great Exhibition, he and Pugin purchased articles in the Indian Collection for the museum at Marlborough as examples of the law of decorating construction.

As mentioned earlier, the noted art historian E. H. Gombrich credited Jones with introducing the psychology of perception into nineteenth-century theory. Gombrich also contrasts the depth of Jones's perception to the void of Ruskin's "graphological expressionism." Gombrich cites explanations of the effects of curving lines and grids underlying pattern construction as examples of Jones's superior understanding. Jones realized that by subdividing and enriching a grid, every line of the pattern produced contributed to the overall effect without interfering with the general form of the item decorated.

Further, grid-based designs produced an attractive appearance from different vantage points. At a distance, only the main lines of the arrangement were visible, but, as the viewer approached the object, the details become evident. The disparity between Ruskin's rhetoric and Jones's perception is apparent in Ruskin's two rules for adapting ornament to sight. The first recommends reducing the size and rudely carving the details farthest from the eye, and the second suggests adopting a design with few parts and simple lines, carved with precision. He admitted flaws in both schemes, saying the first was "a bald execution of a perfect design," while the second showed "a baldness of design with perfect execution."[20] With typical Ruskin oratory and logic, he concludes: "In these very imperfections lies the admirableness of the ornament."[21]

Ruskin also developed a position contrary to Jones with regard to the representation of nature. While Jones rejected the direct imitation of nature, advocating conventionalized images inspired by nature to unify the decoration of each object, Ruskin insisted that man could not "advance in the invention of beauty, without directly imitating natural form."

The conflict extended to the relationship between nature and color. Jones believed color assisted in the perception of form and helped to distinguish objects and parts of objects. He observed that the ancients mirrored nature by distinguishing elements with different colors. Ruskin challenged this hypothesis, saying that color never followed form in nature, but was arranged according to a different system. He cited the stripes of the zebra and the spots of the leopard as evidence and charged that flowers were not variegated with one petal of red and another of white, but with spots of red or zones of white. He argued that color in architecture should be independent from form: columns should be painted with horizontal stripes, not verticals (as in the Crystal Palace), and the divisions of moldings should not be articulated by separate colors as Jones advocated.

Ruskin brought his attack in the open by confessing that he knew his approach to color was "heresy." Undaunted, Jones said Ruskin's position was indeed heresy and championed the bad taste that Jones was trying to eradicate. Humorously, Jones cited horizontal rings of color in ladies' dresses and the broad checks worn by fast men as examples protected "under Mr. Ruskin's assertion, for they just cut the leg into slices in the most approved fashion."[22]

The debate went on. Ruskin continued to oppose the use of color to define form, endorsing constructional, or permanent, polychromy, where a variety of materials in a range of colors produced textured surfaces and patterns independent of form. Although structural elements could be indicated, the purpose of constructional polychromy was not the unity of form and color, but the creation of varied ornamentation in permanent form.

Their dispute involved other aspects of color as well. Jones based his color principles on the scientific studies of Field and Michel-Eugène Chevreul. He articulated these principles in lectures and demonstrated them in the decoration of the Crystal Palace in Hyde Park. He encouraged students to follow these rules and to study Indian textiles to observe examples of the perfect application and balance of color.

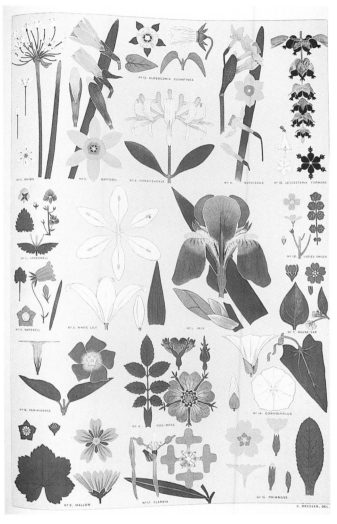

Fig. 5.12. "Leaves & Flowers from Nature No. 8," Pl. XCVIII from The Grammar of Ornament, *1856*

At this point, Ruskin denounced Indian designs and textiles as the work of brutal savages. He also delivered his own set of rules in a lecture entitled "The General Principles of Colour" (December 9, 1854). He began his talk saying he

. . . was most anxious . . . that he should not be understood as depreciating the value of any of those ably illustrated works of Mr. Owen Jones and others who had studied the subject of the law of colour . . . All he meant to convey was that these rules would never teach anyone to color; and the artist who submitted himself to the law of these three primaries was lost forever.[23]

He further castigated Jones's philosophy asserting "Neither he himself nor anybody else could tell anything which would be of the least value, beyond what every person present could find out for himself by the exercise of that noble faculty . . . 'instinct.'" Ruskin defined instinct as "that peculiar faculty by which all creatures did particularly that which it was their function to do, as the bee built its combs." He developed his argument and attack on Jones by explaining that philosophers had studied the hexagonal construction of the bee's honeycombs and "had discovered certain rules, which they had expressed in mathematical and logical formulae. But . . . the bee . . . was perfectly ignorant of the laws of numerical series, by which the principles upon which he acted could be explained and illustrated by the philosopher." Ruskin continued, "The bee did not know, and did not want to know these rules: he built his cells by a higher and a nobler teaching."

Ruskin referred to man's instinctual acts of courage and compassion and declared the case for instinct was especially strong in the arts, where "everything to be well done must be done by instinct." He launched an indirect attack on Jones by saying: "If we went to any noble colourist, to any man of real talent, and asked him why he did such or such a thing, his answer would be, 'I don't know: I do it because it appears to me to look well.'" He said he asked "one of the greatest living colourists, William Hunt, of the Old Water-Colour Society, why he chose a certain color (which appeared to be against all rules) and Hunt responded that 'he did not know; *he was just aiming at it*.'" Ruskin

continued saying he had had frequent opportunities of conversing with J.M.W. Turner, but had never heard him utter a single rule of color, though he had frequently heard him, like all great men, talk of "trying" to do a thing. Ruskin said, "This was ever the language of great genius"; but "a man of no talent, a bad colourist, would be ready to give you mathematical reasons for every colour he put on the canvas."

Ruskin followed these obvious criticisms of Jones with more examples. He said the artist Mulready did not follow rules in painting and that likewise poets, such as Tennyson, and musicians, such as Haydn, were unable to explain how they produced verses or music.

Ruskin professed to be anxious to free his listeners from the idea that they could do nothing without rules. He declared:

We were told, as a rule, that there were three primary colours—red, blue, and yellow—and that these primaries should occur in every composition; that these three colours always existed in a ray of light in the proportions of eight, five, and three, and that in these proportions they neutralised each other, and produced white light. Then said the scientific gentleman, 'Because these colours occur in a ray of light, you should always put them into your compositions in just such a manner as that each colour may be neutralised by its neighbor.' How absurd was all this! Were there not also acids and alkalines in chemistry which neutralised each other? and would it not be equally reasonable for a man to say to his cook, 'Whenever you squeeze a lemon on my veal, put a pinch of magnesia with it, in order that the alkali may neutralise the acid'?[24]

Ruskin pulled out an orange and admired its color. He said a scientific man would color the fruit with eight parts of red and five of blue, but nature had not followed that approach, but had produced the orange color and placed the bright fruit amidst green leaves. Ruskin's audience must have been uneducated with regard to color, since the logic of Ruskin's choice seems to favor Jones's argument rather than Ruskin's, since orange is produced by combining red and yellow and green is created from blue and yellow. He followed with similar specious examples of flowers and the watercolors of Turner, arguing that their beautiful effects had been produced without following arbitrary rules and that adherence to rule would only lead the scholar in a wrong direction and make him moderately conceited.

Ruskin rejected scientific studies of color and instructed artists to ignore all rules and trust to instinct. He recommended studying nature to note attractive combinations of colors and instructed artists, when painting, to put two or three colors into a composition and then the other colors would suggest themselves. He said students hampered by rules would miss the opportunities available at every hour of the day to observe color. Amazingly, in a typical Ruskinian contradiction and reversal of logic, he followed his rejection of rules by imposing a set of his own rules, called "necessities." He assured his audience that these necessities were acknowledged by the most successful of ancient and modern colorists.

These necessities included gradation, subtlety, and surprise. For gradation, Ruskin claimed that no color was valuable until it was gradated or appeared to be dying. He defined gradation as the passing of colors from one to another, becoming paler or darker. He cited examples of gradations experienced in viewing the scarlet cactus at twilight and some of Turner's watercolors.

His concept of subtlety referred to the placement of colors, since he thought a grain more or less of color could harm a composition. He drew an example from a painting by Paul Veronese where he noted a small white hair upon the paw of a cat in the foreground as essential to the complete the picture. His law of surprise centered on the delight experienced from sudden changes, such as unexpected notes in a composition and said that surprise was the principal cause of the pleasure of listening to music. He contradicted an earlier argument by saying that the old masters established laws and then transgressed them playfully and effectively.

He returned to color, saying viewing a sunset, with clouds of scarlet, gold, purple, white, and gray, provided the best lessons. He praised the beauty of crimson and cautioned students to use that sacred color, the symbol of life, with extreme care. These arguments and digressions reveal the contrast between Ruskin's emotional and rhetorical approach to color and Jones's scientifically based logic. Ruskin ignored the fact that reliance upon instinct had produced the inferior and tasteless state of British design. Telling students to copy attractive colors offered no improvement.

Their battle was waged in print and in lectures and critics reported the conflict. An 1857 article entitled "Iron Architecture" in the *Building News* directed readers to ignore Ruskin's lectures and "carefully digest the one that was recently delivered at the Institute by Owen Jones in order to learn that true art consists in idealizing upon, not in copying from, nature."[25]

Similar comparisons continued after Jones's death (1874); for example, in 1889, J. L. Roget told readers of the *Architect* "Mr. Ruskin would obey the presumed injunction of nature by copying the most frequent of her forms, while Mr. Owen Jones would follow her dictates by imitating the most common qualities of her forms."[26] A writer for the *Building News* commented on the strides made in the decorative arts after the Great Exhibition and paid tribute to Jones saying: "The teachings of Ruskin may have done something, but the beautiful works of Owen Jones, and the examples of the true principles of decorative Art he has left us in the courts at Sydenham have largely educated the popular eye and taste in this direction."[27] Dresser echoed this sentiment, describing Jones as "a man who, by his

works, has manifested his knowledge of ornament, and who has given forth more real practical information respecting the decorative art in his propositions . . . than Mr. Ruskin has in his more voluminous writings."[28]

Ruskin was not an architect; consequently, his writings emphasize the aesthetic, rather than the functional, aspects of the built environment. He ignored contemporary problems and contradicted many of his own statements. He died regretting many of his earlier writings and condemning much of the architecture resulting from his recommendations, but the volume of his writings, his popularity, and the fact that he lived twenty-six years after Jones died, contributed to the fact that today he is the better known of the rivals.

WILLIAM MORRIS

Even though Jones and Ruskin were ideologically opposed, many designers drew ideas from both of their philosophies. William Morris is perhaps the best example. Morris identified two functions for the decorative arts and these reflect the dichotomy in the teachings of Jones and Ruskin. The first function, "To give people pleasure in the things they *use*" agrees with Jones; while the second, "To give people pleasure in the things they *make*" follows Ruskin.[29]

Morris followed Ruskin in promoting the art of the craftsman, but adopted Jones's theories of color and pattern

making. Like Dresser, Morris spread Jones's theory through the success of his lectures, writings, and designs (Figs. 5.14–5.16). Unlike Dresser, Morris did not refer to Jones in his writings but did use images from *The Grammar of Ornament* to illustrate the lectures he began giving in 1877 (Fig. 5.13).[30]

Like Jones, Morris discussed the history of design, tracing the symbolism of Egyptian art, the intellectual perfection of the Greeks, the imperialism of the Romans, and the

TOP *Fig. 5.15. William Morris, "Flower Garden" textile design in woven silk, 1879*

ABOVE *Fig. 5.16. William Morris, "Wandle" textile design in printed cotton, 1884*

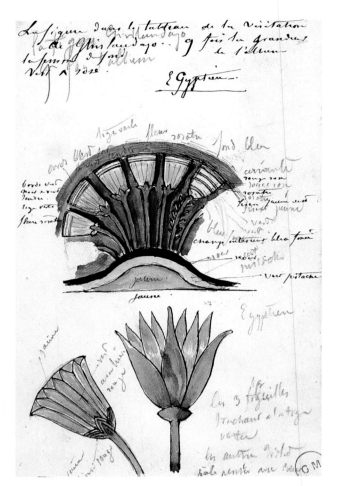

Fig. 5.17. *Copy of an Egyptian fresco after Owen Jones by Gustave Moreau for* Orestes et les Erinyes, *1885–92, and* Salomé tatouée, *1876*

Fig. 5.18. *"Egyptian No. 2," Pl. V, from* The Grammar of Ornament, *1856*

beauty of medieval designs. Both men looked to nature and history as sources for knowledge and inspiration and encouraged students to do the same. Jones said "If a student in the arts, earnest in his search after knowledge . . . will examine for himself the works of the past, compare them with the works of nature, bend his mind to a thorough appreciation of the principles which reign in each, he cannot fail to be himself a creator."[31] Morris gave the same advice, telling students to "follow nature, study antiquity, make your own art."[32]

Jones and Morris also shared the same convictions about beauty. They believed that the conditions of man could be improved through the repose, or serenity, produced by beautiful surroundings composed of well-designed objects. If this condition could be achieved for the general populace, both men believed the mental and physical health of the entire nation would be improved. They recognized the potential to produce aesthetically pleasing, useful, and affordable goods through industrial production.[33] Their desire to make all useful objects beautiful opposed Ruskin's belief in the beautification of useless objects and the restriction of ornament to places of rest and leisure.[34]

Unlike Ruskin, Jones and Morris believed in the importance of art education and encouraged the cultivation of the mind, eye, and hand. They advocated museums and exhibitions in small towns as well as large cities to facilitate the education of designers and manufacturers. Jones was important in developing the collection of Eastern objects in the South Kensington Museum, and Morris's study of that collection led to an appreciation of Eastern design equal to Jones's. Morris described Persia as the Holy Land of designers and developed his later patterns from Persian, Turkish, and Italian designs.[35]

Jones and Morris went beyond most of their contemporaries to study the materials, techniques, and processes used to produce their designs. They even participated in transferring their designs to the large-grid papers required for the machine production of textiles. Jones found the work tedious, but Morris enjoyed coloring in the squares designating the color and position of each thread.

Both designers created two-dimensional abstract patterns inspired by nature. Morris's designs are less abstract than Jones's, since Morris believed that all designs needed some symbolism.[36] He practiced a hierarchy of conventionalization, ranging from the coarsest materials (carpets) in abstract patterns to more realistic designs for tapestries. Basically, however, his guidelines for pattern making and color agree with Jones's theory. For example, Morris agreed that all patterns "should have definite form bounded by a firm outline" and that the lines forming the design should correspond to rational growth, with one thing seeming to grow out of another, which is related to Jones's Proposition Six: "Beauty of form is produced by lines growing out one from the other in gradual undulations . . ."

Morris also described the basic elements of pattern construction as: horizontal lines, block diapers, or checkers (made from lines or circles) and floriated diapers formed by stems with leaves or flowers in the interstices. He used the term "branch" for a diagonal line and "net" to indicate a grid composed of diamond shapes. Like Jones, he arranged his motifs on a grid framework and achieved flatness through his understanding of color (Figs. 5.15 and 5.16). He explained that the relationship between color and relief took two forms. The first type contrasted a light figure on a dark ground or the reverse; in the second, every part of the pattern was outlined with color to distinguish the motif from the ground. He said designers concerned with form adopt the first technique, since the contrast establishes at least two planes in the design. Designers interested in color prefer the second method, where colors are separated but the pattern remains flat. Morris identified the first approach as Western and the second as Eastern. Similar to Jones, Morris recommended the adoption of continuous lines and other techniques developed by Eastern nations to beautify contemporary houses.[37]

His guidelines for wallpapers and the decoration of houses parallel Jones's. For example, he accepts the fashion of dividing walls with dadoes or friezes, but rejects papers imitating pictures, embroidery, or tapestry. Again, like Jones, Morris recommends simplicity achieved through less elaborate designs and the reduction of the number of patterns in a room. He parrots Jones's admonition to refrain from using muddy colors and follows his recommendations for the composition of carpet borders.

These examples represent their philosophic accord. A review of their designs shows a similar concurrence in practice. Morris's biographer Paul Thompson explains that Jones and Pugin had already shifted taste from realistic patterns to highly conventionalized geometric designs before Morris designed his first wallpapers, creating a fashion for "austere diapers, formal fleur-de-lis and acanthus, in almost heraldic colors."[38] Morris's first designs (1864–6) reverted to realism and were largely ignored by consumers and the design community. In 1871, he shifted to geometric patterns closer to prevailing fashion; these include "Diaper," "Indian," and "Venetian." By 1872 he adopted the diagonal grids, flat patterns, and continuous lines characteristic of Eastern designs and the work of Jones, patterns such as the familiar "Jasmine," "Branch," and "Vine."[39]

Jones's designs continued to be preferred over Morris's patterns and continued in production after Jones's death.[40] They were frequently judged superior to contemporary designs, until the preference for formalized patterns waned at the end of the century.

Jones's designs continued to be preferred in the 1870s, but the popularity of Morris's designs in the late twentieth century has overshadowed this fact.[41] The surviving Morris drawings showing motifs borrowed from *The Grammar of Ornament* and the parallels in the theory and method of Morris and Jones, suggests Jones's influence. One thing is

certain, Jones and Morris shared an appreciation of Eastern design and adopted techniques of Eastern pattern making, which contributed significantly to Western design.

LE CORBUSIER AND FRANK LLOYD WRIGHT

While our understanding of Jones's influence on Morris is imprecise, many other designers acknowledged Jones's influence. Some, such as Dresser and Jacob Wrey Mould, were pupils or apprentices of Jones; most, however, assimilated Jones's philosophy and techniques by studying the principles and theory outlined in *The Grammar of Ornament* and copying the plates of the text (Fig. 5.17 and Pl. 5.2). André Evard, a student in the La Chaux-de-Fonds art school in 1905, recalled his first meeting with Professor Charles L'Eplattenier. L'Eplattenier handed Evard a copy of *The Grammar* and told to him to copy the propositions. L'Eplattenier introduced Jones's philosophy to all of his pupils, including Charles-Édouard Jeanneret (Le Corbusier).[42]

Studying the ideas and patterns in *The Grammar of Ornament* gave pupils the techniques, motivation, and confidence to begin experimenting with form and pattern. Frank Lloyd Wright and the young Jeanneret studied the patterns and principles in the book and went on to develop new styles of architecture appropriate to their time and place.[43] An in-depth analysis of Jones's influence on these, and other, designers is beyond the scope of this text, but a few examples indicate the methods and principles they shared with Jones.

The early designs and writings of Wright and Le Corbusier reveal their serious attempts to apply Jones's propositions and follow his mandates to study nature and geometry. As a result, the designs they produced in 1905 show a remarkable similarity and I argue that this is not "a perfect example of the simultaneous manifestation of similar forms (or ideas) occurring among original thinkers at a given moment in different parts of the world," but the direct result of the application of Jones's ideas.[44] Several scholars have shown that Jones's philosophy remained a critical force in the work of Wright and Le Corbusier. I agree with their findings and offer the following examples to support the position that Jones's impact went beyond training the eyes and hands of these designers to inform their theory and approach to design.

Fig. 5.19. Louis Sullivan, drawing of an ornamental motif, 1873

Since Wright admitted few influences, his recognition of Jones and Viollet-le-Duc is significant. In *An Autobiography*, he describes borrowing *The Grammar of Ornament* and Viollet-le-Duc's *Habitations of Man in All Ages* from the library of All Souls Church in Chicago.[45] His initial response to *The Grammar* was the certainty that propositions one through five were "dead right." These are the seminal propositions concerning the derivation of the decorative arts from architecture, the definition of architecture as "the material expression of the wants, the faculties, and the sentiments, of the age in which it is created," the stipulation that architecture and the decorative arts should "possess fitness, proportion, harmony to achieve repose," the understanding that "True beauty results from that repose which the mind feels when the eye, the intellect, and the affections, are satisfied from the absence of any want," and, finally, "Construction should be decorated. Decoration should never be purposely constructed." Although Wright said he was unsure about the other propositions at first, his later work shows that he absorbed their logic as well.

Wright traced the designs from *The Grammar* on nights and Sundays and showed some of the tracings to Louis Sullivan during their first meeting (1887).[46] Wright said Sullivan was unaware of *The Grammar*, but that is unlikely; Sullivan had been employed by Frank Furness and William le Baron Jenney. Jenney's office contained a copy of *The Grammar* and Furness trained in the aetelier of Richard Morris Hunt, where copies of *The Grammar*, *Alhambra*, and other architecture books formed the educational foundation, supplemented with subscriptions to contemporary architecture periodicals. Hunt's students routinely copied from the books in his library, filling sketchbooks with drawings and ornament. This practice explains Furness's conventionalized ornament in the style of Jones and Dresser that "hypnotized" Sullivan.[47] Sullivan prepared drawings in the same style as early as 1873 and one of these drawings survives in the Avery Library (Fig. 5.19). Wright's writing appears on the back, showing that he had studied this work from the hand of Sullivan.[48]

Some historians link the character of Sullivan's ornament to the Celtic motifs and other patterns in *The Grammar*.[49] Thomas Beeby sees a correspondence between nature as the basis of design in Jones's book and Sullivan's *A System of Architectural Ornament*. Sullivan developed his own technique, creating motifs alluding to plant forms derived from geometry, not natural flora. He began with a geometric shape and elaborated the boundary to form radial trajectories at the points of intersection. He then subdivided the main shape and embellished the axial lines and points of intersection with exuberant motifs reminiscent of stems and foliage. This technique produced a complex design with seemingly organic qualities. Wright learned this method of design from *Der Liebe Meister* and boasted that after a year or two Sullivan was often unable to distinguish between Wright's ornament and his own.

Wright, however, also experimented with conventionalizing natural forms, in the manner of Jones, and moved beyond Sullivan's surface decoration to create ornament "*of* the surface, never *on* it.[50] The decorative themes of the Prairie and Usonian Houses represent motifs abstracted from nature, such as the tulip, tree of life, and wingseed patterns devised for the Avery Coonley (Fig. 5.20), Darwin B. Martin (Fig. 5.21), and John and Catherine Christian residences (Fig. 5.23). Wright said these motifs gave each work an organic integrity and provided him with nature's wealth of artistic suggestion.[51] The grid provided the other guiding element in the Prairie and Usonian houses. Wright used the dimensions from the grid to regulate every element of ornament and construction, achieving a proportional relationship between all of the parts and a synthesis of ornament and structure consistent with Jones's theory.

Wright combined ornament and structure in the textile block and Usonian houses (Figs. 5.22 and 5.23), and by late career, the "organic abstractions" became "ornament structuralized," where the program and the structural require-

Fig. 5.22. Frank Lloyd Wright, Ennis House, Los Angeles, California, 1923

Fig. 5.23. Frank Lloyd Wright, view into dining alcove of John and Catherine Christian House, West Lafayette, Indiana, 1954

The Legacy 251

Fig. 5.24. Frank Lloyd Wright, Grady Gammage Memorial Auditorium, Tempe, Arizona, 1959

Fig. 5.25. Frank Lloyd Wright, carpet design from Grady Gammage Memorial Auditorium, Tempe, Arizona, 1959

the text, first in their geometric patterns and later in their architecture. A comparison of a 1905 drawing by Le Corbusier with Wright's contemporaneous piers and capitals at Unity Temple, Oak Park, Illinois, 1905–6, shows both men trying to produce ornament through abstraction (Figs. 5.26 and 5.27).[52]

Pl. 5.2 shows Le Corbusier copying from the plates in The Grammar, probably an assignment for Eugène Schaltenbrand or Charles L'Epplattier, both professors who used Jones's text as the "bible," (Le Corbusier's description) in their courses. Other early designs and structural elements, such as the corbels of the Villa Fallet, can be found in Jones's works and in Persian architecture.[53]

The drawing in the upper right-hand corner of Fig. 5.26 depicts a diaper pattern Le Corbusier formed by repeating a stylized motif of fir trees. This type of diaper is characteristic of other designs by Le Corbusier and Jones. This similarity can be attributed to their use of the diagonal grid and their method of conventionalization.

Like Jones, the works of Wright and Le Corbusier pay particular attention to the use of color to assist in the definition of form and the sensation of the viewer. The research of Mark Wigley and Barbara Klinkhammer indicates Le Corbusier's continuous concern for color. In White Walls, Designer Dresses, Wigley discusses the disparity between Le Corbusier's theory and practice. Wigley points out that although Le Corbusier advocated the elimination of color, he continued to apply a consistent palette throughout his career. Wigley explains that most of Le Corbusier's student drawings and early projects "are indebted to the theory of polychrome ornament presented in Owen Jones's Grammar of Ornament," and that Le Corbusier's later work returns to the privilege of color inherent in the tradition of the decorative arts.[54] For Wigley, this is not surprising; Le Corbusier had accepted Jones's objective of adopting new technologies and materials to create a modern style of architecture.[55]

While the examples above stress an attitude toward and incorporation of color, ornament, and geometry in the work of Wright and Le Corbusier representative of Jones's theory and design methodology, it is also important to consider the influence Jones may have had in inspiring the innovation, order, clarity, proportion (or modularity), and cohesiveness in their work. Evidence of this broader and pervasive influence is suggested in a comparison of two architects: Jacob Wrey Mould and Frank Furness. In 1876, a critic for the American Architect and Building News noted "a curious analogy, without any specific resemblances, between his work [Furness's] in Philadelphia and that which Mr. Mould has done in New York. Both are wonderfully fertile and brilliant in invention, with a keen delight in color, which sometimes makes them forget that architecture is an art of modeling with lights and shadows . . . of both it may be said . . . that the decorator in them tends to overpower the architect."[56] The similar spirit motivating

ments are satisfied but are secondary to the ornamental manipulation of space, volume, and detail. Wright called his approach integral ornament and described it as human imagination giving natural pattern to structure. Wright aimed at making his patterns as articulate in his buildings as structural form is represented in trees and natural phenomena. Wright understood the concept of integral ornament as the expression of the inner rhythm of form (Figs. 5.24 and 5.25).

Although the architecture produced by Wright and Le Corbusier differs substantially, concurrences in their work and thinking point to the influence of Jones. Both men were introduced to the theory of architecture by studying Jones's principles. They produced formal exercises from The Grammar of Ornament and tried to understand and express the universal laws of nature and mathematics expressed in their designs and their interest in color and ornament can be attributed to Jones. Mould was Jones's pupil before moving to New York and Furness was influenced by the work of Dresser. It is impossible to estimate the number of other designers who also assimilated Jones's principles and methods of design and the subsequent generations they influenced. When these numbers are considered, it becomes easy to agree with Dresser that the writings and designs of Jones had a greater influence on the decorative arts and architecture than the more voluminous writings of Ruskin.

When Jones died, one critic wrote "Although he erected few buildings of magnitude, the influence of Mr. Owen Jones's life as a teacher of the philosophy of Art has greatly changed the national taste, and his examples and writings have done more to inculcate a knowledge of true Art than if he had left us a magnitude of buildings."[57] Today the buildings are gone, but Jones's writings, and those of his contemporaries, reveal the substance of his theory and the impact of his ideas and designs during a time of turbulent change in England and of vitriolic debate within the emerging architecture profession. Placed in this context, the significance of Jones's understanding of the problems and the possibilities affecting architecture and society becomes clear and the magnitude of his ideological and practical contributions merit a place in future discussions of architecture theory and history.

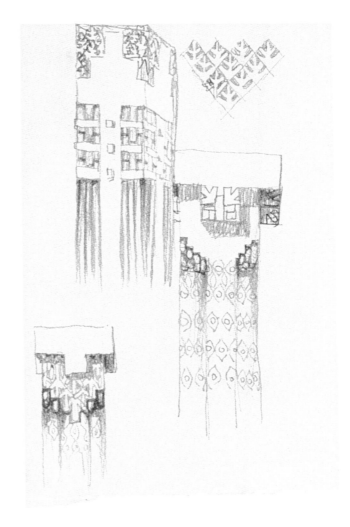

Fig. 5.26. Le Corbusier, studies for piers, columns, and capitals, 1904–5

Fig. 5.27. Frank Lloyd Wright, detail of ornament from Unity Temple, Oak Park, Illinois, 1904

Pl. 5.1. "Egyptian No. 1," Pl. IV from The Grammar of Ornament, 1856

FACING PAGE
Pl. 5.2. Le Corbusier copy of "Egyptian No. 1," Pl. IV from The Grammar of Ornament, 1856

254 Chapter Five

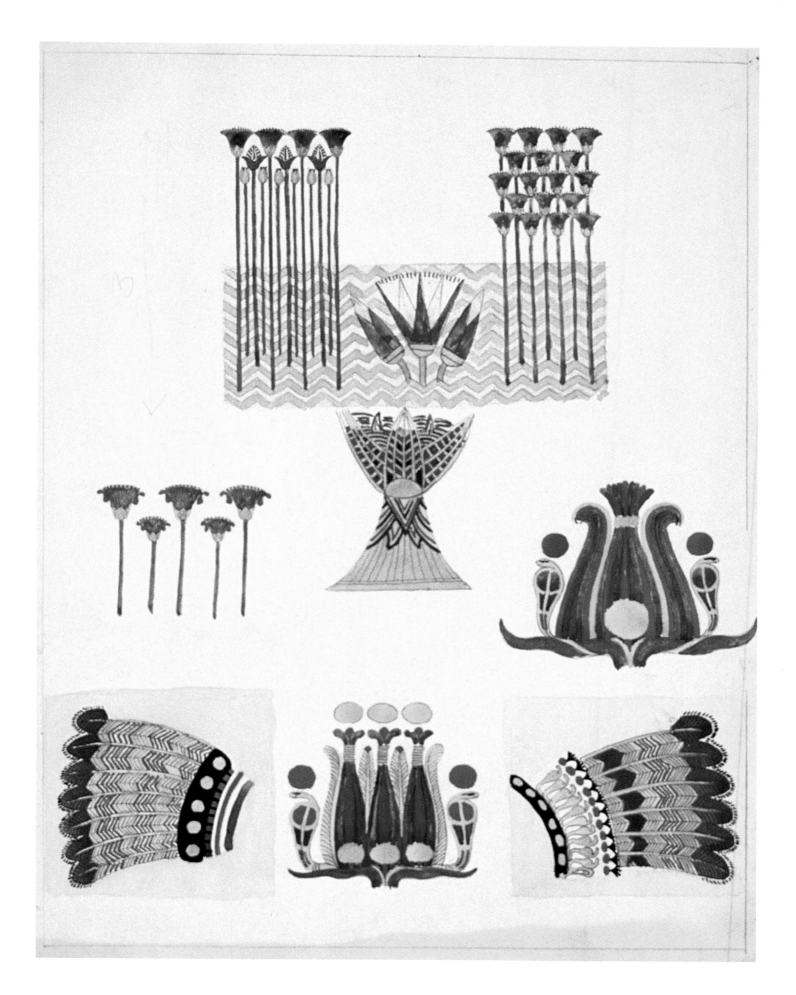

NOTES

INTRODUCTION

1. I am grateful to Dr. Elizabeth Darby for this information.
2. "There is no book on Owen Jones yet—a serious gap in the historiography of Victorian design," Nikolaus Pevsner, *Some Architectural Writers of the Nineteenth Century* (Oxford: Clarendon Press, 1972), 157.

CHAPTER ONE

A NEW UNDERSTANDING
OF ARCHITECTURE

1. John Archer, *The Literature of British Domestic Architecture 1715–1842* (Cambridge, MA: The MIT Press, 1985), 23.
2. David Watkin, *The Rise of Architectural History* (London: The Architectural Press, 1980), 64–9.
3. Matthew Arnold, *The Study of Celtic Literature* (London: Smith, Elder, & Co., 1891), 20–3. A tombstone with an inscription commemorating both Owen Jones Sr. and Jr. located in the churchyard of All Hallows the Less, London, was destroyed by a bomb in World War II according to William Kent, *The Lost Treasures of London* (London: Phoenix House, Ltd., 1947), 90. I am grateful to Jan Piggott for these references.
4. G. M. Trevelyan, *Illustrated English Social History*, vol. 4 (London: Longmans, Green and Co.), 75.
5. Owen Jones Box, John Johnson Collection, New Bodleian Library, Oxford University, Oxford, UK.
6. Vuillamy's best-known works are the Law Society, London (1828–36); the Royal Institution, London (1838); the Dorchester House, London (1863–70); and Westonbirt House (1863–70).
7. Howard Colvin, *A Biographical Dictionary of British Architects 1600–1840*, 3rd ed. (New Haven and London: Yale University Press, 1997), s.v. Lewis Vuillamy, and Adolf K. Placzek, ed., *MacMillan Encyclopedia of Architects* (London: The Free Press, 1982), s.v. Lewis Vuillamy, 353.
8. A letter from A. W. Potter, Royal Academy of Arts, to the author dated August 16, 1995 indicates Jones was admitted to the academy June 25, 1830; a medal in the Owen Jones Box, John Johnson Collection, gives the date of June 26, 1830.
9. *Gentleman's Magazine* (June 1830): 542.
10. List, Owen Jones Box, John Johnson Collection.
11. J. G. Fichte, *Characteristics of the Present Age* (1806); William Hazlitt, *Spirit of the Age* (1825); Thomas Carlyle's "Signs of the Times" (1838) and "Characteristics" (1831); and Mill's "Spirit of the Age," published between 1829 and 1831. A. Dwight Culler, *The Victorian Mirror of History* (New Haven and London: Yale University Press, 1985), 39–66. I am grateful to Rob Craig for the Carlyle reference.
12. J. C. Loudon, *The Architectural Magazine and Journal*, vol. 2 (London: Longman, Rees, Orme, Brown, Green & Longman, 1835), 313–4.
13. Although Frederick Catherwood's study of the Dome of the Rock had been prepared in 1833, it had not been published.
14. Robin D. Middleton, "Hittorff's Polychrome Campaign" in *The Beaux-Arts and Nineteenth-Century French Architecture* (Cambridge, MA: The MIT Press, 1982), 176.
15. *The Builder* (May 9, 1874): 384.
16. Henry Vizetelly, *Glances Back through Seventy Years* (London: Kegan Paul, Trench, Trubner & Co., Ltd., 1893), 200. I am grateful to Robert Thorne for this reference and to Ronald Lewcock for locating the information.
17. Kathryn Ferry, "Printing the Alhambra: Owen Jones and Chromolithography," *Architectural History* 46 (2003): 175–88.
18. Michael Darby, *Owen Jones and the Eastern Ideal* (doctoral dissertation, University of Reading, UK, 1974), 48, 52–3, and Stuart Durant, *Ornament from the Industrial Revolution to Today* (Woodstock and New York: The Overlook Press, 1986), 140.
19. Mildred Archer, *Early Views of India* (London: Thames and Hudson, Ltd., 1980), 234.
20. J. B. Waring, *Masterpieces of Industrial Art and Sculpture at the International Exhibit of 1862* (London: Day and Son, 1863), preface.
21. Antonio Fernández-Puertas, *The Alhambra*, vol. 1 (London: Saqi Books, 1997), 161, 282.
22. The passage from Hugo's *Les Orientales* (1829) reads: L'ALHAMBRA! L'ALHAMBRA! PALAIS QUE LES GENIES / ONT DORÉ COMME UN REVE ET REMPLI D'HARMONIES; / FORTERESSE AUX CRÉNEAUX FESTONNÉS ET CROULANS / OÙ L'ON ENTEND LA NUIT DE MAGIQUES SYLLABES, / QUAND LA LUNE, À TRAVERS LES MILLE ARCEAUX ARABES, / SÈME LES MURS DE TRÈFLES BLANCS! Frederica Harlow-McRae translates this passage as: "The Alhambra! The Alhambra! Palace that genius / Has gilded like a dream and filled with harmony; / Fortress with scalloped and tottering battlements / Where one hears night's magic words [syllables], / When the moon, across its [the Alhambra's] thousand Arabic arches / spreads white clover [*trefle* = trefoil, as in arches] over the walls." The dedication (in English and French) reads: "To the Memory of Jules Goury, Architect / Who died of cholera, at Granada, August XXVIII, MDCCCXXXIV / Whilst engaged in preparing the original drawings. / This work is inscribed, / By his friend, / Owen Jones."
23. Maxim Newmark, *Dictionary of Spanish Literature* (New York: Philosophical Library, 1956), 136–7, and Philip Ward, ed., *The Oxford Companion to Spanish Literature* (Oxford: Clarendon Press, 1978), 238.
24. Owen Jones, *Plans, Elevations, Sections, and Details of the Alhambra* (London: n. p., 1842–5), vol. 1, Pl. I, and Owen Jones "On the Influence of Religion upon Art," (London: n. p., 1863), 18.
25. Jones, *Alhambra*, vol. 1, Pl. X.
26. For ceilings (Pls. VIII and XVIII); column capitals (Pl. XXXIV); spandrels (Pls. XXIII, XXXVI); cornices (Pl. IX); arches (Pls. XXII, XXVII, XXVIII); porticoes and pavilions (Pl. XIII); windows (Pls. IV, XX) and doors (Pl. XXXII) in vol. 1; and lintels (Pl. XXXV, vol. 2) in Jones, *Alhambra*.
27. Jones, *Alhambra*, vol. 1, Pls. III, XIV.
28. Jones, *Alhambra*, vol. 1, text for Pl. XLIV.
29. Middleton, "Hittorff's Polychrome Campaign," 191–5, and Claude Mignot, *Architecture of the Nineteenth Century in Europe* (New York: Rizzoli, 1984), 84.
30. Jones, *Alhambra*, vol. 1, text for Pl. XXXIX.
31. Owen Jones, *Designs for Mosaic and Tessellated Pavements* (London: John Weale, 1842), and Owen Jones, *Encaustic Tiles* (London: n. p., 1843).
32. *The Athenaeum* (1844): 387 and (May 4, 1844): 410.
33. *The Athenaeum* (May 4, 1844): 410.
34. *The Builder* (May 18, 1844): 247.
35. Henry-Russell Hitchcock, *Early Victorian Architecture* (New Haven: Yale University Press, 1954), 37.
36. "Exhibition of Decorative Works at King Street St. James," *The Times* (April 29, 1844).

37. *The Illustrated London News* (April 27, 1844): 266, and *The Civil Engineer and Architect's Journal* (April 1844): 175.

38. T.S.R. Boase, ed., The Oxford History of English Art, vol. 10 (Oxford: Clarendon Press, 1959), 196.

39. Michael Darby, *The Islamic Perspective* (London: The World of Islam Festival Trust, 1983), 20.

40. Oleg Grabar, *The Alhambra* (Cambridge, MA: Harvard University Press, 1978), 103.

41. E. H. Gombrich, *The Sense of Order: A Study in the Psychology of Decorative Art* (originally published 1979; reprinted London: Phaidon Press, Ltd., 1994), 51, 54, 102.

42. Oleg Grabar, *The Mediation of Ornament* (Princeton: Princeton University Press, 1992), 59, and Gombrich, *The Sense of Order*, 237.

43. Jones, *Alhambra*, vol. 1, Pl. XXXVIII; Jones, "On the True and False Principles in the Decorative Arts," delivered at the Marlborough House in 1852.

44. For a discussion of the inscriptions in the Fine Arts courts at Sydenham see Carol A. Hrvol Flores, "Engaging the Mind's Eye: The Use of Inscriptions in the Architecture of Owen Jones and A.W.N. Pugin" *Journal Society of Architectural Historians* vol. 60, no. 2 (June 2001): 158–79 and *Owen Jones, Architect* (doctoral dissertation, Georgia Institute of Technology, 1996).

45. Jones, *Alhambra*, vol. 1, Pls. XL, XLI, and XLII, and Owen Jones, *The Grammar of Ornament* (London: Day and Son, 1856), 72–4.

46. Reviews of the London Exhibition of 1862 credit Jones for the elimination of realism from British wallpapers and textiles and earning awards for some British firms, reversing the trend of the British products displayed in the Great Exhibition of 1851.

47. Jones, *Alhambra*, vol.1, Pl. XXVII.

48. Jones, *Alhambra*, vol. 1, Pl. XXXVIII, and Proposition Twenty-Two from *The Grammar*.

49. Jones, *Alhambra*, vol.1, Pl. XXXVIII.

50. Jones, *Alhambra*, vol. 1, Pl. XXXV.

51. Middleton, "Hittorff's Polychrome Campaign," 206–7.

52. Washington Irving, *The Alhambra* (New York: G. Putnam's Sons, 1865), 64–6.

53. Jones, *Alhambra*, vol. 1, Pl. XXXVIII.

54. Washington Irving, *The Alhambra: A Series of Tales and Sketches of the Moors and Spaniards* (Philadelphia: Carey & Lea, 1832), and Irving, *The Alhambra*, 60.

55. For a discussion of Jones and Pugin, see Flores, "Engaging the Mind's Eye."

56. Augustus-Charles Pugin, *Specimens of Gothic Architecture*, 2 vols. (London: n. p., 1821, 1823); *Gothic Ornaments* (London: n. p., 1831); and *Pugin's Gothic Furniture* (London: R. Ackerman, 1827). Alexandra Wedgwood, "The Early Years" in *Pugin: A Gothic Passion*, eds. Paul Atterbury and Clive Wainwright (New Haven and London: Yale University Press, 1994), 23–5.

57. Wedgwood, "The Early Years," 24, and Jonathan Glancey, "The Great Goth," *Perspectives on Architecture* (June 1994): 26.

58. Many scholars have discussed this, including: Clive Wainwright, "'Not a Style but a Principle': Pugin and His Influence," in *Pugin: A Gothic Passion*, 1; A.W.N. Pugin, *Contrasts, or A Parallel between the Noble Edifices of the Middle Ages, and Corresponding Buildings of the Present Day. Shewing the Present Decay of Taste: Accompanied by Appropriate Text* (London: Charles Dolman, 1841); Phoebe Stanton, "The Sources of Pugin's Contrasts," in *Concerning Architecture: Essays on Architectural Writers and Writing Presented to Nikolaus Pevsner* (London: Allen Lane, The Penguin Press, 1968); Flores, *Owen Jones, Architect*, 28–36; and Rosemary Hill, "Reformation to Millennium: Pugin's *Contrasts* in the History of English Thought," *JSAH* 58 (1999): 26–41.

59. Wainwright, "'Not a Style but a Principle,'" 6, 7.

60. The idea that Byzantine architecture was the basis for both Gothic and Arabic art and architecture was a popular concept. Joseph Gwilt, *The Encyclopedia of Architecture* (1867 edition; reprinted New York: Bonanza Books, 1982), 53.

61. Stanton, *Pugin*, 104

62. Mark Girouard, *The Victorian Country House* (New Haven: Yale University Press, 1985), 112. The Latin translation of "Except the Lord . . ." is *"Nisi Dominus Aedificica Verit Domum in Vanum Labor Averunt qui aeidficant eam."* Pugin prominently exhibited this psalm in Latin in the central lobby of the Palace of Westminster.

63. Nicola Coldstream, *The Decorated Style* (Toronto: University of Toronto Press, 1994).

64. Armando Petrucci, *Public Lettering* (Chicago: The University of Chicago Press, 1993), 12–3.

65. Petrucci, *Public Lettering*, 2.

66. Stanton, *Pugin*, 104.

67. Ibid., 106–7.

68. Ibid., 109–10.

69. Ibid., 107.

70. W. G. Short, *Pugin's Gem: A Brief History of the Roman Catholic Church of Saint Giles, Cheadle* (Stoke-on-Trent, UK: Webberley Ltd., 1981), 11. Gilding is substituted for yellow, a change that Jones often made as well.

71. The riser of the lowest step near the rood screen says: *"Venient ad eam omnes gentes et dicent: Venite et ascendamus ad montem Domini et ad domum Dei Jacob,"* which translates as "All nations will come to it and will say: Come and let us go up to the mountain of the Lord and the house of the God of Jacob." The upper riser displays the words *"Fundata est domus Domini supra verticem montium et exaltata super omnes colles est,"* which translates as: "The house of the Lord is built on the top of the mountains and exalted above all the hills," from Isaiah 2:3. The steps leading into the chapel read: "He gave them bread from heaven. Man ate the bread of angels" taken from Psalm 77 according to Short, *Pugin's Gem*, 12, 15.

72. Roderick O'Donnell, "Pugin as Church Architect," in *Pugin: A Gothic Passion*, 73, and Stanton, *Pugin*, 108.

73. Short, *Pugin's Gem*, 15

74. Jones, *Alhambra*, vol. 1, Pl. II.

75. Marvin Trachtenberg and Isabel Hyman, *Architecture from Prehistory to Postmodernism* (New York: Prentice-Hall/Abrams, 1986), 247–8.

76. Sir Robert Cooke, *The Palace of Westminster* (New York: Burton Skira, 1987), 87–8.

77. Pugin also used Old French for inscriptions on the exterior and interior of the palace.

78. Megan Aldrich, ed., *The Craces: Royal Decorators 1768–1899* (Brighton and London: The Royal Pavilion Art Gallery and Museums, 1990), 74.

79. Rosemary Hill, "The Microcosm of London: Pugin's Parents and His Early Life," presented at the Pugin and the Gothic Revival Conference, Victoria and Albert Museum, July 1994.

80. Wainwright, "'Not a Style but a Principle,'" 1.

81. Alexandra Wedgwood, *Pugin and His Family* (London: Victoria and Albert Museum, 1985), 232.

82. Proposition Four in Jones, *The Grammar*.

83. Stanton, "The Sources of Pugin's *Contrasts*," 120.

84. Ibid., 121.

85. Pugin, *Contrasts*, 1–2, and see Jones, "On the Influence of Religion upon Art," 15.

86. Jones, "On the Influence of Religion upon Art," 16, and Pugin, *Contrasts*, 5–6.

87. Jones, Ibid., 19–20, and Pugin, Ibid., 6.

88. Stanton, *Pugin*, 25–6.

89. Jones, "On the Influence of Religion upon Art," 21.

90. Margaret Belcher, "Pugin Writing," in *Pugin: A Gothic Passion*, 105.

91. A.W.N. Pugin, *An Apology for a Work Entitled* Contrasts (Birmingham, England: R. P. Stone & Son, 1837).

92. Ibid., 4, 7.

93. Joseph Gwilt, *The Encyclopedia of Architecture* (New York: Bonanza Books, 1982), 54, 1142, and John Steegman, *Victorian Taste* (Cambridge, MA: The MIT Press, 1970), 81.

94. *The Athenaeum* (August 4, 1838): 556.

95. *The Athenaeum* (August 20, 1842): 750.

96. The *Revue* had wide distribution in European and American architecture firms, including the atelier of Richard Morris Hunt, giving mature practitioners and young architects such as Frank Furness exposure to Jones's ideas. James F. O'Gorman, *The Architecture of Frank Furness* (Philadelphia: Philadelphia Museum of Art, 1987), 36.

97. *Revue Générale de l'Architecture*, vols. V and VI (1844–5). I am indebted to Frederica Harlow-McRae for translating the *Revue* articles.

98. Simon Houfe, *The Dictionary of 19th-Century British Book Illustrators and Caricaturists* (Woodbridge, England: Antique Collectors' Club, 1978).

99　Letter from Jones to John Murray, December 1839, from Darby, *Owen Jones and the Eastern Ideal*, 191.

100. When issued in October 1841, the price was 2 guineas for a copy with a gold-blocked cover and 2 pounds 13-6 in Morocco leather as printed in the *Athenaeum* (October 16, 1841): 799 and (November 6, 1841): 863. I am grateful to Michael Darby for these references and much of the research on Jones's publishing activities.

101. "Illustrated Publications," from *Chambers' Encyclopedia*, vol. 5. (London: W. and R. Chambers, 1877).

102. Darby, *Owen Jones and the Eastern Ideal*, 129, 138, 145.

103. This material was patented by Leake. Edmund M. B. King, *Victorian Decorated Trade Bindings 1830–1880* (London and New Castle: The British Library and Oak Knoll Press, 2003), xii.

104. Ibid., xiii–xiv.

105. Alan S. Watts, *Dickens at Gad's Hill* (Reading, UK: Cedric Dickens and Elvendon Press, 1989), 39–40.

106. Tom Stoppard, *India Ink* (London and Boston: Faber & Faber, 1995), 14.

107. Catherine Perry Hargrave, *A History of Playing Cards and a Bibliography of Cards and Gaming* (originally published 1930: reprinted New York: Dover Publications, Inc., 1966), 188, 333.

108. Charles Dickens, "A Pack of Playing Cards," in *Household Words* (December 18, 1852): 333, and *Catalogue*, calls 17, number 76, De la Rue Archives, Archives and Special Collections, Reading University.

109. *Furniture Gazette* (September 26, 1874): 1025.

CHAPTER TWO

PRINCIPLES OF ARCHITECTURE AND THE DECORATIVE ARTS

1. Kristine Ottesen Garrigan, *Ruskin on Architecture: His Thought and Influence* (Madison: University of Wisconsin Press, 1973), 166.

2. Stuart Durant, *Ornament, from the Industrial Revolution to Today* (Woodstock and New York: The Overlook Press, 1986), 11.

3. Linda Evans, *Pattern: A Study of Ornament in Western Europe, 1180–1900*, vol. 2 (originally published 1931; reprinted New York: Da Capo Press, 1976), 188–9.

4. All references to *The Grammar of Ornament* are taken from Owen Jones, *The Grammar of Ornament* (London: Day and Son, 1856).

5. Owen Jones, "Gleanings from the Great Exhibition of 1851," *Journal of Design* (June 1851): 90.

6. Owen Jones, "An Attempt to Define the Principles which Should Regulate the Employment of Colour in the Decorative Arts, with a Few Words on the Present Necessity of an Architectural Education on the Part of the Public," (London: David Bogue, 1852), 5. This lecture was read before the Society of Arts, April 28, 1852.

7. A.W.N. Pugin, *Contrasts, or A Parallel between the Noble Edifices of the Middle Ages, and Corresponding Buildings of the Present Day, Shewing the Present Decay of Taste: Accompanied by Appropriate Text* (London: Charles Dolman, 1841), 7.

8. Victor Hugo, *The Hunchback of Notre Dame* (Philadelphia and London: Running Press, 1995; reprint of the 1833 English edition), 241–60.

9. John Claudius Loudon, *Gardener's Magazine* (1828): Entry 187.

10. Owen Jones, "On the True and False in the Decorative Arts," (London: n. p., 1863), 10. This lecture was delivered at the Marlborough House in June 1852.

11. "Beauty is that reasoned harmony of all the parts within a body, so that nothing may be added, taken away, or altered, but for the worse," from Leon Battista Alberti, *On the Art of Building, in Ten Books*, trans. Joseph Rykwert, Neil Leach, and Robert Tavenor (Cambridge, MA and London: The MIT Press, 1988), 156.

12. E. H. Gombrich, *The Sense of Order: A Study in the Psychology of Decorative Art* (London: Phaidon Press, Ltd., 1984), 53–4.

13. George Field, *Chromatography; or, A Treatise on Colours and Pigments, and of Their Powers in Painting* (London: n. p. 1835) and *Chromatics: or, the Analogy, Harmony, and Philosophy of Colours* (London: A. J. Valpy, 1817).

14. Jones, "On the True and False in the Decorative Arts," 28.

15. Gombrich, 54.

16. Michael Brooks, *John Ruskin and Victorian Architecture* (London: Thames and Hudson, Ltd., 1989), 95.

17. Owen Jones, "On the True and False in the Decorative Arts," 18.

18. Gombrich, 122, 191.

19. Ibid.

20. Brooks, 93.

21. John Ruskin, *The Stones of Venice* (New York: Da Capo Press, 1960), 102.

22. César Daly, *Revue Générale* (1845). I am grateful to Frederica Harlow-McRae for translating this material.

23. J. B. Bullen, *Byzantium Rediscovered* (London: Phaidon Press, Ltd, 2003), 135.

24. Henry-Russell Hitchcock, *Early Victorian Architecture in Britain* (New Haven: Yale University Press, 1954), 577.

25. Henry Vizetelly, *Glances Back through Seventy Years*, vol. 1 (London: Kegan Paul, Trench, Trubner & Co., Ltd., 1893), 253.

26. Cole diary entry March 19, 1844. National Art Library, Victoria and Albert Museum.

27. Later, the Royal Society for the Encouragement of Art, Commerce & Manufactures. Jones was proposed for membership by Henry Cole, Richard Redgrave, and John Bell on April 28, 1847 according to minutes of the society in 1846–7.

28. Patrick Beaver, *The Crystal Palace* (Chichester, England: Phillimore & Co., 1993), 14.

29. John McKean presents a different account. McKean reports that Francis Fuller returned to London before Cole and discussed the idea for an international exhibit with Thomas Cubitt who, subsequently, repeated the conversation to the prince. John McKean, *Crystal Palace* (London: Phaidon Press, Ltd., 1994), 5.

30. Other members included: Alderman Thompson, the earl of Rosse; Lord Overstone, the earl of Granville; Right Hon. Henry Labouchere; Sir C. L. Eastlake; Sir C. Lyell; Sir R. Westmacott; Right Hon. W. E. Gladstone; Lord Stanley, the duke of Buccleugh; Thomas Bazley, the earl of Ellesmere; Thomas Baring; Richard Cobden; T. F. Gibson; John Gott; William Hopkins; Philip Pusey; John Shepherd; and Robert Stephenson. Minutes of the Fortieth Meeting of the Royal Commissioners, Windsor Archives, vol. 7., Archives of the Royal Commission for the Exhibition of 1851, Windsor Archives; on permanent loan to the 1851 Commission.

31. *The Builder* (June 8, 1850): 265.

32. George Chadwick, *The Works of Sir Joseph Paxton: 1803–1865* (London: The Architectural Press, 1961): 104–5, and McKean, *Crystal Palace*, 12.

33. Minutes of the Seventeenth Meeting of the Royal Commissioners, May 16, 1850, Archives of the Royal Commission for the Exhibition of 1851, Windsor Archives; on permanent loan to the 1851 Commission.

34. Wyatt's first architectural work was with Brunel on Paddington Station and did not take place until 1852–4. Henry-Russell Hitchcock, *Architecture: Nineteenth and Twentieth Centuries* (originally published 1958; Harmondsworth, England: Penguin Books, 1987), 184.

35. *The Builder* (May 25, 1850): 241.

36. Beaver, *The Crystal Palace*, 15.

37. Hitchcock, *Architecture: Nineteenth and Twentieth Centuries*, 184.

38. Henry-Russell Hitchcock, *The Crystal Palace: The Structure, Its Antecedents and Its Immediate Progeny* (Northampton, MA: Smith College Museum of Art and The MIT Press, 1952), 19.

39. Beaver, *The Crystal Palace*, 15–9.

40. "The Crystal Palace," *The Times*, Windsor Archives, vol. 5, Archives of the Royal Commission for the Exhibition of 1851, Windsor Archives; on permanent loan to the 1851 Commission.

41. Michael Darby, *Owen Jones and the Eastern Ideal* (doctoral dissertation, University of Reading, UK, 1974), 269–70.

42. Hitchcock, *The Crystal Palace*, 23.

43. Ibid., 28.

44. Ibid., 24.

45. *The Illustrated London News* (January 4, 1851): 10, and Darby, 268.

46. *The Times*, Windsor Archives, vol. 5, Archives of the Royal Commission for the Exhibition of 1851, Windsor Archives; on permanent loan to the 1851 Commission, and *The Illustrated London News* (March 8, 1851): 206.

47. Darby, 285.

48. *The Times*, Windsor Archives, vol. 6, Archives of the Royal Commission for the Exhibition of 1851, Windsor Archives; on permanent loan to the 1851 Commission.

49. Letter from Lord Granville to Colonel Grey dated November 11, 1850, Archives of the Royal Commission for the Exhibition of 1851, Windsor Archives; on permanent loan to the 1851 Commission.

50. Letter from Lord Granville to Colonel Grey dated November 22, 1850, Archives of the Royal Commission for the Exhibition of 1851, Windsor Archives; on permanent loan to the 1851 Commission.

51. Letter from Lord Granville to Colonel Grey dated November 25, 1850, Archives of the Royal Commission for the Exhibition of 1851, Windsor Archives; on permanent loan to the 1851 Commission.

52. *The Journal of the Great Exhibition of 1851* (December 7, 1850).

53. "The Crystal Palace in Hyde Park," *The Times*, Windsor Archives, vol. 5, no. 63, Archives of the Royal Commission for the Exhibition of 1851, Windsor Archives; on permanent loan to the 1851 Commission.

54. Owen Jones, "On the Decorations Proposed for the Exhibition Building in Hyde Park," read at the meeting of the Royal Institute of British Architects, December 16, 1850. *The Illustrated London News* (December 28, 1850): 517.

55. *The Furniture Gazette* (March 28, 1874): 432.

56. *The Builder* (January 11, 1851): 18.

57. *Art Journal* (December 1, 1850): 383.

58. *The Expositor* (January 25, 1851): 195. I am indebted to Jan Piggott for this source.

59. *The Builder* (December 7, 1850): 580.

60. Jones, "On the Decorations Proposed for the Exhibition Building in Hyde Park," *Illustrated London News* (December 28, 1850): 518.

61. *The Illustrated London News* (December 21, 1850): 478 and (December 28, 1850): 518; *The Builder* (December 21, 1850): 604–5; *The Athenaeum* (December 21, 1850): 1347–8; and *The Civil Engineer and Architect's Journal* (December 21, 1850): 33.

62. Megan Aldrich, ed., *The Craces: Royal Decorators 1768–1899* (Brighton: The Royal Pavilion Art Gallery and Museums, 1990), and *The Builder* (January 11, 1851): 18.

63. *The Athenaeum* (January 18, 1851): 87.

64. *The Builder* (December 28, 1850): 614.

65. *The Illustrated London News* (January 25, 1851): 58.

66. *The Building News* (April 24, 1874): 440.

67. *The Times* (January 15, 1851). 58.

68. *The Illustrated London News* (January 25, 1851): 58.

69. *The Times* (January 30, 1851).

70. *The Times* (February 3, 1851).

71. *The Times* (January 30, 1851); *The Journal* (February 26, 1851); *Ecclesiologist* (1851): 269–73; and *Art Journal* (1851): 151.

72. *The Times* (February 26, 1851).

73. Windsor Archives, vol. 4, no. 35, Archives of the Royal Commission for the Exhibition of 1851, Windsor Archives; on permanent loan to the 1851 Commission, and "The Great Exhibition," *The Times*, Windsor Archives, vol. 7, no. 2, Archives of the Royal Commission for the 1851 Exhibition, Windsor Archives; on permanent loan to the 1851 Commission.

74. *The Bible Class Magazine* (April 1851): 90, and Hitchcock, *Early Victorian Architecture*, 546.

75. Boris Ford, *The Cambridge Cultural History of Britain Vol. 6: The Romantic Age in Britain* (Cambridge, England: Cambridge University Press, 1992), 282.

76. *Illustrated London News* (May 1, 1851): 392.

77. Ruskin, *The Stones of Venice*, 103.

78. *The Westminster Review* (American edition; New York: Leonard Scott & Co., 1851), 182

79. McKean, *Crystal Palace*, 33.

80. Ibid., 36.

81. Hitchcock, *Early Victorian Architecture*, 546.

82. David Van Zanten, "Architectural Polychromy: Life in Architecture," in *The Beaux-Arts and Nineteenth-Century French Architecture* (Cambridge, MA: The MIT Press, 1982), 215.

83. "On the Painting of the Ancients," *The Civil Engineer and Architect's Journal* (1859): 90.

84. Interestingly, his reputation was greater abroad than in England until the Great Exhibition according to the *Furniture Gazette* (March 28, 1874): 432, and "Literature and Art. *Conversazione* at the Mansion-House," *The Illustrated London News* (July, 23, 185): 4–46.

85. Jones, "An Attempt to Define the Principles which Should Regulate the Employment of Colour in the Decorative Arts," 50–1. The remaining material on color in this chapter is also taken from this lecture.

86. Ibid., 24.

87. Ibid.

88. John Kresten Jespersen, *Owen Jones's* "The Grammar of Ornament" *of 1856: Field Theory in Victorian Design at Mid-Century* (doctoral dissertation, Brown University, 1984), 67.

89. "The Crystal Palace at Sydenham," Archives of the Royal Commission for the Exhibition of 1851, Windsor Archives; on permanent loan to the 1851 Commission. I am grateful to Valerie Phillips, archivist, for this material.

90. Darby, 343, and *The Builder* (June 10, 1854): 297.

91. Philip H. Delamotte, *Photographic Views of the Progress of the Crystal Palace, Sydenham* (London: Crystal Palace Company, 1855).

92. They left England in August 1852 with a budget of 20,000 pounds and letters of introduction from the Secretary of State for Foreign Affairs, Lord Malmesbury. These letters, expressing the sympathy of the English government with their undertaking, an unusual expression of support for a private enterprise, and the participation of the queen and prince consort at the openings of both Crystal Palaces indicates the interest of the monarchy in these projects.

93. J. R. Piggott, *Palace of the People: The Crystal Palace at Sydenham 1854–1936* (London: Hurst & Company, 2004), 87, 90–2.

94. "Opening of the Crystal Palace," *The Illustrated London News* (June 10, 1854): 548.

95. Owen Jones, "An Apology for the Colouring of the Greek Court," in *The Greek Court Erected in the Crystal Palace* (London: Crystal Palace Library, 1854), 7.

96. Ibid.

97. The citation reads "Extracted from an Essay written in 1852, and published in Germany under the title of 'The Four Elements of Architecture.' By Professor Gottfried Semper," in *The Greek Court Erected in the Crystal Palace* (London: Crystal Palace Library, 1854).

98. Delamotte, *Photographic Views of the Progress of the Crystal Palace*, text accompanying Pl. VII.

99. *Illustrated Crystal Palace Gazette* (December 1853): 31, and Delamotte, *Photographic Views of the Progress of the Crystal Palace Sydenham*, Pl. VII.

100. The recommendation to place heraldic shields in the spandrels of the arches is also consistent with Jones's early suggestion for the Crystal Palace in Hyde Park.

101. Margot Gayle, Gretchen Gayle Ellsworth, and Carol Gayle, "The New York Crystal Palace: America's Progress, Power, and Possibilities," *Nineteenth Century* vol. 15, no. 1 (1995): 12, and *The Builder* (December 24, 1853).

102. The material on the London Exhibition of 1862 is taken from Stephen Wildman, "J. G. Crace and the Decoration of the 1862 International Exhibition" in *The Craces: Royal Decorators 1768–1899*, ed. Megan Aldrich, 149–53, and *Survey of London*, vol. 38 (London: Athlone Press, 1975), 144.

103. Crace would have had extreme difficulty in the Crystal Palace at Hyde Park since the laying of the canvas veil was not complete until April 28, three days before the opening of the exhibition. McKean, *Crystal Palace*, 28.

104. *Survey of London*, 145.

105. Geoffrey Best, *Mid-Victorian Britain 1851–1875* (originally published 1971; London: Fontana Press, 1985), 520.

106. *The Building News* (July 3, 1863): 504.

107. *Official Catalogue of the Fine Art Department International Exhibition 1862* (London: Trescott, Son & Simmons, 1862), 88, 129.

108. "The International Exhibition of 1862," *St. James's Magazine* (April–July 1862): 243, 245. I am grateful to Stephen Wildman for material on the Exhibition of 1862 and the Jones chandeliers.

109. The owner of the *Tinted Venus*, Mrs. R. Berthon Preston, insisted that the statue be displayed under a roof structure. The statue is now housed in the Walker Art Gallery, Liverpool, England.

110. I am grateful to Dr. Paul E. Ojennus for these translations.
111. *St. James's Magazine* (April–July 1862): 243, and T. Matthews, *The Biography of John Gibson, R.A., Sculptor, Rome* (London: n.p., 1911).
112. J. B. Waring, *Masterpieces of Industrial Art and Sculpture at the International Exhibition* vol. 3 (London: Day and Son, 1863), text accompanying Pl. 238.
113. Barbara Morris, *Inspiration for Design: The Influence of the Victoria and Albert Museum* (London: Victoria and Albert Museum, 1986), 20–4.
114. Ibid, 25.
115. Durant, 12.
116. Jespersen, 16.
117. Ruskin, *The Seven Lamps of Architecture* (originally published 1849; reprinted New York: Farrar, Straus and Giroux, 1988), 48.
118. Jones, "On the True and False in the Decorative Arts," 81–2.
119. Jones, "Gleanings from the Great Exhibition of 1851" *Journal of Design* (June 1851): 90.
120. I am grateful to Dr. Jessie Poesch for calling my attention to this point. See Ariane Varela-Braga, "L'ornementation primitive dans la Grammar of Ornament d'Owen Jones (1856)," *Histoire de l'art* no. 53 (November 2003): 91–101, and Suzanne Forge and Irvine Green, *Victorian Splendour: Australian Interior Decoration, 1837–1901* (Melbourne and New York: Oxford University Press, 1981), 15.
121. Jones, *The Grammar*, 13.
122. *The Builder* (December 20, 1856): 682–4 and (December 27, 1856): 694–6.
123. James F. O'Gorman, *The Architecture of Frank Furness* (Philadelphia: Philadelphia Museum of Art, 1987), 36–7, and Darby, 363.
124. George Eliot, "Review of *The Grammar of Ornament* by Owen Jones," *Fortnightly Review* (May 15, 1865).

CHAPTER THREE

PUBLIC ARCHITECTURE

1. *Westminster Review* (American edition; New York: Leonard Scott & Co., 1851): 206.
2. *The Athenaeum* (June 1, 1839): 418.
3. *The Civil Engineer and Architect's Journal* (June 1839): 216.
4. *The Athenaeum* (May 30, 1840): 436.
5. *Gentleman's Magazine* (1840): 69.
6. *The Builder* (May 17, 1845): 229.
7. *The Athenaeum* (May 17, 1845): 215.
8. Helen Powell and David Leatherbarrow, *Masterpieces of Architectural Drawing* (New York: Abbeville Press, 1982), 52.
9. Roger H. Harper, *Victorian Architectural Competitions* (London: Mansell Publishing, Ltd, 1983), xi.
10. *The Builder* (May 8, 1847): 213.
11. Harper, *Victorian Architectural Competitions*, xiii–xiv.
12. This contest has been cited as an example of "the glaring mismanagement of national competitions" during the nineteenth century since the design, program, and budget underwent several major changes, and the final building bore almost no relation to the initial scheme that architects had been asked to design. John Wilton-Ely, "The Rise of the Professional Architect in England," in *The Architect*, ed. Spiro Kostof (New York and Oxford: Oxford University Press, 1977), 199.
13. *The Building News* (July 10, 1874): 51.
14. *The Athenaeum* (May 30, 1840): 436.
15. *Gentleman's Magazine* (1840): 69.
16. *The Civil Engineer and Architect's Journal* (1840): 188.
17. *The Builder* (1843): 320.
18. *The Illustrated London News* (April 27, 1844): 266, and *The Athenaeum* (May 4, 1844): 410.
19. The entries were displayed in St. James's Bazaar, King Street, St. James, in April 1844. *The Athenaeum* (1844): 387.
20. *The Builder* (1844): 529, 588, 612 and (January 11, 1845): 13.
21. *The Builder* (May 15, 1845): 122.
22. *The Builder* (February 22, 1845): 88 and (March 15, 1845): 122.
23. *The Builder* (May 8, 1847): 213.
24. *Henry IV*, Part II, Act I, Sc. 3, lines 41–4. I am grateful to Dr. Annibel Jenkins for locating this quotation in Shakespeare's work.
25. *The Athenaeum* (May 1, 1847): 473.

26. Ibid., 496–7.
27. *The Civil Engineer and Architect's Journal* (June 1847): 173.
28. Boris Ford, *The Cambridge Cultural History of Britain Vol. 6: The Romantic Age in Britain* (Cambridge, England: Cambridge University Press, 1992), 193, and *Penny Magazine* vol. 10 (December 25, 1841): 498.
29. *The Architectural Magazine,* vol. II (London: John Weale, 1835), 313, and Michael Darby, *The Islamic Perspective* (London: The World of Islam Festival Trust, 1983), 62.
30. Powell and Leatherbarrow, *Masterpieces of Architectural Drawing*, 53.
31. Frank Lloyd Wright, *An Autobiography* (London: Faber & Faber, 1945), 137.
32. Michael Darby, *Owen Jones and the Eastern Ideal* (doctoral dissertation, University of Reading, UK, 1974), 262–3.
33. *The Builder* (June 21, 1856): 344.
34. *The Builder* (June 28, 1856): 354.
35. *The Builder* (July 19, 1856): 398.
36. *The Builder* (July 5, 1856): 374.
37. *The Builder* (May 30, 1857): 311.
38. *The Civil Engineer and Architect's Journal* (1857): 6, and *The Builder* (January 10, 1857): 22.
39. Darby, *Owen Jones and the Eastern Ideal*, 381.
40. *The Building News* (July 10, 1874): 51.
41. James Fergusson, *History of the Modern Styles of Architecture: Being a Sequel to the Handbook of Architecture* (London: J. Murray, 1862), 472.
42. Hermione Hobhouse, *History of Regent Street* (London: Macdonald and Jane's Ltd., 1975), 84, and *Art Journal* (March 1, 1858): 94.
43. Prospectus printed in *The Illustrated London News* (July 19, 1856): 69.
44. Ibid.
45. *Survey of London*, vol. 32 (London: Athlone Press, 1963).
46. Betty Matthews, "Organs of the London Concert Halls," *The Organ* vol. 67, no. 264 (April 1988): 56, and Andrew Goodman, *Gilbert and Sullivan's London* (Tunbridge Wells, UK: Spellmount and New York: Hippocrene Books, 1988), 76.
47. Stanley Sadie, ed., *The New Grove Dictionary of Music and Musicians* (London: MacMillan, 1980), 195.
48. Robert Elkin, *The Old Concert Rooms of London* (London: Edward Arnold, 1955), 152–4.
49. Goodman, *Gilbert and Sullivan's London*, 76–7. Dickens gave his last reading on March 25, 1870 in St. James's Hall.
50. The organ, manufactured by Gray and Davidson, had pipes in the form of Egyptian columns, probably designed by Jones. Darby, *Owen Jones and the Eastern Ideal*, 375.
51. *The Builder* criticized the narrowness of the treads adjacent to the hand rails in the Surrey Music Hall and called for an alteration in the design of these stairs to avoid future accidents; *The Builder* (July 19, 1856): 396. The changes were not made and witnesses identified the stairs as the cause of a disaster, later that same year, when many people were injured and six people died; *The Builder* (October 25, 1856): 581. For more information on St. James's Hall, see *The Builder* (October 18, 1856): 571 and (March 13, 1858): 171.
52. *The Illustrated London News* (April 3, 1858): 343.
53. *Art Journal* (March 1, 1858): 94.
54. *The Building News* (November 6, 1857): 1171.
55. Ibid. The exterior walls measured 3 feet at the narrowest point, 3 feet 9 inches at the piers, and 4 feet 6 inches on the ends.
56. Ibid. The original estimates projected a total cost of 40,000 pounds; also see *The Illustrated London News* (July 19, 1856): 69.
57. Jones had completed the drawings by August 24, 1855. *The Builder* published three of these drawings in October 1855 and Jones exhibited an interior view of the proposed hall in the architecture exhibition held that winter. Michael Darby suggests these publication efforts may have been undertaken to hasten the negotiations between the company and the commissioners; Darby, *Owen Jones and the Eastern Ideal*, 369–70. Messrs. Lucas were also building the new Italian opera house at the same time; it was scheduled to open May 15, 1851 according to *The Illustrated London News* (April 10, 1858): 369.
58. *The Building News* (February 27, 1857): 209.
59. *The Building News* (November 6, 1857): 1171.
60. *Art Journal* (March 1, 1858): 94.
61. *The Builder* (March 13, 1858): 171.

62. *The Illustrated London News* (April 3, 1858): 343.

63. Darby, *Owen Jones and the Eastern Ideal*, 373.

64. Joseph Gwilt, *The Encyclopedia of Architecture* (1867 edition; reprinted New York: Bonanza Books, 1982), 690.

65. This was a decorative illusion since the Surrey Music Hall (77 feet) was taller than the concert room in St. James's Hall (60 feet).

66. *The Illustrated London News* (April 3, 1858): 343.

67. *The Building News* (March 19, 1858): 290.

68. *The Builder* (April 24, 1858): 282.

69. A statue of the Venus of Milo in plaster cast weighing 320 lbs. would weigh 20 to 25 lbs. in Desachy's fibrous plaster. *The Illustrated London News* (November 6, 1858): 442, and Gwilt, *Encyclopedia of Architecture*, 680, #2251d.

70. St. Giles, Cheadle, offers one example of Pugin's use of this technique.

71. *The Builder* (March 13, 1858): 171.

72. *Art Journal* (March 1, 1858): 94.

73. *The Building News* (March 19, 1858): 290.

74. *The Builder* (April 24, 1858): 282.

75. *The Building News* (March 19, 1858): 290.

76. *The Builder* (April 24, 1858): 282.

77. *Punch* (April 3, 1858): 133.

78. Elkin, *The Old Concert Rooms of London*, 155.

79. *The Building News* (April 24, 1874): 440.

80. Myles B. Foster, *The History of the Philharmonic Society of London 1813–1912* (London: John Lane, 1912), 268, and Elkin, *The Old Concert Rooms of London*, 150.

81. *The Building News* (November 6, 1857): 1171.

82. Foster, *The History of the Philharmonic Society*, 268, and Elkin, *The Old Concert Rooms of London*, 150.

83. Darby, *Owen Jones and the Eastern Ideal*, 378.

84. *Survey of London*, vol. 32 (London: Athlone Press, 1963).

85. Elkin, *The Old Concert Rooms of London*, 155.

86. "True architecture does not admit iron as a constructive material," John Ruskin, *The Seven Lamps of Architecture*, (originally published 1849; reprinted New York: Farrar, Straus and Giroux, 1988), 16–7, 44.

87. *The Illustrated London News* reported the population of the working classes on the north side of London to be four times the number of those on the south; in addition, the major railroad terminals of the Great Northern, the London and North-Western, the Eastern Counties, and the Great Western Railways were located on the northern side of the city, so that it wasn't "only the teeming population of the metropolis which will benefit by the erection of the Palace of the People, but nine-tenths of the United Kingdom are interested in its success, as excursion trains can bring up visitors from all the manufacturing districts, and convey them back to their homes, without the annoyance, delay, and expense of working their way through the crowded streets of London." *The Illustrated London News* (February 12, 1859): 168.

88. *The Building News* (December 24, 1858): 1278.

89. *Catalogue for the Architectural Exhibition* (n.p., 1859), 14.

90. *The Building News* (February 11, 1859): 132.

91. The Alexandra Palace Working Party, *Alexandra Palace* (n. p., 1979), 7.

92. *The Building News* (February 11, 1859): 131.

93. *The Illustrated London News* (March 17, 1860): 266.

94. The dome measured 200 feet on the interior and 216 feet on the exterior, the same interior dimensions as the building committee's dome for the 1851 Exhibition Building in Hyde Park. This reintroduces the idea of attribution for the building committee's design and Jones's attempts to promote it. The masonry walls supporting the dome rose 36 feet above the ground floor and 48 feet from the general level of the building.

95. *The Illustrated London News* (March 17, 1860): 266 and (March 5, 1859): 226.

96. Problems at Sydenham resulted from raising the heat to a level adequate for tropical plants, but which was harmful to the fabric of the building and uncomfortable for visitors. The humidity required in a hothouse configuration was also injurious to artwork and other exhibits.

97. *The Building News* (February 11, 1859): 132.

98. *Floral World and Garden Guide* (May 1859): 98–9.

99. *The Illustrated London News* (March 17, 1860): 266.

100. *The Building News* (February 11, 1859): 132.

101. *The Illustrated London News* (February 12, 1859): 168; (March 5, 1859): 226; (March 17, 1860): 252; and *The Builder* (December 25, 1858): 869 and (March 12, 1859): 199.

102. *Art Journal* (April 2, 1859): 125.

103. *The Athenaeum* (January 1, 1859).

104. The Alexandra Palace Working Party, *Alexandra Palace*, 7.

105. Darby's research recognized the second scheme as the prototype for Paxton's St. Cloud design in the possession of the Yale University Art Gallery. Darby suggests that both Jones and Paxton were members of a company formed to erect a permanent exhibition facility in the St. Cloud project; the company was dissolved in 1862. Michael Darby and David Van Zanten, "Owen Jones's Iron Buildings of the 1850s," *Architectura: Zeitschrift fur Geschichte der Architektur* no. 1 (1974): 64.

106. Walter Benjamin, *Reflections* (New York: Schocken Books, 1978), 151–2.

107. Ibid., 94–5.

108. Kathryn A. Morrison, *English Shops and Shopping* (New Haven, CT and London: Yale University Press, 2003), 99.

109. *Art Journal* (December 1, 1858): 366.

110. *The Building News* (August 6, 1858): 797, and *The Illustrated London News* (November 6, 1858): 440.

111. Henry-Russell Hitchcock reproduced the interior illustration of the Crystal Palace Bazaar printed in the *Illustrated London News* (1858) and discussed this shopping area as an important example of cast-iron architecture in "Early Cast Iron Facades," *Architectural Review* (1951), and in *Early Victorian Architecture in Britain* (New Haven: Yale University Press, 1954), 403.

112. *The Illustrated London News* (November 6, 1858): 440. The galleries were covered with coved ceilings of corrugated iron. The galleries were 9 feet wide; *The Building News* (August 6, 1858): 797, and *The Builder* (October 30, 1858): 720.

113. *The Illustrated London News* (November 6, 1858): 442.

114. Minutes of the Royal Society for the Encouragement of Arts, Manufactures & Commerce, November 8, 1850 and November 29, 1850; Morrison, *English Shops and Shopping*, 99.

115. *The Builder* (October 30, 1858): 719.

116. *Journal of Design* (1851): 12–3

117. The Houbigant address was 216 Regent Street (demolished) and Jay's, established by William Chickall Jay in 1841, was located on the southwest corner of Oxford Circus and nos. 247, 249, and 251 Regent Street (demolished). Alison Adburgham, *Shops and Shopping: 1800–1914* (London: George Allen and Unwin, Ltd., 2003), 65.

118. *The Building News* (June 3, 1859): 510.

119. *The Building News* (January 13, 1860): 20.

120. John Smith, *Osler's Crystal for Royalty and Rajahs* (London: Mallett, 1991), 9.

121. *Getting London in Perspective* (London: The Barbican Art Gallery, 1984), 69; "The London Show-rooms" from John P. Smith's files Birmingham Art Gallery, Birmingham, UK. I am indebted to John P. Smith for this information and for other material on Osler's, as well as Stephen Wildman, Glynns Wild, Michael Darby, and the late Gordon Cherry.

122. *Indian Daily News* (February 24, 1883).

123. *The Building News* (May 17, 1861): 412–4. Jones exhibited an elevation of the facade of Osler's showroom in the London Exhibition of 1862, and a drawing of the showroom in the Paris Exhibition of 1867. Darby, *Owen Jones and the Eastern Ideal*, 387, and *Art Journal* (1862): 211. The Osler premises were demolished in 1926 during a remodeling.

124. Darby, *Owen Jones and the Eastern Ideal*, 443.

125. *The Illustrated London News* (November 1, 1862): 482.

126. Nikolaus Pevsner, *The Buildings of England: London and Westminster* (Harmondsworth, England: Penguin Books, 1957), 515.

127. Mary Cathcart Borer, *The British Hotel through the Ages* (Guildford: Lutterworth Press, 1972), 190.

128. Robert Thorne, "The Langham Hotel," internal documents from the Greater London Council, Department of Architecture and Civic Design, Historic Buildings Division, November 1982, 1, 2, 6.

129. Nikolaus Pevsner, *A History of Building Types* (Princeton: Princeton University Press, 1976), 173–89.

130. Thorne, "The Langham Hotel," 2.
131. *The Building News* (June 16, 1863): 422. See also *The Illustrated London News* (July 8, 1865): 5, 12, and *The Builder* (July 26, 1863): 531–3 and (June 17, 1863): 433.
132. Darby, *Owen Jones and the Eastern Ideal*, 428.
133. *The Builder* (December 24, 1864): 931, and Jack Simmons, *St. Pancras Station* (London: George Allen and Unwin, Ltd., 2003), 48.
134. Oliver Carter, *British Railway Hotels 1838–1983* (St. Michael's, Lancashire: Silver Link Publishing, 1990), 56.
135. *The Builder* (January 13, 1866): 33.
136. The other estimates submitted were: Scott, 316,000 pounds; Hine & Evans, 255,000 pounds; Sorby, 245,000 pounds; Barry, 236,487 pounds; Walters & Barker, 190,000 pounds; Jones, 187,000 pounds; Clarke, 164,500 pounds; Cockerell, 155,000 pounds; Lloyd, 150,000 pounds; Lockwood & Mawson, 135,792 pounds; Darbishire, no estimate. Simmons, *St. Pancras Station*, 49.
137. *The Builder* (May 5, 1866): 318.
138. Priscilla Metcalf, *The Halls of the Fishmongers' Company* (London: Phillimore, 1977), 163–6, 178, 203, and Michael Darby, *Owen Jones and the Eastern Ideal*, 431–5.
139. M. H. Port, *Imperial London: Civil Government Building in London 1850–1915* (New Haven and London: Yale University Press, 1995), 175.
140. Although twelve architects were invited, only the following participated: Jones; Brodrick; G. E. Street; F. P. Cockerell; J. Murray; E. M. Barry; F. C. Penrose; G. S. Clarke; M. Digby Wyatt; and Banks & Barry. Harper, *Victorian Architectural Competitions*, 96. G. G. Scott and S. Smirke were invited but did not participate; *The Builder* (May 1, 1866): 354.
141. Port, *Imperial London*, 175.
142. The judges included: Viscount Hardinge; Lord Elcho; A.J.B. Beresford-Hope; W. Tite; W. Russell; W. Boxall; D. Brandon; T. Gambier Parry; and R. Redgrave. Harper, 96.
143. Tite pronounced the drawings "'of eminent beauty and excellent as works of high art', but not suitable for a National Gallery." Harper, *Victorian Architectural Competitions*, 175–6.
144. Darby, *Owen Jones and the Eastern Ideal*, 409.
145. *The Builder* (May 5, 1866): 318.
146. Owen Jones, "Designs for the Proposed Enlargement of the National Gallery," unpublished. Royal Institute of British Architects.
147. Joseph Bonomi Papers, add. 9389/2/J/41, Manuscripts Room, Cambridge University Library.
148. *The Phoenix Foundry Company, Limited Catalogue* (n. p., 1897), 3, 26.
149. *The Architect* (May 18, 1872): 256b.
150. J. Mordaunt Crook, *Victorian Architecture: A Visual Anthology* (New York and London: Johnson Reprint Corporation, 1971), Pl. 252.
151. *The Builder* (November 10, 1866): 832–3 and (December 1, 1866): 885, and *The Building News* (August 25, 1866): 578.

CHAPTER FOUR

INTERIOR DESIGN, DECORATIVE ARTS, AND PRIVATE ARCHITECTURE

1. Gill Saunders, *Wallpaper in Interior Decoration* (London: V & A Publications, 2002), 12.
2. Lesley Hoskins, ed., *The Papered Wall* (London: Thames and Hudson, Ltd., 1994), 138.
3. Marilyn Oliver Hapgood, *Wallpaper and the Artist* (New York, London, and Paris: Abbeville Press, 1992), 90.
4. Saunders, *Wallpaper in Interior Decoration*, 107–8.
5. Samples of Jones's papers are maintained at the Victoria and Albert Museum, Sanderson & Co., the Public Record Office at Kew, Cole & Son, and the Whitworth Art Gallery. Cole & Son also has some of the original blocks for printing wallpapers designed by Jones.
6. The extensive copying and imitation complicate design attribution. Jones's designs for Jeffrey & Co. are stamped with his initials and a registration mark on the reverse of the printed pattern, but most other manufacturing designs do not have this distinction.
7. Hoskins, *The Papered Wall*, 145.
8. *Architectural Exhibition Catalogue* (n.p., 1859).
9. Christine Woods, "Jeffrey & Co.," in *Encyclopedia of Interior Design*, eds. Joanna Banham and Leanda Shrimpton, vol. 1 (London and Chicago: Fitzroy Dearborn Publishers, 1997), 651–2.
10. Hapgood, *Wallpaper and the Artist*, 46.
11. Woods, "Jeffrey & Co.," 653.
12. Saunders, *Wallpaper in Interior Decoration*, 107.
13. Charles C. Oman and Jean Hamilton, *Wallpapers: A History and Illustrated Catalogue of the Collection of the Victoria and Albert Museum* (London: Sotheby Publications, 1982), 63.
14. Saunders, *Wallpaper in Interior Decoration*, 107, and Jean Hamilton, *An Introduction to Wallpaper* (London: Her Majesty's Stationery Office, 1983), 33.
15. *The Furniture Gazette* (May 13, 1876): 301.
16. Hoskins, *The Papered Wall*, 145.
17. Nikolaus Pevsner, *Pioneers of Modern Design* (originally published 1936; reprinted London: Peregrine Books, 1986), 46–7.
18. The company was known as Warner, Sillet & Co. from March 1870 to January 1871; Warner, Sillet & Ramm from 1871 to 1874; Warner & Ramm from 1874 to 1891; and Warner & Sons until 1897; and Warner Fabrics plc. from 1897 until today. The Warner Archive is housed in the Braintree District Museum, Braintree, Essex, England.
19. According to Sue Kerry, archivist, Benjamin Warner purchased this design from Jones in 1868, two years prior to the establishment of Warner & Sons.
20. Mary Schoeser, "Owen Jones' Silks," in *Disentangling Textiles: Techniques for the Study of Designed Objects*, eds. Mary Schoeser and Christine Boydell (London: Middlesex University Press, 2002), 159.
21. Warner's acquired the patterns of Daniel Walters & Sons and Charles Norris & Co. Schoeser, "Owen Jones' Silks," 158–62.
22. Sanderson's no. 19573; Cole & Sons: BT 43/90 85746.
23. Forty-three York Terrace is now 20 York Terrace; Entries for February 20 and March 22, 1877 in the Warner account book. I am grateful to Mary Schoeser for informing about this book and to the Royal College of Art for giving me access to the book when it was in their possession.
24. *Furniture Gazette* (November 16, 1878): 336.
25. T.40-1916, Warner Archive and excerpt from a letter written by Sir Frank Warner to the Victoria and Albert Museum to explain a drawing in the museum's collection for T.40-1916.
26. Schoeser, "Owen Jones' Silks," 160.
27. *The Builder* (July 18, 1874): 601.
28. *The Art Journal Illustrated Catalogue* incorrectly credits a Mr. Paton as the designer. Three of the patterns are by Paton, but "Arabesque," "Vine," and "Alhambra" are by Jones. Letter from Marin Norgate, Dunfernline Museum, Scotland, to Michael Darby, October 25, 1973.
29. Jones, "On the True and False in the Decorative Arts," (London: n. p., 1863), 83–5.
30. Jones credited Graham for valuable design suggestions. Clive Edwards, "The Firm of Jackson and Graham," *Furniture History* vol. XXXIV (1998): 238–62.
31. *The Builder* (May 9, 1874): 385.
32. Edwards, "The Firm of Jackson and Graham," 248–53, and "Extract from Report of the Jury," *London Suburban Directory* (1863): 800.
33. Michael Darby, *Owen Jones and the Eastern Ideal* (doctoral dissertation, University of Reading, UK, 1974), 422.
34. *Furniture Gazette* (September 36, 1874): 1025, and *The Builder* (July 18, 1874): 600.
35. Moncure Daniel Conway, *Travels in South Kensington* (London: Trubner & Co., 1882), 158.
36. *Journal of the Society of Arts* (July 10, 1874): 763.
37. I am grateful to Martin Levy for this information.
38. *The Building News* (July 10, 1874): 51.
39. *The Architect* (September 16, 1874): 159–60.
40. "The International Exhibition," from an unidentified newspaper from the files of Michael Darby.
41. I am grateful to Max Donnelly for this information and to the Library Company of Philadelphia for providing the illustration.
42. Jones, "On the True and False in the Decorative Arts," 89, 92, 94.
43. *The Civil Engineer and Architect's Journal* (July 1840): 226.
44. Darby, *Owen Jones and the Eastern Ideal*, 150, and *The Civil Engineer and Architect's Journal* (July 1840): 226–7.

45. Hugh Clout, ed., *The Times London History Atlas* (London: Times Books, 1994), 84.

46. "The Crown Estate in Kensington Palace Gardens," *Survey of London*, vol. 37 (London: Athlone Press, 1975), 154.

47. Mark Girouard, "Gilded Preserves for the Rich: Kensington Palace Gardens—I" *Country Life* (November 11, 1971): 1269. He adds, "If all thirty-three plots were let at the minimum rents proposed, the estate would have yielded an annual revenue of over two thousand three hundred pounds."

48. *Survey of London*, vol. 37, 153–4, 156.

49. *The Illustrated London News* (January 31, 1846): 78.

50. *The British Almanac for the Society of the Diffusion of Useful Knowledge* (London: Cassell, 1846), 245.

51. Darby, *Owen Jones and the Eastern Ideal*, 356.

52. Girouard, "Gilded Preserves for the Rich: Kensington Palace Gardens—I," 1270.

53. Darby, *Owen Jones and the Eastern Ideal*, 170.

54. *The British Almanac* (London: Cassell, 1846), 245.

55. C. R. Cockerell had used a central skylight of this type previously, but without colored glass. Geoffrey Beard, *The English House Interior* (London: The Penguin Group, 1990), 221.

56. Mark Girouard, *The Victorian Country House* (New Haven and London: Yale University Press, 1985), 36.

57. Darby, *Owen Jones and the Eastern Ideal*, 173.

58. Ibid., 174–5. See also *Survey of London*, vol. 7 (London: Athlone Press, 1975), 184.

59. Phillip Hardwick (no. 10), Sydney Smirke (nos. 9 and 11), and Charles Barry (nos. 12, 18, 19, and 20); Charlotte Gere, *Nineteenth-Century Design* (New York: Harry N. Abrams, Inc., 1994), 68. Four houses (nos. 12, 18, 19, and 20) built to designs attributed to Charles Barry were produced for the contractors Thomas Grissell and Samuel Morton Peto, but the four designs were probably produced by architects on Barry's staff; Girouard, "Gilded Preserves for the Rich: Kensington Palace Gardens—I," 1270, and *The British Almanac*, 243.

60. Mark Girouard, "Gilded Preserves for the Rich: Kensington Palace Gardens—II." *Country Life* (November 18, 1971): 1360–1.

61. Michael Jenner, *London Heritage* (London: Penguin Books, 1991), 213.

62. James Steven Curl, *Victorian Architecture* (Newton Abbot and London: David & Charles, 1990), 92.

63. The initial construction was begun in October 1845 but was not finished in July 1847 when the house was included in the sale of Blashfield's estate held as part of his bankruptcy proceedings. James Ponford, a builder in Bayswater, St. John's Wood, and Belgravia purchased the house for 3400 pounds, completed it, and used it for his residence. *Survey of London*, vol. 37, 183–4.

64. Darby, *Owen Jones and the Eastern Ideal*, 172.

65. For example, Barry's Traveller's Club (1829–32), Reform Club (1837–41), and Trentham Hall, Staffordshire (1834–42). For discussions on this see Girouard, *The Victorian Country House*, 48–50; *The British Almanac*, 243; Stephan Muthesius, *The English Terraced House* (New Haven and London: Yale University Press, 1982); John Summerson, *The Unromantic Castle* (London: Thames and Hudson, Ltd., 1990), 222–6; and Gordon Toplis, "Urban Classicism in Decline," *Country Life* (November 15, 1973): 1526–8.

66. Owen Jones Box, John Johnson Collection, New Bodleian Library, Oxford University, Oxford, UK.

67. *The Athenaeum* (January 3, 1846): 4.

68. *The British Almanac*, 243.

69. Darby, *Owen Jones and the Eastern Ideal*, 155.

70. Although the beginning of the relationship is unknown, Lewes had contributed an essay to Jones's "Apology for the Colouring of the Greek Court" a decade earlier and apparently visited Jones regularly. Gordon S. Haight, *George Eliot: A Biography* (Oxford, London, and New York: Oxford University Press, 1968), 371.

71. *The Westminster Review* vol. 135 (American edition; New York: Leonard Scott & Co., 1858), 136.

72. J. W. Cross, ed., *George Eliot's Life as Related in Her Letters and Journals*, 3 vols. (New York: Harper & Brothers, 1885), 221, 373.

73. Gordon S. Haight, ed., *The George Eliot Letters* (New Haven: Yale University Press), 111–2.

74. Ibid., 442.

75. The palace exists in a partially restored state today as the Marriott Hotel in Cairo. Letter from Mohammad al-Asad to the author dated August 31, 1995, lists Julius Franz, De Curel Del Rosso, and Carl von Diebitsch as architects associated with the building. Von Diebitsch was an architect of the Schinkel School who shared an appreciation for Islamic architecture with Jones. Like his English contemporary, von Diebitsch conducted a six-month on-site study of the Alhambra that influenced his later work.

76. *A Handbook For Travellers in Egypt* (London: John Murray, 1875), 143.

77. *The Illustrated London News* (1856): 537

78. Elke Pflugradt-Abdel Aziz, *A Prussian Palace in Egypt*, exh. cat. (Cairo: Embassy of the Federal Republic of Germany and Museum of Egyptian Modern Art, 1993), 11–6. I am grateful to Ronald B. Lewcock for this information.

79. *The Builder* (May 9, 1874): 385

80. Darby, *Owen Jones and the Eastern Ideal*, 430–1.

81. Clive Wainwright, "Alfred Morrison: A Forgotten Patron and Collector," in *The Grosvenor House Art and Antiques Fair 1995 Handbook* (London: Burlington Magazine, 1995), 27.

82. *The Builder* (May 9, 1874): 385.

83. I am grateful to the Crown Estate Commissioners for photography and for allowing me to study the interiors on several occasions.

84. *The Builder* (February 21, 1885): 265.

85. Conway, *Travels in South Kensington*, 154, and Mrs. Haweis, *Beautiful Houses* (London: Sampson Low, Marston, Searle & Rivington, 1882), 53–60.

86. John Cornforth, "Arabian Nights in the Mall," *Country Life* (May 18, 1989): 246–9.

87. Michael Darby also believes that the gold-on-red coves of the former drawing room date only from the 1960s.

88. *The Builder* (May 9, 1874): 385. David Mason, the great-grandson of James Mason, explains that his ancestor's character was such that he would have given Jones a free hand in the design, but would have insisted on the highest standards. Letter to the author from David Mason, May 25, 1995.

89. Mrs. Haweis remarked on "the great winding staircase, with a solid balustrade of polished woods, far handsomer than rails," in 16 Carlton House Terrace; *Beautiful Houses*, 57. See also Girouard, *The Victorian Country House*, 14.

90. The installation of gas lighting involved a considerable commitment on the part of the property owner. James Mason commissioned the construction of a gasworks and brickworks to produce the gas and necessary building materials. Three gas-holding tanks, approximately 25 feet in diameter, constructed of brick and lined with metal, were buried near the house. Letter from James Mason to the author dated June 22, 1995. See also drawings 14 and 17, Eynsham Hall, Special Collections, Reading University Library.

91. Girouard, *The Victorian Country House*, 9, 26.

92. One pattern in silk woven by Warners remained on two chairs from Eynsham Hall received by the Victoria and Albert Museum in 1953. These fragments in the "Sutherland" pattern are referenced as "T. 225" and "A-1953" in the Textiles Collection, Victoria and Albert Museum. Letter to the author from Wendy Hefford, deputy curator of textiles and dress, Victoria and Albert Museum, dated November 10, 1995. See also *Furniture Gazette* (January 3, 1880) and (October 30, 1880).

93. Garden layout dated January 24, 1872, Prints and Drawings, Victoria and Albert Museum, E.499–1952.

94. Letter from David Mason to the author dated May 25, 1995. Moldings by Jones have been reused in two rooms of the present Eynsham Hall, completed in 1908 to the designs of Sir Ernest George, R. A. (1839–1922).

95. Jones, "On the True and False in the Decorative Arts," (London: n. p., 1863), 105–8.

96. Jones and Semper met in Greece in 1832. Later, when Semper moved to London, he and Jones were both involved with the Department of Practical Art, professional architecture associations, and the Crystal Palaces in Hyde Park and Sydenham. Jones published Semper's "On the Origin of Polychromy in Architecture" (excerpted from Semper's "The Four Elements of Architecture") as part of the instructional doc-

umentation on the Greek Court at the Crystal Palace, Sydenham, 1852.

CHAPTER FIVE

THE LEGACY

1. Many scholars have discussed this, including: David Van Zanten, *Architectural Polychromy of the 1830s* (New York: Garland Publishing, Inc., 1977), 222–3; Barry Bergdoll, "'The synthesis of all I have seen': The Architecture of Edmund Duthoit (1837–1889)" in *The Beaux-Arts and Nineteenth-Century French Architecture*, ed. Robin Middleton (Cambridge, MA: The MIT Press, 1982), 236; Jeffrey A. Cohen, "Styles and Motives," in *Frank Furness: The Complete Works* (New York: Princeton Architectural Press, 1991), 118–20; and Anne Monahan, "'Of a Doubtful Gothic': Islamic Sources for the Pennsylvania Academy of the Fine Arts," *Nineteenth Century* vol. 18, no. 2 (Fall 1998): 33.

2. Christopher Dresser, *The Art of Decorative Design* (originally published in 1862; reprinted Watkins Glen: The American Life Foundation & Study Institute, 1977), 10.

3. On May 24, 1905, Mary Dresser offered to sell the following items from Dresser's collection to the Victoria and Albert Museum: ten unframed drawings of the Alhambra by Jones, fifteen framed drawings by Owen Jones, Jones's artwork for *Paradise and the Peri*, and an exterior of the Crystal Palace by Jones. These were offered at 60 pounds for the group or sold individually. Stuart Durant, *Christopher Dresser* (London: Academy Editions, 1993), 42.

4. Ibid., 42–3.

5. Jones gave Viollet-le-Duc at least one tour of the Crystal Palace.

6. James Rosser Johnson, *The Radiance of Chartres: Studies in the Early Stained Glass of the Cathedral* (New York: Random House, 1965), 47–50.

7. Ibid., 86.

8. Viollet-le-Duc's library contained a copy of Jones's *Alhambra*. Nikolaus Pevsner, *Some Architectural Writers of the Nineteenth Century* (Oxford: Clarendon Press, 1972), 215.

9. Mark Crinson, *Empire Building: Orientalism and Victorian Architecture* (London and New York: Routledge, 1996).

10. John Ruskin, *The Works of John Ruskin*, eds. E. T. Cook and Alexander Wedderburn, vol. 16 (London: George Allen; New York: Longmans, Green, and Co., 1903), 307.

11. John Ruskin, *The Seven Lamps of Architecture* (originally published 1849; reprinted New York: Farrar, Straus and Giroux, 1988), 191.

12. Ibid., 197.

13. Ibid., 15, 43.

14. Ibid., 191.

15. Ibid., 194.

16. Ibid., 194–5.

17. E. H. Gombrich, *The Sense of Order: A Study in the Psychology of Decorative Art* (Oxford: Oxford University Press, 1979), 39.

18. Ruskin, *The Works of John Ruskin*, 501.

19. Kristine Ottesen Garrigan, *Ruskin on Architecture: His Thought and Influence* (Madison: University of Wisconsin Press, 1973), 167.

20. John Ruskin, *The Stones of Venice* (New York: Da Capo Press, 1960), 114–5.

21. Ibid., 115.

22. Owen Jones, "On the True and False in the Decorative Arts," (London: n. p., 1863), 10.

23. Ruskin, *The Works of John Ruskin*, vol. 8, 502.

24. Ibid., 499–502.

25. Michael W. Brooks, *John Ruskin and Victorian Architecture* (London: Thames and Hudson, Ltd., 1989), 91–3, and *Building News* (January 9, 1857): 34.

26. Brooks, 93, and J. L. Roget, "Tesserae," *Architect* (March 27, 1889): 179–80.

27. *The Building News* (April 24, 1874): 440.

28. Christopher Dresser, *The Art of Decorative Design* (London: Day and Son, 1862), 149.

29. William Morris, "Lecture on the Decorative Arts," in *The Collected Works of William Morris*, vol. XII (London and New York: Longmans, 1914), 5.

30. Linda Parry, *William Morris Textiles* (London: Weidenfeld & Nicholson, 1983), 48, 183, and Mary Schoeser, "Owen Jones' Silks," in *Disentangling Textiles: Techniques for the Study of Designed Objects*, eds. Mary Schoeser and Christine Boydell (London: Middlesex University Press, 2002), 160–1.

31. Owen Jones, *The Grammar of Ornament* (London: Bernard Quaritch, 1868), 156.

32. Morris, *The Collected Works of William Morris*, 28.

33. Morris and Company used machines in their production and Morris emphasized that machines should be used to save human labor. Paul Thompson, *The Work of William Morris* (London: Heinemann, 1967), 86–7.

34. Reginald Turnor, *Nineteenth Century Architecture in Britain* (London and New York: Batsford, 1950), 97.

35. Morris, *The Collected Works of William Morris*, 180, and Thompson, *The Work of William Morris*, 88. Also see Jon Catleugh, *William De Morgan Tiles* (Ilminster: Richard Dennis, 2002), 75.

36. Thompson, *The Work of William Morris*, 89, 103.

37. William Morris, "Some Hints on Pattern-Designing," in *The Collected Works of William Morris*, 20.

38. Although Pugin died in 1852, the impact of his wallpaper designs for the Palace of Westminster continued to be recognized along with Jones's contemporary designs.

39. Thompson, *The Work of William Morris*, 91–3.

40. Warner's, Sanderson's, and Cole & Son continue to produce designs by Jones.

41. Katharine A. Lochnan, "Wallpaper," in *Earthly Paradise*, eds. Katharine A. Lochnan, Douglas E. Schoenherr, and Carole Silver (Toronto: Key Porter Books Ltd., 1993), 125.

42. Mary Patricia May Sekler, *The Early Drawings of Charles-Edouard Jeanneret (Le Corbusier) 1902–1908* (doctoral dissertation, Harvard University, Cambridge, 1973), 101, n. 40.

43. Marilyn Oliver Hapgood, *Wallpaper and the Artist* (New York, London, and Paris: Abbeville Press, 1992), 137, 139–41.

44. H. Allen Brooks, *Le Corbusier's Formative Years: Charles-Édouard Jeanneret at La Chaux-de-Fonds* (Chicago and London: The University of Chicago Press, 1997), 60–1.

45. Frank Lloyd Wright, *An Autobiography: Frank Lloyd Wright* (New York: Horizon Press, 1977), 97.

46. Grant Manson, *Frank Lloyd Wright to 1909: The First Golden Age* (New York: Van Nostrand Reinhold Company, 1958), 22.

47. Monahan, "'Of a Doubtful Gothic,'" 30–1. For other discussions of Jones's influence on Frank Furness see James F. O'Gorman, *The Architecture of Frank Furness* (Philadelphia: Philadelphia Museum of Art, 1973), 24–7, 36, and Zeynep Çelik, *Displaying the Orient: Architecture of Islam at Nineteenth Century World's Fairs* (Berkeley: University of California Press, 1992), 168.

48. Several scholars have discussed this, including: Thomas H. Beeby, "The Grammar of Ornament/Ornament as Grammar," *Ornament, Via III* (1977): xx; O'Gorman, *The Architecture of Frank Furness*, 36–7; Robert Twombly, *Louis Sullivan: His Life and Work* (Chicago: The University of Chicago Press, 1987), 42; and David Hanks, *The Decorative Designs of Frank Lloyd Wright* (Mineola, NY: Dover Publications, Inc., 1979), 4–5.

49. Manson, *Frank Lloyd Wright*, 10.

50. Frank Lloyd Wright, "In the Cause of Architecture," *The Architectural Record* (March 1908): 161.

51. Ibid., 161–2.

52. Brooks, *Le Corbusier's Formative Years*, 61, and Stanislaus von Moos, *Le Corbusier, Elements of a Synthesis* (Cambridge, MA and London: The MIT Press, 1979), 4.

53. Brooks, *Le Corbusier's Formative Years*, 76.

54. Mark Wigley, *White Walls, Designer Dresses: The Fashioning of Modern Architecture* (Cambridge, MA and London: The MIT Press, 1995): 191–2.

55. Ibid., 191.

56. "Jacob Wrey Mould," *American Architect and Building News* (October 14, 1876): 335.

57. *The Building News* (April 24, 1874): 440.

APPENDIX A

PUBLISHING ACTIVITIES

Works Authored, Edited, Designed, Printed, or Containing Plates,
Pages, Endpapers, or Bindings (Covers) by Owen Jones

Adams, E. *The Polychromatic Ornament of Italy*. London: n.p., 1846. (Printed)

Ashley, A. *The Art of Etching*. London: n.p., 1849. (Designed binding)

Bacon, M. A. *Flowers and Their Kindred Thoughts*. London: Longman and Co., 1847. (Designed interior and binding and printed binding)

_____. *Fruits from the Garden and Field*. London: Longman and Co., 1850. (Designed and printed)

_____. *Little Goody Two Shoes*. London: n.p., 1850. (Designed binding possibly)

_____. *Winged Thoughts*. London: Longman and Co., 1851. (Designed and printed interior and designed binding)

The Book of Common Prayer. London: John Murray, 1845, 1846, 1850. (Designed various decorative elements, and chromolithographed title pages and binding)

Calabrella, E. C. de. *The Prism of Imagination*. London: Longman, Brown, Green, and Longmans, 1842, 1843, 1844. (Designed and printed borders and ornamental titles)

Carleton, W. *The Black Prophet*. London: n.p., 1847. (Designed binding)

Catherwood, F. *Views of Ancient Monuments in Central America, Chiapas, and Yucatan*. London: n.p., 1844. (Printed; designed title page)

Essex, W. R. H. *Illustrations . . . of the Temple Church*. London: n.p., 1845. (Printed various plates)

The Floral Almanack. London: n.p., 1846. (Designed and printed)

Gray, Thomas. *Gray's Elegy*. London: Longmans and Co., and New York: Wiley and Putnam, 1846. (Illuminated; designed binding)

Hay, Robert. *Illustrations of Cairo*. London: n.p., 1840. (Designed title page and printed possibly)

Hayter, C. *An Introduction to Perspective, Practical Geometry, Drawing and Painting*. 6th edition. London: n.p., 1845. (Printed various plates)

The History of Joseph and His Brethren: Genesis Chapters XXXVII, XXXVIII, XL. London: Day and Son, 1862. (Designed plates and binding)

Holy Bible. London: n.p., 1862. (Designed binding)

Holy Matrimony. London: Longman and Co., 1849. (Illuminated and printed)

Humphreys, H. N. *The Illuminated Books of the Middle Ages*. London: n.p., 1849. (Printed)

_____. *The Illuminated Calendar and Home Diary for 1845*. London: n.p., 1845. (Printed flower borders)

_____. *The Illuminated Diary and Calendar*. London: n.p., 1846. (Printed possibly)

Hunt, L. *A Jar of Honey from Mount Hybla, Illustrated by Richard Doyle*. London: Smith, Elder & Co., 1848. (Designed binding)

Jones, Owen. *Designs for Mosaic and Tessellated Pavements by Owen Jones, Archt*. London: John Weale, 1842. (Printed plates)

_____. *Encaustic Tiles*. London: n.p., 1843. (Printed plates)

_____. *Examples of Chinese Ornament*. London: S. & T. Gilbert, 1867. (Designed)

_____. *The Grammar of Ornament*. London: Day and Son, 1856. (Designed)

_____. *One Thousand and One Initial Letters Designed and Illuminated by Owen Jones*. London: Day and Son, 1864. (Designed binding also)

_____. *702 Monograms*. London: Thomas De la Rue, 1864. (Designed)

_____, and Jules Goury. *Plans, Elevations, Sections, and Details of the Alhambra: from drawings taken on the spot in 1834 by the late M. Jules Goury and in 1834 and 1837 by Owen Jones, Archt. with a complete translation of the Arabic inscriptions, and an Historical Notice of the Kings of Granada, from the Conquest of that City by the Arabs to the Expulsion of the Moors, by Mr. Pasqual de Gayangos*. 2 vols. London: n.p., 1842–5. (Designed and printed both volumes)

_____. *Views on the Nile from Cairo to the Second Cataract*. London: n.p., 1843. (Designed)

Knight, Henry Gally. *The Ecclesiastical Architecture of Italy*. London: Bohn, 1842, 1843. (Designed and printed title page and printed plates)

Lockhart, J. G. *Ancient Spanish Ballads*. London: John Murray, 1841, 1842, 1853, 1856, 1859. (Designed, including borders and motifs, and printed several title pages; designed endpapers for 1842 edition)

Maw and Company's Tile Patterns. London: n.p., 1871. (Designed binding)

Miller, T. *A Treatise on Water-Colour Painting*. London: n.p., 1848. (Printed various plates)

Milman, Dean. *The Works of Quintus Horatius Flaccus*. London: John Murray, 1849. (Designed borders, title pages, and binding)

Moore, Thomas. *Paradise and the Peri*. London: Day and Son, 1860. (Illuminated with Henry Warren; designed borders and binding)

The Musical Bijou. London: D'Almaine & Co., 1842. (Designed binding and title page and printed various plates)

The Preacher. London: Longman and Co., 1849. (Designed plates, endpapers, and binding)

Roberts, J. C. *A Few Words to School Boys about Christmas*. London: n.p., 1851. (Designed and printed)

The Sermon on the Mount. London: Longman and Co., 1844, 1845. (Designed and printed plates)

Shakespeare, William. *Scenes from the Winter's Tale*. London: Day and Son, 1866. (Designed; illuminated with Henry Warren)

Simpson, W. *India Ancient and Modern*. London: n.p., 1867. (Designed title page)

Society of Arts. *Transactions*. London: n.p., 1852. (Printed twelve plates of tile designs)

The Song of Songs. London: Longman and Co., 1849. (Designed and printed plates, endpapers, and designed binding)

The Sunday Alphabet. London: Day and Son, 1861. (Designed and illuminated plates)

Talbot, Willliam Henry Fox. *The Pencil of Nature*. London: n.p., 1844. (Designed various elements, printed various plates, and designed parts of title page)

Taylor, Tom. *Birket Foster's Pictures of English Landscape: (Engraved by the Brothers Dalziel) With Pictures in words by Tom Taylor*. London: Routledge, Warne, and Routledge, 1863. (Designed binding)

Tennyson, Alfred. *A Welcome to Her Royal Highness the Princess of Wales from the Poet Laureate. Owen Jones illuminator*. London: Day and Son, 1863. (Designed and illuminated interior and designed binding)

The Thousand and One Nights. Translated by E. W. Lane. 2nd ed. London: n.p., 1847. (Designed and printed title pages)

A Treasury of Pleasure Books for Young Children. London: Grant & Griffith and Joseph Cundall, 1850 (Designed binding and endpapers)

The Victorian Psalter. London: n.p., 1861. (Designed and illuminated interior and designed binding)

Weale, John. *Divers Works of the Early Masters in Christian Decoration*. London: John Weale, 1846. (Printed various plates)

_____. *Quarterly Papers on Architecture*. Volume II. London: John Weale, 1844. (Printed plates on St. Jacques and Temple Church)

Westwood, J. O. *Palaeographia Sacra Pictoria*. London: William Smith, 1843–5. (Printed plates)

Wilkinson, J. G. *The Manners and Customs of the Ancient Egyptians*. London: John Murray, 1836. (Printed various plates)

PROJECTS AND COMMISSIONS

1830	Competition entry, Birmingham Town Hall
1839	Competition entry, St. George's Hall, Liverpool
1840s	Showroom decoration, Houbigant, Regent Street, London
1840	Four houses, Westbourne Terrace, London
	Interior decoration, Wimborne House, 22 Arlington Street, London
1842	Designs for book covers, title pages, etc., Longmans, London
	Tile designs for John Marriott Blashfield published
1843	8 Kensington Palace Gardens, London, demolished 1961
1844	Competition entry, Houses of Parliament floors, London
	Begins designing products for De la Rue, London
1845	Competition for Baths and Wash-houses, London
	24 Kensington Palace Gardens, London
	7 Sussex Terrace, London
	12 Westbourne Terrace, London
	Entertainment complex for Antenor Joly, Leicester Square, London
	James Morrison dairy and cottages, London
1847	Competition entry, Army and Navy Club, London
	Floor patterns, Little Wodehouse Hall, 3 Hyde Terrace, Leeds
1848	Pavement for 3 Hyde Terrace in association with Bateman/Corson, Leeds
1849	Villa Alderman Moon, London
	Alhambra stove for Hoole (manufacturer), Birmingham Exhibition
1850	Chappell's, Bond Street, London
	84 Westbourne Terrace, London
	Interior decoration, Lewis Vuillamy's All Saints Ennismore Gardens, London
1851	Interior decoration, James Wild's Christ Church, Streatham, restored
	Superintendent of Works and Interior Scheme, Great Exhibition, London
	Gold Medal for Chromolithography, Great Exhibition, London
	Table linens for Erkskine Beveridge displayed in the Great Exhibition, London
	Book-binding tools for De la Rue displayed in the Great Exhibition, London
1852	Addiscombe, Surrey, demolished
1852–4	Interior and Fine Arts courts, Crystal Palace, Sydenham, destroyed
1854	Interior decoration, St. Bartholomew, Sutton Waldron, Dorset, restored
	Consultant to I. K. Brunel and M. Digby Wyatt, Paddington Station, London
1856	Color consulting, Carlisle Cathedral
	Interior decoration, Jay's, 247–249 Regent Street, London, rebuilt 1923
	Competition entry, Manchester Art Treasures Exhibition Building
1857	Interior stencil designs, St. Mark's Church, Wrexham, demolished
1858	Crystal Palace Bazaar, London, demolished 1890
	St. James's Hall, Piccadilly, London, demolished 1905
	Unexecuted project, Palace of the People Muswell Hill, London
1859	Unexecuted project, United Service Club, 116 Pall Mall, London
	John Trumble & Company advertises as the sole manufacturer of Jones's wallpaper designs
1860s	Iron gates manufactured by Andrew Handyside & Company
1860	Osler's, 76 Oxford Street, London, demolished 1926
	Proposals, Exhibition Building, St. Cloud, Paris, France
	Tombstone for William and Margaret Chappell, Kensal Green Cemetery
1861	Showroom decoration, Hancock's, Bruton Street, London, demolished
	Plans, elevations, shops, and cottages for Hancock, London, demolished
1862	Osler's wing addition, London, demolished 1926

	Decoration, Overstone Hall (Lockinge), Northampton; Jones's work doesn't survive
	Facade and concert room, Collard and Collard, 16 Grosvenor Street, rebuilt
	Sculpture Pavilion for London Exhibition of 1862
	Exhibition stand, Osler's, London, destroyed
1863	Indian, Chinese, and Japanese courts, South Kensington Museum, removed
	Decoration, the Priory, 21 Northbank, Regent's Park, London, destroyed
	Decoration, Chapel, Cornwall Road, Notting Vale, demolished
	Decoration, Charing Cross Hotel, London; Jones's work doesn't survive
	Interior, Fonthill House, Gifford, Wiltshire, demolished
1864	Interior, Viceroy's Palace, Cairo, Egypt, now the Marriott Hotel
	Interior decoration, Langham Hotel, London, altered
	Interior decoration, 12A Kensington Palace Gardens, altered
1865	Interior, 16 Carlton House Terrace, London, restored
	Interior decoration, Fishmonger's Hall, London, destroyed in World War II, but rebuilt with some sympathy for Jones's earlier work
	J. and G. Haywood shopfront, Derby, demolished 1924, Jackson and Graham
	Competition entry, St. Pancras, London
	Crystal Palace decoration, Portuguese International Exhibition, Oporto, Portugal
	Paxton Memorial, Crystal Palace, Sydenham, survives in place
	Cast-iron fascia design, Derby Market Hall
1866	Kiosk for Bombay, India, with Ordish, whereabouts unknown
	Interior decoration, Preston Hall, Kent, two ceilings survive
	Tombstone, Thomas De la Rue, Kensal Green Cemetery, London
1867	Competition entry, National Gallery, London
	Silver vase for Hancock's with R. Monti
	Furniture exhibited, Gold Medal of Honor with Jackson and Graham, Paris Exhibition
1868	Silver ewer for Hancock's with R. Monti
1869	Facade and interiors, Jackson and Graham, 36–38 Oxford Street, London
1870	Billiard room addition and decoration, 43 York Terrace, London, demolished 1941
1872	Major expansion and renovation, Eynsham Hall, Oxfordshire, building demolished 1904
1873	Abbotsfield, Wivelscombe, Somerset, altered
	Gold Medal with Jackson and Graham for cabinet, Vienna Exhibition
	Exhibition stand for Huntley & Palmer, Vienna Exhibition, destroyed
1874	Color consulting and chimney design, Star Works, Huntley & Palmer, Bunhill Row, London, demolished
n.d.	Drawing room and conservatory, Douglas Castle, Lanarkshire, Scotland, demolished
n.d.	Conservatory, Mr. Fiden; more information is not known
n.d.	Interior, Beech Grove, Newcastle-upon-Tyne, demolished
n.d.	Gallery for Edward Benzon
n.d.	Drawing rooms, 60 Prince's Gate, London
n.d.	Interior, Lancaster Gate for Baron Rendel

SELECTED BIBLIOGRAPHY

Beeby, Thomas H. "The Grammar of Ornament/Ornament as Grammar." *Ornament, VIA III* (1977): 11–29.

Catalogue of the Drawings Collection of the Royal Institute of British Architects. Fairborough: Gregg, 1973.

Crinson, Mark. *Empire Building: Orientalism and Victorian Architecture.* London and New York: Routledge, 1996.

Darby, Michael. *The Islamic Perspective.* London: The World of Islam Festival Trust, 1983.

_____. *Owen Jones and the Eastern Ideal.* PhD diss., University of Reading, 1974.

_____, and John Physick. *Marble Halls: Drawings and Models for the Victorian Secula Buildings Exhibition.* London: Victoria and Albert Museum, 1973.

_____, and David Van Zanten. "Owen Jones's Iron Buildings of the 1850s." *Architectura: Zeitschrift fur Geschichte der Architektur* no. 1 (1974): 53–75.

Eliot, George. "Review of *The Grammar of Ornament* by Owen Jones." *Fortnightly Review* (May 15, 1865).

Ferry, Kathryn. "Printing the Alhambra: Owen Jones and Chromolithography." *Architectural History* 46 (2003).

Flores, Carol A. Hrvol. "A Colorful Context: Owen Jones's Design for the Manchester Art Treasures Exhibition Building." *Elvehjem Museum of Art Bulletin 1999–2001.*

_____. "Engaging the Mind's Eye: The Use of Inscriptions in the Architecture of Owen Jones and A.W.N. Pugin." *Journal Society of Architectural Historians* vol. 60, no. 2 (June 2001).

_____. *Owen Jones, Architect.* PhD diss., Georgia Institute of Technology, 1996

Jervis, Simon. "Owen Jones." In *Dictionary of Design and Designers.* London: Penguin Books, 1984.

Jespersen, John Kresten. *Owen Jones's "The Grammar of Ornament" of 1856: Field Theory in Victorian Design at the Mid-Century.* PhD. diss., Brown University, 1984.

Jones, Owen. *The Alhambra Court Erected in the Crystal Palace.* London: Crystal Palace Library, 1854.

_____. "An Attempt to Define the Principles which Should Regulate the Employment of Colour in the Decorative Arts." London: David Bogue, 1852. Lecture originally read before the Society of Arts, April 28, 1852.

_____. *Designs for Mosaic and Tessellated Pavements.* With an essay by F. O. Ward. London: John Weale, 1842.

_____. "Designs for the Proposed Enlargement of the National Gallery." London: n.p., 1865.

_____. *Examples of Chinese Ornament.* Originally published London: S. & T. Gilbert, 1867. Reprinted as *The Grammar of Chinese Ornament.* New York: Portland House, 1987.

_____. "Gleanings from the Great Exhibition of 1851." *Journal of Design* (June 1851).

_____. *The Grammar of Ornament.* London: Day and Son, 1856.

_____. *Lectures on Architecture and the Decorative Arts.* London: n.p., 1863.

_____. *Lectures on Articles in the Museum of the Department of Science and Art.* London: n.p., 1852.

_____. "On the Decorations Proposed for the Exhibition Building in Hyde Park." Lecture read at the meeting of the Royal Institute of British Architects, December 16, 1850.

_____. "On the Influence of Religion upon Art." London: n.p., 1863.

_____. "On the Leading Principles in the Composition of Ornament from Every Period." Lecture read before the Royal Society of British Architects, December 15, 1856.

_____. "On the Necessity of an Architectural Education on the Part of the Public." *Civil Engineer and Architect's Journal* (1852).

_____. "On the True and the False in the Decorative Arts." London: n. p., 1863. Lecture originally delivered at Marlborough House, June 1852.

_____. *One Thousand and One Initial Letters Designed and Illuminated by Owen Jones.* London: Day and Son, 1864.

_____. *702 Monograms.* London: n.p., 1864.

_____. "Textile Art." In *Art Treasures of the United Kingdom.* Edited by J. B. Waring. London: Day and Son, 1858.

_____, and Joseph Bonomi. *Description of the Egyptian Court Erected in the Crystal Palace.* London: Crystal Palace Library, 1854.

_____, and Jules Goury. *Plans, Elevations, Sections, and Details of the Alhambra: from drawings taken on the spot in 1834 by the late M. Jules Goury and in 1834 and 1837 by Owen Jones, Archt. with a complete translation of the Arabic inscriptions, and an Historical Notice of the Kings of Granada, from the Conquest of that City by the Arabs to the Expulsion of the Moors, by Mr. Pasqual de Gayangos.* 2 vols. London: n.p., 1842–5.

_____. *Views on the Nile from Cairo to the Second Cataract.* London: n.p., 1843.

_____, and G. H. Lewes. *An Apology for the Colouring of the Greek Court in the Crystal Palace.* London: Crystal Palace Library, 1854.

_____, and Sir G. Scharf. *The Greek Court Erected in the Crystal Palace.* London: Crystal Palace Library, 1854.

_____. *The Roman Court Erected in the Crystal Palace.* London: Crystal Palace Library, 1854.

"The Late Mr. Owen Jones." *The Builder* (May 9, 1874): 383–5.

Middleton, Robin. "Hittorff's Polychrome Campaign." In *The Beaux-Arts and Nineteenth-Century French Architecture.* Cambridge, MA: The MIT Press, 1982.

"Owen Jones's Obituary." *The Architect (London)* (1874): 174, 235.

"Owen Jones's Obituary." *The Athenaeum* (1874): 269.

Piggott, J. R. *Palace of the People: The Crystal Palace at Sydenham 1854–1936.* London: Hurst & Company, 2004.

Redgrave, Richard, M. Digby Wyatt, and Owen Jones. *Catalogue of the Articles of Ornamental Art selected from the Exhibition of the Works of Industry of all Nations in 1851 and purchased by the Government.* London: n.p., 1852.

Schoeser, Mary. *Owen Jones' Silks.* Braintree: Warner & Sons, 1987.

_____. "Owen Jones' Silks." In *Disentangling Textiles: Techniques for the Study of Designed Objects.* Edited by Mary Schoeser and Christine Boydell. London: Middlesex University Press, 2002.

Seroux D'Agincourt, Jean-Baptiste. *History of Art by Its Monuments.* Translated by Owen Jones. London: Longman and Co., 1847.

Sweetman, John. *The Oriental Obsession: Islamic Inspiration in British and American Art and Architecture 1500–1920.* Cambridge, MA: Cambridge University Press, 1987.

Van Zanten, David. *The Architectural Polychromy of the 1830s.* New York: Garland Publishing, Inc., 1977.

_____. "Architectural Polychromy: Life in Architecture." In *The Beaux-Arts and Nineteenth-Century French Architecture.* Edited by Robin Middleton. Cambridge, MA: The MIT Press, 1982.

_____. "Jacob Wrey Mould: Echoes of Owen Jones and the High Victorian Styles in New York 1835–1986." *Journal of the Society of Architectural Historians* vol. 28 (1969).

Varela-Braga, Ariane. "L'ornementation primitive dans la *Grammar of Ornament* d'Owen Jones (1856)."' *Histoire de l'art* no. 53 (November 2003): 91–101.

RELATED WORKS

Aldrich, Megan, ed. *The Craces: Royal Decorators 1768–1899*. Brighton: The Royal Pavilion Art Gallery and Museums, 1990.

Archer, John. *Art and Architecture in Victorian Manchester*. Manchester, England: Manchester University Press, 1985.

————. *The Literature of British Domestic Architecture 1715–1842*. Cambridge, MA: The MIT Press, 1985.

Atterbury, Paul, ed. *Master of Gothic Revival*. New Haven, CT and London: Yale University Press, 1995.

————, and Clive Wainwright, eds. *Pugin: A Gothic Passion*. New Haven, CT and London: Yale University Press, 1994.

Baker, Malcolm, and Brenda Richardson. *A Grand Design: The Art of the Victoria and Albert Museum*. New York: Harry N. Abrams, Inc., 1997.

Barrucand, Marianne, and Achim Bednorz. *Moorish Architecture in Andalusia*. Hohenzollernring, Germany: Benedikt Taschen Verlag, 1992.

Beaver, Patrick. *The Crystal Palace: A Portrait of Victorian Enterprise*. Chichester, England: Phillimore & Co., 1993.

Bell, Quentin. *The Schools of Design*. London: Routledge and Kegan Paul, Ltd., 1863.

Benjamin, Walter. *Illuminations*. Edited by Hannah Arendt; translated by Harry Zohn. New York: Schocken Books, 1968.

————. *Reflections*. New York: Schocken Books, 1978.

Blau, Eve. *Ruskinian Gothic*. Princeton: Princeton University Press, 1982.

Bloomer, Kent. "Botanical Ornament: The Continuity and the Transformation of a Tradition." *Perspecta* vol. 23 (1986).

Boe, Alf. *From Gothic Revival to Functional Form: A Study in Victorian Theories of Design*. New York: Da Capo Press, 1979.

Bonython, Elizabeth, and Anthony Burton. *The Great Exhibitor: The Life and Work of Henry Cole*. London: V & A Publications, 2003.

Bourbon, Fabio. *The Lost Cities of the Mayas: The Life, Art, and Discoveries of Frederick Catherwood*. Shrewsbury: Swan Hill Press, 1999.

Brolin, Brent C. *Architectural Ornament: Banishment and Return*. New York and London: W. W. Norton & Company, 1985.

Brooks, H. Allen. *Le Corbusier's Formative Years Charles-Édouard Jeanneret at La Chaux-de-Fonds*. Chicago and London: The University of Chicago Press, 1997.

Brooks, Michael W. *John Ruskin and Victorian Architecture*. London: Thames and Hudson, Ltd., 1989.

Bullen, J. B. *Byzantium Rediscovered*. London: Phaidon Press, Ltd., 2003.

Calvert, Albert Frederick. *The Alhambra: Being a Brief Record of the Arabian Conquest of the Peninsula*. London: John Lane, 1906.

Carter, Oliver. *British Railway Hotels 1838–1983*. St. Michael's, Lancashire: Silver Link Publishing, 1990.

Çelik, Zeynep. *Displaying the Orient: Architecture of Islam at Nineteenth-Century World's Fairs*. Berkeley: University of California Press, 1992.

Chadwick, George F. *The Works of Sir Joseph Paxton*. London: The Architectural Press, 1961.

Chevreul, M. E. *The Principles of Harmony and Contrast of Colors and Their Applications to the Arts*. Translated by Charles Martel. London: Thomas Delf, 1854.

Christensen, Ellen. *The Significance of Owen Jones's* The Grammar of Ornament *for the Development of Architectural Ornament in Twentieth-Century Europe and America*. Master's thesis, University of Cincinnati, 1986.

Collins, Michael. *Towards Post-Modernism: Decorative Arts and Design Since 1851*. Boston: Little, Brown, and Company, 1987.

Collins, Peter. *Changing Ideals in Modern Architecture 1750–1950*. Montreal: McGill-Queen's University Press, 1965.

Connelly, Frances S. *The Sleep of Reason: Primitivism in Modern European Art and Aesthetics, 1725–1907*. University Park: The Pennsylvania State University Press, 1999.

Conway, Moncure Daniel. *Travels in South Kensington*. London: Trubner & Co., 1882.

Cooper, Jeremy. *Victorian and Edwardian Furniture and Interiors*. London: Thames and Hudson, Ltd., 1998.

Cornforth, John. "Arabian Nights in the Mall." *Country Life* (May 18, 1989).

Crary, Jonathan. *Techniques of the Observer: On Vision and Modernity in the Nineteenth Century*. Cambridge, MA: The MIT Press, 1990.

Crook, J. Mordaunt. *The Dilemma of Style*. London: John Murray, 1987.

————. *Victorian Architecture: A Visual Anthology*. New York and London: Johnson Reprint Corporation, 1971.

Cross, J. W., ed. *George Eliot's Life as Related in Her Letters and Journals*. 3 vols. New York: Harper & Brothers, 1885.

"The Crown Estate in Kensington Palace Gardens." In *Survey of London*, vol. 37. London: The Athlone Press, 1975.

Curl, James Stevens. *Kensal Green Cemetery*. Chichester, England: Phillimore & Co., 2001.

Daniels, Morna. *Victorian Book Illustration*. London: The British Library, 1988.

Davies, Philip. *Splendours of the Raj, British Architecture in India 1660 to 1947*. London: John Murray, 1985.

Delamotte, Philip H. *Photographic Views of the Progress of the Crystal Palace Sydenham*. London: Crystal Palace Company, 1855.

De Maré, Eric. *London 1851: The Year of the Great Exhibition*. London: The Folio Press, 1973.

————. *Victorian London Revealed: Gustave Doré's Metropolis*. London: Penguin Books, 1973.

Dennis, James, and Lu Wenneker. "Ornamentation and the Organic Architecture of Frank Lloyd Wright." *Art Journal* (Fall 1965).

Dresser, Christopher. *The Art of Decorative Design*. London: Day and Son, 1862.

————. *Principles of Victorian Decorative Design*. Originally published 1873; reprinted New York: Dover Publications, Inc., 1995.

————. *Studies in Design*. Originally published 1874; reprinted London: Gibbs Smith, 2002.

Durant, Stuart. *Christopher Dresser*. London: Academy Editions, 1993.

————. *Ornament from the Industrial Revolution to Today*. Woodstock and New York: The Overlook Press, 1986.

Edwards, Clive. "The Firm of Jackson and Graham." *Furniture History* vol. XXXIV (1998): 238–65.

Edwards, Ralph, and L. G. G. Ramsey, eds. *The Early Victorian Period 1830–1860*. London: The Connoisseur, 1958.

Elliott, Brent. *Victorian Gardens*. London: Batsford, 1986.

Frampton, Kenneth. *Studies in Tectonic Culture: The Poetics of Construction in Nineteenth and Twentieth Century Architecture*. Cambridge, MA: The MIT Press, 1995.

French, Yvonne. *The Great Exhibition: 1851*. London: n.p., 1950.

Gage, John. *Color and Culture*. Boston, Toronto, and London: Little, Brown, and Company, 1993.

Garrigan, Kristine Ottesen. *Ruskin on Architecture: His Thought and Influence*. Madison: University of Wisconsin Press, 1973.

Gascoigne, Bamber. *Milestones in Colour Printing 1457–1859*. Cambridge, England: Cambridge University Press, 1997.

Gayle, Margot, Gretchen Gayle Ellsworth, and Carol Gayle. "The New York Crystal Palace: America's Progress, Power, and Possibilities." *Nineteenth Century* vol. 15, no. 1 (1995).

Gere, Charlotte. *Nineteenth-Century Decoration*. New York: Harry N. Abrams, Inc., 1989.

————, and Michael Whiteway. *Nineteenth-Century Design*. New York: Harry N. Abrams, Inc., 1994.

Getting London in Perspective. London: The Barbican Art Gallery, 1984.

Gibbs-Smith, C. H. *The Great Exhibition of 1851*. London: Her Majesty's Stationery Office, 1981.

Girouard, Mark. "Gilded Preserves for the Rich: Kensington Palace Gardens—I." *Country Life* (November 11, 1971).

————. "Gilded Preserves for the Rich: Kensington Palace Gardens—II." *Country Life* (November 18, 1971).

————. *Life in the English Country House*. Harmondsworth, England: Penguin Books, 1980.

————. *The Victorian Country House*. New Haven, CT and London: Yale University Press, 1985.

Gloag, John, ed. *The Crystal Palace Exhibition Illustrated Catalog*. New York: Dover Publications, Inc., 1970.

Gombrich, E. H. *The Sense of Order: A Study in the Psychology of Decorative Art*. Oxford: Oxford University Press, 1979.

Good Victorian Furniture. London: Sotheby's, 1984.

Gore, Alan, and Ann Gore. *The History of English Interiors*. London: Phaidon Press, Ltd., 1991.

Grabar, Oleg. *The Alhambra*. Cambridge, MA: Harvard University Press, 1978.

_____. *The Mediation of Ornament*. Princeton: Princeton University Press, 1992.

Graves, Algernon. *The Royal Academy of Arts*. Vol. 4. London: Henry Graves & Co., Ltd., and George Bell and Sons, 1906.

Gray, Nicolette. "Prophets of the Modern Movement." *Architectural Review (London)* vol. 81 (1937).

The Great Exhibition: London's Crystal Palace Exposition of 1851. New York: Gramercy Books, 1995.

Great Exhibition of the Works of Industry of All Nations 1851: Official Descriptive and Illustrated Catalogue in Three Volumes. London: W. Clowes & Sons, 1851.

Haight, Gordon S., ed. *George Eliot: A Biography*. Oxford, London, and New York: Oxford University Press, 1968.

Halen, Widar. *Christopher Dresser*. London: Phaidon Press, Ltd., 1993.

_____. "Ornamentation Seen as High Art." *Scandinavian Journal of Design History* vol. 1 (1991).

Hamilton, Jean. *Playing Cards in the Victorian and Albert Museum*. London: Her Majesty's Stationery Office, 1988.

Hanks, David. *The Decorative Designs of Frank Lloyd Wright*. Mineola, NY: Dover Publications, Inc., 1979.

Hapgood, Marilyn Oliver. *Wallpaper and the Artist*. New York, London, and Paris: Abbeville Press, 1992.

Hardie, Martin. *English Coloured Books*. Originally published 1906; reprinted London: Fitzhouse Books, 1990.

Hargrave, Catherine Perry. *A History of Playing Cards and a Bibliography of Cards and Gaming*. Originally published 1930; reprinted New York: Dover Publications, Inc., 1966.

Harper, Roger H. *Victorian Architectural Competitions*. London: Mansell Publishing, Ltd., 1983.

Haweis, Mrs. *Beautiful Houses*. London: Sampson Low, Marston, Searle & Rivington, 1882.

Herbert, Tony, and Kathryn Huggins. *The Decorative Tile*. London: Phaidon Press, Ltd., 1995.

Hitchcock, Henry-Russell. *Architecture: Nineteenth and Twentieth Centuries*. Originally published 1958; Harmondsworth, England: Penguin Books, 1987.

_____. *The Crystal Palace: The Structure, Its Antecedents and Its Immediate Progeny*. Northampton, MA: Smith College Museum of Art and The MIT Press, 1952.

_____. "Early Cast Iron Facades." *Architectural Review* (1951).

_____. *Early Victorian Architecture in Britain*. New Haven, CT: Yale University Press, 1954.

Hix, John. *The Glass House*. Cambridge, MA: The MIT Press, 1974.

Hobhouse, Hermione. *History of Regent Street*. London: Macdonald and Jane's, 1975.

_____. *Lost London*. New York: Weathervane Books, 1971.

Hoskins, Lesley, ed. *The Papered Wall*. London: Thames and Hudson, Ltd., 1994.

Houseman, Lorna. *The House That Thomas Built: The Story of De la Rue*. London: Chatto & Windus, 1968.

Howell, Peter, and Ian Sutton. *The Faber Guide to Victorian Churches*. London and Boston: Faber & Faber, 1989.

Hugo, Victor. *The Hunchback of Notre Dame*. Philadelphia and London: Running Press, 1995; reprint of the 1833 English edition.

_____. *The Works of Victor Hugo*. Vol. I. Boston and New York: The Jefferson Press, 1900.

Hunt, Arnold, Giles Mandelbrote, and Alison Shell. *The Book Trade & Its Customers 1450–1900*. Winchester: St. Paul's Bibliographies, 1997.

Irving, Washington. *The Alhambra*. New York: G. Putnam's Sons, 1865.

_____. *The Alhambra: A Series of Tales and Sketches of the Moors and the Spaniards*. Philadelphia: Carey & Lea, 1832.

Jackson, Neil. "Christ Church, Streatham, and the Rise of Constructional Polychromy." *Architectural History* vol. 43 (2000): 219–52.

Jeans, Herbert. *The Periods in Interior Decoration*. London: The Trade Papers Publishing Co., Ltd., 1921.

Jenkins, R. T., and Helen M. Ramage. *A History of the Honourable Society of Cymmrodorion*. London: n.p., 1951.

Jenkyns, Richard. *Dignity and Decadence*. Cambridge, MA: Harvard University Press, 1992.

Jervis, Simon. *High Victorian Design*. Woodbridge: Boydell Press, 1983.

King, Edmund M. B. *Victorian Decorated Trade Bindings 1830–1880: A Descriptive Bibliography*. London and New Castle: The British Library and Oak Knoll Press, 2003.

Kohlmaier, Georg, and Bana von Sartory. *Houses of Glass*. Cambridge, MA and London: The MIT Press, 1991.

Leathart, William Davies. *The Origin and Progress of the Gwyneddigion Society of London*. London: n.p., 1831.

Lehmann, Karl. "The Dome of Heaven." *Art Bulletin* vol. 27 (1995): 1–27.

Lemmen, Hans van. *Tiles: 1000 Years of Architectural Decoration*. New York: Harry N. Abrams, Inc., 1988.

Lester, David. "Fishmongers' Hall." *The Journal of the London Society* vol. 436 (Autumn 1998): 16–8.

Levine, Neil. "The Book and the Building: Hugo's Theory of Architecture and Labrouste's Bibliothèque Ste-Geneviève." In *The Beaux-Arts and Nineteenth-Century French Architecture*. Edited by Robin Middleton. Cambridge, MA: The MIT Press, 1982.

Lichten, Frances. *Decorative Art of Victoria's Era*. New York and London: Charles Scribner's and Sons, 1950.

London—World City, 1800–1840. New Haven, CT and London: Yale University Press, 1992.

Lubbock, Jules. *The Tyranny of Taste*. New Haven, CT and London: Yale University Press, 1995.

Lyons, Harry, and Christopher Morley. *Ch. Dresser: People's Designer 1834–1904, Exhibition by New Century, 2nd–19th June 1999*. Worcestershire: Alastair Carew-Cox, 1999.

MacKenzie, John M. *Orientalism: History, Theory and the Arts*. Manchester: Manchester University Press, 1995.

March, Lionel, and Philip Steadman. *The Geometry of Environment*. London: RIBA Publications Ltd., 1971.

McKean, John. *Crystal Palace*. London: Phaidon Press, Ltd., 1994.

McLean, Ruari. *Victorian Book Design and Color Printing*. London: Faber & Faber, 1963.

Middleton, Robin, ed. *The Beaux-Arts and Nineteenth-Century French Architecture*. Cambridge, MA: MIT Press, 1982.

_____, and David Watkin. *Neoclassical and 19th-Century Architecture*. New York: Rizzoli, 1987.

Mignot, Claude. *Architecture of the Nineteenth Century in Europe*. New York: Rizzoli, 1984.

Monahan, Anne. "'Of a Doubtful Gothic': Islamic Sources for the Pennsylvania Academy of the Fine Arts." *Nineteenth Century* vol. 18, no. 2 (Fall 1998): 28–36.

Morris, Barbara. *Inspiration for Design, The Influence of the Victoria and Albert Museum*. London: Victoria and Albert Museum, 1986.

_____. "The 1952 Exhibition of Victorian and Edwardian Decorative Arts at the Victoria and Albert Museum: A Personal Recollection." *The Decorative Arts Society: 1850 to the Present* (January 25, 2001): 11–24.

Morrison, Kathryn A. *English Shops and Shopping*. New Haven, CT and London: Yale University Press, 2003.

Murphy, James Cavanaugh. *The Arabian Antiquities of Spain*. Zurich: TRI Publishing, 1982.

Muthesius, Stephan. *The English Terraced House*. New Haven, CT and London: Yale University Press, 1982.

Newton, Charles. *Victorian Designs for the Home*. London: V & A Publications, 1999.

O'Gorman, James F. *The Architecture of Frank Furness*. Philadelphia: The University of Pennsylvania Press, 1973.

Parry, Linda. *Textiles of the Arts and Crafts Movement*. London: Thames and Hudson, Ltd., 1988.

_____. *The Victoria & Albert Museum's Textile Collection: British Textiles from 1850 to 1900*. New York: Canopy Books, 1993.

Payne, Joan. *Christ Church Streatham: A History and Guide*. Streatham, England: Streatham Society, 1986.

Peters, Tom F. *Building the Nineteenth Century*. Cambridge, MA: The MIT Press, 1996.

Pevsner, Nikolaus. *The Buildings of England: London and Westminster*. Harmondsworth, England: Penguin Books, 1957.

————. "Christopher Dresser, Industrial Designer." *Architectural Review (London)* vol. 81 (1937).

————. *High Victorian Design: A Study of the Exhibits of 1851*. London: Architectural Press, 1951.

————. *A History of Building Types*. Princeton: Princeton University Press, 1976.

————. *Pioneers of Modern Design*. Originally published 1936; reprinted London: Peregrine Books, 1986.

————. "Ruskin and Viollet-le-Duc." *On the Methodology of Architectural History*. Edited by Demetri Porphyrios. London: Architectural Design, and New York: St. Martin's Press, 1981.

————. *Some Architectural Writers of the Nineteenth Century*. Oxford: Clarendon Press, 1972.

————. *The Sources of Modern Architecture and Design*. London: Thames and Hudson, Ltd., 1968.

————. *Studies in Art, Architecture, and Design, Victorian and After*. Princeton: Princeton University Press, 1968.

Pflugradt-Abdel Aziz, Elke. *A Prussian Palace in Egypt*. Exhibition catalogue. Cairo: Embassy of the Federal Republic of Germany and Museum of Egyptian Modern Art, 1993.

Physick, John. *The Victoria and Albert Museum: The History of Its Building*. London: Victoria and Albert Museum, 1982.

Polak, Ada. *Glass: Its Makers and Its Public*. London: Weidenfeld & Nicholson, 1975.

Port, M. H. *Imperial London: Civil Government Building in London 1850–1915*. New Haven, CT and London: Yale University Press, 1995.

Powell, Helen, and David Leatherbarrow. *Masterpieces of Architectural Drawing*. New York: Abbeville Press, 1982.

Pugin, A.W.N. *Contrasts, or, A Parallel between the Noble Edifices of the Fourteenth and Fifteenth Centuries, and Corresponding Buildings of the Present Day; Shewing the Present Decay of Taste: Accompanied by Appropriate Text*. London: Charles Dolman, 1841.

————. *Floriated Ornament*. London: n.p., 1849.

————. *Glossary of Ecclesiastical Ornament and Costume*. London: n.p., 1844.

————. *The True Principles of Pointed or Christian Architecture*. London: n.p., 1841.

Redinger, Ruby V. *George Eliot: The Emergent Self*. New York: Alfred A. Knopf, 1975.

Ridening, William H. *Thackeray's London*. Boston: Cupples, Upham and Company, 1885.

Rossetti, William Michael. *Fine Art, Chiefly Contemporary: Notices Re-printed, with Revisions*. Originally published 1867; reprinted New York: Ames Press, Inc., 1970.

Rowe, Colin. "Character and Composition; or Some Vicissitudes of Architectural Vocabulary in the Nineteenth Century." *Oppositions* vol. 2 (February 1974).

Ruskin, John. *Diaries*. Edited by Joan Evans and John Howard Whitehouse. Oxford: Clarendon Press, 1956–9.

————. *Lectures on Architecture and Painting (Edinburgh 1853) with Other Papers (1844–1854)*. London: George Allen, 1904.

————. *The Seven Lamps of Architecture*. Originally published 1849; reprinted New York: Farrar, Straus, and Giroux, 1988.

————. *The Stones of Venice*. New York: Da Capo Press, 1960.

————. *The Works of John Ruskin*. Edited by E. T. Cook and Alexander Wedderburn. London: George Allen and New York: Longmans, Green, and Co., 1903.

Saunders, Gill. *Wallpaper in Interior Decoration*. London: V & A Publications, 2002.

Schafter, Debra. *The Order of Ornament, The Structure of Style: Theoretical Foundations of Modern Art and Architecture*. Cambridge, England: Cambridge University Press, 2003.

Semper, Gottfried. "On the Origin of Polychromy in Architecture." In *The Greek Court Erected in the Crystal Palace*. By Owen Jones. London: Crystal Palace Library, 1854.

Shand, Morton. "The Crystal Palace as Structure and Precedent." *Architectural Review* vol. 81 (1937).

Simmons, Jack. *St. Pancras Station*. London: George Allen and Unwin, Ltd., 2003.

Smith, John P. *Osler's Crystal for Royalty and Rajahs*. London: Mallett, 1991.

Snodin, Michael, and Maurice Howard. *Ornament: A Social History Since 1450*. New Haven, CT and London: Yale University Press, 1996.

Sotheby, Wilkinson & Hodge. *Catalogue of the Valuable Library of the late Owen Jones, Esq*. Auction catalogue. April 10, 1875.

Stanton, Phoebe. *Pugin*. New York: The Viking Press, 1971.

————. "The Sources of Pugin's Contrasts." In *Concerning Architecture: Essays on Architectural Writers and Writing Presented to Nikolaus Pevsner*. Edited by John Summerson. London: Allen Lane, The Penguin Press, 1968.

Sugden, Alan V., and J. L. Edmondson. *A History of English Wallpaper, 1509–1914*. London: Batsford, 1926.

Summerson, John. *The Architectural Association, 1847–1947*. London: Architectural Association and Pleiades Books, Ltd., 1947.

————. *Architecture in Britain 1530–1830*. New York: Penguin Books, 1983.

————, ed. *Concerning Architecture: Essays on Architectural Writers and Writing Presented to Nikolaus Pevsner*. London: Allen Lane, The Penguin Press, 1968.

————. *The Unromantic Castle*. London: Thames and Hudson, Ltd., 1990.

Survey of London: The Museum Area of South Kensington and Westminster. Vol. 38. Edited by F.H.W. Sheppard. London: The Athlone Press, 1975.

Thompson, Paul. *The Work of William Morris*. London: Heinemann, 1967.

Thorne, Robert. "The Langham Hotel." London: Greater London Council, 1982.

————. "Paxton and Prefabrication." *Architectural Design* vol. 57, no. 11/12 (1987).

Trilling, James. *The Language of Ornament*. London: Thames & Hudson, Ltd., 2001.

Twyman, Michael. *Printing 1770–1970: An Illustrated History of its Development and Uses in England*. London: The British Library, 1998.

Tyack, Geoffrey. *Sir James Pennethorne and the Making of Victorian London*. Cambridge, MA: Cambridge University Press, 1993.

Vidler, Anthony. *The Writing of the Walls*. New York: Princeton Architectural Press, 1987.

Vivant, Dominique (Baron Denant). *Voyage dans la Basse et Haute Égypte*. 1802.

Vizetelly, Henry. *Glances Back through Seventy Years*. Vol. 1. London: Kegan Paul, Trench, Trubner & Co., Ltd., 1893.

Wainwright, Clive. "Alfred Morrison: A Forgotten Patron and Collector." In *The Grosvenor House Art and Antiques Fair 1995 Handbook*. London: Burlington Magazine, 1995.

————. "Principles True and False: Pugin and the Foundation of the Museum of Manufactures." *Burlington Magazine* (1993).

Waring, J. B. *Masterpieces of Industrial Art and Sculpture at the International Exhibit of 1862*. London: Day and Son, 1863.

Watanabe, Toshio. "The World Market of Ornament." *Daidolos* vol. 54 (December 1994): 84–93.

Watkin, David. *The Rise of Architectural History*. London: The Architectural Press, 1980.

Watts, Alan S. *Dickens at Gad's Hill*. Reading, UK: Cedric Dickens and Elvendon Press, 1989.

Wedgwood, Alexandra. *A.W.N. Pugin and the Pugin Family*. London: Victoria and Albert Museum, 1985.

Whiteway, Michael. *Shock of the Old: Christopher Dresser's Design Revolution*. London: Victoria and Albert Museum, 2004.

Wigley, Mark. *White Walls, Designer Dresses: The Fashioning of Modern Architecture*. Cambridge, MA and London: The MIT Press, 1995.

Wildman, Stephen. "J. G. Crace and the Decoration of the 1862 International Exhibition." In *The Craces: Royal Decorators 1768–1899*. Edited by Megan Aldrich. Brighton: The Royal Pavilion Art Gallery and Museums, 1990.

Wilton-Ely, John. "The Rise of the Professional Architect in England." In *The Architect*. Edited by Spiro Kostof. New York and Oxford: Oxford University Press, 1977.

Wyatt, M. Digby. *Great Exhibition of the Works of Industry of All Nations 1851: Official Descriptive and Illustrated Catalogue in Three Volumes*. London: W. Clowes & Sons, 1851.

————. *The Industrial Arts of the Nineteenth Century*. London: n.p., 1851–3.

INDEX

Numbers in *italics* indicate images.

PHOTOGRAPHY CREDITS

Last page from The Sunday Alphabet, *1861*